Teaching with Harry Potter

ALSO BY VALERIE ESTELLE FRANKEL

Buffy and the Heroine's Journey: Vampire Slayer as Feminine Chosen One (McFarland, 2012)

From Girl to Goddess: The Heroine's Journey through Myth and Legend (McFarland, 2010)

Teaching with Harry Potter

Essays on Classroom Wizardry from Elementary School to College

Edited by VALERIE ESTELLE FRANKEL

McFarland & Company, Inc., Publishers
Jefferson, North Carolina, and London

LIBRARY OF CONGRESS CATALOGUING-IN-PUBLICATION DATA

Teaching with Harry Potter : essays on classroom wizardry from elementary school to college / edited by Valerie Estelle Frankel.
    p.   cm.
Includes bibliographical references and index.

ISBN 978-0-7864-7201-7
softcover : acid free paper ∞

1. Rowling, J.K.— Study and teaching. 2. Young adult fiction, English — Study and teaching. 3. Creative teaching. 4. Children — Books and reading. 5. Young adults — Books and reading. 6. Potter, Harry (Fictitious character) I. Frankel, Valerie Estelle, 1980– editor of compilation.
PR6068.O93Z8885 2013
823'.914—dc23   2013001850

BRITISH LIBRARY CATALOGUING DATA ARE AVAILABLE

© 2013 Valerie Estelle Frankel. All rights reserved

No part of this book may be reproduced or transmitted in any form or by any means, electronic or mechanical, including photocopying or recording, or by any information storage and retrieval system, without permission in writing from the publisher.

On the cover: owl drawing by Robin Bauguess; other images © 2013 Shutterstock

Manufactured in the United States of America

McFarland & Company, Inc., Publishers
* Box 611, Jefferson, North Carolina 28640*
* www.mcfarlandpub.com*

To all those teachers who work so tirelessly and
still make the classroom a fun place to be.

Table of Contents

Introduction   1

Part I: Reaching Kids — A New Wave of Young Readers

From Hogwarts Academy to the Hero's Journey
    LANA A. WHITED   4

The Nuances of Rule-Breaking
    TENILLE NOWAK   21

Harry Potter and the Child with Autism
    DENISE DWYER D'ERRICO   32

Strange Apostle: Assessing the Conflict Between Today's Christianity and Modern Culture
    J. MALCOLM STEWART   42

Boy Wizards and Girl Scientists: Rowling's Contributions to Science Outreach
    KRISTINE LARSEN   56

Part II: Innovative Approaches for the Internet Generation

Two Boy Heroes (and a Sparkly Vampire) Teach the SAT
    VALERIE ESTELLE FRANKEL   70

Fan Fiction, Remix Culture, and the Potter Games
    JEN SCOTT CURWOOD   81

The Battle to Save Australian Teen Spirituality
    CLARE DIVINY   93

J.K. Rowling's Innovative and Authoritative Online Presence
    SAVANNAH SHARP   107

Exploring eNotes.com: A Grounded Theory of Harry's Place in Language Arts Pedagogy
    JAMES B. KELLEY   117

Part III: Meaning in Children's Books Within the University

Legit Lit: Of Spells and Serious Scholarship
    J. STEVE LEE   130

Scribere Paedegogia: The Magical Art of Teaching Composition
    CYNTHIA K. O'MALLEY   141

Getting Medieval in the Classroom
    RENEÉ WARD   152

To Grow Up Blake in a Potter World: Teaching *Songs of Innocence and of Experience*
    WHITNEY E. JONES FRANCIS   168

Casting *Lumos* on Critical Cultural Studies: Gender, Hegemony and Other Social Stereotypes
    AMANDA FIRESTONE   179

Introducing English Literature in Pakistan
    ASMA MANSOOR   188

Portkey to the Scholarly Disciplines
    ELISABETH C. GUMNIOR   196

The Queen City Muggles: Town and Gown Go to Hogwarts
    SUSAN JOHNSTON   209

Appendix: Worksheets and Supplemental Materials   219
Bibliography   255
About the Contributors   267
Index   271

Introduction

There is an entire genre out there of aca-fans: those who participate in academic fandom. These scholars and professors read the text, love it, and then analyze its deeper meanings and what it divulges about our society. This scholarly interest in such a mainstream series as *Harry Potter* is immense: Bookstores teem with *Harry Potter* collections focusing on gender roles, tropes, and the series' influence on today's children. Conferences appear across the world, inviting scholars of all disciplines to present deeply thoughtful works. However, many academics today are taking *Harry Potter* much further — bringing it with them into the classroom itself.

Composition and literature teachers mention Harry as a familiar, simplified example of concepts like third-person limited narration or cross-genre fiction. The books are used to teach the classics from Shakespeare, Blake, and Dickens to Arthurian romances. Likewise, creative writing teachers embrace the series as their students struggle to master Joseph Campbell's hero's journey and write their own epics. Education majors construct lesson plans for the K-8 curriculum using the series. Introductory freshman classes, too, focus on *Harry Potter* as a fun transition class, welcoming students to university with a taste of the familiar. Jungian archetypes and concepts of good and evil shine in all seven books, producing fodder for philosophy and psychology. Nonetheless, these are all predictable, well-trodden paths, ones that have been broken already with *Alice in Wonderland, Star Wars,* the Narnia books, and other popular series.

The fascinating part is how many subjects outside literature the books can teach. Romance language teachers and SAT instructors find a wealth of memory aids in the Latin roots of Rowling's spells. Medieval studies too fits well into the Potter series, with its emphasis on alchemy and ancient bestiaries. Even modern history classes reference the blood purity laws and ghettos of *Deathly Hallows,* exploring the false propaganda and racism of World War II. In fact, issues of race, gender, class, marginalization, and stereotypes permeate the series, bringing Harry and his friends into sociology, gender studies, and other social science classrooms. Universities also welcome Harry into theology classes as they debate concepts of the soul, the afterlife, and concepts of true righteousness.

The hard sciences too take their place in this spectrum: Hermione's fascination with logic, arithmancy, and astronomy guides other girls on those paths, while science professors speculate whether antigravity research could someday create the brooms and flying cars of Harry's world. The 100-person class "Harry Potter and Genetics," taught at Sun Yat-sen University in China, clarifies that the series is stretching far beyond its origin as a work of children's fiction.

The books also offer moral and social values for children, guiding them to make the right choices, deal with bullies, and find friends, channeling shyness and disabilities to find empowerment. Those unable to connect with today's religions are turning to Harry for spiritual guidance and emotional well-being as well as entertainment. Other children are having a delightful time at Hogwarts "camps" held at colleges and community centers. Kids learn "spells" (Latin roots), "potions" (cooking or chemistry), astronomy, herbology, and care of magical creatures — or exotic creatures at least.

Online, Rowling is pioneering the web as a new kind of author, creating a virtual community and computer game in one: Pottermore teaches readers of all ages a new way to interact and enjoy the series, while releasing hidden gems of the author's original notes. Readers respond by creating fan fiction, art, video mash-ups and more, building a fandom made up of their creative work as much as their favorite author's. By comparing the series with *The Hunger Games*, *Twilight*, and other franchises, fans perform a new style of literary criticism for a new century, even as they remake the works as they desire. As Enotes.com reveals, these teens are truly engaging with the Potter series, discussing and dissecting literature with an effort they rarely devote to their classroom anthologies of classics, and the ease of the web allows them to become a new kind of active readers — creators themselves.

As the finished series is superseded by new franchises, will this cultural icon last? It's difficult to guarantee. However, *The Lord of the Rings* and *The Chronicles of Narnia* did. *Alice in Wonderland* and *The Wizard of Oz* did. In a world of books, the best and most beloved continue to entice new readers each year. And with a new theme park in Florida, one coming in California, a burgeoning new Pottermore website, and a new literary novel by Rowling herself, it seems likely Harry's popularity will be endless. Thus its classroom potential for succeeding generations of students can only grow.

Part I

Reaching Kids — A New Wave of Young Readers

From Hogwarts Academy to the Hero's Journey

Lana A. Whited

Imagine a group of middle schoolers wearing gloves and goggles, peering intently into cauldrons, smoke rising around their ears. This is a scene not from Potions class in the Hogwarts dungeon but from a Ferrum College Summer Enrichment Camp class called "Hogwarts Academy." The class is *Harry Potter* immersion, from the first-day sorting through the distribution of O.W.L. certificates at the end of the week. Its participants are academically talented 10- to 13-year-olds for whom hanging out at the pool isn't a sufficiently challenging way to spend summer vacation. Although the curriculum has changed little (a problem to be discussed shortly), young "witches" and "wizards" are returning for their second and third years.

In fall 2011, I had my first opportunity to teach an entire undergraduate course themed around the *Harry Potter* books, a topics course offered primarily for sophomores pursuing completion of the college's general education requirement in literature. The course, Harry Potter and the Hero Myth, is a survey of Western hero stories, starting with *The Epic of Gilgamesh* and ending with the *Harry Potter* saga. The focus of the course is the hero archetype, following Joseph Campbell's *The Hero with a Thousand Faces*. The undergraduates who take this course do not get sorted, have a Defense Against the Dark Arts lesson, or earn house points and O.W. L. certificates (although they would probably like to). Instead, they learn how to perform literary analysis using both classic and contemporary texts.

In some ways, these two classes would seem to have little in common, other than dealing with the *Harry Potter* saga. The Summer Enrichment Program is largely a "doing" program, while the college course is primarily a reading, critical thinking, and writing scholastic experience, with measured outcomes. The two audiences are obviously different in age, maturity, and educational experience, although it turns out that all students in both groups have often read much of the same literature, and sometimes the younger students have read *more*. The Summer Enrichment campers are also consistently more enthusiastic, which is understandable, considering the limited scope of their course and the fact that it involves no required reading or homework. Despite the differences in the two classes, however, they have been enriching for me to teach and to consider how one experience might inform the other: what I can learn from tweens about teaching *Harry Potter* to undergraduates, and vice versa.

Hogwarts Academy (Ferrum College Summer Enrichment Camp)

On the first day of Hogwarts Academy, I don a master's robe (which resembles a Hogwarts costume far more than my doctoral regalia) and a witches' hat and await the arrival of my charges, who come en masse, escorted by their college student counselor. The classroom door, bearing a large "Hogwarts Academy" sign, is closed, the counselor advised in advance to knock. I open the door, greet the students, and recite Professor Minerva McGonagall's speech preceding the Sorting: "Welcome to Hogwarts. The start-of-term banquet will begin shortly, but before you take your seats in the Great Hall, you will be sorted into your houses" (*SS* 114).

The Sorting is one of students' favorite parts of Hogwarts Academy, and students who have returned for the second or third year invariably want to be re-sorted into the same house as before, although I do not insist upon it. In alphabetical order, I call students' names in Hogwarts fashion, last name first: "Stein, Madison!" The summoned student sits on a tall stool at the front of the room, wearing my Sorting Hat, in front of a backdrop of Harry Potter book jackets (this makes a delightful photo, which I hand out the second or third day as keepsakes).

The hat originally called out house names, courtesy of an electronic mechanism in the crown. But after a few years of use, the mechanism failed, and there was a period of about a year when the hat, sitting on a windowsill in my office, would occasionally call out the name with no warning and without my touching it. This was always startling and, especially when a student happened to be in my office, downright funny.

Because the Sorting Hat was always somewhat unreliable and because real flesh-and-blood *Harry Potter* fans don't want their Sorting to be random, I have had to devise another method of conducting our ceremony. For the first year, I had the student simply whisper the name of the desired house in the ear of the aide, who then called it out, and we all applauded. But this was not suitably dramatic, as there was no element of surprise for the student being Sorted. So I began having students in turn complete an online Sorting quiz with preference questions such as "What is your favorite Hogwarts subject?" and personality/character questions such as whether you would keep a lost wallet if no one saw you find it.

We also begin wand-making on the first day, and while one student is taking the quiz (which takes three to four minutes), the others are painting varying lengths of thin dowel sticks. Afterward, I give a mini-lecture on Celtic wandlore with an introduction to the Celtic lunar cycle and the association of certain wood types with certain moons or months, so that students can find their appropriate wands and consider the religious and pagan symbolism. For example, the wood associated with the July moon would be holly, Harry Potter's wand wood (for his July 31 birthday).[1]

After painting their wands, students clean up the painting area and prepare for the Sorting ceremony. Because the computerized quiz generates the house selection, students do not know their assignment until it is announced, and there are surprises (and sometimes disappointments). After the Sorting, the classroom is rearranged, one or two rows of seats per house, and I ask each house to make a banner (using 11 × 17 paper and the colored pencils, crayons, and markers on the crafts table) to be used for the entire week. We tape each banner on the wall behind its table and conclude the class with as many rounds of *Harry Potter* trivia questions as we have time for, with house points awarded for correct answers. Each house gets the same number of turns, and anyone who blurts out an answer out of order loses house points. Trivia questions always reflect the days' lesson, and, on the first day, the questions cover Hogwarts houses, characters' house assignments, and wands. (For a sample list of trivia questions, see the Appendix.) By the end of the first day, students are generally so immersed in the experience that they leave calling me "Professor McGonagall" rather than "Dr. Whited." The fact that I am what Brits call a "ginger"—a redhead—probably contributes to students' fantasy.

We should note that Hogwarts Academy classes are 90 minutes long, and I usually have two before lunch and one or two after. It is important, from the first day, to have projects students can work on if they're finished with an assigned task or awaiting a turn at the crafts table. For example, first-year students have the opportunity to earn an Ordinary Wizarding Levels (O.W.L.) certificate by completing a chart listing all eight core subjects, along with the instructors, textbooks, and required supplies for each subject (see the Appendix). Their final marks of O (outstanding), E (exceeds expectations), A (acceptable), P (poor), D (dreadful), and T (Troll) are determined by the accuracy and thoroughness of the information they provide.

In addition, students are always welcome to read or use resources from our classroom library, which includes all seven *Harry Potter* books and non–English editions of a few, as well as about two dozen secondary sources on *Harry Potter*, one of which is the volume I edited, *The Ivory Tower and Harry Potter*.[2] The library also includes *Harry Potter*–themed board games, such as *Uno*, *Scene It?* and *Clue*, which students are invited to play in pairs or groups during transitions. I display my Potter paraphernalia on another table: figurines, Christmas ornaments, kaleidoscope boxes, stuffed creatures, and Lego kits; in three years of nearly twenty classes, no artifact has ever disappeared. I also decorate the walls with the films' photographs, most from old calendars. In other words, there is a lot to look at in the classroom. I decided before the first class that if a student claimed to have finished all the projects and wanted something to do, I would suggest drawing an alternate cover illustration, but to date I have never had to use this suggestion.

The wand project is also a good occupier of transition time, as the wand is created in several stages. On the first day, students only paint the wand, often using their house colors or a natural color. After the paint is dry, on the second day, students can apply ribbon, glitter, feathers, or other ornaments, and then wait for the glue to dry. This project also involves the completion of a Wand Registration Certificate for the Ministry of Magic, listing the wood type, core ingredients, and quality of motion. For example, Mr. Ollivander, the wand maker, describes Lily Potter's wand as "Ten and a quarter inches long, swishy, made of willow. Nice wand for charm work" (*SS* 82). The student also draws a picture of the wand, using colored pencils. This step generally takes the student 15–20 minutes. (For a copy of the certificate, see the Appendix.)

Although the first and last days of Hogwarts Academy have always followed the same format, the lessons on days two, three, and four depend on external scheduling. When available, Dr. Jason Powell (who comes to class in his own homemade Severus Snape costume) conducts Potions from a laboratory in the science building, and students don goggles and gloves for the lesson (this is one of the best photo-ops for both the Summer Enrichment staff and the college's Public Relations Office, and we have also had a local news crew in the class twice. Photos are available on the Ferrum College website at http://www.ferrum.edu/fcsec and on the Facebook page "Ferrum College Summer Enrichment Camp.") Using his best Severus Snape imitation, Dr. Powell gives a few demonstrates involving changing the color of liquids and causing substances to make loud noises, before asking students to undertake several projects. Two experiments result in edible outcomes: Dr. Powell freezes marshmallows in liquid nitrogen, and he makes vanilla ice cream using the liquid nitrogen, not an ice cream maker! One of my goals for the entire week is to impress upon students the broad nature of the Hogwarts education, and the Potions lesson is our natural sciences exemplar.

History of magic is among the easiest of the Hogwarts subjects to present, and I try to be more energetic than Professor Binns, the ghost professor who drones on while generations of students slumber. I adapt the subject to talk about the tradition of books—particularly British ones—about the education of young witches and wizards. Examples include the *Worst Witch* series by Jill Murphy and Anthony Horowitz's *Groosham Grange* (both set in boarding schools), as well as Ursula K. LeGuin's Earthsea saga, Monica Furlong's *Wise Child*, and Diana Wynne Jones's Chrestomanci series. We also discuss elements of the history of magic such as alchemy.

This lesson is the most academic and traditional of the week, and I have been somewhat dissatisfied with my methodology in presenting it. However, our discussion of alchemist Nicholas Flamel's career took a more local and interesting turn in Summer 2010 when a colleague in religion traveled to Spain to undertake a portion of the pilgrimage of St. James—the Camino de Santiago. According to sources, Flamel undertook the same pilgrimage in the late fourteenth century in an effort to obtain a translator for *The Book of Abraham the Mage*. The book, which Flamel said he first saw in a dream, was written in an ancient form of Hebrew and was said to contain instructions for using the Philosopher's Stone to perform a transmutation of other substances into gold.[3] My colleague's photographs made this lesson considerably more compelling. Adolescent readers are also familiar with Michael Scott's very popular five-part series *The Secrets of the Immortal Nicholas Flamel,* and consequently are very conversant with Flamel's life. Some, for example, will have heard the legend that Flamel's grave was opened and no body found, adding evidence for those who wanted to believe that the alchemist had, in fact, discovered the secret of immortality. If my presentation of this material relies on a largely traditional talk-and-PowerPoint methodology, my students still seem to find it more interesting than Professor Binns' lectures, and some who have not read Michael Scott's *Nicholas Flamel* series go home vowing to do so.

Among the more difficult Hogwarts subjects to address in a brick-and-mortar classroom building is Defense Against the Dark Arts. I cannot ask the Summer Enrichment Camp organizers to find me a boggart in a wardrobe on which students can practice Patronus-conjuring spells, and I can only imagine what the college's insurance underwriters and liability consultants might have to say if they could. But DADA is Harry's favorite subject, and at some point every year after the wands are finished, students pretend to duel while yelling hexes and jinxes. (Their Latin pronunciation is first rate.) In lieu of the real action, we watch the scene in *Harry Potter and the Prisoner of Azkaban* when

Remus Lupin teaches students how to conjure the Patronus, and I ask the students, using the art supplies in the room, to draw what they would see if they released their boggarts from the wardrobe. The range of responses always includes a variety of predictable but nevertheless well-executed snakes and spiders, as well as interesting representations of fear of the dark, of being lost, and — not surprising for this group — of bad grades.

A few students in every group produce a representation of themselves alone in the world, having lost their parents; one student drew a page with newspaper obituaries, featuring her mother's and father's names. This appears to be a far greater fear for my students than the possibility of their own deaths, a phenomenon that developmental psychology explains. I ask students to name (or, if we've been talking for a while and need movement, to write on the board) the names of other fictional or mythical characters who are separated from one or both parents. I usually cut this discussion off after five minutes, after students have compiled a long list that includes Cinderella and Moses. I embellish their list only if they are unable to think of non–Western examples, in order to make the point that the theme of the parentless or inadequately parented hero is universal. Then I ask them to explain why this theme is so prevalent, particularly in juvenile fiction. Using the discussion, I can steer the class toward understanding that being adrift in the world without parents is the greatest fear for most young readers and that works such as Cinderella variants and the *Harry Potter* saga can help them to work through this fear vicariously.

As a final activity for DADA, I ask each student to produce a drawing of his or her Patronus. What animal does each perceive to be his or her guardian or source of strength? Like Harry, whose Patronus takes the form of a stag, students convey in their drawings a desire for superior strength or ability and always produce lions, eagles, owls, dragons, unicorns, and a surprising number of turtles (which they appear to view as invulnerable, compared with most other animals).

The animals that populate the *Harry Potter* series were the focus of a Care of Magical Creatures class during one year of my Hogwarts Academy experience. My colleague Tina Hanlon maintains a website about dragons in art and literature (available at http://www2.ferrum.edu/thanlon/dragons) and adapted a PowerPoint presentation for my students. Because I like to have an interactive class, I began by inviting them to write on the chalkboard the names of all the creatures, real and magical, that appear in the novels. Then I introduced Dr. Hanlon. We supplemented the presentation by bringing to class copies of several bestiaries, both in print and online (including Rowling's *Fantastic Beasts and Where to Find Them* and others available in Renée Ward's List of Medieval Resources in the Appendix). In another year of Hogwarts

Academy, when Dr. Hanlon was unavailable, I talked the class through her slideshow and asked our class aide, Ben Lavon, to summarize a college paper he'd written on how Rowling uses the phoenix as both a symbol and a plot device. The *Harry Potter Lexicon* includes a useful bestiary that distinguishes which creatures Rowling borrows from myth and folklore and which ones she made up or adapted, such as House-elves (http://www.hp-lexicon.org/bestiary/bestiary.html). This class, like the segment on Nicholas Flamel, is a valuable lesson for students in how writers combine research with their own imaginations.

Not all of my best classes in Hogwarts Academy are carefully planned. One evolved quite extemporaneously the day after a group of campers had seen a performance by Ferrum College's Jack Tale Players, a theatrical troupe that has been performing the traditional stories and music of the Blue Ridge region for 35 years. I was walking in from the parking lot the following morning, thinking about how to jazz up a forthcoming discussion on spells and charms and their Latinate roots. It suddenly occurred to me that a folk tale plays a pivotal role in the culmination of the *Harry Potter* saga and that among the books in our classroom library was *The Tales of Beedle the Bard*. What would happen if I directed the students to dramatize "The Tale of the Three Brothers," Jack Tales style? The result became one of my very best Hogwarts Academy experiences, one that I am eager to repeat.

The Jack Tale Players use a traditional mountain storytelling style, with actors performing the scenes as the narrator describes them. The actors use minimal props, sometimes play animals, and even assume the shapes of objects such as a door or bush. The resulting style seems both rehearsed and improvisational. We began our class that morning with a discussion of the performance style, and the students were astute analysts. We decided that I would first read the story while a student volunteer wrote the roles on the chalkboard. Then we cast the roles, including a narrator, and read the story a second time, working out what lines characters would actually say, as well as their movements and any props. Our three primary props were the Elder wand, the Resurrection Stone, and the Cloak of Invisibility. For the first, we used a wand I had made during my first Hogwarts Academy class (although once we used a wand bought at the Wizarding World of Harry Potter in Orlando). For the second, we used a small coal turtle with green eyes. And for the third, we used the master's robe I had worn as Professor McGonagall on the first day (which I leave in the room in case students want to be photographed in a robe with the Sorting Hat).

We rehearsed once, and the second time I filmed the performance for the Summer Enrichment Camp website and Facebook page. In subsequent classes that day, I decided to leave the room for 10–15 minutes during the students' rehearsal under the direction of the student counselor. My departure and return seemed to increase students' sense that they were performing the folktale for a true audience. We concluded each class with a discussion of why Rowling decided to make a folktale central to the resolution of her series, and I believe the discussion enhanced students' understanding of the Jack Tale Players' performance, of folktales in general, and of the *Harry Potter* saga. I knew we had been successful when I overheard students from the morning classes enthusiastically telling their friends at lunch what we'd done—several asked me when the videos would be uploaded and where their parents might view them. Although I will have to deal with the complication that students do not see a Jack Tales performance in every week of the program, I have several videotaped Jack Tales that I can show as a starting point.

The last day of Hogwarts Academy, like the first day, is always the same: it is a day for the awarding of O.W.L. certificates (and, sometimes, N.E.W.T. certificates—more on this later), for drinking butterbeer (which I make from a recipe using mostly cream soda and butterscotch syrup), and for playing *Harry Potter*–themed games, including a house-against-house *Harry Potter Scene It?* Match. At the end of the match, the house points for the week are tallied and the winner declared. The prize is being first in line for butterbeer. I also give a brief presentation (primarily via websites) on *Harry Potter* in popular culture, including the following: the International Quidditch Association (IQA) and the inroads quidditch has made as an international (and NCAA) sport; *Harry Potter*–themed popular music, including such wizard rock bands as Neville's Froggy Girl and Draco and the Malfoys; Harry Potter merchandise; and Harry Potter tourism, including the Wizarding World of Harry Potter (which at least one student in each class has visited). Then I allow five to ten minutes for students to recommend websites and pull up a few. Popular choices are the *Harry Potter Puppet Pals* videos on YouTube ("The Mysterious Ticking Noise" is a special favorite [http://www.youtube.com/watch?v= Tx1XIm6q4r4]) and some pages on a Lego site featuring *Harry Potter*–themed Lego kits. Beginning with the next class, I will add J. K. Rowling's *Pottermore*.

After the O.W.L. certificates are distributed, I call students' attention to the fact that the series never includes a graduation ceremony and ask them to speculate on what they imagine a Hogwarts Commencement would be like. They generally describe something like the Start-of-Term or End-of-Term feast, with diploma presentations and speeches. Then we talk briefly about *why* Rowling never wrote a graduation ceremony. (In fact, in the United Kingdom, there is no formal graduation ceremony until students complete university.) Regardless, students have mixed opinions about Rowling's writing off a final year set at Hogwarts: some are disappointed and say they miss the familiar setting, and some say they have grown weary of mention of the same classes and welcome the change. Because this particular group of students tends to be academically advanced, they also have mixed feelings about Harry's not having finished his Hogwarts education.

There are several changes or additions I would like to make to the class. Because there are sessions when my chemistry colleague is not available, I would like to develop a Herbology lesson featuring a member of our horticulture faculty. The college has a nice greenhouse, and students would undoubtedly enjoy learning that the idea of covering one's ears to avoid hearing a Mandrake scream actually has a long history in English folklore, or that the American Mandrake or "May Apple" has cytotoxic (cell-killing) properties and is used in chemotherapy.[4] I also have a strong hankering to play quidditch with students. Equipped with the IQA website's rulebook, I believe the students and I could figure out how to assign positions and devise a match. Although the *IQA Rulebook* is intended for a college-aged population, it includes an appendix about adapting the rules for middle school and high school players (essentially, minimizing aggression). Quidditch would give campers a greater sense of a Hogwarts-like experience, I believe. The greatest obstacle may be whether the number of broomsticks required is within the FCSEC budget!

The biggest challenge I currently face in offering Hogwarts Academy stems, ironically, from the fact that the class has been so popular that students are returning for a second and even third Hogwarts experience. I anticipate that it won't be long before I work with counselors who have themselves attended Hogwarts Academy. The students rarely complain about repeating activities, but I am currently at work on devising a multilayered experience. The idea is that new students would study selections from the eight core subjects offered to Hogwarts students in the first year: Astronomy, Charms, Defense Against the Dark Arts, Flying (no textbook!), Herbology, History of Magic, Potions, and Transfiguration. Provided the curriculum could become more fixed, students attending for the second year could study any of the core subjects not available during their first year, with the addition of quidditch, as it is not allowed for first-year students (except Harry). Third-year students could be offered the Hogwarts elective subjects, which include Ancient Runes, Arithmancy, Care of Magical Creatures, Divination (a tea party, with leaf-reading and astrology chart drawing!), Muggle Studies, and, for the very advanced students, Apparition. While I hope no students would actually disappear, they would probably be intrigued to learn that researchers at the University of Dallas (Texas) have attempted to create a cloaking or mirage effect that temporarily hides objects from view by using changes in temperature to cause light rays to bend.[5] I also allow returning students who have already earned O.W.L. certificates to complete a N.E.W.T.s chart listing text, teacher, and supplies needed for the elective courses.

The hurdle to establishing a fixed, multi-layered Hogwarts program is the unpredictability of class size after the first year, as, ideally, second- and third-year students would have their own separate classes. A compromise might be to have a combined returning class in which the third-year students work more independently. In summer 2011, for example, when I had three third-year students in the same class, I asked them to devise a presentation, including PowerPoint, for the class on Harry Potter in Popular Culture, and they were excused from some first-year activities to work in an adjacent classroom and the library under the supervision of the class aide.

Children who are not in my classes stop me at lunch and tell me that they had wanted to take the class, but it was full, so they'll register for camp earlier next year. Other teachers and counselors also gleefully discuss my activities. For a few days, I feel a little like a rock star—all because of a series of books.

Harry Potter and the Hero Myth (Ferrum College Undergraduate Course)

After three years as the headmistress of Hogwarts Academy, I had my first opportunity to teach a college-level *Harry Potter* course in fall 2011. The course, offered on the sophomore level, was one of five choices for students meeting the core requirement in literature, with the other choices being the far more traditional World, British, American, and African-American literatures. The student learning outcomes for the "sophomore" literature courses include demonstrating competence in the reading, interpretation, analysis, and evaluation of texts; writing about literature with unity, coherence, and adherence to standard rules and conventions; employing independent critical thinking skills; and demonstrating an understanding of cultural differences. In addition, my course was designed to meet three hours of the college's writing-intensive requirement for students who had already taken three hours of 200-level literature, which means that the quantity of writing had to exceed fifteen pages, be undertaken via a recursive process (with multiple drafts), and incorporate both primary and secondary sources. In addition, students were expected to maintain an average of "C" or better on the required writing assignments.

Eighteen students enrolled in the class, five of them English majors and one an English minor. Of five students who earned A's, three were English majors (the other two were criminal justice majors). The two English majors who did not earn A's earned B's. Ten students said they took the class predominately to meet the core requirement in literature, while the other eight had already met the requirement and were taking it as an English elective or for the subject matter. One student wrote on her student profile form, "I am a major *Harry Potter* fan [and] usually get into detailed discussions about it with my friends." In addition, several students indicated a general interest in fantasy. Three students said that they had already written a fantasy novel themselves, and one young man is such an avid reader of fantasy that he covered, in his research presentation, the plot of Brian Jacques and Gary Chalk's twenty-two novel *Redwall* series. In other words, the students as a group were remarkably immersed in fantasy in general and the *Harry Potter* novels specifically.

The course description for English 207: Harry Potter and the Hero Myth is as follows:

> A study of the Harry Potter saga, focusing on the tradition of fantasy in literature in English and the hero myth in Western culture. Students should be familiar with the first six Harry Potter novels *prior to* the start of the course, and during the course students will read the last book in the series as well as works that represent Rowling's antecedents, influences, and contemporaries.

Students wrote three short analytical essays in the course, followed by a research project, which included both a paper of 8–10 pages and a class presentation with PowerPoint (more on the research project later). In addition, during the reading and discussion of each novel, students completed a study sheet for that novel (see the Appendix) and were expected to come to class each day with a five-by-seven index card with two or three questions and a selected quotation.

We generally began each discussion with these cards, after I gave a brief lecture of historical or critical relevance to the week's reading. For example, when we started *Gilgamesh*, I spoke briefly about the nineteenth-century discovery of the twelve Sumerian tablets containing the epic. Interestingly, a student had seen the tablets on a visit to the British Museum during the previous May term, so she knew more about them than I did (I love it when this happens).

We began the course with discussion of the terms *fantasy*, *myth*, and *the hero*. The ambiguous use of the term *hero* to mean both "admirable person" and "main character" set up a subsequent discussion about whether it is necessary for a protagonist to be admirable. Then we launched right into *Harry Potter and the Deathly Hallows*, discussing the book as both a self-contained entity and the culmination of the *Harry Potter* saga.

One of the chief luxuries, for me, was having students who were mostly already familiar with the main text. Consequently, our discussion could begin on a higher plane and go further than with any other literature course I have taught. Coming into the course, fifteen of eighteen students had read all seven books, some of them more than once. Of the other three, one student had read six and started book seven; one had read *Sorcerer's Stone* and half of *Chamber of Secrets*, and only one had read none.

After the *Harry Potter* discussion, we read course texts chronologically: *Gilgamesh* (circa 2750–2500 B.C.E.); *The Odyssey* (circa 700 B.C.E.); *The Sword in the Stone* (1938, but, of course, based on Arthurian legend, which traces its roots all the way to Celtic mythology); *The Lion, the Witch, and the Wardrobe* (1950); and *The Hunger Games* (2008). It is a shame to have such a limited reading list for such a major topic, and it was difficult to choose texts from such a broad range of possibilities. Nonetheless, the student presentations involved eighteen other works in the hero subgenre and provided students with an opportunity to hear a little about these other epics. Our presentation schedule included texts (chosen by students) covering a very broad time frame: *Sundiata: An Epic of Old Mali* (1210–1260); *The Twelve Labors of Hercules* (600 B.C.E.); *The Merry Adventures of Robin Hood* (Howard Pyle, 1883); *The Wonderful Wizard of Oz* (L. Frank Baum, 1900); *Peter Pan* (J. M. Barrie, stage play, 1904; book, 1911); *The Hobbit* (J.R.R Tolkien, 1937); the *Redwall* Series (Brian Jacques and Gary Chalk, 1986–2011); *The Eye of the World* (Robert Jordan, 1990); *The Golden Compass* (Philip Pullman, 1995); *Eragon* (Christopher Paolini, 2002); *Trickster's Choice* (Tamora Pierce, 2003); *The Lightning Thief* (Rick Riordan, 2005); *Twilight* (Stephenie Meyer, 2005); *The Alchemyst* (Michael Scott, 2007); *Fell* (David Clement-Davies, 2007); *Eon* (Alison Goodman, 2008); *Test of Metal* (Matthew Stover, 2010); and *The Son of Neptune* (Rick Riordan, 2011).

It is abundantly clear from the students' choices that they grew up reading avidly, as nearly half of these books were published during their youth or adolescence, and few are likely to have ever been assigned reading. The aim of the research project assignment was twofold: first, to provide each student with the opportunity to apply concepts from our secondary readings to a work of fantasy not discussed by the entire class; and second, to acquaint the class with a much broader range of hero stories than simply the six assigned texts. Many students seemed to regard the presentations as an opportunity to compile future reading lists, and they frequently noted on their peer evaluations that they planned to read the works their classmates had selected.

In addition to the six primary texts, we also read two secondary works: a selection from *The Myth of the Birth of the Hero* by Austrian psychoanalyst Otto Rank (a close associate of Sigmund Freud), and one from American comparative mythologist Joseph Campbell's *The Hero with a Thousand Faces*. I asked all students, as homework assignments, to produce outlines of both Rank's stages of the hero saga and Campbell's monomyth of the hero's journey.

The outlines became the foundation for the research project, in which the student was expected to apply either Rank's or Campbell's ideas to the primary text he or she chose.

One of the best responses to the assignment was Carey Elson Kimbrough's paper "The Hero's Journey and *Eragon*." Kimbrough condenses Campbell's monomyth into several key steps applicable to *Eragon*, while acknowledging that it is difficult to impose a pattern designed for an entire myth on what is merely the first novel in Paolini's *Inheritance Cycle*. His facility with Campbell's system is aptly illustrated by his explanation of how Campbell's "Crossing the First Threshold" stage (in which the hero encounters a "threshold guardian at the entrance to a zone of magnified power,"[6]) applies to *Eragon* as a figurative, not a literal, crossing:

> This threshold does not take the form of a physical place in Eragon's life; rather it is an event. Eragon crosses his threshold when he inadvertently casts his first spell.... During a fight with these fierce beasts [in Yazuac], Eragon accidently discovers magic in a moment of desperation by uttering the word "brisingr"; upon uttering this word, Eragon's arrow ignites in a blue flame and strikes the Urgals, causing an explosion.... With Eragon's budding knowledge of magic and the ancient language, he fully immerses himself in the legacy and culture of the nearly forgotten Dragon Riders. Before Eragon knew of magic and the ancient language, he was in a transition of sorts. As a Dragon Rider, he was no longer in Campbell's proposed ordinary world; but because he was not fully aware of all the secrets of Dragon Riders, he was not in Campbell's idea of a special world, either; he was stuck in between. With this new magical knowledge, Eragon officially completes his transition from the ordinary world into the special world of the Dragon Riders.[7]

In addition to students' excellent use of Rank and Campbell in their individual papers, we also had an interesting discussion about how the stages of Campbell's monomyth are illustrated in the progression of *Harry Potter* novels as a complete hero saga. Campbell's three general categories of the monomyth are "Separation/Departure," "Initiation," and "Return": Harry's *departure* or separation from the "normal" world and entry into the "special" world comes when he receives his Hogwarts invitation and leaves for the wizard school, where his *initiation* largely occurs. During his final confrontation with Voldemort in *Deathly Hallows*, he returns, if not to the "normal" world, then to Hogwarts, which by this time has become home to Harry, and achieves, by virtue of Voldemort's defeat, what Campbell calls "Freedom to Live."

The success of Carey Kimbrough's paper was eclipsed by his class presentation. In the conclusion of the paper, he began formulating a theory of a hero subtype when he noted Eragon's relative youth:

> Eragon is a very interesting character because unlike most classical literary heroes, he is not an adult; rather, he is an awkward teenager. This portrayal of the awkward,

moody teenage hero that embarks on not only a hero's journey, but also a coming of age story, is something many contemporary authors have begun to favor, rather than the older, more traditional heroes of ages past.[8]

By the time of his presentation, he had fully developed his theory of the hero subtype and given it a name: "the angsty teenage hero" (subtitled "Coming of Age While Saving the World"). In a discussion encompassing primarily Eragon, Percy Jackson, Harry Potter, and Katniss Everdeen, Kimbrough outlines the peculiar characteristics of his hero type:

- has "daddy issues," lives with the mother or mother's family, and acquires a mentor who becomes a father figure
- ventures away from the safe and familiar into the scary unknown
- is "marked" with a special designation (Shur'tugal, The Boy Who Lived, The Girl on Fire, the Lightning Thief)
- has a destiny outside himself or herself, beyond his or her individual control
- begins the journey as apathetic but becomes increasingly passionate
- is dominated by the moodiness or angst typical of adolescence
- acquires a "semi-perfect love interest" (Arya, Ginny, Peeta) and has both an "angsty" best friend (Murtagh, Ron, Gale) and a "non-angsty" best friend (Saphira, Hermione, Prim)
- encounters a "Big Bad," or antagonist (Galbatorix, Voldemort, President Snow) who is politically powerful and deeply talented, but paranoid and unstable
- experiences some psychological deterioration after the midpoint of the saga
- matures and accepts, even reclaims, his or her fate prior to triumphing

The critical thinking skills illustrated in Kimbrough's presentation were outstanding, and the presentation moved beyond the application of Campbell's ideas to the next steps in Bloom's Taxonomy: analysis, synthesis, and evaluation. Ultimately, the special adaptation of hero theory that Kimbrough achieved was an exemplar for his classmates, who also enjoyed the quirky critical vocabulary he formulated in terms such as "angsty teenaged hero" and "big bad."

I was very pleased with several other aspects of the presentations, as a group. The presentation on *Sundiata* provided us with an example of a story from a culture not otherwise represented on our reading list. That presentation and the one on *The Twelve Labors of Hercules*, combined with the required readings of *Gilgamesh* and *The Odyssey*, gave us four very old hero stories and a good discussion on the origins and oral nature of many early myths. We were lucky that students in a Theatre Arts class studying oral interpretation of texts presented staged readings (complete with a fire pit) from *Gilgamesh* while our course was in progress. We also enjoyed a nice balance of classics (*Robin Hood, Peter Pan, The Hobbit, The Wonderful Wizard of Oz*) with very contemporary texts by authors such as Pierce, Paolini, Pullman, Riordan, and Scott, all of whom have drawn a wide readership, and some of whom draw on myth and other medieval traditions.

The only complaint in the student evaluations concerned difficulty keeping up with the reading. At the risk of sounding like an old-timer, I recall an average of a novel a week in undergraduate English courses, and I believe that six young adult novels in thirteen and a half weeks is not a demanding load. However, I believe that if I distributed the required reading list by email prior to the start of the term (perhaps right after pre-registration), students could use the summer or winter break to begin the reading. I also like the suggestion made my students in my Novel I class that I assign a certain number of pages for each class day rather than just telling students to finish it by a certain date. This tells me that students want me to pace their reading, and those who read faster will feel advanced.

Transfiguration — Lessons from Intertwined Classes

As noted earlier, the populations in my two *Harry Potter* teaching experiences are different in many respects. But I believe there are lessons I can learn from each experience to improve the other. Adding a component of more traditional age-appropriate literary analysis to Hogwarts Academy could increase my summer campers' (and their parents') sense that our *Harry Potter* experience is useful academic enrichment, and infusing my Harry Potter and the Hero Myth class with the spirit of play so central to Hogwarts Academy might inspire my undergraduates to do even better work (and would just be downright fun!).

This sense of play might cause college students to engage on a deeper level in the course and feel more motivation to keep up with the reading. Early in the semester, I commented that I keep a Sorting Hat in my office and that students could feel free to stop by to be sorted. Only two or three did. If I brought the hat and stool to class on the first day, I might prompt student participation in the course earlier. I might introduce other lighter activities (perhaps as extra credit), and have students draw an illustration for a scene or an alternate book jacket cover. The dramatization my Hogwarts Academy students did using "The Tale of the Three Brothers" would be a good activity late in our discussion of *Deathly Hallows*, as the folktale illustrates the theme not only of that novel but of the entire *Harry* Potter series: there are at least three ways of responding to the inevitability of death, through forced confrontation (the elder wand), through denial (the resurrection stone), and through determined avoidance (the invisibility cloak). Ultimately, Rowling appears to be recommending determined avoidance: that we go about our lives minimizing the harm we do to others until the time for death is appropriate, when we welcome death "as an old friend" (*DH* 409).

In my recent Novel I class, I piloted a strategy of reading aloud to the class (or asking students to read) the first few pages of the *next week's* novel. I believe oral interpretation reflects so much of a student's understanding of a text that I could virtually predict my students' final grades by having them read a few pages. When I teach the *Harry Potter* class next, I want to try this preview strategy, as I believe it will whet students' appetites for the next novel as well as giving them a sense that they've already begun the reading and need only continue—starting is a bigger threshold than continuing. While I am sure my undergraduates would enjoy drinking butterbeer and playing Quidditch as well, there is obviously only time for so much play in a college-level course, in which the O.W.L.s and N.E.W.T.s have real weight.

If my Hogwarts Academy class has a flaw, it is that every session is tightly scheduled and activity-oriented, so there is little time for just sitting around and talking about *Harry Potter* the way one might do with a book club. During breaks, students often start these discussions: Which is your favorite book? Your least favorite? What do you think of the films? Have you been on Pottermore? Do you read fanfiction? Partially because of the richness of my undergraduate course's discussions, I would like to carve out space in the Summer Enrichment schedule for "The Common Room": open discussion of the texts that form the basis for our experience. Perhaps I will designate a receptacle or classroom wall for students' questions and ideas and encourage them to use any free time to contribute written selections. A similar in-class critical thinking strategy called "Gallery Walk" would serve the very same purpose: groups of students propose, develop, refine, and evaluate ideas about a common subject of study by posting on flip charts in succession, in rotating groups. The Gallery Walk strategy also allows shy students to share ideas without the stress of talking before a group (the middle school campers are less shy than some of my undergraduates). Another positive outcome of our Common Room discussion would be a reading list, compiled communally, that students could take home. Students in Hogwarts Academy are almost universally readers.

My long-term goal is to facilitate the transformation of these enthusiastic young readers into college students adept at and passionate about the analysis of literature. I fervently hope that they will populate all my courses and go on to become literary scholars or authors in their own right, all without losing the spirit of play that characterizes Hogwarts Academy.

Among the three objects willed by Albus Dumbledore to Harry, Ron, and Hermione is a collection of folktales. The three friends ultimately figure out that Dumbledore has bequeathed Hermione literature not just because of her tremendous intellect, but also because the stories are familiar to Ron from childhood. They were his bedtime stories, and he knows them by heart. The success of my two *Harry Potter* experiences affirms both ways of "knowing" literature — by the head and by the heart. The centrality of books is declared in what Ron recognizes as Hermione's mantra: "When in doubt, go to the library" (*COS* 255).

Notes

1. Mary Jones, "The Celtic Tree Calendar," *Jones' Celtic Encyclopedia,* 2004, http://www.maryjones.us/jce/celtictreecalendar.html.

2. Lana A. Whited, *The Ivory Tower and Harry Potter* (Columbia: University of Missouri Press, 2002).

3. Maurice Magre, "Nicolas Flamel et la Pierre Philosophale," in *Magiciens et Illuminés (Magicians, Seers, and Mystics),* trans. Reginald Merton, 1930. *Alchemylab.com,* accessed May 22, 2012, http://www.alchemylab.com/flamel.htm.

4. Thomas Baurley, "American Mandrake," *Naturally Science and Lore,* Nov. 7, 2010, http://www.technogypsie.com/science/?cat=22.

5. "Real Life 'Invisibility Cloak' Makes Objects Vanish," *International Business Times,* Oct. 5, 2011, http://au.ibtimes.com/articles/225375/20111005/invisibility-cloak-refaction-mirage-effect.htm.

6. Joseph Campbell, *The Hero with a Thousand Faces* (New York: Bollingen, 1949), 77.

7. Carey Kimbrough, "The Hero's Journey and *Eragon*" (unpublished paper, Ferrum College, 2011), 4–5.

8. Ibid., 9.

The Nuances of Rule-Breaking

Tenille Nowak

Fifteen years have passed since the first *Harry Potter* novel was released, and during that time, the boy wizard has become a prominent and controversial pop culture icon in America. A generation of young readers grew up following the adventures of Harry and his friends. For the parents of those young readers, ensuring that their children were reading age-appropriate material was not much of a concern since a significant amount of time passed before the next novel was released. Though this delay heightened anticipation and increased frustration for older readers, it also ensured that many who were the same age as Harry was in the first novel when they began reading matured along with him.

But what about today's young readers? Many parents recognize that it is their responsibility to ensure that their children are reading age-appropriate books. Some people may wonder why there is unease over how old children should be when they pick up the first *Harry Potter* novel. However, for parents of children aged seven to ten, there is plenty of reason for concern. After teaching several semesters of a college writing class in which we focused on the early *Harry Potter* novels for our major writing assignments, I discovered an interesting trend. One essay asked students to argue whether the first three *Harry Potter* novels were appropriate for children between seven and ten years old. Much to my surprise, a large number of students argued that the novels were not, in fact, appropriate for young readers. The majority of these students cited the same point: The rule-breaking by Harry and his friends and the inconsistency of the consequences for doing so presented a serious problem for parents trying to teach their children that they must conform to the rules. Multiple students argued that seeing an admired protagonist break the rules and frequently escape punishment would teach young readers that similar behavior was acceptable. This would place parents in a difficult position since, as Edmund Kern notes in *The Wisdom of Harry Potter*, children are "drawn to his magical world but then won over by his qualities, [and thus they] ... want to emulate Harry Potter."[1]

Undoubtedly, the *Harry Potter* novels have much to offer in the way of entertainment, moral development, and help with reading skills, but how could a parent explain to her child that sometimes it's okay to break the rules? Wouldn't it be better, my students argued, to simply prevent young children from reading the *Harry Potter* novels until they were older and more capable of understanding the subtle nuances of society?

Preventing young children from reading the books until they are perhaps 12 or 13 is one method of handling this issue. However, telling a child that he can't read the books when he's surrounded by *Harry Potter* commercials, movies, and merchandise is perhaps unrealistic and may instead encourage the child to read the books on the sly with no parental guidance. There is an alternative: Reading the novels with the young child so that parents may take the opportunity to discuss the scenes which may prove problematic had the child read them by himself. As Daniel Handler, author of the Lemony Snicket books, notes, "young readers are not only finding a diversion in the melodrama of the [characters'] lives, but they are also finding ways of contemplating our current troubles through stories."[2] Furthermore, he maintains that "we can find value in stories that admit the world is tumultuous, instead of reassuring us that it is not."[3] Therefore, instead of banning the books, parents and children can discuss various examples of rule-breaking in the early novels and specifically focus on the motivations behind those choices and the nature of the resulting consequences.

Handler is not the only one who recognizes the intrinsic value of fantasy stories like *Harry Potter*. Bruno Bettelheim addresses this idea in his text *The Uses of Enchantment*. He notes that "[s]ome parents fear that their children may get carried away by their fantasies; that when exposed to fairy tales, they will come to believe in magic ... [or that] a child's mind may become so overfed by fairy-tale fantasies as to neglect learning to cope with reality."[4] However, Bettelheim goes on to explain that children eventually grow out of this belief and he argues that fantasy tales are, in fact, a necessary part of a child's development. By engaging in fantasy, he argues, the child's imagination is nurtured, and his ability to interpret and cope with complex situations is enhanced. I agree with Bettelheim, and argue that the *Harry Potter* novels provide the perfect bridge for children who are just starting to crave more than the traditional "bedtime story" fairy tales. *Harry Potter* offers an intriguing blend of fantasy and reality as the wizarding world in which Harry lives is full of fun, adventure, and magical things ... but is also plagued with very real problems and turmoil. Thus, instead of avoiding conversations on challenging topics like rule-breaking, parents should, as psychologist Lawrence

Kohlberg argues, give children the chance to "work through the difficulties of moral conflict to have a better sense of ethical problems and solutions."[5] Discussion on issues like following rules is becoming increasingly crucial as the world changes and the lines of communication between parents and their children are often difficult to forge. Therefore, reading *Harry Potter* together and discussing the events that take place allows parents and children to not only lay the groundwork for future communication but also help children develop a better moral and ethical awareness.

For young readers, perhaps the most challenging aspect of understanding the ambiguities involved with rule-breaking in the early *Harry Potter* novels is that they must develop the ability to think critically and look beyond the characters' actions and the consequences. For many children, the world is black and white: If someone breaks the rules, he should get punished. Many of them do not yet understand that a person's *motivations* often have a profound impact on how authority figures react to the alleged infraction. However, for some parents, figuring out how to get their children to think critically about a text and understand this issue may prove challenging. In their article "To Find Yourself, Think for Yourself," Barbara Fink Chorzempa and Laurie Lapidus discuss a method of helping young children develop these critical thinking skills. They advocate the use of the Socratic method in inclusive elementary classrooms, noting that "teachers often struggle with developing students' abilities to think for themselves. As a result, students may find analyzing a piece of literature ... to be a daunting task."[6] Lapidus as quite successful using the Socratic method to encourage her students to read a text and then formulate questions and explore ideas in a discussion-based format. Students were able to control the discussion by formulating their own questions and providing answers by examining the text to find evidence to support those answers.

This was another key element of Lapidus' Socratic approach. Asking the "students to analyze the text critically and require them to provide support for their statements with details from the text"[7] required them to find proof of their conclusions and thus gave said conclusions more significance and validity. Overall, Chorzempa and Lapidus concluded that the Socratic method worked because it gave younger readers a sense of ownership over the text and their encounter with it. It also fostered a deeper, more critical understanding of the story's more subtle points and it helped them develop the skills to engage more profoundly with the text. As such, I suggest that parents who are uncertain of how to approach the *Harry Potter* texts with their young readers employ a modified version of Lapidus' Socratic approach.

While Lapidus encouraged her students to develop their own critical thinking questions, we must recognize that some younger readers may not be intellectually prepared to do so. Therefore, and since most parents may not be familiar with the Socratic method, the remainder of this article will offer a sampling of scenes from the first three *Harry Potter* novels which are appropriate for a discussion about rule-breaking and motivation, along with a series of corresponding questions that parents may use (and modify as they see fit) when discussing those scenes with their children. It is my belief that using this modified Socratic approach will allow children to begin developing their critical thinking skills and gain a more solid understanding of society's variable views on rule-breaking and its consequences.

Our first scene occurs in *Harry Potter and the Sorcerer's Stone* when Harry and his friends get their first lesson on how to ride a broomstick. During the lesson, Neville Longbottom, a sweet, shy, and clumsy wizard, is injured. Madame Hooch tells the students, "None of you is to move while I take this boy to the hospital wing! You leave those brooms where they are or you'll be out of Hogwarts before you can say 'Quidditch'" (*SS* 147). The consequences are clear and forbidding: instant expulsion. However, Malfoy steals Neville's dropped Remembrall and flies off, taunting the other students. Despite Hermione's warnings ("No! ... Madam Hooch told us not to move — you'll get us all into trouble"), Harry leaps on his broom and pursues Malfoy. He gets the Remembrall back, but has quite obviously broken the no flying rule. Professor McGonagall pounces on him and, like the reader, Harry is convinced that he "was going to be expelled... He hadn't even lasted two weeks. He'd be packing his bags in ten minutes" (*SS* 150). However, much to Harry's surprise, he isn't expelled but is instead recruited as the Seeker for the Gryffindor House Quidditch team.

Though adults may exult in Harry getting the best of the odious Malfoy, young readers may question why he wasn't punished. Their confusion is certainly understandable because the consequences were clearly laid out and Harry was caught red-handed. This scene is an excellent example of how a character's motivations can have a strong influence on an authority figure's decision to suspend punishment. Asking the following basic questions can help the child look beyond the plot to understand Professor McGonagall's decision. Why did Malfoy steal Neville's Remembrall? Is stealing a nice thing to do? Is it okay to let someone steal another person's property if we can stop them? How would you feel if it was your toy that was stolen and nobody helped you? Do you think someone should be punished if he got your toy back for you from the bully? As parents will notice, these questions are designed to progressively build on the hypothetical responses that children will likely give. Although it may be tempting for parents to provide an answer, Chorzempa and Lapidus note that "teachers [and parents] must refrain from sharing their thoughts through the discussion to allow the [children] to develop their own critical thinking skills."⁸ Allowing the child time to think and formulate his own responses not only helps him develop critical thinking skills but also solidifies his conclusions in his mind because he came to them *himself.*

Parents should encourage the child to recognize that Harry's motivation is the key element that influenced McGonagall's decision, and may want to emphasize this idea by continuing with these additional questions: Did Harry fly his broomstick just to disobey Madame Hooch? If he wasn't trying to disobey, why did Harry fly his broomstick? Does Harry deserve to be punished for helping Neville? Do we think that Professor McGonagall is a wise woman? Would she be able to understand why Harry flew on his broomstick?

The goal of these first two sets of questions is to subtly encourage the child to come to several important conclusions. First, Malfoy was being a bully, and tolerating bullies is never acceptable. Second, Neville was helpless to defend himself, and it is always important to stand up for the weak. Third, Harry's actions were done to help a friend. If parents can coach their children into providing answers that bring out these ideas, they will have concluded that Harry's rule-breaking does not deserve punishment because it was done with the sole intent of helping a friend, and standing up to bullies should be rewarded, not punished.

Another episode in *Harry Potter and the Sorcerer's Stone* that provides a good opportunity to engage children in a critical conversation about rule-breaking and consequences is when Harry and Hermione help Hagrid relocate the illegal dragon that he is hiding in his cottage. After Harry and Hermione send the baby dragon off with Charlie Weasley, they are discovered sneaking back to their dormitories. Professor McGonagall berates them and snarls that she's "disgusted... Four students out of bed in one night! I've never heard of such a thing before!" (*SS* 243). (Draco Malfoy and Neville Longbottom were also caught. Draco was trying to alert McGonagall that Harry and Hermione were out of bed, Neville was trying to warn them about Draco.) She immediately docks each student 50 points and sentences them to a detention.

Although Harry is once again breaking the rules to help a friend, there is a significant element in this scene which clearly demonstrates when breaking the rules to help a friend is right, and when doing so is wrong. While Harry and Hermione's efforts to assist Hagrid are motivated by the desire to help a friend, children need to understand that in the context of the situation, Hagrid's possession of an illegal baby dragon can also have a significant impact on whether punishment is administered or not. Earlier, when Harry, Ron, and Hermione first discover that Hagrid has obtained a dragon egg, Ron notes, "it's against our laws... Dragon breeding was outlawed by the Warlocks' Convention of 1709 ... anyway, you can't tame dragons, it's dangerous" (*SS* 230).

Even worse, Hagrid is an adult who not only has illegal actions but also asks children to break the rules on his behalf. This scene can help children understand that assisting another person to engage in illegal behavior cannot be tolerated. The fact that Harry and Hermione are punished provides clear evidence that the context of a situation sometimes supersedes one's good intentions.

This is a fairly complex scene to deal with because the child has just been encouraged to think that he should always help a friend in need. To help navigate this scenario, the following set of questions, again using a modified Socratic approach and building on the child's likely responses, may help the child realize the impact that illegality has on potential consequences: Is it okay for Hagrid to own a baby dragon? Why not? Is it okay for Harry and Hermione to help Hagrid break the law? Why not? If they are breaking the law by doing something illegal and dangerous, should they be punished? Why?

The key element here is that, although Harry and Hermione are helping a friend and Hagrid is trying to right a wrong that he has committed, covering up someone else's illegal actions is not acceptable. It is still breaking the law, and society's laws exist to protect people from harm and to prevent dangerous behavior that may injure others or their property. The wizard law against owning dragons is a perfect example. According to Harry's schoolbook *Fantastic Beasts and Where to Find Them*, dragons are "the most difficult [magical beasts] to hide. The female is generally larger and more aggressive than the male, though neither should be approached by any but highly skilled and trained wizards."[9] The textbook gives a description of the different types of dragons, and the picture becomes clear: Dragons are incredibly dangerous. For young readers, seeing Harry and Hermione get punished for helping Hagrid should show them that getting involved with illegal and dangerous actions will have serious consequences. However, by reading about it and analyzing (with their parents' assistance) the characters' motivations, the situation's context, and the consequences they must endure, children may become better prepared to recognize and cope with similar real-life scenarios.

Harry Potter and the Chamber of Secrets also provides several episodes that may help parents discuss rule-breaking and consequences with their young readers. Two scenes which are particularly instructive are Harry's and Ron's unorthodox arrival at Hogwarts and their actions at the end of the novel. Discussing these scenes can help children develop a mature consciousness. Harry's and Ron's arrival at Hogwarts in Mr. Weasley's flying car is an important scene for several reasons. First, it enforces the idea that rules should be followed. Second, it encourages young children to think before they act. And third, it sets up a scene at the end of the novel that demonstrates that adults are not always infallible and that sometimes extenuating circumstances influence an authority figure's reaction to rule-breaking. These lessons are valuable because they can assist children in developing the inner resources they will need to navigate their way through the complex adult world.

When Harry and Ron find themselves apparently stranded at King's Cross station, they believe that they must get to Hogwarts in any way possible. Ron notes, "We're stuck, right? And we've got to get to school, haven't we? And even underage wizards are allowed to use magic if it's a real emergency" (*COS* 69). Ron's reasoning seems sound, but it soon becomes clear that using the flying car demonstrates hasty and poor judgment. Flying the car may have seemed like their only option, but this has several serious repercussions. First, they are seen by several muggles. Second, Ron's father owns the car and is now facing an inquiry at work. Third, when the car crashes into the Whomping Willow, it causes considerable damage to school property.

But it was an emergency, young readers may say. They *had* to get to school, didn't they? Perhaps, but Professor McGonagall's response offers an alternative solution: "Why didn't you send us a letter by owl?" she asks (*COS* 80). Even Harry has to admit that sending a letter "seemed the most obvious thing to have done. 'I—I didn't think—'" he explained (*COS* 80). The fact that Harry and Ron didn't stop to think through their options clearly indicates that they are still young and have not yet grasped that each situation may have multiple courses of action which can be taken. A flying car is certainly the most exciting option, but as Professor Snape points out, it is also one with serious consequences. In contrast, sending a letter by owl or simply waiting for Mr. and Mrs. Weasley to return would have been far more practical. Pausing to discuss this scene will emphasize that most situations have several potential courses of action, and the following questions are designed to help the child discover that he must think before he acts. What he would do if he was in Harry's situation? What if he was supposed to take the bus to school and missed it? What possible courses of action could he follow? Can he come up with more options? Asking the child to come up with several possible solutions is important because it can lead to a conversation on the pros and cons of each potential choice. The child can begin to understand that pouncing on the first option is not always smart.

Parents may also point out that the professors' reactions emphasize the need to think through one's possible options before acting. Snape demands that Harry and Ron receive the severest of consequences because they "flouted the Decree for the Restriction of Underage Wizardry, [and] caused serious damage to an old and valuable tree..." (*COS* 81). He is correct, but Dumbledore's and McGonagall's quiet voices and serious faces demonstrate even more clearly that the choices Harry and Ron made were poorly thought out.

Harry recognizes that he has let down those whom he most admires, and Dumbledore confirms this when he notes that "I must impress upon both of you the seriousness of what you have done... I must also warn you that if you do anything like this again, I will have no choice but to expel you" (*COS* 81). McGonagall adds to the punishment by assigning Harry and Ron a detention (*COS* 82). The message is clear: Harry and Ron did not think through their options and broke the rules; therefore, they must pay the price.

Parents may continue this discussion by posing another series of questions to their child. Why did Harry and Ron break the rules? Did their actions result in any bad things happening? What were those bad things? Do they deserve to be punished? At this point, parents can emphasize *why* this particular case of rule-breaking must result in punishment. It is not simply that Harry and Ron broke the rules; instead, it is the unintended repercussions of their hasty actions that make the situation so serious. Even the youngest child would probably agree that these are serious (albeit unintended) consequences and that they wouldn't have happened if Harry and Ron had stopped to think about what they were doing. Once a child comes to this conclusion, parents can emphasize that, if he ever finds himself in a similar situation (say, for example, missing the school bus), he should learn from Harry and Ron, and think before he acts.

This leads into another scenario in which Harry and Ron have very clearly broken many school rules, yet instead of getting punished or expelled (as Dumbledore had promised earlier in the novel), they both receive Special Awards for Service to the School. Dumbledore himself notes that "I seem to remember telling you both that I would have to expel you if you broke any more school rules" (*COS* 330). However, motivation and context are once again key elements in Dumbledore's decision to reward them instead of administering punishment.

Despite being repeatedly warned that they needed to follow the rules, when Harry and Ron discover that Ron's sister Ginny has been abducted by the monster, they make the conscious decision to ignore the order to return to their House dormitories. Interestingly, instead of immediately trying to handle the situation on their own, Harry and Ron demonstrate their growing wisdom in attempting to alert a professor to what they have discovered. Unfortunately, that professor proves to be uncooperative. Thus, Harry and Ron venture into the Chamber of Secrets on their own, realizing that Ginny likely does not have much time. Once in the Chamber, they manage to rescue Ginny and return to the safety of Hogwarts. Admirable actions, no doubt, but again, they have clearly broken the rules.

Harry's and Ron's attempt to alert an adult first demonstrates their intellectual growth, and shows that they recognize this is a situation they should not attempt to handle themselves. However, when faced with the adult's refusal to assist, they also realize that they must act immediately or Ginny will die. Although they put themselves into a dangerous and potentially deadly situation, their actions are directly responsible for several positive outcomes: Ginny's life is saved and Hagrid is proved to have never opened the Chamber of Secrets. Although these outcomes were not guaranteed, parents need to help their children understand that Harry and Ron provided Dumbledore with enough positive context to forego any punishment.

The following questions can help the child discover for himself why Harry and Ron were not punished for breaking the rules: What did Harry and Ron first do when they knew Ginny was in danger? Why was this a smart action? What else could they have done when that adult refused to help? Was there enough time to follow any other courses of action? At this point, parents need to emphasize that alerting another adult is the best course of action. They may continue with other questions: What happens if there is no time to seek out another adult? Is it okay to attempt a rescue if the child feels he can help? Admittedly, this is a tricky situation. No parent wants to encourage her child to plunge into danger, and it may be worthwhile to remind the young reader that Harry and Ron have magic on their side. Fawkes comes to their rescue, but Fawkes is magical and creatures like him cannot provide help in the real/muggle world. Although Harry's and Ron's rescue of Ginny is admirable, young readers should remember that it is always best to enlist the aid of an adult. If the first won't help, find another.

If necessary, parents may continue to break the situation down into questions that can lead the young reader to a deeper understanding of the "gray" nuances of life. Was Ginny in mortal danger? Would Tom Riddle (aka Lord Voldemort) have killed her? Did Harry and Ron save her life? Should people be punished for saving someone's life? What's more important: following the rules or saving someone's life? This last question may help young readers understand that sometimes, in very special circumstances or contexts, breaking the rules is necessary when a person's life is at stake. Even Dumbledore recognizes this when he claims that "the best of us must sometimes eat our words" (*COS* 331), and decides to reward Harry and Ron instead of expelling them.

Harry Potter and the Prisoner of Azkaban provides yet another notable episode that can be used in a discussion on rule-breaking and its consequences. By the end of the novel, Harry and Hermione have shattered many school rules, and have even broken one of the most important Wizarding Laws, that one must not tamper with time (*POA* 393–396), in order to release a condemned murderer from prison. For those who have not read the novel, Harry's and Hermione's actions may seem reprehensible, but Rowling carefully establishes a clear context for their behavior. Even the youngest reader can understand that Sirius Black did not commit the murders for which he has been imprisoned. Thus, an innocent man has been jailed and will face the Dementor's kiss if someone doesn't act. When Harry and Hermione discover his innocence, they demonstrate their intellectual growth by attempting to inform the Minister of Magic, but he refuses to believe them so they inform another adult: Dumbledore. He, of course, recognizes the truth, but laments that "the word of two thirteen-year-old wizards will not convince anybody" (*POA* 392). Instead of arguing with the other adult wizards, Dumbledore grants Harry and Hermione unspoken permission to do what they can to rescue Sirius Black (*POA* 393). Because of the Time Turner, Harry and Hermione are the only two who know that Black is innocent *and* can act upon that knowledge.

A key element in this scenario is that an innocent man's life is at stake. Young children may have difficulty understanding why an authority figure like Dumbledore would ever give children permission to so blatantly break the rules, but the politics behind Dumbledore's position are complex. The following questions can help the child understand why Dumbledore didn't save Sirius himself and what role context and motivation play in the aftermath: Did Harry and Hermione try to inform the authorities of the mistake that had been made? Were they believed? Could they have eventually convinced the authorities of their mistake? Was there enough time to do so? What would happen if it took a long time to convince the Ministry that they had the wrong man? Did they have the ability to rescue Sirius themselves? Was it okay to do so? Should Harry and Hermione have been punished for saving the life of an innocent man when everyone who had the ability to put a stop to the sentence refused to listen? At this point, parents should shift the discussion to reality lest the child think it would be okay to break people out of jail.

These questions should encourage the child to realize that Harry and Hermione first did everything they could to convince the authorities that they were wrong, and when that failed, they turned to another trusted adult. In the real world, this is an excellent pattern to follow; when children know someone has been unjustly or incorrectly accused of a crime, it is their responsibility to do everything in their power to right the wrong. In Harry's and Hermione's case, it eventually meant breaking Sirius out of jail. In the real world, it will likely mean taking a different course of action, but the motivation is still the same. Parents may continue their discussion with the following questions: Does this mean that we can go around breaking people out of jail just because we think the prisoners are innocent? Why not? What could we do instead? Getting the child to focus on what he could do in a real life situation will help him develop the awareness that Harry's actions do not always translate well into our real life, but there are important lessons to be learned from his actions.

Helping young children begin to develop the intellectual maturity necessary to understand the complexities of the adult world can be a challenge for many parents. While some adults fear that the *Harry Potter* novels encourage disobedience and rule-breaking, I have attempted to demonstrate how parents can use the novels and a modified version of the Socratic method to teach their children how to look beyond the surface to discover how motivation and context can have an impact on whether rule-breaking should be punished or not. As Bruno Bettelheim notes, "[w]e grow, we find meaning in life, and security in ourselves by having understood and solved personal problems on our own, not by having them explained to us by others."[10] By following the modified Socratic questions I have offered above, parents have the opportunity to allow their young readers to solve the "problems" faced by Harry and his friends and, as a result, find meaning and develop a clear security in their future decisions. Rather than ignoring or banning the novels, parents can engage their children in a conversation about rule-breaking, motivations, and context, an important step towards helping them develop critical thinking skills that will help them successfully navigate life's difficulties.

Notes

1. Edmund Kern, *The Wisdom of Harry Potter* (Amherst, New York: Prometheus Books, 2003), 41.
2. Daniel Handler, "Frightening News," *New York Times,* Oct. 30, 2001, 17.
3. Ibid., 17.
4. Bruno Bettelheim, *The Uses of Enchantment* (New York: Random House, 1976), 118.
5. Kern, *The Wisdom of Harry Potter*, 40.
6. Barbara Fink Chorzempa and Laurie Lapidus, "To Find Yourself, Think for Yourself," *Teaching Exceptional Children* 41, no 3 (January 2009): 55, *Academic Search Complete*.
7. Ibid., 56.
8. Ibid., 57.
9. Newt Scamander (J.K. Rowling), *Fantastic Beasts and Where to Find Them* (New York: Scholastic, 2001), 10.
10. Bettelheim, *The Uses of Enchantment*, 19.

Harry Potter and the Child with Autism

Denise Dwyer D'Errico

In this essay, I will describe how *Harry Potter* has helped my son with the challenges of having autism. He has grown from being almost completely non-verbal to becoming a confident, high-functioning nine-year-old. As Harry's lessons have become my son's lessons, I hope that our story may help other families with autism spectrum disorders.

First, a very brief background on my son's development and diagnosis: my son seemed to achieve developmental milestones up until he was fifteen months of age, when his speech actually regressed. And so began our family's journey into the labyrinth of autism. After successful hearing tests and unsuccessful speech therapy, we were flummoxed. The pediatrician suggested an autism evaluation "just to rule it out." We were shocked when that evaluation was positive, and we received a twelve page clinical diagnosis report including words and phrases we had never seen or heard before, such as hypotonia (low muscle tone) and apraxia of speech (lack of oral motor skill needed to form speech). It was such scrutiny at the tender age of two — it hardly seemed fair.

The doctor looked me in the eye and said, "This diagnosis is like a golden ticket. Many services are free. And the therapy won't hurt him." We were astonished to find that there were so many service providers in our area and so many dedicated professionals and students who were absolutely devoted to helping our son learn and grow. He had three A.B.A. (Applied Behavioral Analysis) therapists, an occupational therapist, and a speech therapist who all came to our home for a total of 25 hours a week. — It was as if preschool was making house calls. My son enjoyed the play-based therapy and progressed very well.

Autism is a developmental disorder affecting 1 out of 88 children in the United States.[1] Its definition has broadened in recent years to include a range of symptoms and characteristics, which is why it is now called the Autism Spectrum Disorder (ASD). No longer the stereotypical Rainman as depicted in the Tom Cruise movie, autism is not that black and white; rather, it is the whole spectrum with shades of gray in between. For this reason, it's far more polite to refer to those with autism with the more sensitive and accurate description of "children who are on the spectrum." A child could have a low Verbal IQ (lack of speech) and a high nonverbal IQ (exhibit empathy), and another child could have high verbal IQ (many words) and low nonverbal IQ (lack of social sensitivity) sometimes associated with Asperger's Syndrome. Both descriptions are on the spectrum. Likewise, it's appropriate to use the term "typically developing" for someone not on the spectrum. Labeling those children as "normal" is impolite.

Autism awareness is increasing, with celebrities like Holly Robinson Peete and Jenny McCarthy speaking out about their family experiences. Persons with Autism/Asperger's are often shown on television as successful: "J-Mac" Jason McElwain (the boy who scored six three-pointers in the final three minutes of his high school basketball game), contestant Zev Glassenberg on *The Amazing Race*, and singer James Durbin on *American Idol*. Let us not forget autism advocates Stephen Shore and Temple Grandin, who are on the spectrum as well.

Returning to my son's story, it wasn't long before one of my son's therapists observed his hyperlexia. Hyperlexia combines the super-ability to read with a deficiency in self-help skills. Hyperlexic children have an extreme fascination with letters and numbers, so they decode words much earlier than their peers, reading precociously, though not fully understanding what they are reading. As one might expect, hyperlexia is commonly observed in families in which the mother is a bibliophile.[2]

My own journey with *Harry Potter* began as I read the first four novels in quick succession. I remember well, as I read and reread the books, how my dear son at age three, previously non-verbal, would climb onto my lap and "sound out" the letters on the cover. I longed for the day we could read them together. But I shelved this idea for a later time.

Fast forward to two summers ago, when a behavior analyst observed my seven-year-old son watching too much *Dora the Explorer* (and similar programming) with his then two-year-old sister, thereby hindering the likelihood of his socializing appropriately with his peers in the third grade. I confess that I was somewhat shocked at this revelation. Although I knew such shows were "young" for him, I had thought them harmless. Every parent has challenges; how could I keep my son socially age-appropriate without introducing more obsessions (such as video games)? I had noticed that some of his peers at school had *Star Wars: Clone Wars* backpacks, so I introduced him to the *Star*

Wars saga. After watching the six *Star Wars* movies, he wrote a detailed list of major plot events in his journal. After seeing how well he understood them, I decided he was ready for *Harry Potter*.

As we began to read the books together, I realized just how much *Harry Potter* had to offer our family. I read aloud as he read along. I encouraged him to read Harry's lines aloud at key scenes, and he did so with emotion and drama that I had never heard from him before. I gave him an official Hogwarts blank journal, which he completed from Harry's point of view, detailing names and dates from the stories. He invented a fifth House called "Queaselpops," for those with queasy stomachs, and wrote out class schedules and professors for the whole year.

We soon started inventing our own spells for use in our daily life: "Zipperus Unstuckus," was my first spell, necessity being the mother of invention. And you should have seen his sweet face light up! Not only had I just made up our own spell, but it was a set of funny sounding, hard consonant words, *and* it worked. The previously stubborn zipper glided easily. Once while we were goofing around, his too-big sweatpants slid down a little, exposing his Hanes. "Uh-Oh!" I said, "What happened here? Pantus Falldownus!" He laughed gleefully. My son tends to squirm a lot and doesn't sit properly for more than five seconds, so naturally I said to him, "Yourbuttus Sitdownus." Suddenly it was fun to sit down and my reminder didn't sound like nagging. We had a shared text and a pattern of Noun-us Verb-us. Even my husband, a Muggle, dropped a bar of soap and exclaimed "Soapus Dropus!"

We sang the triple triplet melody from the first film (as Harry first enters the Great Hall) with common phrases, such as: "Pick it up, Pick it up, Pick it up!" Even my then two-year-old daughter did this. As a mnemonic device, it softens an otherwise undesirable message or task. We also employed a points based rewards system, saying: "Ten points for Gryffindor!" All these creative additions to our family life are what autism therapy calls generalizing: applying learned skills to real life situations.

Children on the autism spectrum often have areas of extreme interest, with an intensity and focus beyond the typically developing child's obsessions. For my son, first it was cars, then maps. Rather than let the obsession cloud social interaction, autism therapy suggests directing the child's special interest in a positive way, such as naming the child the class subject matter expert (see *Just Give Him the Whale!* on the list of autism resources in the Appendix). Indeed, I was delighted to point out to my son that the second book featured a Ford Anglica and the third book featured a map.

Upon reading *Harry Potter and the Sorcerer's Stone*, my son asked the following insightful questions: "Why does Hagrid live in such a small hut if he's so big? Why do owls deliver mail?" (To which I replied: "Just like the birds deliver flowers in Disney's *Enchanted*, owls deliver letters in *Harry Potter*.") He innocently asked, "Why would anybody want to study the Dark Arts?" Most interesting to me were his observations about the climax. He told me he had been predicting there would be something under the turban, and since Quirrell called Voldy "Lord," that made him think of Lord Vader, and so he wondered who Voldy's apprentice was. All these questions demonstrate reading comprehension and reflection, which is an area of challenge for hyperlexic and ASD children.

My son has identified with Harry and delights in how closely he physically resembles the films' young Daniel Radcliffe. In fact, Daniel Radcliffe has said he has the challenge of dyspraxia, which is the inability to see layers necessary in order to tie one's shoes.[3] This disability has not held him back. Some days I would find my son wearing his Harry Potter glasses from his Halloween costume. "Good Morning, Harry," I would say to him, and surprisingly he did not correct me, as one would expect a child on the spectrum to do, for they are extremely logical (see *The Funny Side of Autism,* also in the list of autism resources). "Good morning, Mommy," he said and smiled as he returned to his task. He even slept with said glasses near his bed, as if he really needed them.

I encouraged this connection, and it has been most helpful in a variety of situations, such as the time when he fell and broke his arm. "Wow, you're so brave!" I told him. "Just like a true Gryffindor. Now you have something else in common with Harry — you both broke your right arms. Good thing Professor Lockhart isn't here to accidentally erase your bones!" And he smiled, the pain and discomfort of the situation forgotten for the moment. Similarly, when my son resisted returning to the orthodontist's office to resume making the pre-braces study mold, I said to him: "Remember when Harry had to drink Skele-Gro all night in order to regrow his vanished bones? You're so lucky; all you have to do is bite into that awful-tasting putty for like, five seconds!" It was just the encouragement and perspective he needed.

Now my son's ninth birthday approaches. He's only read books one through three at this point; after all he's still rather young. I decided that I wanted him to have a little more life experience and maturity before approaching the fourth book, which we readers know is a significant turning point in the series, as everything becomes much darker from that point on. I expect that we will read the fourth book aloud together, as we did the first three.

We continue referring to the books at every opportunity: My son has dressed as Harry for the last two Halloweens and had *Harry Potter*-themed birthday parties. This year the favor bags included Harry's glasses, gold coin chocolate "galleons," every flavor beans, and a light-up glow-stick "wand."

We have talked about how important friendship is and how lucky he is to have such good friends, as I make them all friendship bracelets woven to resemble Gryffindor scarves.

My children and I also are creating a music playlist honoring significant themes in the series: "Place in This World" by Michael W. Smith, "You're My Best Friend" by Queen, "New Soul" by Yael Naim, "Don't Stop Believin'" by Journey, and "Firework" by Katy Perry. It is my hope that by identifying the meaning of the lyrics and linking them with the *Harry Potter* themes, characters, and stories, he will become more aware of the themes in his own life and in his own development. (Please refer to the Appendix for a sample worksheet. Visual learners will benefit from the parallel boxes in the chart and recognize the parallels from their own life examples.)

But the most extraordinary lessons have been within the stories. In addition to providing typical growing-up lessons, the books provide fantastic examples for a child on the spectrum. Autism research shows that in contrast to the challenges of executive function (ability to plan and focus) and theory of mind (understanding that everyone thinks individually), people on the spectrum possess a talent for systemizing (analyzing and creating systems).[4] Patterns in *Harry Potter* are evident: the hero's journey, doppelgangers, mirror images and ring composition (symmetry of plot development and resolution), etc. Discussion of these patterns heightens awareness, and this skill can be applied to other areas of life.

Most significant are the social and personal awareness lessons embedded within, for these address the primary challenges for children with autism. Firstly, "Have Friends." This is something we might take for granted, but cannot be emphasized enough for a child who is apt to play alone. (Remember the very word "Autism" literally means "towards one's self.") Harry's success in his yearly quests at Hogwarts School of Witchcraft and Wizardry are in part due to the help he receives from his friends Ron and Hermione, dramatized especially in the pursuit of the stone in the first book, and in the hunt for the hallows and horcruxes in the last book. Hermione's logic and wit allow Harry to pass through the potions barrier en route to the stone, as does Ron's talent at playing wizard chess. Likewise, Ron, Hermione, and Neville's devotion and bravery assist Harry in the final book, as they each dispatch one of the horcruxes. This lesson is also echoed in the pop culture surrounding the books. Familiarity with *Harry Potter* is a common interest, helping to identify potential friends, as well as providing subject matter for conversation. Indeed, my son was pleasantly surprised to find that some of his current friends are also *Harry Potter* readers.

Another lesson shown within the *Harry Potter* novels is "Identify Friendly Types." Ironically, when Draco Malfoy offers to help Harry find "the right sort," Harry coolly replies, "I think I can tell who the wrong sort are for myself, thanks" (*SS* 109). Even friendly characters aren't always what they seem. Conversely, the alleged murderer escaped from prison may just be the wrongfully accused loving godfather you never knew, while unpopular misfits such as the delightful Luna Lovegood and the once-hapless Neville Longbottom can be the most loyal and heroic of companions.

The stories also demonstrate how bullies often were bullied themselves. Draco is bullied by his father Lucius. Lucius is bullied by Voldemort. Children with autism have difficulty reading social cues and nuances; therefore, taunting and mean-spiritedness are not recognized as inappropriate play, especially if the other children are smiling as they are taunting. Recently I heard that my son was being taunted by some children after school. We talked about Harry's first flying lesson in which Draco steals Neville's Remembrall and flies away with it. Harry is compelled to fly after him (despite not having had his first flying lesson yet) and yell, "Give it *here*!" (*SS* 148). So I told my son about mean-spirited kids: "Don't let them get all Draco on you."

Behavioral therapy for the hyperlexic child includes the use of flashcards as well as social stories. These social stories, designed for the children with close to average reading skills, describe settings and situations and include specific dialogue. They are scripts designed for the autism spectrum child, which therapists hope the child will apply as a guide for real-life social interactions. In the fantastic comic-book-style *SuperFlex* series by Michelle Garcia Winner, the child is plagued by villains such as "Rock Brain," "Body Snatcher," and "Space Invader," which are negative behaviors. The child thwarts said villains by being flexible, hence SuperFlex. The parent or therapist can also create an original, personalized social story with the child's name in the script. Naturally, as a parent of an autism spectrum child, I began to see the Harry stories as potential social stories, for the social awareness lessons they present.

Social awareness lessons in *Harry Potter* include the following: Do the right thing. Between doing nothing, and something, do something. Make the right choices. Ask for help.

1. Do the right thing: Harry is compelled to warn Hermione of the lurking mountain troll in the first novel, even before they become friends.

2. Between doing something and nothing, do something: Also in the first book, Harry is inspired to chase Draco despite never having flown on a broom before, in order to defend Neville Longbottom and protect Neville's Remembrall.

3. Make the right choices: Headmaster Dumbledore articulates another theme of J.K. Rowling's in the second book. Quite simply and poignantly,

the good professor says this gem: "It is our choices, Harry, that show what we truly are, far more than our abilities" (*COS* 333).

4. Ask for help: Throughout the series, Harry often forgets to seek help. Again, it is Professor Dumbledore who articulates this social awareness lesson. "You will also find that help will always be given at Hogwarts for those who ask for it" (*COS* 264).

To read the story of *Harry Potter* is to discover Harry's personal journey. Personal awareness lessons include many useful thoughts: You are unique. You have special talents. You can contribute to your community. You have a place in this world. Have faith.

These are lessons in the human condition: what Carl Jung called individuation,[5] and Joseph Campbell called the hero's journey.[6] Individuation can be described as discovering one's true identity, while the hero's journey is the pattern of the quest. Harry's journey is a quest of individuation and personal awareness.

The first personal awareness lesson is "You are unique." Harry is shown to be a wizard among Muggles. Additionally, he is also unique among wizards, as denoted by his scar. When my son recognizes his own diagnosis as being on the autism spectrum, he will perceive his own uniqueness. Also, because he is "high-functioning" and exhibits some empathy, he is unique even among spectrum kids.

"You have special talents." Harry discovers he can fly. This comes naturally to him, without training. I have reminded my son that he is a great reader; he could read well at a very young age. Because he could read easily, spelling comes naturally to him, as does math and geography.

"You can contribute to your community." Soon after Harry learns he can fly, he is called upon to play Quidditch, representing his house. In the fourth book, Harry is likewise chosen to represent his school in the Tri-Wizard Tournament. I remind my son that his strengths in academics make him a good candidate for the class Spelling Bee and Geography Bee. The day of his class Geo Bee I told him, "This is like your Quidditch!" He replied with quiet confidence, "Yeah." Then we sang the chorus of "Firework" (by pop singer Katy Perry) before I dropped him off at school. He was one of two winners in his class bee, and went on to compete in the school Geo Bee. Just before the latter event, I reminded him that just as Harry was the youngest Seeker in a century, he would be the youngest in the school bee. I also told him that we were so proud of him already, and that he should remember that even Harry Potter fell off his broom, but that he came back to play in the next match. This seemed to relax him a bit, and he asked how many days were between Quidditch matches. I suggested we reread the books and chart the match dates. His eyes sparkled. I am delighted to report that my son actually won his school Geo Bee and will be entered in the State Geo Bee. He also finished fifth in the School Spelling Bee.

"You have a place in this world." This lesson is related to the previous one, but on a much larger scale. Harry learns throughout the novels that he belongs within the wizarding world, at Hogwarts. Then in the fifth book, he's devastated to learn of the prophecy that has defined his life in others' eyes. Voldemort chose to believe the prophecy concerned Harry, thereby giving him power. From Dumbledore, however, Harry learns that the prophecy means nothing without interpretation: he can let others dictate his fate, or he can claim it and use the prophecy as a tool. When Harry chooses to accept the prophecy, he gains a confidence, the power of intent. I continue to show my son examples of spectrum kids who have risen beyond their diagnoses to find significant success.

"Have faith." In these stories, spells are more than mere recitation of specific words; the witch/wizard must have intent. Young Harry is able to find the Stone in the first novel because his intent is to find it, but not use it (*SS* 300). In the third book, Harry works extra hard to learn how to conjure a Patronus and to summon his broom. Bellatrix Lestrange taunts Harry about his attempt to use an Unforgiveable Curse in the fifth novel: "You need to *mean* them, Potter!" (*OOTP* 810). In fact, when Harry pretends to give his friend Ron a bit of Felix Felicitus, Ron becomes confident and therefore successful because he *believes* he has been given "liquid luck." Clearly, the correct frame of mind, the intent, and the belief produce magic. Most importantly, throughout the series, Harry learns to believe in himself.

Dumbledore's Dilemma

As of this writing, my dear son has not become aware of his own placement on the autism spectrum. And as his mother, I find myself in a curious Dumbledore dilemma: when do I tell him of his own diagnosis? I simply can't. I keep thinking a suitable opportunity will present itself; alas it hasn't yet. I decided when he was entering mainstream kindergarten at age four that that was entirely too young to carry such a burden. Each succeeding grade I have asked myself the question again.

I have decided that the best thing I can do is prepare him for when he is ready to know. Meanwhile, we refer to our shared understanding of the *Harry Potter* stories in many ways so that it is a not only a color of life but the foundation of it. Harry's lessons are tools for successful growing up, for children in general. How many times have I heard myself saying, "Be Brave," "You're a Gryffindor" and "What's the pattern in this situation?"

I hope that when the time comes, and he learns of his own diagnosis, he too will realize that in a way, he has always known. It will be a moment like the one in which Harry learns he is a wizard, and suddenly the odd happenings of his childhood make sense. Likewise, when Harry learns of the prophecy, it's not so much the prophecy itself that matters, it's the underlying truth. Harry's realization of the following reminds us that we always have a choice to accept our destiny and even to thrive in it:

> But he understood at last what Dumbledore had been trying to tell him. It was, he thought, the difference between being dragged into the arena to face a battle to the death and walking into the arena with your head held high. Some people, perhaps would say that there was little to choose between the two ways, but Dumbledore knew—*and so do I*, thought Harry, with a rush of fierce pride, *and so did my parents*—that there was all the difference in the world [*HBP* 512].

For Harry, this is the difference between merely accepting his fate versus claiming his choice. For my son and others living with Autism, it is the difference between resigning oneself to one's diagnosis and embracing it.

When my son does begin to recognize his own diagnosis, there is a series of steps we will follow. From the excellent resource *Talking Together about an Autism Diagnosis*[7] we will complete an "All About Me" booklet, which lists and describes his strengths and interests, in addition to his particular challenges.

I will share many of the best references with him, and I am certain he will find them reassuring, as the authors are kindred spirits. In *Asperger Syndrome, The Universe, and Everything*, the ten-year-old author Kenneth Hall, himself on the spectrum, describes having read the *Harry Potter* stories many times over. When my son is ready to perceive his own diagnosis, he will enjoy reading the author's account of what it is like to be on the spectrum. And he will feel something in common with him: familiarity and appreciation of *Harry Potter*. James Williams, a young person with autism, likewise references *Harry Potter* characters and stories when describing to students what it is like having autism.[8] He compares Harry's learning he's a wizard with the initial diagnosis, and Hermione's obsession with books and history with the interests of people on the Spectrum. It is nothing short of miraculous to note that both these young individuals on the autism spectrum have both not only successfully navigated their individual challenges, but in very public ways are bringing Autism Awareness and Autism Acceptance to the masses. Here is evidence that even spectrum kids can and will achieve personal growth and social success.

Additionally, I will host an autism awareness party. My son will be the guest of honor, of course. I hope to bring his "All About Me" project to display, as well as many other resources listed in the Appendix. The party decor will be the now familiar Hogwarts Gryffindor colors of red and gold, for we will be celebrating my son and his accomplishments. It is at this event that my husband and I will present to him a personalized, framed Hogwarts acceptance letter. It is our hope that he will remember the moment as something significant, special, and most of all, positive.

Throughout this journey, my son has taught me that Harry echoes his own quest into personal and social awareness. As we face obstacles, hurdles and fears in our own lives, we need only remember the boggart, and imagine it silly and laugh. Should we suffer loss of a loved one, we need only remember that love lives. Should we be burdened with psychological disease or trauma, we need only remember that conjuring our happiest memories will drive away those dementors. We can practice visualization (similar to using the Mirror of Erised) when setting goals for ourselves. Recognizing the tools and utilizing the skills is a kind of magic in itself. This has been documented in the article "Putting Harry Potter on the Couch" by psychotherapist Colman Noctor,[9] and detailed by author Julie Sykley in *Harry Potter Power*, which is an "it gets better" book designed for teens.[10]

Such concepts are very applicable in personal growth for all ages. But most of all, the feeling of confidence and belonging is significant for everyone — imagine how empowering this can be for a child on the autism spectrum. *Alohamora!*

Notes

1. "Autism Spectrum Disorders (ASDs)" *Centers for Disease Control and Prevention*, March 29, 2012, http://www.cdc.gov/ncbddd/autism/data.html.
2. Susan Martins Miller, *Reading Too Soon: How to Understand and Help the Hyperlexic Child* (USA: Center for Speech and Language, 1993), 16.
3. Chris Irvine, "Harry Potter's Daniel Radcliffe has Dyspraxia," *The Telegraph*, August 17, 2008, http://www.telegraph.co.uk/news/celebritynews/2573230/Harry-Potters-Daniel-Radcliffe-has-dyspraxia.html.
4. Simon Baron-Cohen, *Autism and Asperger Syndrome: The Facts* (New York: Oxford University Press, 2008), 62–68.
5. A.S. Petridis, "Jung's Individuation Process," *Soul Therapy Now*, December 5, 2008, http://southerapynow.com/articles/individuation.html.
6. Christopher Vogler, "Hero's Journey," *Storytech Literary Consulting*, http://www.thewritersjourney.com/hero's_journey.htm#Heronine.
7. Rachel Pike, *Talking Together About an Autism Diagnosis* (London: National Autistic Society, 2008).
8. James Williams, "Harry Potter and the Chamber of Autism," *Jamesmw.com*, 2005, http://www.jamesmw.com/harry.htm.
9. Colman Noctor, "Putting Harry Potter on the Couch," *Clinical Child Psychology and Psychiatry* 11, no. 4 (2006): 685.
10. Julie-Anne Sykley, *Harry Potter Power* (USA: Glass House Books, 2009).

Strange Apostle: Assessing the Conflict Between Today's Christianity and Modern Culture

J. Malcolm Stewart

From the fall of 1998 and forward, Christian educators, youth leaders and Sunday-School teachers began to take notice of a peculiar phenomenon. Many of our students were *reading*.

Now, this phenomenon was shocking not just for the mere fact they were reading (though it was certainly against the recent trend), but it was *what* they were reading. Not the six-to-eight page tract pamphlets that many Christian publishers insisted were the way to reach modern "short attention span" kids. Not the multi-colored, large print, message-scrubbed, young adult "life guides" that were all the rage for churches in the late '90's. No, these students were reading a 309 page monster-tome quite out of the norm for younger readers.

Many of the readers of this mysterious book would often complain to the aforementioned teachers of not having time to memorize five verse Scripture readings with seven days to complete the task. Now these same students were tearing through chapters of this super-book at home, at school and in church, as if discovering the printed word for the first time.

The puzzlement was widespread. I can report this because I was one those mystified teachers who watched J.K. Rowling's *Sorcerer's Stone* explode on the scene like no other "children's" book of our era. The appetite for the story of Harry Potter, a seemingly normal English pre-teen who is transported to Hogwarts School of Witchcraft and Wizardry after discovering his parents' magical heritage, was insatiable. The response to the Potter phenomenon ended up speaking volumes about the issues facing the modern Christian movement. And for Christians involved in working with youth, making sense of the arguments and counter-arguments about Rowling and Harry Potter became an industry unto itself.

Much of the response from Christian leaders in the wake of the series was negative. The use of magic themes and spells was decried as "un–Christian" and many prominent religious leaders argued that Rowling's character was doing everything from promoting Wicca to embodying the earthly manifestation of the Anti-Christ. Even when some acknowledged *Harry Potter's* classic theme of the young and brave finding their identity in overcoming evil, much of the public face of American Christianity still found fault.

Much of the basis of opposition to *Harry Potter* by critics is found in the warnings against the use of magic in the writings of Moses. Several of the prohibitions found in the five-volume Pentateuch, the books of Genesis, Exodus, Leviticus, Numbers and Deuteronomy, deal with the practice of "sorcery" and "witchcraft" as defined by what many scholars call the Holiness Code, which was revealed during the Israelite Exodus and Wilderness Wanderings. To many Christian critics, one of the pertinent passages reads as so: There shall not be found among you anyone who makes his son or his daughter pass through the fire, one who uses divination, one who practices witchcraft, or one who interprets omens or a sorcerer, or one who casts a spell or a medium, a spiritist, or one who calls up the dead (Deuteronomy 18:10–12 NASB).[1]

Throughout the text of the Pentateuch, "magic" and "sorcery" are seen as forces in direct opposition to the God of the Bible. This opposition is manifested in form of giving tribute or worship to any other supernatural forces other than that of God Himself.

First to be denounced in the Pentateuch are the "sorcerers" and "wise men" of Egypt for opposing the freedom message of Moses. Next in line for condemnation are the "practices of the nations," specifically those who follow the Canaanite deity Moloch, whose cultic worship rites are explicitly denounced in Deut. 18:10–12. Additionally, the Mosaic writings attack a brand of "sorcery" either officiated over or promoted by unreformed Israelite women. This type of "witchcraft" was considered especially noxious. Under the Mosaic statutes, such women were to be executed upon proffered evidence of their crimes: You shall not allow a sorceress to live (Exodus 22:18 NASB).

While the terminology of Exodus 22:18 is explicitly feminine in the Hebrew text, other provisions against magical or idolatrous practices in the Pentateuch also applied to males, making this pattern of biblical prohibition relevant to the *Harry Potter* series.

> If there is found in your midst, in any of your towns, which the LORD your God is giving you, a *man* or a *woman* [my emphasis] who does what is evil in the sight of the LORD your God, by transgressing His covenant, and has gone to serve other gods and worshiped them, or the sun or moon or any of the heavenly host,

which I have not commanded,.... Behold if it is true ... then you shall bring out that man or that woman who has done this evil deed ... and you shall stone them to death [Deuteronomy 17:2–5 NASB].

To critics, these bright-line prohibitions in the Mosaic writings make depictions of heroic characters using magic impermissible. Author Richard Abanes in his 2001 book *Harry Potter and the Bible* claims that Rowling's characters through the course of the series gleefully violate the prohibitions found in Deut. 18:10. In his analysis, some character, either Potter or another Hogwarts student at some time or other uses divination, interprets omens, communicates with the dead, etc. Coupled with this was the idea that the *Harry Potter* novels gave license for Christian youth and others to become involved with idolatrous worship offensive to the God of the Bible by calling upon occult forces for aid, guidance and protection. To Abenes, Rowling's character was a wolf dressed up in hero's clothing, misleading Christian readers into accepting occultism.

Some defenders of *Harry Potter* within the Christian community did bring forth the argument that the Mosaic commandments were time and place sensitive and that many of their provisions (the dietary laws, the prescribed High Holy days, legal concessions to slavery) were not considered binding on modern Christians. However, when challenged, Abenes and others claimed ample evidence against the use of "magical" items or "spell casting" with the context of the Greek-language New Testament writings.

Paul of Tarsus, often considered by scholars as the prime figure of doctrinarian Christianity, restated the Mosaic teaching as so: Now the deeds of the flesh are evident, which are: immorality, impurity, sensuality, idolatry, *sorcery*, [my emphasis] enmities, strife, jealousy, outbursts of anger... And things like these of which I forewarn you ... that those who practice this things will not inherit the kingdom of God (Galatians 5:19–21 NASB). Again, the presence of what was deemed "sorcery" was aligned with forces that prevented whole-hearted devotion to the faith, this time to the Church and the message of Jesus of Nazareth. And again, "magic" is linked to false or idolatrous worship of other deities. Those who decried *Harry Potter* on the basis of the New Testament teachings pointed also to the events recorded in Acts 19:11 where Greco-Roman converts to Christianity "who practiced magic brought their books together and began burning them in the sight of everyone," as a sign of their newfound devotion to the Church. To the Potter critics, the line was clear. Magic equaled idolatry, which in turn equated to evil.

Paul Hetrick of the political advocacy group Focus on the Family summed up this attitude in his 1999 comments dealing with efforts to ban the book from school libraries. It contains some powerful and valuable lessons about love and courage and the ultimate victory of good over evil. However, the positive messages are packaged in a medium — witchcraft — that is directly denounced in Scripture.²

Rowling's books were given similar critiques by leaders and spokesmen from across the spectrum of the Christian faith, from convicted-Watergate-conspirator-turned- prisoner-reformer Charles Colson to then Cardinal Joseph Ratzinger, who later became Pope Benedict XVI. Potter-bashing became a cause that for a brief moment united differing and oftentimes opposed branches of the Christian tree.

Rowling's personal beliefs also came under scrutiny despite her status as practicing member of the Church of Scotland. Some found her general affirmation about "believing in God" was too vague to be genuine. Her critics continued to assert that her personal beliefs mirrored the environment of the fictional Hogwarts, a "playground" of the neo-occult, with nary a hint of Christian ethic or doctrine.

Some critics accused Rowling personally of being a Wiccan or an Occultist, whose underlying goal in writing the Potter books was to subvert faith in Christian message. This belief was reported to have extended as far as the White House as former presidential spokesman Matt Latimer related in his 2009 memoir *Speech-Less*. In the book, Latimer reveals that Rowling was denied consideration for the Presidential Medal of Freedom by the administration of George W. Bush because the Potter books in their view promoted "witchcraft."³

These rejections of *Harry Potter* might have been the final word from most mainstream Christians. But a strange thing happened on the way to final consensus. In 2005, while the Harry Potter books were nearing their completion and the equally popular film series was underway, C.S. Lewis' classic tale *The Lion, the Witch and the Wardrobe* was put into wide release by Walden Media and Disney Pictures. This event, as they say, tipped over the rhetorical apple cart. Foes of Rowling's magic based heroes and heroines became zealous advocates for the fantasy world of Narnia and the supernatural occurrences contained therein.

On one level, the dichotomy was easily explained. Lewis' place as one of the twentieth century's most revered Christian thinkers and writers is unquestioned and his influence over modern Christian leaders is considerable (I've met some who treat his 1952 apologetic *Mere Christianity* as a de-facto book of the Bible). He also produced one of the best received fantasy series of all time as his complex Bible-based allegory *The Chronicles of Narnia* is practically required reading for literature-lovers of all backgrounds. The fact that a series based on his fiction would soon be in theaters was welcome news to scores of Christian parents who commented about being overwhelmed by "secular-themed" entertainment.

However, the release of the *Narnia* movie revived the same problem for many Christian leaders as *Harry Potter*. What *is* the position of the Church on the use of magic? Scores of prominent leaders had lined up to condemn Rowling's use of spells, wands and incantations in the *Harry Potter* series. But given the same opportunity to condemn "magical" wardrobes, talking animals and supernatural weaponry in the *Narnia* film, many of Rowling's critics seemed to take a 180 degree turn. In the wake of the movie's release, sermons encouraging Christian parents to see *The Lion, the Witch and the Wardrobe* were being given from pulpits across the land and viewing parties were being organized, many times at the behest of church leaders. Were Christians now "double minded" when it came to use of magic in popular fiction?

The explanation offered by Christian leaders usually came in the form of two mitigating factors. Some blatantly couched their acceptance of the magic-themed heroes of Narnia in the argument that Lewis was one of "us" while Rowling was considered to be one of "them."

Lewis' background, method and motives were clear to mainstream Christians, while in the case of Rowling; well, frankly, who *really* knew what she was about? If some of what Lewis' Narnia was about smacked of "magic" or "sorcery" it could be overlooked given his other good works. Rowling would be held to another standard.

While spurious on many grounds, this particular argument failed the standard described by no less a figure than Jesus of Nazareth: But let your statement be "Yes, yes" or "No, no." Anything beyond that is of evil (Gospel of Matthew 5:37 NASB). Clearly, Christians could not adhere to a standard that magic was permissible only when self-identified Christians used it in a story. If that was the case, then Rowling's public discussions of her Christian faith would place her in the same hallowed territory as Lewis. While one could certainly argue (and many did) that Rowling's brief statements on her faith were minuscule when compared to Lewis' volumes of theological defense of the Church, the fact remained that two professing Christians were using the same device — magic — to tell a story. One had encountered waves of hostility from many Christians. The other was getting Sunday-morning sermons in favor of his works.

Some critics, sensing the facile hypocrisy of this argument, turned to the qualitative "use" of magic as the basis of their denunciation of Rowling and *Harry Potter*. The problem with Harry didn't lie with just the use of magic, but it was the "type" of magic described by Rowling's that was the problem. To them, the magic and the sources of magic used by Harry Potter and the Hogwarts students were based in real occultism and not in fantasy.

The previously mentioned Rowling critic Richard Abanes argued for a quantitative difference between Lewis' and Tolkien's fantasy-world "magic" and what he believed was Rowling's use of real-world, occult "magick" in a 2007 interview with the Christian Broadcasting Network:

> One of the easiest ways to know whether a fantasy book or film has real world magick in it is to just ask a simple question: "Can my child find information in a library or bookstore that will enable them to replicate what they are seeing in the film or the book?" If you go to *The Chronicles of Narnia* and the *Lord of the Rings* what you see in, story magic and imagination, it is not real. You can't replicate it. But if you go to something like *Harry Potter*, you can find references to astrology, clairvoyance, and numerology. It takes seconds to go into a bookstore or library and get books on that and start investigating it, researching it, and doing it. In fact, that's why real Wiccans, real witches, and real occultists are using the popularity of *Harry Potter* to lure kids toward real world occultism. They actually have advertisements for their own books that use Harry Potter as their appeal.[4]

When pressed on some of the particulars, Abanes continued to define what he perceived as the differences between the intent of Rowling and previous Christian fantasists.

> It is a very new trend for children's fiction to be dark, to be sinister, to be anti–Christian, to be filled with occult imagery. That is something that actually started when there was a changeover in Hollywood from the classic portrayal of demons, witches, and things like that in a negative light. You started getting movies around the late 1980s and early 1990s that were starting to portray witchcraft, the occult, and the paranormal in a positive way. And that started piquing an interest of the community and of kids. You know, Hollywood targets children a lot because there is a lot of money to be made there. So that started this trend toward the popularity of that. Then you get the television shows, like "Buffy the Vampire Slayer" and "Charmed," that presented these types of things in a very positive, fun, stimulating, exciting way, and that has caused this interest. Then there are books like the R.L. Stine books that have contributed greatly to this horror genre for children. That's how that started.[5]

While quick to point out that he is not for the censorship or banning of the Potter series, Abanes goes on to reiterate that parents should be informed of the qualitative differences between the types of magic presented to their children.

Abanes's critique of Rowling's approach opened up an interesting area of discussion on both sides of the debate. It is true that the *Harry Potter* series delves into "real-world" occult practices such as astrology, communication with spirits and divining the future through supernatural means. While the scientific validity of all three is left to question, Christians and many members of other religious faiths consider these practices to have an active influence in the modern world. On some level, it *is* conceivable that a reader of the *Harry Potter* books might out of curiosity seek out more information about these religiously unsanctioned activities.

It is equally true that an acute reader of the Bible might find his interest piqued in supernatural matters from reading such accounts as the transformation of rods into serpents by Egyptian "sorcerers," or the summoning of the spirit of Samuel the Judge from Sheol by the Medium of Endor, or the "wise men" of the East who use astrology to determine the birthplace and time of Jesus. These occurrences of the occult, found within the pages of Scripture, also await eager eyes.

Abanes's strongest point may be the "dark" trend of modern youth literature. Many who follow the patterns found modern YA literature have noticed a shift away from the reliably "moral" protagonist in favor of delving into areas many would describe as controversial or morally ambiguous. A quick comparison between the eighteen-year-old sleuth Nancy Drew, created in 1928, and the fifteen-year-old slayer Buffy Summers, created in 1992, gives a telling illustration of the changes in the values, worldview and cultural expectations for heroes that took place during the nearly seventy years that divided their debuts.

Nancy Drew, it could be said, has been a character almost absent of inner conflict for the majority of her existence. In the course of her detective adventures, Nancy generally listens to parents, works with law enforcement, and projects the image of a stable, well-adjusted, naturally curious but still "within-the rules" female hero. In comparison, Buffy Summers in her role as a slayer misleads or deceives adults, cuts classes, engages in deals with demons, has sex with vampires and wrestles with enough personal monsters to make Nietzsche sympathetic.

Such modern heroes as Bella Swan (The *Twilight* novels), Katniss Everdeen (*The Hunger Games* novels), Lyra Belacqua (*His Dark Materials* novels) and others present to traditional-culture critics new and unwanted heroes, delving into subjects previously off-limits for youthful readers. The conflicts confronting these heroines are such things as economic class divisions, wartime ethics, non-traditional sex and marriage and even the questioning of God and religious morality. These are issues that Nancy Drew likely never heard discussed around the dinner table in River Heights.

This "darkening" trend, while uncertainly not unheard of in heroic literature, does represent a break in the majority of the twentieth century youth literature in which pop-culture heroes were expected to have at least nominal allegiance to mainstream values. While correctly noting the growing influence of the "dark theme" in youth culture, Abanes and many others of Rowling's critics tend to downplay the moral fiber that Harry and his fellow students display in confronting and overcoming the challenge of evil. Voldemort and his minions present themselves at times as an overwhelming force of destruction, making the Hogwarts students' opposition of them the classic "lost cause." Yet Harry, in particular, rarely bemoans his destiny as the opponent of the Dark Lord, and unlike the modern anti-hero, he does not fall prey to the temptation to use his abilities for self-enrichment or revenge. Nor can he be seduced by the idea of seizing the power of the Dark Lord for himself, despite several opportunities near the end of the series.

While there are images of evil and threats of danger, the young hero and his crew for the most part seem to be unambiguously loyal, optimistic, dedicated to the cause of opposing evil and free of higher ambition. This theme of "dark temptation," a mainstay elsewhere in modern youth literature, is consistently rejected. These qualities should, to both supporter and critic alike, represent the some best character traits that younger readers can emulate.

Further muddying the waters on the question of "good" or "bad" magic is the growing viewpoint that Rowling crafted the character of Harry as a stand-in for the life and suffering of Jesus in a manner similar to Lewis' allegorical use of the lion Aslan in the *Narnia* novels. Rowling herself furthered this viewpoint in her 2007 interview after the release of *Harry Potter and the Deathly Hallows*: "To me, the religious *parallels* have always been obvious. But I never wanted to talk too openly about it because I thought it might show people who just wanted the story where we were going."[6]

To many Rowling's supporters, the climactic battle in which Harry returns from the afterlife to defeat Voldemort after offering himself as a willing sacrifice to save his friends speaks to a powerful parallel with the Gospel accounts of the resurrection of Christ. In this final battle, many readers saw echoes of Jesus' triumph over death and the power of the Devil that form the basis of the Christian faith.

As additional evidence of her allegorical leanings, the gravestone markers of Harry's parents that provide two New Testament verses, Matthew 6:19 ("Where your treasure is, there will your heart be also.") and 1 Corinthians 15:26, ("The last enemy that shall be destroyed is death"). These dramatic verses were intended to foreshadow Rowling's final theme of the Potter series.

In his book, *Looking for God in Harry Potter*, author and literature professor John Granger argues that critics such as Abanes and Hetrick are completely wrong in their analysis of Harry Potter's use of magic (specifically alchemy), the overall theme of the Potter novels and even the very idea of what constitutes an acceptably Christian hero. Rowling, in Granger's view, has not just produced a heroic figure sympathetic to Christian values, but an actual, twenty-first century, "Christian" heroic figure. He states in the book's first chapter that the criticism of Rowling's use of magic is wrongheaded:

> If there is anything tragic in this misunderstanding of Harry Potter by well-intentioned Christians, it is the tragedy of "friendly fire." Just as foot soldiers are sometimes hit by misdirected artillery fire from their own troops, so Harry has been

> condemned by the side he is serving. Because we mistake fictional magic for sorcery, we misconstrue a well-aimed blow at atheistic naturalism as an invitation to the occult. This only serves to attack a new and valuable ally in the spiritual warfare against our common enemy. If the "magical trees" in Harry Potter are of any help in retaking ground lost to those who would burn down the spiritual forest, then Rowling has done Christian communities everywhere a very good deed.[7]

Granger goes on to make the case that Rowling's intent was to continue the work of the great Christian fantasists, making her almost a de-facto member of the Inklings, the Oxford-based writing group to which such professing Christians as Tolkien, Lewis and Charles Williams belonged. To him, the actions of Harry and his fellows in the novels are steeped in the overtones of Christian theology and Harry himself is a "Hero-Christian" in the mode of Percival or Galahad, or even a figure paired with Jesus Himself.

> If there is a single meaning to the Potter books ... it is that love conquers all. And of all loves, sacrificial love is the most important, because it has conquered death. Harry's protection against the assault of the evil one is the love shown years ago by someone who made the greatest sacrifice for him. His bond with that sacrifice and the love it demonstrated permeates his person and repels all evil. Voldemort cannot touch him because of Harry's worthiness to receive the Stone (Christ), and because of the Christ-like love and sacrifice that shield him.[8]

While his analysis is perhaps too willing to impart hidden Christian overtones in the books, the popularity of *Harry Potter* with Christian readers and the mitigating influence of Disney's *Narnia* release might have allowed Granger's "Hero-Christian" thesis to create some common ground between supporters and detractors. However, after the release of *Harry Potter and the Deathly Hallows*, Rowling herself perhaps re-stoked the fire of distrust towards the Potter series with a final crackling, cultural log. "I always thought of Dumbledore as gay. ... Dumbledore fell in love with Gellert Grindelwald, and that added to his horror when Grindelwald showed himself to be what he was..."[9] This statement, given in answer to a fan's question at an event at Carnegie Hall in 2007, in many ways renewed the tidal wave of criticism of the Potter books. While fans of the series, for the most part, received the news of Professor Dumbledore's sexual orientation with varying levels of enthusiasm or indifference, conservative critics took it as new salvo in the culture war. Many of the same voices that had denounced Rowling for her use of the occult — and who had been greeted with debate — now felt vindicated in slamming the books as promoting a "homosexual rights" agenda, proof positive again of the author's allegedly sinister intent. Pat Roberson, the leader of the influential evangelical 700 Club television program, renewed calls for the Potter novels to be banned from schools and many new sermons were prepared to freshly denounce Rowling and her "un–Christian" writings.

This new wrinkle in the debate left even some Rowling supporters scratching their heads. All clear-headed commentators certainly concede it is within Rowling's rights to give her creations whatever traits she deems fit. And given the complex nature of human sexuality, the placement of a single gay character into the *Harry Potter* mythos was unlikely to spur anyone into the "homosexual lifestyle" by their presence on the page. However, misgivings with her announcement remained.

If Dumbledore was indeed a gay man in love with Grindelwald for many years and his unrequited emotions lead to decisions that were central to the plot of the series, why was this never explicitly stated anywhere in the narrative? Even very meticulous readers of the series (readers far more dedicated than I) commented that no overt mention of Dumbledore's sexual preference could be found. If this detail wasn't worth mentioning in the novels, then why issue this pronouncement in the aftermath of *The Deathly Hallows*?

Some conspiracy minded observers put forth the idea that Rowling succumbed to a final urge to "stick it" to her traditional-values critics by revealing what was to some a minor controversy in the novel's backstory. After nearly ten years of attacks by opponents of *Harry Potter*, perhaps Rowling was using her spotlight to get the ultimate blow in for her side of the culture wars. Some critics (and even some supporters) offered an even more cynical theory. Rowling was engaging in a "just-spell-my-name-right" controversy-driven marketing campaign aimed at getting previously uninterested parties into buying the Potter novels. These arguments dealing with Rowling's inner motivations have waxed and waned in the years since the completion of the novels and movies.

The dizzying turns in the debate left many teachers and youth leaders in a bit of a quandary. As is too often the case in modern Christianity, the debate of religious leaders often times does little to inform laity about how to deal with nuanced controversy. Certainly, every informed Christian understands we have a Scriptural basis for the idea "Thou Shalt Not." It's something every church-going child gets a dose of at a tender age. However, when leaders get into subjects that are not as well-defined and rhetoric becomes heated, their Biblical sense of True-North has the potential to become fuzzy.

Many churches gave thundering sermons against *Harry Potter* and Rowling *ad nauseam* throughout the 2000's (though I can report this was not the norm at the non-denominational church where I spend my Sundays). However, these same leaders many times ignored the fact that if they wanted to find these subversive *Harry Potter* books, all they would have had to do is leave the pulpit and request a copy from one of the youths who were supposed to be listening to their sermonizing. (Spotting kids with a copy of a

Harry Potter book open during the occasional slow-moving Sunday morning sermon became a bit of a personal pastime, even when I was the sermonizing offender.)

Telling people something is "bad" for them is not the same as telling them why it is "bad" for them. More importantly, unconsidered, uniformed "Thou Shall Not" statements tend to have an opposite effect than the one intended, especially in kids. I decided that to figure this issue out, I would have to make my own inquiries.

At twenty-seven years of age when the debates over *Harry Potter* began and with no children of my own, I will admit to being a Johnny-come-lately to the phenomenon. I knew nothing about the books until I saw my Sunday-School students reading them when they should have been doing other things (like paying attention to their wonderful teacher). But when I saw how intently they were reading the Rowling books, the literary side of my personality was piqued. I borrowed a copy of *Harry Potter and the Sorcerer's Stone* from a student and took a few days to read through it.

What I found there was a fairly engaging story about a young hero, near in age to most of the students I was teaching, swept up into a magical realm that set the stage for fantastic adventures with others in his same age group. I certainly could see the appeal of the story. The use of magic I found there was not overly realistic and certainly not terribly detailed for use as a repeatable occult practice. While *Harry Potter* did describe magic usage, it seemed to be based on stringing together Ancient Latin prefixes rather than calling upon occult powers. I found no evidence that verbalizing the spells would conjure up anything except a few giggles for the speaker.

If I saw any objectionable use of magic (and this general objection continued throughout the series and with the movies) it was in the belief that any problem or obstacle could be overcome quickly with the application of skillful spellcasting. While Rowling does address the facility of magic to solve problems at different times, the first impression left in my mind was that "magic" and its clever use was the instant solution to life's ups-and-downs. While blunted a little by the plot turns of the series, Rowling, given my personal reading, never directly debunks this "ease-of-magic" device.

Additionally, the idea of being separated from the world of the "muggles" and somehow being more gifted than normal humans touched the nerve of some vague egalitarian impulse. While certainly the heroes of the series defend the world of the muggles, they also continue a pattern of separatism from them as well. Even the term "muggle" carried the hint of some personal distaste for, if not bigotry against, ordinary non-magical humans

I recognize that many teens and pre-teens who enjoy fantasy could readily accept the concept of fleeing a world filled with unrefined peers and absent parents for a stimulating, magical one because that worldview mirrors their own desires. However, a value system that does not have at its core respect for the uniqueness of human existence and a fundamental desire to love others and seek out the highest expression of good towards them does not seem Christian in its definition to me.

These misgivings aside, I saw nothing permanently harmful in the text of the books. I returned the tome with thanks to my student, asking him again not to read the book during class time.

But what stayed with me from Rowling's book was powerful. The kids in question had become engrossed in the story of Harry and his Hogwarts fellows, to such an extent that they could not wait to read the next paragraph, the next chapter, the next book in the series. To my mind, and confirmed by later questioning of students, the idea of Harry and his fellow characters dealing with the important issues of maturity and identity while forging bonds of loyalty and friendship was something they responded to. To make a Shakespearean allusion, the story was the thing that was hooking the kids. The use of magic, not so much.

The idea of storytelling began to appeal to me in a way I had not considered. One of the most interesting dichotomies present in modern Christian education is the lack of storytelling as an educational tool. This is not to say there are not stories relating to Scripture being taught. The students in my classes could have easily repeated to me Bible lessons about Adam and Eve, Noah's Ark, David and Goliath and others. But the idea of internalizing the moral themes of these portions of Scripture seemed very foreign to them. Sadly, many could tell me the various details of the stories, but were not engaged enough with their themes to analyze the decision-making of the participants or to delve into moral applications of their decisions.

Storytelling in ancient times engaged the mind of the listener to consider not just the details of the story, but created a framework that encouraged response to the themes presented. This process of engaging the hearer's (or in this case, the reader's) imagination with the concepts used helped students form identifiable, concrete associations with the principles of the lessons. Oral histories, fables, myths, word "riddles" and folk tales were all used throughout antiquity as signposts of cultures, transmitting the values of a group of people to the next generation.

In an unorthodox way, Rowling's *Harry Potter* seemed to make contact with these elements of culture, telling the story of a hero (with guidance from teachers and support from peers) who is forced to confront life's moral challenges at a young age. Despite the fantastical setting and the supernatural powers, readers, even very young readers, could identify with Harry and relate to his personal challenges and the testing of his core values. Harry was that rarest of figures in modern literature: an everyman who through the course of his fictional coming-of-age story had a touchstone event for almost everyone who read the novels. It was more than people just wanted to be Harry. They saw themselves living the story with him, being in his shoes, stumbling through adolescence, confronted by need to make solid moral decisions while trying to find their way in the world.

After considering it, I believed I'd identified a part of the appeal of the *Harry Potter* novels. The next step was to ponder how to best harness this powerful tool of personal engagement for my students' benefit. How could I engage them with the Christian message the way they'd engaged with Harry?

This led me to ponder at length about the way my faith is generally taught. While contemporary Christian teaching often focuses on retention of direct, bright line doctrine-related verses, the Gospel accounts are replete with fictional stories attributed to Jesus, specifically, the method of rabbinical storytelling known to Christians as the Parables. The Greek New Testament provides us with over 50 interpretations of the unique short-stories told by Jesus to His disciples and those lay-people who were interested in His itinerant ministry. Plainly put, had one seen Jesus in the road or in the marketplace, He likely would have being telling a story.

For a storyteller, getting the listener (or the reader) to identify with the hero can be an important step toward engaging them with the larger theme, or in my case, having them apply the moral teachings of the Bible. Rowling had found a compelling way to engage readers in the drama of Harry Potter. Now I took the challenge of finding a way to connect my students with the lessons I was trying to teach. It was to be in the Parables I would find my inspiration.

During the start of a new class session in 2000, I announced that the final project that summer would be staging a reading of several of Jesus' parables with each student acting out a part of the story. Each student would have to, through performance, demonstrate how his or her "role" in the parable was essential to the overall lesson. While many of the parts were non-speaking roles (i.e. students were called upon to portray inanimate objects or animals) each student was encouraged to put a personal twist or element into the performance. The students finished their project with a flourish, putting on a very engaging half-hour show for the congregation, complete with props and staging designed by the participants.

While religious drama is certainly not a new teaching device, the emphasis of being immersed in character I believed helped the students connect with the narrative of the Bible. That's not to say that one should abandon such techniques as memorization or public reading of Scripture (I'm still infamous with the kids of my church for making them do this in my class). Still, the power of putting a student in the "shoes" of the protagonist gives an insight into the personal conflicts and decision-making process that rarely comes from reciting events.

The exercise also, I believe, impressed upon the students a way of looking at their faith in a new light. A former student from that summer class session, now into her twenties with a young child of her own, remarked to me lately that she looked back on that class with fondness because I had demonstrated that the Parables were more than just words on the page. While flattered, I pointed out that what engaged her with the project was the power of the story.

If Rowling and other YA authors have proven anything, it is that modern readers still are searching for a heroic figure who speaks to their lives and experiences and will follow a well-crafted story for months and years, past the days of youth and into adulthood. As for the impact of the books, I can gladly report that the majority of the students I worked with are now productive, engaging adults who mostly still attend church services and are not agents of Moloch or any other occult power. Some of them even have children of their own who have a high probability of being exposed to the *Harry Potter* novels in our vast world of ideas. My hope is that those entrusted with the Gospel message will also consider how to use the magical power of storytelling to stimulate them always toward faith and good deeds.

Notes

1. All Scripture quotations provided from The New American Standard Translation, USA, Lockman Foundation, 1995.

2. Holly Kurtz, "Harry Potter Expelled from School," *Denver Rocky Mountain News*, November 6, 1999, http://www.cesnur.org/recens/potter_06.htm.

3. Matt Latimer, *Speech-Less: Tales of a White House Survivor* (New York: Crown, 2009), 201.

4. Belinda Elliott, "Harry Potter: Harmless Christian Novel or Doorway to the Occult?" *Christian Broadcasting Network.com*, October 2007, http://www.cbn.com/spirituallife/OnlineDiscipleship/HarryPotterControversy/elliott_RichardAbanes.aspx.

5. Ibid.

6. Jonathan Petre, "J.K. Rowling: Christianity Inspired Harry Potter," *The Telegraph*, October 20, 2007, http://www.telegraph.co.uk/culture/books/fictionreviews/3668658/J-K-Rowling-Christianity-inspired-Harry-Potter.

7. John Granger, *Looking for God in Harry Potter* (USA: Tyndale/Zondervan Publishing, 2004), 9–10.

8. Ibid., 124–125.

9. Raju Mudhar, "Outing Dumbledore as Gay," *The Toronto Star*, October 23, 2007, http://www.thestar.com/entertainment/Books/article/269449.

Boy Wizards and Girl Scientists: Rowling's Contributions to Science Outreach

KRISTINE LARSEN

Interesting Girls in Science: A Call to Action

In the 21st century, the need for a scientifically engaged and literate populace is increasingly apparent. Not only is there a growing job market for scientists, engineers, and other highly skilled practitioners, but citizens in all walks of life often come face-to-face with scientific discoveries and controversies, from climate change to genetic engineering to nuclear power. Therefore it is vital that high school and college graduates have at the very least a basic understanding of the process of science, and that science educators at all levels make a concerted effort to encourage students to consider careers in STEM (science, technology, engineering, and mathematics). Part of this is making science seem relevant and exciting to young people, and a proven methodology is the use of popular culture in the science classroom. From analyzing science fiction film scenes for their scientific content[1] to using episodes of *Star Trek: The Next Generation* to teach science,[2] science education journals routinely publish "how-to" articles on using some science fiction television series, novel, or film to interest students in science content. Fantasy and horror works can also be used, such as the works of J.R.R. Tolkien[3] and even zombie films.[4] The *Harry Potter* novels and films are no exception to this trend; for example, Blickenstaff explained that teachers could use segments of *Harry Potter and the Deathly Hallows, Part 1* to show their earth science students examples of geological formations in the British Isles that are not common in the U.S.[5]

While the use of popular culture in teaching science has certainly proven successful, the formal science classroom is not the only place where science learning occurs. Just as important are so-called informal science education opportunities, also termed outreach activities, including after school and weekend programs, museums exhibits, and planetarium shows, among others. The National Science Teachers Association (NSTA) "strongly advocates informal science education because we share a common mission and vision."[6] Lynn Dierking and John Falk coined the term "free-choice learning" to encompass these communal activities, as well as more solitary ones such as an individual seeking out information about science in books or on the internet. Free-choice learning "is guided by learners' needs and interests — the learning that people engage in throughout their lives to find out more about what is useful, compelling, or just plain interesting to them. This type of learning is intrinsically motivated and largely under the choice and control of the learner."[7]

While the *Harry Potter* novels have rightly been lauded for interesting children in reading, emphasis has usually been placed on the series' particular ability to get normally reticent male readers off the internet and video games and into the pages of a book. (E.g. http://blogs.wsj.com/juggle/2009/08/07/harry-potters-magic-how-to-get-boys-to-read-more). As international studies have demonstrated,[8] there is indeed a gender gap in terms of reading: girls read more than boys and comprehend what they read at a higher level. But I argue that in the case of the intersection of *Harry Potter* and science, it is the potential impact on girls' interest in science on which we should focus. For while both boys' and girls' interest in science wanes between elementary and high school, girls lose interest at a greater rate than boys, an important issue for those seeking a gender balance in the STEM careers. For example, while roughly equal percentages of boys and girls like science in fourth grade, by eighth grade girls trail boys in science interest two-to-one.[9] Thus Sneider urges that the "critical period for influencing students is between 8 and 13 years old."[10] Informal out-of-school programs have been shown to increase girls' interest and participation in science, and studies suggest that the most successful programs incorporate "hands-on activities, role models, an emphasis on practical applications, and practices that promote equitable learning environments for girls."[11]

Since *Harry Potter* fans already take part in free-choice learning, through their reading, fan fiction writing, movie viewing, and, in some cases, a wider participation in the fandom online and at conventions, science educators have a unique opportunity to bring science directly to girls in an exciting and personally relevant way.[12] This essay will not only give concrete examples of the science in the series (focusing on astronomy) but more importantly share examples of informal science learning based on the series conducted by planetariums, professional organizations, and individuals. My goal is to convince the reader to take up the baton (or should I say wand) themselves, and to use what others have already done to share the science of the Potterverse with the girls in their lives.

"Mars Is Bright Tonight": Astronomy in the Potterverse

Astronomy is one of the subjects taught at Hogwarts, the only one that corresponds to a "Muggle" field of study. J.K. Rowling could have chosen to be vague in her descriptions of the curriculum, but instead not only includes a number of specific astronomical tasks the students must complete on the way to earning their O.W.L. (Ordinary Wizardly Level), but utilized an obvious astronomical theme in the naming of many of her wizards. Luna Lovegood, the moon-eyed girl, is named for earth's natural satellite, and astronomy professor Aurora Sinistra's first name derives from the Northern Lights, an atmospheric effect created when the solar wind interacts with earth's magnetic field. Bellatrix Lestrange is named for a bright star in Orion (Bellatrix "the Female Warrior" or "the Amazon Star"[13]) while Tom Riddle's mother Merope Gaunt is named for one of the Pleiades (or Seven Sisters) in Taurus. Draco Malfoy's name is borrowed from the dragon that snakes its way between the Big and Little Dipper, while his son Scorpius Malfoy is named for the scorpion seen in the summer sky. Sirius Black is named for the brightest star in the night sky, the so-called Dog Star that marks the collar of Canis Major, the large dog, a fit name for a character that can transform himself into a canine. Alphard Black, Arcturus Black, Pollux Black, and Regulus Black are likewise named after other bright stars in the sky, while Andromeda Tonks, Cassiopeia Black, Cygnus Black, and Orion Black owe their names to prominent constellations.

These rather obvious astronomical references are widely known in the Potter fandom, thanks in part to online essays such as Mike Weinstein's "Astronomy in the Harry Potter Series" (in *The Harry Potter Lexicon*, July 6, 2011, http://www.hp-lexicon.org/essays/essay-astronomy.html). Astronomy educators have realized the outreach potential of these "stars" of the Potterverse, using them as a hook to interest fans of *Harry Potter* in learning about these bodies. Examples include C. Renee James's article "The Real Stars of Harry Potter" (in *Mercury* 36, no. 4 (2007): 22) in the Astronomical Society of the Pacific's popular level periodical *Mercury*, amateur astronomer Marc Keelan Bishop's "Harry Potter AstronaKazam! Page" (http://www.marcs observatory.com/mo_harrypotter.html) and Bates College student Bev Levene's "Harry Potter and the Night Sky" podcast (based on an original planetarium show, available at http://365daysofastronomy.org/2010/11/13/november-13th-harry-potter-and-the-night-sky/).

But the astronomy of Hogwarts is not limited to celestial names. Students in Professor Sinistra's classes have to write a "long and difficult essay about Jupiter's moons" (*OOTP* 295). Ron and Harry both struggle with the assignment, and it is up to Hermione, the better astronomer, to set them straight. She corrects several errors in Ron's essay, noting that Jupiter's largest moon is "Ganymede, not Callisto," and that "it's Io that's got the volcanoes" (*OOTP* 295). She later also corrects a rather silly error in Harry's essay, noting "you must have misheard Professor Sinistra... Europa's covered in ice, not mice!" (*OOTP* 300). Hermione (and therefore Rowling) are correct on all counts in this case. As a result, NASA based a public outreach article on the moons of Jupiter on this scene (http://science.nasa.gov/science-news/science-at-nasa/2003/02jul_harrypotter).

But Rowling's astronomy is not always so perfect. For example, in *Harry Potter and the Sorcerer's Stone* (253) Ronan asserts that Mars is "unusually bright" that night. Weinstein shows that based on the dates in the Lexicon Timeline, Mars was actually not especially bright on the night in question. Weinstein catches a similar mistake made in *Harry Potter and the Order of the Phoenix* (602) where Mars is described as looking like a "twinkling red star" when Mars normally does not twinkle. Interested readers are directed to Weinstein's article (in the bibliography) for additional examples of astronomical gaffs.

One often-repeated error in Rowling's astronomy deserves special attention. For their astronomy final exam, Hogwarts students must observe the heavens with their individual telescopes and fill out a star chart with the position of important bodies such as the planet Venus and the constellation Orion (*OOTP* 718–19). However, Orion is not viewable near midnight in June, the timing of the exam in question. Numerous internet posts and astronomical articles have picked up on Rowling's error; one could easily turn this into a teachable moment by using a planetarium or star chart to show a young person why Rowling was in error, rather than merely complaining that her astronomy was imprecise. For example, the Morehead Planetarium and Science Center in North Carolina used these references to interest the public in their regular night sky show, entitling their July 19, 2011, blog "Harry Potter's Impossible Astronomy Exam" and describing the error of seeing Orion in the June sky. (http://moreheadplanetarium.org/blog/?p=1387).

But one should not rush to proclaim Rowling's astronomy wrong without careful consideration. Venus — the Morning Star or Evening Star — is generally never seen in the sky so close to midnight, prompting astronomer Kevin Krisciunas to investigate Rowling's claim further. What he found surprised him — Venus technically can be visible from central England around midnight in certain years, including 2007, the year the film treatment of *Harry Potter and the Order of the Phoenix* was released.[14]

It should be noted that although the astronomical references are generally not depicted in the films, the astronomy tower itself is front and center in important scenes (such as the death of Dumbledore). Therefore, while viewers of the film will not have the same astronomical exposure as readers of the series, characters named Sirius, Draco, and Bellatrix are still central to the mythology, and can still serve as a hook to draw movie viewers into the greater astronomical universe in Rowling's fiction.

Informal Science Education and Harry Potter: Examples from the Trenches

C. Renee James noted that "J.K. Rowling might not have known it, but she provided a vast new avenue for astronomy outreach by doing some good research into mythology and naming plenty of characters after things you can find in the night sky."[15] Since a representation of the current night sky is often featured as part of public planetarium shows, Rowling's celestial nomenclature caught the interest of numerous planetarium professionals. Some took a simple approach, weaving references into pre-existing shows. For example, Tanja Diederich described in her blog how she delighted her audience with mentions of Sirius and Draco. In her words, "With the Harry Potter stories, we have new stories to tell in the sky and a new generation to introduce to the wonders of the night."[16]

Some planetariums took the next step, developing entire planetarium shows around the references in Rowling's works. These shows typically targeted a younger audience (and their Potter-savvy parents). For example, the planetarium at the New Jersey Astronomy Center for Education at Raritan Valley Community College has occasionally offered a special Harry Potter-themed show, "The Skies Over Hogwarts," (http://www.raritanval.edu/about/news/pr/2008-2009/PR243RVCCPlanetariumSetsHarryPotter-Themed-Shows.html) while the Silverman Planetarium at the Milton J. Rubenstein Museum of Science & Technology in Syracuse, New York, developed "Astronomy 101¾: Astronomy and Harry Potter" (http://www.most.org/2_ee_planetarium_ss.cfm#5). "The Secret Stars of Harry Potter" has been shown at the George E. Coleman, Sr. Planetarium at North Georgia College and State University (http://www.northgeorgia.edu/Planetarium/Default_1col.aspx?id=4294970297), and the BYU Astronomical Society has presented "The Astronomy of Harry Potter" show at the Derrick Planetarium (Provo, Utah) several times since 2006 (http://nightsky.jpl.nasa.gov/event-view.cfm?Event_ID=5303; http://events.fox13now.com/Planetarium_Shows_Astronomy_in_Harry_Potter/224385308.html).

Another popular type of astronomical informal education is the star party, where telescopes are set up for the public to directly view the heavens. As previously noted, the Hogwarts students were expected to be able to handle a telescope and make their own observations. For this reason, *Harry Potter*-themed star parties (especially as a tie-in to the release of the books) began to pop up around the world. For example, the staff at Jodrell Bank Observatory in England have held events to coincide with the release of *Harry Potter and the Half-Blood Prince* and *Harry Potter and the Deathly Hallows*. At each event, the attendees were divided by the robed astronomers into four "houses" named for the constellations Aquila, Cygnus, Lepus, and Delphinus, and took part in hands-on activities including viewing through telescopes. At midnight, the attendees received their long-awaited copies of the novel.[17]

Jane Houston Jones, Senior Outreach Specialist for the Cassini Program at NASA's Jet Propulsion Laboratory and past president of the Astronomical Association of Northern California, has also hosted several star parties to coincide with the release of *Harry Potter and the Goblet of Fire* and *Harry Potter and the Deathly Hallows*, and used her blog to recruit others with personal telescopes to do the same at their local bookstores (http://www.whiteoaks.com/pipermail/sfevents/2003-June/000226.html; http://mail.otastro.org/pipermail/otevents/2007-June/000112.html). Jones combined her astronomical knowledge and outreach expertise to craft (along with Caroline Sagaguchi Kunioka) the "Harry Potter Objects" stargazing project website, an excellent resource for backyard observers wishing to view all the astronomical objects related to *Harry Potter*. Most are visible to the unaided eye; while others require a telescope, interested Potter fans can certainly download the list and bring it to their local observatory in order to see these objects themselves, or request that the observatory or local astronomy club host special *Harry Potter* star parties based on the list. As Jones and Kunioka explain, "this list might just be the 'hook' to get your favorite muggle or wizard to step outside for a night of stargazing."[18]

My personal offerings in the field of *Harry Potter*-based astronomy outreach have been varied, and intersect with those already discussed. I am fortunate to have both a planetarium and observatory at my disposal, as well as long-standing outreach programs into which I could integrate *Harry Potter* astronomy activities. In April 2008 I developed a series of hands-on activities based on astronomical references in *Harry Potter*, as well as a *Harry Potter* themed planetarium show entitled "The Stars of Hogwarts." The activities and planetarium show were first done as part of CCSU's Partners in Science Saturday morning science enrichment program for seventh graders that targets girls and students of color. The activities were later also conducted with children attending the 2008 Stellafane amateur telescope makers convention in Springfield, Vermont, and both the activities and planetarium show were offered a number of times to the general public as part of CCSU's International Year of Astronomy activities in 2009. The activities include using a starfinder to explore the astronomical names in the Potterverse (and Rowling's Orion error), making a scale model of Jupiter and its moons, and exploring Sagittarius the Centaur and the structure of our galaxy (in honor of the centaurs in the Potterverse). Details and templates for these activities can be found on the NSTA website in the form of a PowerPoint presentation. (For a detailed description of the activities, see http://www.nsta.org/conferences/schedule.aspx?id=2011har. Search for the keyword "Hogwarts.") Additional Potter-related activities were developed by attendees to a workshop presented by myself and Science Education Professor Marsha Bednarski at the Preparing for the International Year of Astronomy Symposium in 2008. One activity centered on predicting and analyzing planetary alignments, and the other used references to astrology and divination within the novels as a prompt to test whether or not divination is scientific.[19]

Sometimes great outreach ideas go up in flames, thanks to powers beyond our control. In September 2008 I published an article in the *Communicating Astronomy with the Public* Journal encouraging astronomers to use the scheduled November 2008 release of the film version of *Harry Potter and the Half-Blood Prince* to their benefit.[20] The idea was to host sidewalk observing sessions of the November 30/December 1, 2008 Venus-Jupiter conjunction at local movie theaters running the film. Since Venus and Jupiter both appear in the Hogwarts astronomy curriculum, and the books make references to planetary conjunctions, Potter fans would be delighted to follow in the footsteps of their idols and view these objects in a telescope with their own eyes. Unfortunately the movie's release was changed to July 2009, but I still managed to connect Hogwarts to our public observing sessions of the December 2008 conjunction on campus, handing out O.W.L. Astronomy certificates to young people who visited our observatory to view Venus and Jupiter.

Ken Brandt, Director of the Robeson Planetarium and Science Center in Lumberton, NC, took my article to heart, and, dubbing himself "The Resident Astronomer of the Ministry of Magic," brought a telescope to his local theater's opening night of *Harry Potter and the Deathly Hallows, Part 2*. He showed those waiting in line Saturn and other objects, and taught basic celestial navigation. Those who could identify the North Star were given Astronomy O.W.L. certificates (http://nightsky.jpl.nasa.gov/event-view.cfm?Event_ID=28762; https://solarsystem.nasa.gov/calendar/event-view.cfm?EV_ID=11921). Certificates were also awarded to attendees of the CIT Blackrock Castle Observatory (Cork, Ireland) Halloween 2012 season Harry Potter astronomy workshops. (http://www.science.ie/science-events/halloween-hogwarts-workshops.html).

Harry Potter also afforded me the opportunity to work with our campus librarians in bringing a special exhibit to our institution. In July 2007 the U.S. National Library of Medicine launched an exhibition entitled "Medicine and Magic in Harry Potter," which explored depictions of Renaissance science within the series (http://www.nlm.nih.gov/exhibition/harrypottersworld). A traveling version of the exhibit toured libraries on a competitive basis, and CCSU's Elihu Burritt Library hosted the exhibit in October and November 2009 as part of our International Year of Astronomy activities (http://web.ccsu.edu/astronomy/iyaoct.htm; http://articles.courant.com/2009-09-27/news/potter1004.art_1_harry-potter-s-world-renaissance-science-medicine). The excitement generated by this event mirrors that seen every time I offer a *Harry Potter* science activity, because people are clearly wild about Harry. It's my job to make them equally wild about science.

Gender, Science, and Harry Potter: Moving Beyond the Feminist Critiques

Any discussion of using *Harry Potter* to engage girls in a nontraditional field must address the elephant in the room, namely the fact that numerous feminist authors have panned the series as being steeped in classic gender biases and stereotypes. For example, Heilman and Donaldson point out that while the last three books showcase richer roles and more powerful females, we find that women are still marginalized, stereotyped, and even mocked. The overall message related to power and gender still conforms to the stereotypical, hackneyed, and sexist patterns of the first four books, which reflect rather than challenge the worst elements of patriarchy.[21] On the other hand, Mayes-Elman noted that although traditional gender roles are common in the series, there were also "female characters who were nurturing, strong, and intelligent, while resisting the fairy tale formula. I do not believe that either Professor McGonagall or Hermione would be found in a fairy tale; overall they are too strong."[22]

One of Heilman and Donaldson's complaints is that Hermione "is primarily an enabler of Harry's and Ron's adventures, rather than an adventurer herself"[23] and that Hermione only uses her "advanced knowledge of magic ... to aid Harry's quests rather than focusing on her own career. He is the hero; she is but an assistant."[24] This is unarguably true; after all, the series is named *Harry Potter and,* not *Hermione and.* However, it can be argued that Hermione's intelligence and basic knowledge are required for Harry's success; in addition, the series emphasizes the importance of cooperation among groups of people in order to accomplish tasks. This message is nothing less than a fundamental lesson in the way science is generally done in the 21st century. Since it has been proposed that girls may feel less inclined to go into STEM careers because they perceive those fields as "providing few opportunities for social interaction,"[25] the depiction of science in *Harry Potter* as a group activity in which boys and girls both take a hands-on role may help break those erroneous stereotypes of the scientific endeavor.

Having Hermione be the best science student also confronts and confounds deep-rooted stereotypes of scientists. (Julie Darbyshire does an excellent job in summarizing research on depictions of women scientists in popular culture. See www.lablit.com/article/523). For example, a study of over 1500 middle school students asked the children to draw a picture of a scientist. Students generally drew "white males with laboratory coats, eyeglasses, and facial hair" and only a quarter included a female scientist in their drawing.[26] The fact that Hogwarts' astronomy professor is a woman — Aurora Sinistra — also breaks the stereotype of astronomy as a male-only profession.

While Sinistra's first name is known among the online fandom, it is not stated in the books; rather, Rowling included it (and noted Sinistra's gender) in the "More idle jottings (Page 1)" easter egg extra on her official website. (Text transcribed at http://www.hp-lexicon.org/about/sources/jkr.com/jkr-com-trans-jottings1.html). The "Harry Potter Lexicon" page on wizards and witches notes the question of Sinistra's gender came up during the translation of *Order of the Phoenix* into Portuguese. "The translation team contacted the Lexicon for an answer to the question, but I couldn't answer for sure, since it never says one way or the other in the books. I suggested they contact Rowling, which they did. Rowling's reps responded that Sinistra was in fact a woman."[27]

Without a first name, it is certainly less obvious that the character is female; she is called merely "Professor Sinistra" in the books. For example, in *Goblet of Fire* (175) we read that "Professor Sprout, the Herbology teacher, whose hat was askew over her flyaway gray hair ... was talking to Professor Sinistra of the Astronomy department. On Professor Sinistra's other side was a sallow-faced, hook-nosed, greasy-haired Potions master." However, young readers may naturally assume that Sinistra is a woman when the character is described as dancing with a male character: "Mad-Eye Moody was doing an extremely ungainly two-step with Professor Sinistra, who was nervously avoiding his wooden leg" (*GOF* 420). Even if young readers do not pick up on Sinistra's gender on their own, there is no reason why adults can't mention the fact, perhaps in the wider context of teaching examples of women in the history of science. (Biographies of women scientists can be found at http://www.sdsc.edu/ScienceWomen; http://www.astr.ua.edu/4000WS/summary.shtml; http://www.eiu.edu/wism/about_biographies.php.)

Interestingly, Sinistra possibly appears (unidentified) in the film version of *Harry Potter and the Philosopher's Stone*. What makes this noteworthy is that the character is portrayed by an African-American actress. If this is the case, it is indeed unfortunate that she is not clearly identified in the film, as the percentage of minority women in science is far less than that of women in general. If Rowling herself pictured Sinistra as African-American, it would make the character even more noteworthy as a role model for young girls. While fans argue whether or not this extra is truly Sinistra, the official Lego minifigure for Sinistra is indeed black. (See fan discussion at http://harrypotter.wikia.com/wiki/Talk:Aurora_Sinistra.) The Harry Potter Wiki uses a picture of the unidentified film character to illustrate its article on Sinistra; therefore fans searching for information on her will come to the conclusion that not only is Sinistra a woman, but a black woman at that (http://harrypotter.wikia.com/wiki/Aurora_Sinistra). "The Leaky Cauldron" website does not use a picture of the unidentified actress in its page, but does describe the character as having "dark skin and dark hair" (http://www.the-leaky-cauldron.org/wiki/index.php?title=Aurora_Sinistra).

In 2003, women earned only 18 percent of American Ph.D.s in Physics and 26 percent in Astronomy.[28] Three years later, a study conducted by the Society of Women Engineers found that while 95 percent of girls thought STEM careers were "cool" a full two-thirds said these careers were "not for them."[29] These statistics are disturbing, and lead us to believe that the next generation of scientists may be nearly as male-dominated as those preceding it. It is therefore vital that we make concerted efforts to interest girls *in* science, and make them confident about their ability *to do* science. Any means of accomplishing this should be cultivated, and widely disseminated, among educators (both formal and informal), community leaders, and parents. Heilman and Donaldson ask that readers of the series "think about these portrayals" of women. In the case of astronomer Aurora Sinistra and her student Hermione, I heartily concur.[30]

Conclusion: Turning Muggles into Science Wizards

In her 2004 World Book Day Chat, J.K. Rowling claimed, "I don't think I'd be very good at science fiction; you need to know some science!"[31] Clearly Rowling was being modest, because she not only incorporated school-age appropriate science into her series, but also pushed the envelope, in incorporating medieval science and, as Roger Highfield noted in *The Science of Harry Potter,* playing at the edges of such cutting edge science (or science fiction) as time travel, antigravity, and dark energy. Even when Rowling gets it wrong, her science can be used to not only interest young people in the study of the natural world, but give girls the confidence to trust in their ability to do science. For example, in *Harry Potter and the Prisoner of Azkaban*, Hermione figures out that Lupin is a werewolf based in part on her observation that he is sick when the moon is full (346). While Weinstein has pointed out that Rowling's dates for events in the series do not match with the 29.5 day lunar phase cycle, the error is the author's, not Hermione's.[32] For as Lupin adds, "You're the cleverest witch of your age I've ever met, Hermione" (*POA* 346). Not only is she a clever witch, she is undoubtedly an astronomer as well. As such, she serves as a role model to girls her age who are in danger of becoming disenchanted with scientific fields. Girls who remain interested in science into high school have far more career opportunities open to them, including high paying STEM careers.

Interesting young women in science means making science relevant and exciting; it also means making it personal. Science educators need to be creative to accomplish this—we need to channel our inner wizards. I recently tapped into my wizard side when students from a performing arts magnet high school visited our planetarium. I role-played Sinistra for the first half of the show in a costume of academic robes and a pointed star-studded hat. As the students were leaving, one female student joyfully exclaimed to her teacher, "I'm so glad this had a *Harry Potter* theme. That made it so much cooler." I couldn't agree more.

Mercury Journal assistant art director Meg Hove wrote of her daughters' interest in the astronomy in *Harry Potter*: Tracking the phases of the Moon to watch for werewolves, finding characters they loved (or loved-to-hate) in the sky, and learning that Europa is covered in ice, not mice, were adventures, not educational chores. With each star chart filled out, essay written and exam taken, they learned more about the world above us. To a parent, that is a magic in itself.[33]

We have the opportunity to create a generation of professional women scientists who were first introduced to, and excited by, the field through *Harry Potter*, and, equally important, were confident that they could excel in science, thanks to Hermione Granger and her boy (and girl) wizard companions.

Notes

1. Michael Barnett and Alan Kafka, "Using Science Fiction Movie Sciences to Support Critical Analysis of Science," *Journal of College Science Teaching* 36, no. 4 (2006): 31–35.

2. Leroy W. Dubeck and Rose Tatlow, "Using *Star Trek: The Next Generation* Television Episodes to Teach Science," *Journal of College Science Teaching* 27 no. 5 (1998): 319–23.

3. Kristine Larsen, "The Astronomy of Middle-Earth: Teaching Astronomy through Tolkien," in *Cosmos in the Classroom 2004*, eds. Andrew Fraknoi and William Waller (San Francisco: Astronomical Society of the Pacific, 2004), 237–45.

4. Kristine Larsen, "Zombies A̶t̶e̶ Are My Science Homework: Enticing Reluctant Science Students with the Undead," *Connecticut Journal of Science Education* 48, no. 2 (2011): 11–13.

5. Jacob Clark Blickenstaff, "Muggle or Wizard? Science in *Harry Potter and the Deathly Hallows (Part 1)*," *NSTA Reports* 22, no. 5 (2011): 20–21.

6. NSTA Board of Directors, "Informal Science Education," *Journal of College Science Teaching* 28, no. 1 (1998): 17.

7. Lynn D. Dierking and John H. Falk, "Optimizing Out-of-School Time: The Role of Free-choice Learning," *New Directions for Youth Development* no. 97 (2003): 77.

8. David Booth, Susan Elliott-Johns, and Fiona Bruce. *Boys' Literacy Attainment: Research and Related Practice* (North Bay, Canada: Centre for Literacy at Nipissing University, 2009), http://www.edu.gov.on.ca/eng/research/boys_literacy.pdf.

9. Yupin Bae, Susan Choy, Claire Geddes, Jennifer Sable, and Thomas Snyder, *Trends in Educational Equity of Girls and Women* (Washington, DC: National Center for Education Statistics, 2000), 54, http://nces.ed.gov/pubs2000/2000030.pdf

10. Cary Sneider, "Reversing the Swing from Science: Implications from a Century of Research" (paper presented at the ITEST Convening on *Advancing Research on Youth Motivation in STEM*, Boston College, Boston, Massachusetts, September 9–11, 2011). http://www.noycefdn.org/documents/Sneider-The%20Swing%20from%20Science.pdf, 8.

11. Sheryl A. Tucker, Deborah L. Hanuscin and Constance J. Bearnes, "Igniting Girls' Interest in Science," *Science* 319 no. 5870 (2008): 1621.

12. Kristine Larsen, "Hobbits, Hogwarts, and the Heavens: the Use of Fantasy Literature and Films in Astronomy Education and Outreach," in *Proceedings of IAU-UNESCO Symposium 260*, eds. D. Valls-Gabaud and A. Bokensberg (Cambridge: Cambridge University Press, 2001), 306–10.

13. Richard Hinkley Allen, *Star Names: Their Lore and Meaning* (New York: Dover, 1963), 313.

14. Kevin Krisciunas, "Rowling Gets it Right," *Sky and Telescope* 106, no. 6 (2003): 12.

15. C. Renee James, "The Real Stars of Harry Potter," *Mercury* 36, no. 4 (2007): 22.

16. Tanja Diederich, "Harry Potter and Astronomy: Sirius, Draco, Bellatrix and Merope Share a Place in the Night Sky," Jul 17, 2009, http://voices.yahoo.com/harry-potter-astronomy-3802114.html

17. Stuart Lowe, "Harry Potter and the Telescopes of Doom," Feb 12, 2007,http://www.strudel.org.uk/blog/astro/000596.shtml; http://www.strudel.org.uk/blog/astro/000676.shtml; http://www.strudel.org.uk/blog/astro/000680.shtml.

18. Jane Houston Jones and Caroline Sagaguchi Kunioka, "The Harry Potter Objects — a Year-Round Literary Stargazing Project," July 2011, http://jane.whiteoaks.com/2009/07/09/the-harry-potter-objects-a-year-round-literary-stargazing-project.

19. Kristine Larsen and Marsha Bednarski, "Muggles, Meteoritic Armor, and Menelmacar: Using Fantasy Series in Astronomy Education and Outreach," in *Preparing for the 2009 International Year of Astronomy*, eds. M.G. Gibbs, J. Barnes, J.G. Manning, and B. Partridge (San Francisco: Astronomical Society of the Pacific, 2008), 82–90.

20. Kristine Larsen, "Harry Potter and the Upcoming Venus-Jupiter Conjunction: A Unique Outreach Opportunity." *Communicating Astronomy to the Public Journal* no. 4, (2008): 16–17.

21. Elizabeth E. Heilman and Trevor Donaldson, "From Sexist to (sort of) Feminist Representations of Gender in the Harry Potter Series," in *Critical Perspectives on Harry Potter*, 2nd, ed. Elizabeth E. Heilman (NY: Routledge, 2009), 140.

22. Ruthann Mayes-Elman, *Females and Harry Potter: Not All That Empowering* (Lanham, MD: Rowman and Littlefield, 2006), 119.

23. Heilman and Donaldson, "From Sexist," 146.

24. Ibid., 145

25. Sean Cavanagh, "Educators Revisit Girls' Loss of Math, Science Interest," *Education Week* 24, no. 34 (2005): 6.

26. Charles R. Barman, "Students' Views of Scientists and Science: Results from a National Study," *Science and Children* 35, no. 1 (1997): 18–23.

27. *The Harry Potter Lexicon*, "Wizards, Witches, and Beings: S.," August 2, 2011, http://www.hp-lexicon.org/wizards/a-z/s.html.

28. Rachel Ivie and Kim Nies Ray. *Women in Physics and Astronomy 2005* (College Park, MD: American Institute of Physics, 2005), 1.

29. Ronald Roach, "Survey: American Girls Aren't Interested in STEM Careers," *Diverse: Issues in Higher Education* 23, no. 4 (2006): 54.

30. Heilman and Donaldson, "From Sexist," 159.

31. J.K. Rowling, "World Book Day Chat," *Accio-Quote,* Mar. 4, 2004, http://www.accio-quote.org/articles/2004/0304-wbd.htm.

32. Mike Weinstein, "Astronomy in the Harry Potter Series," *The Harry Potter Lexicon,* July 6, 2011, http://www.hp-lexicon.org/essays/essay-astronomy.html.

33. Megan Hove, "The Magic Above," *Mercury* 36, no. 4 (2007): 24.

PART II

Innovative Approaches for the Internet Generation

Two Boy Heroes (and a Sparkly Vampire) Teach the SAT

Valerie Estelle Frankel

I tutor many foreign-born students from around fifth grade up past high school, living as I do in Silicon Valley. The younger ones learn writing skills, the older ones SAT vocabulary and grammar. And they all find the finer points of English a serious challenge. The language breaks its own spelling and pronunciation rules too frequently to count. (I mean, really. Where's the "i" in "women"? Or the "f" in "rough"?) The question frequently comes up: Why is English so inconsistent? Is it harder than other languages? I'm forced to explain that, yes, English, with a truly enormous vocabulary of an estimated 500,000 words (with an estimated 500,000 additional scientific and technical terms) compared to 185,000 German words or fewer than 100,000 French words,[1] is more complicated than most languages for one simple reason: England is an island.

My statement may seem the ultimate non sequitur, but it's actually quite fundamental to the modern English language and its development. Water is easy to traverse. So historically, every culture imaginable sailed in and conquered England, or parts of it, bringing their own language and culture to merge with those already present. England was invaded by the Celts, Romans, Scots, Angles, Saxons, Jutes, Frisians, Vikings, Normans, missionaries, and possibly others. Each brought their own language, and their words mixed into the hodge-podge that was slowly becoming Modern English. When William the Conqueror invaded in 1066, he established a noble ruling class (of mostly his friends) who spoke only French. The heavy French influence of the Norman court became the final staple of English, making up about a third of our current language.

So much for history. What does all this have to do with SAT words? Glad you asked. William the Conqueror and his friends brought over the complex, pompous words of the leisure class. Most of English's convoluted, four-syllable SAT words thus derive from the French court (court itself is a French word). These were the words the aristocrats spoke, while the peasants continued to "think" and "speak," not bothering with "contemplate" or "extemporize." Therefore, if you're good with French, or the Latin roots that form its base, you have an advantage on the SAT.

Furthermore, J.K. Rowling, bless her academic heart, constructed her spells out of the same Latin roots that form SAT words. For instance, even the most casual of *Harry Potter* fans knows "Expelliarmus," the spell that sends a wand flying across the room. And it contains *three* Latin roots. "Ex" means "out" (exit, excite, expel), while "pel" means "push" (propel, repel, dispel, propeller). The Latin "arma" (weapon) relates to the Constitutional "right to bear arms" as well as words like armor or armaments. So if students can remember "Expelliarmus," they already know three Latin roots: "Out-push-weapon." When confronted with an obscure word like excise or armature, they have the tools they need to take it apart.

There are so many simple, well-known Potter spells that offer memory aids for Latin roots. "Lumos" (the light spell) contains the root "lum," meaning light (illuminate, luminous, luminescent). The Fidelius Charm (also known as the Secret-Keeper charm of book three) has a "fid," Latin for trust or faithful (fidelity, confide, perfidy).

Avada Kedavra, mangled Aramaic, isn't much help, but the other two Unforgivable Curses are quite useful. Imperio, the curse of commanding, gives us the Latin root "imper": to govern or command (emperor, imperative, imperious). Crucio is Latin for torture (crucible, crucify, excruciating). One might argue that these roots won't give a dictionary definition, only more of a related meaning. But on the multiple-choice SAT, knowledge of roots will give that general meaning clearly enough to pick from five choices.

Sample SAT Question:

He was writhing on the ground in _____ pain because he had severely broken his arm.

(A) photogenic (B) contemplative (C) immutable (D) neoclassic (E) excruciating

Even with only the knowledge of roots, the choice is obvious. In fact, all five of these words can be taken apart and understood using a basic knowledge of roots. "Photo" (light), "con" (with), "temp" (time), "im/in" (not), "mut" (change), and "neo" (new) all indicate the words' meanings well enough for an educated guess.

There are a variety of activities one can do with these roots, all based on the principle that makes life the easiest for teachers: the kids are interested. Students already seek out, collect, and memorize the more famous *Harry Potter* spells and they want to learn more. I've created basic worksheets like the "Vol" and "Mort" one in the Appendix, and we've expanded from there.

I've also had excellent results with asking students to make up their own *Harry Potter*-style spells and share them with the class, or pretend to cast them on one another. "Porc-morph" (turn into a pig) is popular, as is mobifin (stop moving). Students who have been sitting for hours, memorizing vocabulary lists and working with flash cards, are happy to try this as a break to routine. Sometimes they even wave their pencils as wands.

There are countless lists of Latin roots and/or *Harry Potter* spells on the web (for the latter, the *Harry Potter Lexicon* (http://www.hp-lexicon.org) is popular, though I've also had good luck with Wikipedia). Since there are thousands of these roots (of varying levels of usefulness), it's important to start with those most widely appearing in English vocabulary and those that students already know. *Harry Potter*'s "Alohamora" opens a locked door, but the Hawaiian "Aloha" is useless for this purpose, and "mora" (Latin for obstacle), teaches only the single vocabulary word "moratorium." Magic-related roots like "magus" or "incantatum" are less useful than "therm" (heat) or "temp" (time). By contrast, "gnos" (to know) gives us cognition, ignoble, diagnosis, incognito, agnostic, prognosticate, recognizance, and many more. "Spir" (soul/breath) becomes inspiration, aspirant, suspire, sprightly, dispirit, expiratory, perspire, and spiritual. The Appendix offers a list of some of the more useful *Harry Potter* spells and roots I've given students.

In class, it's also interesting to point out how many roots students already know. They can count in Latin after they've had geometry class (ask high school students what uni, bi, tri, quad, penta mean. They know). Of course, they're ready for more complex words after they've counted from the pentagon through the decagon and listed the months (Julius Caesar and Caesar Augustus created July and August respectively, pushing months September through December down from their original seven-through-ten slots of the calendar):

1. Unus/Mono: Unique, Unanimous, Unitary, Universal, Monogamy, Monopod, Monochrome, Monopoly
2. Bi: Bilingual, Bisect, Bigamy, Bicentenary, Bicentennial, Bicycle
3. Tri: Triad, Triangle, Triangulation, Trident, Tricolor, Tricky
4. Quad/Quat: Quadrilateral, Quadruplets, Quadrangle, Quadrupeds, Quadrant
5. Pent: Pentagon, Pentagram, Pentathlon
6. Hex/Sex: Hexagon, Hexagram, Sextet, Sextuplets, Sexagenarian.
7. Sept: September, Septuagenarian, Septillion, Septenary, Septante
8. Oct: October, Octagon, Octave, Octopus, Octillion

9. Non: November, Nanosecond, Nonagenarian
10. Dec/Deca: Decimal, Decade, Decathlon, Decimate
100. Cent: Century, Centennial, Centenary, Centipede, Cents
1000. Milli: Millennium, Millenarian, Million, Millipede, Millisecond

Modern subjects and inventions are often named with Latin roots — the following simple words make teaching roots easy as, like spells, the students already know them. There are school subjects like bio-logy (life study), geo-metry (earth measuring), geo-graphy (earth-writing or mapmaking). There are common words like soph-more (wise fool), dental (dent means teeth), and solar (sol means sun). And modern inventions: tele-phone (far-sound), micro-scope (small-see), sub-marine (under-water). I list words like these to indicate how comfortable the students already are with roots. When I tell them the word, they can often figure out the root meanings themselves. Of course, the following roots can be mixed and matched into many other familiar words, or recombined to make new ones:

Mono-rail	one-rail
Bi-cycle	two-wheels
Tri-dent	three-teeth
Quadr-angle	four-angles
Penta-gon	five-sides
Mega-phone	big-sound
Micro-scope	small-see
Peri-meter	around-measure
Tele-vision	far-see
Bio-logy	life-study
Auto-mobile	self-move
Geo-graphy	earth-write
Circum-scribe	around-write

Enter Greek Mythology

In the past few years, my teaching with Greek and Latin roots has expanded to use kids' obsession with *Harry Potter*'s literary successor, *Percy Jackson*. Rick Riordan, the series' now-famous author, was a reluctant reader until he discovered mythology and fantasy in junior high.[2] In fact, many junior high students now are reluctant readers until they discover Riordan and his boy hero, an ordinary American kid who's really the half-divine son of Poseidon. "Mythology is a natural draw for kids. It has magic, mystery, adventure — everything you could want," Riordan comments. "I hear from librarians all the time that the 200 section is getting a real workout these days. That's fantastic!"[3] The books about a hero with ADHD were written for Riordan's son who also has ADHD and was having trouble reading, though he loved mythology. They're bursting with action and offer a young hero struggling with school (and frequently blowing it up!) whom boys just want to be. As Riordan's later series branch out from the Greek myths into Egyptian and Roman, kids today are expanding their interest into collections of classical mythology.

Many Greek and Roman gods have lent their names to English words. Chronos, father of Zeus, gives us the root "chron" (time) along with chronology, chronograph, and synchronize. "Martial" comes from Mars, god of war; "Saturnine" and "Saturnalia" from Saturn; "Jovial" from Jove, another name for Jupiter. Atropos, the Fate who cuts the thread of life, gives us Atrophy, while "Lethargic" and "Lethal" come from the Greek river of the underworld, Lethe. Ceres, goddess of grain (cereal, cerium) or Vulcan the smith god (volcanology, vulcanize) join the list. Once again, as with *Harry Potter*, the advantage is that kids already know these lists of mythic names. Several of my fifth to ninth graders have become mythology experts and lecture *me* on who these gods were and what they could do. So I've made lists of the Greek gods who gave their names to English vocabulary words (also available in the Appendix) and urged the kids to use these words in their own stories and essays.

It's a slow method, but telling the stories can teach the associated words: Following my retelling of, say, the Greek tale of Arachne, I mention the connection to "arachnid." And then there's Tantalus, punished in the underworld by being surrounded by food and water but unable to taste it (tantalized much?). If the kids have already read the story, it's much quicker to simply remind them where the word "tantalize" comes from and give them a mental picture to draw on. Of course, Draco, Cerberus, Narcissus, Merope, Andromeda, and others of these mythological names show up in *Harry Potter* as well.

My students are dragging out their own mythology books and memorizing the contents, and they'll even go research on theoi.com, one of Rick Riordan's own favorite sites for Greek myth.[4] Theoi.com is an amazing resource for teachers as well as students. It contains all the classical mythology texts (in English) and an enormous encyclopedia of all the gods and heroes. Further, it contains *all* the versions: Ovid's hundred-headed hydra, Ptolemy's golden-headed hydra, the nine-headed hydra of Hesiod, the fifty-headed one of Simonides.[5] For me, this has ended far too much squabbling with students who are sure they've read the "correct" version. And even reluctant readers are interested when I suggest they browse Theoi and find out something interesting about Greek gods and monsters.

Popular Boardgames

In class, I try to teach Latin roots and vocabulary with methods other than ponderous drilling. We sometimes play games of Pictionary on the whiteboard with vocabulary words like "specter" and "arboreal." For more active games, charades works well, as does taping a word to each kid's back and having them all walk around the room playing twenty questions.

Another successful activity I created to vary the monotony was Trivial Pursuit: The SAT Version. I took my old *Trivial Pursuit* board and bought colored paper to match the six colors of squares. Then I made up cards in six categories: vocabulary, grammar, reading comprehension, diction, rhetorical devices, and tone. I built reading comprehension questions by having the kids work out a very difficult SAT word's meaning in a sentence (admittedly, more of a vocabulary question than comprehension, but these were short answer). Diction cards asked students to differentiate between homophones and other confusable words, such as stationery and stationary or pour and pore. Grammar cards contained a sentence error for students to find (with the harder ones containing the painful "no error" as an option). Rhetorical device and tone questions were multiple choice. Here are a few sample questions:

> Reading Comprehension:
> Since I have no car or bike, I must PEREGRINATE to school today.
>   Define the capitalized word.
>
> Tone:
> He went down in the darkness, and felt his way to the parlor, and then to the mantel-piece. The talisman was in its place, and a horrible fear that the unspoken wish might bring his mutilated son before him ere he could escape from the room seized upon him, and he caught his breath as he found that he had lost the direction of the door. His brow cold with sweat, he felt his way round the table...
> (Qtd. from "The Monkey's Paw" by W.W. Jacobs)
>   What is the tone of this piece: (a) euphoric, (b) sinister, (c) appreciative, (d) resentful, (e) melancholic
>
> Rhetorical Devices:
> The Sounds of Silence
>   Is this: (a) antithesis (b) oxymoron (c) paradox (d) hyperbole (e) personification

I printed these cards in Microsoft Word, eight to a page with the answers on the backs, and then cut them apart. Presto! A game was born. While it took some time to set up, I saved effort by copying some of the questions from existing SAT tests, and to date, I've been using the same set of cards for over ten years. Dividing the entire class into two teams worked well for classroom play, and allowed me to make very hard questions indeed, as ten students could work together to solve them.

When I discovered my seventh graders and even younger students were interested, I made easier question cards for them. Some categories, such as guessing a vocabulary word's meaning from context, weren't too hard. Rhetorical device and tone cards worked too, once I defined the multiple choices (and as the words "euphoric" or "antithesis" showed up on multiple cards, students soon learned them). But if students had no clue what an SAT word meant, they lacked the tools to figure out the vocabulary cards. Here the Latin roots proved invaluable, as I could make question cards with hints for students. Giving them the roots and also explaining what part of speech each word was generally guided students to the right answer. Here are a few sample cards:

Protégé
   Define this word. Clue: noun, root of *prot*, meaning protect.
Imperturbable
   Define this word. Clue: adj, root of *turb*, meaning stirred up.
Vociferous
   Define this word. Clue: adj, root of *voc*, meaning voice, and *ferre*, meaning to bear.
Attenuate
   Define this word. Clue: verb, root of *ten*, meaning thin.

The students could figure these words out with the clues, and I often point out other familiar words containing these roots. There are other ways to adapt popular games or create them for grammar lessons and play them on a blackboard or overhead for the class. Cynthia O'Malley's Grammar Quidditch in the Appendix is one of many examples.

Games like *Apples to Apples* also worked well when I substituted my own vocabulary cards. To play *Apples to Apples* (available at game stores or online shops), everyone takes a pile of noun cards. The leader names an adjective like "delightful," and everyone plays a noun card that they think best matches the adjective (or is a funny and absurd fit): "Chocolate," "Long walks on the beach," "Landfills." Whichever noun card the leader chooses gets a point for the one who played it. Then another kid becomes leader. This is a large group or party game that is played to five points, or more with a smaller group. (The rules are also available online at http://www.com-www.com/applestoapples/applestoapples-rules-official-basicset.html.) Of course, noun cards out of a box of SAT word flashcards from the store can be substituted in for a harder, more rewarding game. (Though my Spark Notes cards are no longer available, Barrons, Kaplan, and Princeton Review still sell boxes of cards in bookstores and online.)

I actually prefer the similar game *Attribute* from Z-Man Games (http://www.zmangames.com/cardgames/attribute.htm). I pass out piles of adjective cards (while the original game comes with easy words, I usually substitute the adjective cards out of my SAT flash card set) and ask a student leader to make up a noun like "this classroom" or "Harry Potter." Then each kid in the group picks the best adjective card to describe it, from "venerable" to "grotesque." The best one (according to the leader) gets a point. (These are the simplified rules — more complex ones are available at http://www.zmangames.com/cardgames/files/attribute/attribute_rules.pdf. I should add that while adults often complain to me about the counter-intuitive scoring system, my fifth graders pick it up without a problem. I also keep the scoring system written on the board or on scratch paper, so we can constantly refer to it.) We usually play with the flashcard definitions visible; as kids hastily read the definitions and apply them, the words stick.

A final beloved game for teachers is *Once Upon a Time: The Storytelling Card Game* (again, available in game stores or online from Atlas Games. A teacher's guide is free at http://www.atlas-games.com/onceuponatime). Students have cards that read "princess" or "an enchantment is broken" or "beautiful." One student tells a story, endeavoring to use up his cards as he names them in his tale. But if he names a card someone else is holding, that student can use that card to take over the story. It's good training for creative writing, fast thinking, team building, and so forth, but can also be adapted for vocabulary training. I fish many sets of synonyms from my box of SAT word cards: (noisome, putrid, noxious, malodorous, and fetid, for instance) and pass these out. A student tells his story, throwing down words like "noxious" and "putrid," with definitions up so he and the other students can see what they mean. If another student has the synonym "fetid," he can interrupt and take over the story. The advantage for many of these games is that I can join in and play with the kids, unlike the *Trivial Pursuit* game, for which I know all the answers.

Branching Out: Reading, Writing, and More

Even *Twilight* has helped me teach. Aloud, I take examples from *Harry Potter, Twilight,* and fairytales, as many teachers do, simply because all the students are so familiar with them (though I mix in *Romeo and Juliet,* the book most freshmen have already studied). But there are more directed uses. When I instruct students in the art of writing SAT-style essays, I give them a generalized prompt like "Do you think actions speak louder than words?" which they should explicate in a one-page, twenty-five minute essay using a strong thesis and specific examples. I remember telling one teenager her examples weren't specific enough and asking her to use a classic she remembered from school ... the problem was, she didn't remember any! She had little interest in reading and even less retention of the so-called "boring" classics she'd read, and her English grades reflected as much. Could she write about current events? No. History? No. "What's your favorite book?" I asked in desperation. Oh it was *Twilight*, and of course she remembered Bella flinging herself off cliffs and riding a dangerous motorcycle after begging Edward to stick around was useless. With that concept, she could write an example paragraph. Of course, an essay on *Twilight* won't impress the SAT graders. But I was pleased I could at least show her how to write an essay, before I assigned her some easy classics to read. (I keep lists of these at http://vefrankel.com/EasyClassics.htm and http://vefrankel.com/WatchingClassics.htm.)

While the high schoolers mostly get SAT training, I'm asked to practice general reading comprehension and all kinds of writing with the younger students, in roughly fifth through eighth grade. While they'll obediently write short essays on topics of my choice, fiction is much more fun for all concerned — kids will write enormous books and actually enjoy the writing.

Whenever I ask this age what they'd like to write on, they describe first person "Chosen One" plots with magic, weapons, and tons of action — clearly *Percy Jackson* imitations. While the kids delight in describing monster beheadings and sword fights in great detail, these stories often lack description, thoughts, motivations, and emotions, all things I must remind students to include. I generally have them start by describing with details from the five senses, bringing a beach or forest to life. Throughout their writing, I remind students to mix description into the action scenes and introduce new characters and settings.

Reading is another problematic area for kids. Many read a great deal — if they can find books in their genre. When I offer to recommend books to kids, they most commonly request "something like *Percy Jackson* or *The Hunger Games*" or at least "something first person with lots of action." Sometimes, I've apologetically told students that some books like *The Hunger Games* stand out for their writing style and that's why they're bestsellers — even books in the same genre often aren't as entertaining. At the same time, I've had great luck leading kids from children's books into harder novels.

Mythology up to and including *The Odyssey, King Arthur*, and related classics is an obvious way to go for *Percy Jackson* and *Harry Potter* fans alike. However, the young readers often are seeking more of the same epic fantasy, and instead of going to classics with their outmoded prose, one can go to today's popular fiction ... even books written for adults. I recently offered one *Percy Jackson* fan *The DaVinci Code*, as a book of page-turning action. He loved it. I was likewise browsing a fantasy booth at a conference, and this back cover caught my eye:

> My name is Kvothe, pronounced nearly the same as "quothe." ... I have stolen princesses back from sleeping barrow kings. I burned down the town of Trebon. I have spent the night with Felurian and left with both my sanity and my life. I was expelled from the University at a younger age than most people are allowed in. I tread paths by moonlight that others fear to speak of during day. I have talked to gods, loved women, and written songs that make the minstrels weep.
> You may have heard of me.[6]

It was *The Name of the Wind* by Patrick Rothfuss, which I bought immediately and read — it was a first-person boy-centered fantasy after all, rare among the adult fiction shelves. As it turned out, it was actually about an orphaned smart-aleck teen attending wizard school. However, unlike so many kids' books, it had depth and fantastic writing. I lent it to my student, and it soon became his favorite. Unfortunately, the sequel *The Wise Man's Fear* had a somewhat explicit romance, so I knew that it would be inappropriate for someone his age. (With adult books for kids, someone really should be monitoring the content.) I frankly told him the problem, just as I told him *The DaVinci Code* had some grisly murders that were equivalent to perhaps a PG-13 movie. He decided on that basis that he'd try *The Da Vinci Code* but not *The Wise Man's Fear* (yet). He went on to enjoy other Dan Brown books along with the *Mistborn* fantasy series by Brandon Sanderson. A list of these and similar books is available in the Appendix, for kids and teens ready to try PG-rated, action-packed adult fantasy.

Teachers can similarly respond to *Twilight* fans, offering them the *Romeo and Juliet* or *Pride and Prejudice* on which the books are based or giving them adult vampire fiction from *Dracula* to Anne Rice. The trick is building on the children's and teens' reading interests rather than assigning "classics" arbitrarily. I remember, a high schooler once told me that all classics are depressing. "That's not true," I said. "Give me your list." However, after skimming it, I had to admit that her teacher's preferences were, in fact, all depressing. As for myself, I enjoy the lighthearted adventures of centuries past: *Ivanhoe, The Three Musketeers, Sherlock Holmes, Cyrano de Bergerac,* and especially *The Scarlet Pimpernel*, masked superhero of his time. With books like these, students can learn that classics don't have to be dull.

In Conclusion

Today, I'm a popular SAT and English tutor across the Bay Area. I rely on knowledge the students already have and love for the books that motivates their extracurricular activities. As students devour *Percy Jackson*, I take them to the best Greek and Roman mythology sites and teach them about the gods and goddesses lending their names to today's vocabulary. But *Harry Potter* so ingrained itself in the minds of kids who are today's high schoolers and SAT students that it's a wonderful tool for teachers to employ. I've used it to teach plot diagrams, the hero's journey, reading, writing, satire, and especially vocabulary. And their faces just light up when I tell them they're about to learn the SAT with Harry.

Notes

1. Robert McCrum, William Cran, & Robert MacNeil, *The Story of English* (New York: Penguin, 1992), 1.
2. J. Larson, "Talking with Rick Riordan," *Book Links* 18, no. 5 (May 2009): 18.
3. Ibid., 19.
4. Ibid., 18.
5. Aaron J. Atsma, ed., "Hydra," *The Theoi Project: Greek Mythology*, 2011, http://www.theoi.com/Ther/DrakonHydra.html.
6. Patrick Rothfuss, "Back Cover," *The Name of the Wind* (USA: DAW, 2007).

Fan Fiction, Remix Culture, and the Potter Games

JEN SCOTT CURWOOD

Introduction

The dynamic interplay of literature, literacy, and technology is evident in how youth engage with J.K. Rowling's *Harry Potter* and Suzanne Collins' *The Hunger Games*. Young fans use online affinity spaces related to young adult literature to deepen their understanding of the narrative structures and themes. At the same time, these spaces encourage their creative responses to literature. Around the world, fans are writing *Harry Potter*-based and *Hunger Games*-inspired stories, creating art, producing videos, composing music, and designing role-playing games. Fans draw on a variety of modes, semiotic resources, and literacy practices throughout this process. By actively participating in affinity spaces around a shared passion, young people have an authentic audience who reads, responds to, and even critiques their creative work.[1]

This chapter draws on my ethnographic research of adolescent literacy, online affinity spaces, and young adult literature. Affinity space ethnography is a powerful methodology that can shed light on the culture of physical, virtual, and blended spheres that adolescents inhabit.[2] In particular, affinity space ethnography affords access to participants around the world, a readily available web-based historical record of the affinity space's practices, and a way to trace adolescent literacy practices across sites, texts, and discourses. As part of an affinity space ethnography, I explored how youth, ages 11 to 17, in the United States, Canada, and Australia engaged with *The Hunger Games*. Cassie (a pseudonym) was one participant in the study, and this chapter analyzes her experience with writing fan fiction based on *Harry Potter* and *The Hunger Games*.

With fan fiction, fans take the characters or settings from an original work, such as a book or film, and incorporate them into a creative story. In this respect, fan fiction and remix culture can support how young people read and respond to literature. Drawing on my ethnographic research of online affinity spaces, I analyzed Cassie's writing process as she remixed the characters *Harry Potter* and settings from *The Hunger Games*. As an avid participant in *The Hunger Games* affinity space, Cassie was invited to contribute to *The Potter Games*, an online choose-your-own adventure game. She was assigned the character of Colin Creevey, who was one of 24 Harry Potter characters within *The Potter Games*.

In order to write her story, Cassie chose to closely analyze ten novels, create a character study, and critically consider how to use language and literary techniques within her remixed story. Each *Potter Games* writer had their own process and final product. Cassie's writing process was shaped by her prior school experiences and her experience within *The Hunger Games* affinity space. I argue that her motivation to engage in creative writing is closely linked to her passion for young adult literature as well as the availability of having an authentic audience for her work. For researchers and educators, this raises new questions about the role of motivation in shaping young people's literacy development. In the following sections, I consider the relationship among young adult literature, fan fiction, and remix culture.

Young Adult Literature

According to the Cooperative Children's Book Center, recent years have seen a marked increase in the number of novels published for young adults, particularly in the science fiction and fantasy genre.[3] This includes *Harry Potter* and *The Hunger Games* as well as *Divergent, Matched, Delirium, Twilight, Uglies,* and *The Knife of Never Letting Go*. These novels are often set in the future, in a parallel world, or in a historical past. They may feature characters that are wizards, mutants, robots, or genetically engineered humans. Within this genre, readers may encounter novel scientific principles, technological advancements, political systems, and social cultures.

Suzanne Collins' dystopian trilogy includes *The Hunger Games, Catching Fire,* and *Mockingjay,* initially published between 2008 and 2010. Set in a post-apocalyptic world, Panem is an affluent capital, surrounded by thirteen impoverished districts. In the Dark Days, the districts rose up against the Capitol; twelve districts were defeated and one was obliterated. To remind the citizens of Panem that such a revolution must never happen again, they are subjected to the Hunger Games each year. Each of the districts must provide two tributes, one boy and one girl, to participate. Over a period of several weeks, the tributes fight to the death. The Hunger Games is televised throughout Panem, from the glittering streets of the Capitol to the coal mining towns. The protagonist, sixteen-year-old Katniss Everdeen, must decide whether to kill or be killed — and later, whether to lead a revolution.

Harry Potter and *The Hunger Games* offer young people the opportunity to immerse themselves in new worlds. From Voldemort's quest for power to Panem's effort to suppress rebellion, fans ask themselves, "What do power and privilege mean? How can someone make an impossible choice? Is violence ever justified?" These questions often turn inward, as readers contemplate their own lived experiences, beliefs, and values. In this way, literary response involves both reading the word and reading the world.[4]

Jenkins argues that J.K. Rowling's richly detailed world provides youth with many points of entry to literature.

> Some kids imagine themselves as related to the characters — the primary ones like Harry Potter or Snape, of course, but also minor background figures — the inventors of the Quidditch brooms, the authors of the textbooks, the heads of referenced agencies, classmates of Harry's mother and father, any affiliation that allows them to claim a special place for themselves in the story.[5]

Young people can put themselves into the story through writing and sharing fan fiction in online affinity spaces. Fan fiction, in this sense, provides a way *into* the story — and a point of entry to the *Harry Potter* and *Hunger Games* fandoms.

Fan Fiction

Research on fan culture has examined how fans write stories, create art, produce songs, and engage in role-plays. In effect, these practices blur "any clear-cut distinction between media producer and media spectator, since any spectator may potentially participate in the creation of new artworks."[6] Online affinity spaces offer a way for young people to actively engage with this aspect of fan culture. In recent years, literacy scholars have considered how young fans use the characters, settings, and themes within popular culture texts as inspiration for their own creative work. Thomas' study, for instance, shows how fan fiction can promote collaborative writing and role-playing across a range of real-life and virtual spaces.[7] Black's research on Fan fiction.net highlights adolescent English language learners' process of writing anime-based stories.[8] She posits that their writing skills develop through peer review and by having a global audience of readers.

Fan fiction offers many opportunities for writers to engage with modes and genres. Magnifico's study of *Neopets*, a virtual pet site, demonstrates how some fans use identity profiles and role-plays to situate themselves in the world of Neopia. They can then take on the role of writers, editors, and artists for the *Neopian Times*, a weekly online newspaper.[9] Due to readily available digital tools, fan fiction is increasingly multimodal and hybrid.[10] In her research, Lammers shows how fans use visual representations of characters and settings from *The Sims* game to write stories. These are shared, critiqued, and revised within an online space.[11] Within online affinity spaces, fan fiction writing involves the interaction of semiotic resources and the public dissemination of creative work.

Affinity spaces offer new ways for fans to engage with young adult literature. These affinity spaces are not just created for young fans — they are also created *by* young fans. Jenkins' research on fan culture highlights how one *Harry Potter* fan launched *The Daily Prophet*, an online "school newspaper" for Hogwarts. At its peak, this young woman managed an international staff of over a hundred writers who produced fan fiction stories on everything from the latest Quidditch match to Muggle cuisine. Jenkins explains, "Heather personally edits each story, getting it ready for publication. She encourages her staff to closely compare their original submission with the edited versions and consults with them on issues of style and grammar as needed."[12] Therefore, online affinity spaces provide ways for fans to write, edit, design, and review stories. But fan fiction writing can also be understood within remix culture.

Remix Culture

Remix is a practice of taking cultural artifacts and combining them in new and creative ways.[13] With the increasing availability of digital tools and online spaces, remixing has flourished in recent years. However, the practice of remixing literary texts is much older than the Internet. Pugh argues that the practice was evident in the 1400s, with Robert Henryson's sequels to some of Geoffrey Chaucer's poetry.[14] Today, Lessig sees remix as a core part of the secondary English curriculum.

> You read a book by Hemingway, *For Whom the Bell Tolls*, you read a book by F. Scott Fitzgerald, *Tender Is the Night*, and then you take bits from each of these books and you put them together in an essay. You take and combine, and that's the writing, the creative writing, which constitutes education about writing: to take and to remix as a way of creating something new.[15]

Remix, in this sense, can be a cultural, a literary, and/or a digital practice. It involves taking artifacts (including paper-based artifacts like stories or digital artifacts like images), combining them in new and provocative ways, and even adding in original content.[16] Online affinity spaces offer ways to readily disseminate remixes to a global audience.

Research by the Pew Internet and American Life Project indicates that 73 percent of adolescents use online social network sites and 64 percent participate in content-creating activities.[17] For many fans, social media allows them to engage in affinity spaces and share creative work, which may span any number of genres and modes. For example, fans have used characters from *The Sims* to illustrate their *Harry Potter*–based fan stories that are then posted on LiveJournal. Stein explains that fans used the home-based interactions inherent in *The Sims* to consider *Potter* characters' domestic lives. This emphasizes "the expansiveness of fan imagination rather than the limitations of canon."[18] When young fans engage in remix, their only limit is their imagination. While they may begin with literature like *The Hunger Games* or *Harry Potter*, they can draw on other texts and tools. Fan culture embraces both the process and the product of remixing, which is evident in fan fiction. In the following section, I share my research on fan culture and young adult literature.

Researching Literacy, Literature, and Fandom

In my ethnographic study, data collection began with systematic observation to gain insight into the dynamics of communication and semiotic production in portals to the *Hunger Games* affinity space. Portals provide a way to access the affinity space, and include websites such as HungerGamesTrilogy.net, HungerGamesRPG.com, and Mockingjay.net. To delve deeper into the fan culture associated with *The Hunger Games*, I conducted multiple interviews with focal participants via Skype, email, or instant messenger. Since I was interested in understanding the factors that shaped their literacy development, I also examined artifacts. Because online affinity spaces are socially constructed, an analysis of artifacts can provide insight into the culture. I collected and analyzed artifacts such as codes of conduct, role-play game rules, online discussions, and social media posts as well as fan-created stories, videos, songs, and artwork.

In this essay, I focus on a young woman named Cassie. She is sixteen years old and lives in the northeastern United States. At the suggestion of her middle school librarian, Cassie read *The Hunger Games* and was enthralled by the dystopian world of Panem, the brutality of the Hunger Games, and Katniss' quest for survival. Eager to discuss the novels with others, she turned to the Internet. Soon, Cassie discovered the ever-growing *Hunger Games* fandom, and she took on the role as co-administrator on a popular fansite. In this role, she designs interactive features, creates videos, shares news, manages social media accounts, and participates in podcasts. Cassie has an active role within the affinity space; other fans may write stories, share artwork, participate in online discussions, or simply lurk as passive participants. She explains that the online *Hunger Games* fandom has changed her understanding of the trilogy, and "it allowed me to explore perspectives other than my own... I see more of the world that the author has created." For Cassie, remixing the *Hunger Games* and *Harry Potter* was a powerful experience.

Writing Fan Fiction and Remixing Young Adult Literature

Due to Cassie's active involvement in *The Hunger Games* fandom, she has met many others who share her passion for young adult literature. In 2011, she was invited to contribute to *The Potter Games*, an online choose-your-own adventure game that situates *Harry Potter* characters within the *Hunger Games*. ThePotterGames.com is part of TheFandom.net. It was created by Adam Spunberg, Savanna New, Sam Cushion, and Shylah Addante, and currently overseen by Kait Silva and Natasha Baucas. Cassie had previously met Adam and Savanna through their involvement in *The Hunger Games Fireside Chat*, a popular podcast. Cassie shared, "I love writing! I think my love of writing helped me through this project, but the reason I participated in *The Potter Games* in the first place was because I thought it was a unique project. Having my writing included was incredible. It was so neat to be able to see that I'd contributed to a project of this magnitude that other fans enjoyed."

Like all *Potter Games* writers, Cassie was assigned a specific character and required to use a choose-your-own adventure format, but she had total control of her writing process and her storyline. In order to remix *Harry Potter* and *The Hunger Games*, Cassie had to build on textual evidence and consider how her assigned character, Colin Creevey, might change when he was put in life-threatening circumstances. Using a choose-your-own adventure storyline, Cassie wrote her story and included key choices that directly engaged her audience. If Colin is to survive the Hunger Games, what choices will he make? Will he betray his friends, sacrifice his principles, or commit violent acts? Cassie's writing process shows how she drew on the original settings and characters as well as her command of language and genre to answer these questions.

Drawing on Mentor Texts

Like many writers before her, Cassie began by consulting mentor texts.[19] While mentor texts can provide writers with insight into a particular genre, they also offer expertly crafted examples of how another writer uses descriptive language, draws on literary techniques, and builds a narrative arc. For Cassie, these mentor texts were written by J.K. Rowling and Suzanne Collins. She initially reviewed all *Harry Potter* books in order to learn more about Colin Creevey as a character. Cassie explained, "He isn't mentioned much in the books, so I tried to take the motivations for things that he did in the *Harry Potter* books and create a bit of a background story for him. This character, with the filled-in background, was the one that I used in the *Potter Games*." Since Colin wasn't a main character in the *Harry Potter* books, writing a fan fiction story required that Cassie use her imagination and her artistic license.

Cassie began her story as Colin prepared to risk his life in the Hunger Games. At the Cornucopia, waiting for the Games to start, Colin was surrounded by his friends. Cassie chose to use the second person to draw her readers into the story and help them identify with Colin.

> Standing on a small platform, trying to stay as still as possible for the seconds that you must wait before you are free to enter the arena, you look around you at the other tributes. You can't focus on the tense goodbye you said to your stylists and mentor, or the moment you waited in the hovercraft, feeling your heart skip a beat as you realized maybe you wanted to die early; save your parents the grieving. Of course, as you stand on the platform, you look across at the other tributes, from Harry Potter to Cedric to Cormac, the Quidditch players who constantly inspire you at school with their athleticism and utter wizardry. The way you looked up to them was the same way your brother looks up to you. If you need to try for anyone, you need to try for your brother and the future of the world.

While Cassie drew on *Harry Potter* and *The Hunger Games* as mentor texts, she was also aware that she was writing her own story.

In order to situate Colin in the Hunger Games, Cassie had to develop his identity and his background story. "I did try to keep his main morals and values, but filling him in really gave me insight to the type of alliances he might make and the type of things he might do once put into the Hunger Games," she stated. "After all, the Hunger Games are a fight-to-the-death situation, and the goal of the character writer is to create separate paths, including victory paths and dead ends." The genre of a choose-your-own-adventure story is perfectly suited to this endeavor. Cassie saw herself as a character writer, and she knew that she was remixing *Harry Potter* and *The Hunger Games*. Because of the genre, the task, and the audience, Cassie realized from the onset that she had specific writing goals.

The Process of Writing and Remixing

Drawing on her prior school-based experiences, Cassie set several writing goals for herself. Cassie shared that her first goal was to create a victory path for Colin Creevey. While he may be an unlikely victor of the Hunger Games, Cassie knew that if it were to happen, she would need to embrace his strongest traits. Based on her analysis of *Harry Potter*, she believed that Colin would be good at hiding. In the Hunger Games arena, if Colin could camouflage, he might outlive his enemies. But Cassie thought that hiding wouldn't be enough and Colin would "have to be a bit tougher at some points." She imagined how devastated Colin would be at the prospect of hearing of Harry's death — let alone being responsible for it.

Cassie concluded that she would need to have Colin confront this weakness, and she did so by making Harry and Ron seem uncharacteristically heartless. She reflected, "Who knows what would have made Harry and Ron become mean in the arena. I was just writing for Colin, and I needed him to toughen up by having them be tougher." *The Potter Games* offers readers 24 stories, written by different authors; for that reason, Cassie's characterization of Colin, Harry, and Ron was different from other writers' portrayal of them.

By developing Colin's character — and showing some unsavory sides of Harry and Ron's characters — Cassie laid the groundwork for her story. As she remixed *Harry Potter* and *The Hunger Games*, she drew on textual details, including spells from the wizarding world and lethal "muttations" from the Hunger Games arena. Cassie found that these details added to the authenticity of her story. However, since her audience was avid fans of both series, she strived for accuracy. She shared, "I would check my books or the *Harry Potter* encyclopedia to make sure I had the details right." In this respect, Cassie used mentor texts as well as other resources to remix the two worlds. Even though she wrote her story by herself, she was keenly aware of her prospective audience.

At one point in her story, Cassie puts Colin in an impossible situation: he must kill or be killed. In both *Harry Potter* and *The Hunger Games*, this was not an unfamiliar situation for the characters. But it was one that Colin had never faced — at least not in this way.

> You and Harry are now the last two standing. You decide to walk where you think he will be: the camp where he allied with and then abandoned you. For better or for worse, you must now face him and put an end to these Games. You must fight Harry Potter.
>
> Harry Potter. The Boy Who Lived. The Chosen One. Your friend. Your mentor. Your idol.
>
> *Was your idol,* you think bitterly. Over the course of these Games, you have seen a different side of Harry. You would have never expected him to need saving ...

or abandon a friend. You reach the camp, and find Harry standing there. He is bloody and burned, but his wand isn't drawn. More than anything else, he just looks tired.

As a writer, Cassie knew that she needed to craft two paths for Colin, which she conceptualized as "a victory path and a dead end." In order for Colin to win the Hunger Games, he must kill Harry Potter. To make this an easier choice for him, Cassie had previously depicted some of Harry's less-than-enviable traits. But at this moment, she also made the audience sympathetic toward Harry's plight. As a choose-your-own-adventure story, the audience had full control of the denouement. Will Colin murder Harry and emerge victorious from the Hunger Games? Or will he remain loyal to Harry and sacrifice his own life?

Writing for an Authentic Audience

As a writer, Cassie used mentor texts and literary resources as well as rich language and literary techniques to craft Colin's story. When *The Potter Games* was released in 2011, it was marketed within online affinity spaces, including on fansites and through social media. Youth from both the *Harry Potter* and *The Hunger Games* fandoms eagerly read — and critiqued — *The Potter Games*. Cassie recalled, "Some of the Facebook fans didn't like it because they said the main trio was too out-of-character. However, I wanted to make Colin become a whole different person, to grow into someone who saw his own strengths." As an avid reader of J.K. Rowling's books, Cassie knew that Colin couldn't just outright murder Harry, Ron, or Hermione. As she put it, "He had to have some change in perspective about them." By making them more heartless, and consequently, less sympathetic to readers, Cassie was able to craft a scenario in which Colin truly had the choice whether or not to murder Harry.

Through *The Potter Games*, Cassie had an opportunity to share her writing with a public audience. Within the first nine months of its release, *The Potter Games* had been visited half a million times and had 40,000 Facebook likes. Released just before *Harry Potter and the Deathly Hallows: Part Two*, *The Potter Games* was poised to draw readers from two burgeoning fan cultures. Cassie felt it was an incredible honor to be asked to contribute Colin's story. As a fan herself, she knew that her readers would be smart, be concerned about authenticity, and have high expectations of any *Harry Potter* and *Hunger Games* remix. As a writer, Cassie was motivated by the opportunity to learn from mentor texts penned by J.K. Rowling and Suzanne Collins. She specifically talked about her goals as a writer, and she readily drew on resources that existed within the fandoms and affinity spaces. Moreover, Cassie was eager to share her work with a global audience. Through the process of remixing, Cassie deepened her knowledge of the *Harry Potter* and *Hunger Games* canons at the same time that she honed her craft as a writer.

Implications for Teachers

In 2004, the National Endowment for the Arts warned of a marked decline in adolescents' engagement with literature. *Reading at Risk: A Survey of Literary Reading in America* contrasted books with digital media and argued that the latter "often require no more than passive participation" and "foster shorter attention spans and accelerated gratification."[20] In contrast, scholars have argued that digital literacy practices are more participatory, collaborative, and distributed than conventional print-based literacy practices.[21] My ethnographic research on online affinity spaces suggests that remixing can be an opportunity for young people like Cassie to critically engage with young adult literature and develop their writing skills.

Today, youth are no longer limited to primarily writing for their teachers in school settings.[22] With online fan communities, they can (and do) write for greater audiences. Young people's interest in and skills around fan culture are a valuable resource for teachers. In particular, fan fiction can be a way to "reposition some adolescents as capable literacy learners."[23] Many young people readily watch movies and television shows and read books, comics, and graphic novels. Fan culture, in many ways, encourages young people to shift from being passive consumers to active producers. Online affinity spaces offer multiple ways that fans can connect with others, share creative work, and remix cultural artifacts.

Agee argues, "How high school teachers approach literature sends messages to their students not only about what kinds of literature are valued but also who is valued."[24] Young adult literature, including *Harry Potter* and *The Hunger Games*, offers a way *into* the curriculum for many students. Motivation has a tremendous (and often underestimated) impact on literacy. Through young adult literature, students can immerse themselves in new worlds and critically engage with words, ideas, and themes. Fan fiction offers an opportunity for them to respond to literature by remixing characters, settings, and events. They can make the story their own in new and exciting ways, and share their work with a global audience. Bean and Moni add that both accomplished and struggling students need opportunities to make personal and intertextual connections with young adult literature.[25] By valuing the practices of writing, designing, and remixing, teachers can bring fan culture into the classroom in new and powerful ways.

NOTES

1. James Paul Gee, *Situated Language and Learning: A Critique of Traditional Schooling* (New York: Routledge, 2004).
2. Jayne C. Lammers, Jen Scott Curwood, & Alecia Marie Magnifico, "Toward an Affinity Space Methodology: Considerations for Literacy Research," *English Teaching: Practice and Critique,* forthcoming.
3. Cooperative Children's Book Center, *Thoughts on Publishing in 2010,* 2011, http://www.education.wisc.edu/ccbc/books/choiceintro11.asp.
4. Paulo Freire, *Pedagogy of the Oppressed* (New York: Continuum, 1970).
5. Henry Jenkins, *Convergence Culture: Where Old and New Media Collide* (New York: New York University Press, 2006), 182.
6. Henry Jenkins, *Textual Poachers: Television Fans and Participatory Culture* (New York: Routledge, 1992), 247.
7. Angela Thomas, *Youth Online: Identity and Literacy in the Digital Age* (New York: Peter Lang, 2007).
8. Rebecca W. Black, *Adolescents and Online Fan Fiction* (New York: Peter Lang, 2008).
9. Alecia Marie Magnifico, "The Game of Neopian Writing," in *Videogames, Affinity Spaces, and New Media Literacies,* ed. S.C. Duncan & E.R. Hayes (New York: Peter Lang, forthcoming).
10. Gunther R. Kress, *Literacy in the New Media Age* (New York: Routledge, 2003).
11. Jayne. C. Lammers, "'Is the Hangout…the Hangout?' Exploring Tensions in an Online Gaming-Related Fan Site," in *Videogames, Affinity Spaces, and New Media Literacies,* ed. S.C. Duncan & E.R. Hayes (New York: Peter Lang, forthcoming).
12. Jenkins, *Convergence Culture,* 178.
13. Collin Lankshear, & Michelle Knobel, *New Literacies: Everyday Practices and Classroom Learning* (New York: Open University Press, 2006).
14. Sheenagh Pugh, *The Democratic Genre: Fan Fiction in a Literary Context* (Bridgend: Seren, 2006).
15. L. Lessig, "Creative Commons" (paper presented at the annual ITU conference: Network for IT-Research and Competence in Education, University of Oslo, Norway, 2005).
16. Jen Scott Curwood & Damiana Gibbons, "'Just Like I Have Felt': Multimodal Counternarratives in Youth-Produced Digital Media," *International Journal of Learning and Media* 1, no. 4 (2009): 59–77.
17. A. Lenhart, M. Madden, A. Smith, & A.R. Macgill, "Teens and Social Media," *Pew Internet and American Life Project* (Washington D.C.: Pew Charitable Trusts, 2007), http://www.pewinternet.org/Reports/2007/Teens-and-Social-Media.aspx and A. Lenhart, K. Purcell, A. Smith, & K. Zickuhr, "Social Media and Young Adults," *Pew Internet and American Life Project* (Washington D.C.: Pew Charitable Trusts, 2010), http://www.pewinternet.org/Reports/2010/Social-Media-and-Young-Adults.aspx.
18. L. E. Stein, "'This Dratted Thing': Fannish Storytelling through New Media," in *Fan Fiction and Fan Communities in the Age of the Internet,* ed. Karen Hellekson & Kristina Busse (Jefferson, N.C.: McFarland, 2006), 256.
19. Lucy Calkins, *The Art of Teaching Writing* (Portsmouth, NH: Heinemann, 1994) and Katie Wood Ray, *Wondrous Words: Writers and Writing in the Elementary Classroom* (Urbana, IL: National Council of Teachers of English, 1999).
20. Tom Bradshaw & Bonnie Nichols, *Reading at Risk: A Survey of Literary Reading in America.* Research Division Report No. 46. (Washington, D.C.: National Endowment for the Arts, 2004), vii.
21. Jen Scott Curwood & Laura Lee H. Cowell, "iPoetry: Creating Space for New Literacies in the English Curriculum," *Journal of Adolescent and Adult Literacy* 55 no. 2 (2011):

107–117; M.L. Gomez, M.B. Schieble, J.S. Curwood, & D.D. Hassett, "Technology, Learning, and Instruction: Distributed Cognition in the Secondary English Classroom," *Literacy* 44, no. 1 (2010): 20–27; and Collin Lankshear & Michelle Knobel, *New Literacies: Everyday Practices and Classroom Learning* (New York: Open University Press, 2006).

22. Alecia Marie Magnifico, "Writing for Whom: Cognition, Motivation, and a Writer's Audience," *Educational Psychologist* 45, no.3 (2010): 167–184.

23. K., Chandler-Olcott, & D. Mahar, "Adolescents' Anime-Inspired 'Fan fictions': An Exploration of Multiliteracies," *Journal of Adolescent and Adult Literacy* 46, no. 7 (2003): 565.

24. J. Agee, "What is Effective Literature Instruction? A Study of Experienced High School English Teachers in Differing Grade- and Ability-Level Classes," *Journal of Literacy Research* 32, no. 3 (2000): 306.

25. Thomas W. Bean & Karen Moni, "Developing Students' Critical Literacy: Exploring Identity Construction in Young Adult Fiction," *Journal of Adolescent and Adult Literacy* 46, no. 8 (2003): 638–648.

The Battle to Save Australian Teen Spirituality

CLARE DIVINY

Introduction: Harry Potter and Spiritual Malaise in the Digital Age

There is no denying the enormous success and popularity of the *Harry Potter* franchise. The books have sold over 450 million copies[1] and the final film, *Harry Potter and the Deathly Hallows Part 2*, received $476 million USD in box office sales worldwide in the weekend of its release.[2] The books are so popular that they have been translated into 67 languages[3] and they are cited as being responsible for revitalizing an interest in reading amongst the teen/young adult demographic.[4] Australia has mirrored the worldwide obsession with all things *Harry Potter*, spawning an Australian National Quidditch team, the Harry Potter Fan Zone, Mugglespace and several popular fan clubs, such as the Melbourne Muggles and the Sydney Muggles United. At the time of the final film release in Australia 2011, local newspapers were awash with fan interviews bemoaning the end of the films. These Australian fans (like many around the world) shared just how significant a role the books played in their lives. What is interesting is that this enduring love affair with the boy wizard has coincided with Australia's spiritual crisis.

Over the past few decades, there has been a rise in spiritual uncertainty amidst Australia's younger population. More recent studies indicate that Australia's youth do not strongly identify as possessing a spiritual identity. Statistics report that more and more people are leaving organized religions and that developing one's spirituality is no longer a popular pastime for Australian teens. In an attempt to resolve this slump, in 2010 the Australian government committed further funding into the National School Chaplaincy Program (NSCP) to provide more "chaplaincy and pastoral care services"[5] to more public schools. However, is providing these services or even more religious education the answer? Can educating contemporary teens with religious stories and parables written over a thousand years ago remedy our current predicament? Certainly many religions have "updated" these historical teachings in order to appeal to a younger audience, but even so in Australia teens are showing very little interest in spiritual matters.

However, Australian fans can't seem to get enough of *Harry Potter*. That fact is hardly surprising given the universal appeal and popularity of the franchise. What is interesting is that the release of the book series has coincided with a gradual decline in Australian youth's interest in their spirituality. Could *Harry Potter* be a contemporary balm to soothe our Australian spiritual crisis as it addresses many issues beyond that of just entertainment? Like parables in The Bible and other sacred religious books, *Harry Potter* presents tales and trials of life and death, good and evil, resurrection and rebirth and faith and nihilism. These tests take place in a fantastic world where magic and mysticism are the norm. Yet it also deals with the more mundane everyday issues of being a teenager, such as falling in love, fighting with friends and struggling to stay focused in school. The spiritual tests and challenges in *Harry Potter* provide Australia's teens with the opportunity to explore these complex and philosophical conundrums via playful, magical adventures. Relatable characters, humor, magic and mysticism are seductive enticements to draw fans in; yet is it possible that it is the underlying spiritual challenges that function as the impetus for these teens to explore their spirituality? Is part of *Harry Potter*'s popularity due to the spiritual engagement that these books provide?

Harry Potter and the Magic of Fiction

Although J.K. Rowling's successful book series has rejuvenated the children's fantasy genre, a number of authors have introduced fantastic and magical characters and stories into children's (and adult's) imaginations pre–Potter. Ostling cites "J. R. R. Tolkien, C. S. Lewis, and Ursula Le Guin"[6] as influential contributors to this genre. Another noteworthy author is Enid Blyton, who was a significant producer of early twentieth century children's fantasy fiction. The concept of a human boy entering a magical world is certainly not original or new. This basic story has been told before and *Harry Potter* shares parallels with Blyton's 1943 book *The Magic Faraway Tree* and C.S. Lewis' 1950 *The Lion, the Witch and the Wardrobe*. In both works, an ordinary human child or teen discovers another realm where magic is the norm. Themes of heroism and being the "chosen one" are particularly prevalent in Lewis' book. The fact that Harry is a wizard in training has also been previously explored in

Ursula Le Guin's 1968 book *A Wizard of Earthsea*. This echoing of elements from previous works has not diminished the appeal or popularity of the *Harry Potter* series. Retelling familiar tales is not a new practice nor does it detract from the originality and ingenuity of the series. In fact McAvan argues that it is the recycling and resuscitation of familiar elements, an evocation of old charm that lies at the heart of Harry Potter's popularity.[7]

McAvan contends that fans are reassured and comforted by the familiar, stating that "much of the appeal of the *Harry Potter* series lies in its nostalgic recreation of the boarding school stories, of creating a timeless and eternal Merry Old England existing parallel to the present."[8] This is an advertising technique that functions to engage consumers by highlighting more current "social concerns" via these repeated nostalgic elements.[9] In our current Western technology-centric society in which multitasking and time saving are de rigueur, writing notes with a quill and ink pot seems both laborious and indulgent. When technology allows us to communicate around the clock instantly via digital smart phones and slick A4 size computers, sending and receiving messages by owl is unreliable and clumsy but at the same time quaint. On a larger societal level, this recycling of old and familiar rituals provides a stark contrast to our current fast-paced digital world. However, on a more personal scale, fiction has always been an entertaining means of escaping our current life and entering a fantasy realm of adventure. Whilst Harry's world of old English castles brought to life by ghosts and magic is certainly enchanting, reading fiction plays a far more significant role than mere entertainment.

Fiction allows us to mentally explore not only other worlds, but characters in a range of different situations. These characters represent various combinations of moral, ethical, psychological, emotional and personality elements that can mirror real life.[10] In order to engage with the text and become interested in the story as readers, we need to relate to the characters, imagine their motivation for certain behaviors, and even predict what the character will do next. The act of "trying on" these various "mental states" allows us to contemplate a different perspective beyond our own.[11] Zunshine argues that there are "cognitive rewards" to reading fiction and that these stories allow us to entertain different states of mind in more playful and imaginative ways.[12] In the fictitious world the pressures of our daily lives do not dissolve completely but are perhaps put on hold or in the least held at arm's length. Whilst in this fantasy realm, readers can pretend to become someone else, identify with a character's plight or consider different outcomes to a problem without real-life consequences. For young teens struggling to come to terms with many life-changing events, reading fiction can offer a safe world in which to explore difficult issues.

Australia's Spiritual Crisis

Australia's youth appear to be experiencing a spiritual crisis. ABS statistics (Australian Bureau of Statistics) reveal that over the past twenty years more Australians are categorizing their religious status as "no religion," and numbers for Christian-based religions are on the decline over the same period.[13] Studies show that in Australia "most young people have little interest in religious organizations."[14] In a 2005 study of religious practices around the world, Burkimsher found that in Australia only 17.1 percent of people between the ages of 18–29 years attended a religious service once a month.[15] The same study found attendance rates were much higher in other countries with the highest being for the Philippines at 88.2 percent.[16] In other Western countries rates were still significantly higher than those for Australia. In the United States attendance rates were 40.5 percent, Ireland 37.6 percent, and Canada 28.8 percent.[17] From 2003–2007, Mason, Singleton and Webber conducted a nationwide survey of 1,219 people aged between 13–24 years of age to determine their views on religion and spirituality. They found that 59 percent of respondents had no "interest in and involvement with religion or spirituality," 17 percent of those surveyed did not believe in God and 19 percent believed that "there is very little truth in any religion."[18]

In an attempt to stem this tide of spiritual malaise, on the May 10, 2011, the federal government announced that they would commit $222 million AUD to boost the existing National School Chaplaincy Program (NSCP).[19] Education minister the Hon. Peter Garrett stated that the program "assists schools and their communities to support the spiritual wellbeing of their students."[20] This boost in funding to the NSCP has sparked heated debate in the education, politics, child welfare and religious communities. The main problem is that at the time of the announcement 98.5 percent of the chaplains in this scheme were Christian.[21] Although 63.9 percent of the population still identifies as Christian,[22] as a multicultural country, Australia's current population is comprised of people from a mix of various religions and faiths from around the world. There is still a lot of debate in Australia about whether children should receive religious instruction in public schools. However, despite varying opinions, many teachers, psychologists and social workers agree that during their school years, young people benefit from some type of spiritual nourishment.[23] The problem with the NSCP is that the main focus has become about the politics of religion rather than fostering a schooling environment where children are safe to explore their spirituality. Furthermore, the NSCP cannot be a fix-all for the broader social changes that have been instrumental in fostering a society that promotes the pursuit of more superficial and less mystical pastimes.

This teen disinterest in the divine is a result of a series of subtle and more overt social influences. It is not possible to conclusively pinpoint the exact cause for this current trend. However, there are larger social patterns and changes that have created an environment where more superficial and entertaining pastimes are readily available and more highly prized than pursuing one's spiritual path. In our current digital technology era, games, social networking platforms, films, blogs, chat rooms and various other online applications stream advertising, information and entertainment 24/7. In Australia, like many children, young people and adults around the world, young people have embraced technological advances such as the internet, mobile phones, computer games and PDAs with gusto. (According to the ABS 76 percent of twelve to fourteen year olds own a mobile phone. 96 percent of twelve to fourteen year olds use the internet and 77 percent of five to eight year olds regularly play games online [Australian Bureau of Statistics 2011]). The advent of digital technologies has changed how we as a society work, spend our leisure time, communicate, relate to each other; understand the world and ultimately perceive ourselves.[24] Part of the problem is that as a result of our current digital age, we are overwhelmed by too much information. This information overload means that quantity is valued over quality. In other words, because we are exposed to such an amount of news, information and even emotions, we become almost immune to their significance due to the sheer volume.[25] DeSouza & Hyde argue that teenagers today are far more skeptical and have a greater tendency to trivialize important events, information and even emotions.[26]

This is further exacerbated by the consumer values promoted in our Western culture,[27] where teens receive the message that owning products is social currency. Our consumer society promotes that, for example, possessing the latest mobile phone can elevate your social status. This constant streaming of information and materialism promotes the notion that there is an endless supply of content and material items. This excess and glut reduce their exclusivity and value, thus resulting in trivialization and skepticism. Furthermore, the omnipresent accessibility of digital technologies fosters a need for instant gratification in these teens.[28] The ease with which many tasks can be accomplished in a blink of an eye adds to this notion of trivialization. The combination of these influences encourages these teens to adopt "an outward façade of complacency" which can serve to "mask or conceal their genuine values and feelings."[29] Trivializing their true emotions makes it very difficult for young people to develop emotionally, psychologically and spiritually. DeSouza & Hyde argue that consumerism, trivialization and skepticism are key factors which inhibit "children's expression of their spirituality."[30]

What is interesting to note is that in this digital age of consumerism, trivialization and skepticism, it is a fictitious boy wizard that has captured the hearts and imagination of young Australians. *Harry Potter* has evoked almost a fanatical dedication of biblical proportions as Australia's youth flocked in droves to see the final film. Around the time of the release of *Harry Potter and the Deathly Hallows Part 2*, in Australia (July 13, 2011), local newspapers were filled with all things *Harry Potter*. As to be expected with wildly successful popular cultural texts, there were articles attesting to the enormity of the series' success, interviews with Rowling and the film cast, academics commenting on various merits and flaws of the phenomenon, and interviews with the fans. What was interesting about these fan interviews was the impact that *Harry Potter* had on these fans' lives. Younger fans who grew up as the books were being published related to Harry's growing pains. Australian fan Samantha Landy was seven years old when *Harry Potter and the Philosopher's Stone* was first published in 1997. She identifies herself as part of Generation Potter or "Gen Potter" who grew up reading the books, watched the films and who have embraced Potter and his magical Hogwarts world into their lives.[31] Fans speak candidly about using this text to escape their troubled childhoods and enter a world vastly different from their own dreary reality. Another Australian fan, Adam Shelley, who is shown in one article wearing a black cape, Gryffindor tie, and scarf, states; "I didn't have the best childhood. I guess I could identify with Harry wanting to get away to this magical place where anything was possible."[32]

However, these fantasy novels and films do more than transport fans into another realm. At the heart of the *Harry Potter* controversy is concern over the impact these texts have on developing minds. Evans argues that the books "served as a moral compass, informing young reader's choices on how to live."[33] Christian groups appear to be divided on the magical and moral messages extolled in the series. However, whatever position one adopts in the debate, there is no denying the overwhelming popularity and verve with which fans have taken to these texts. Founder of the Melbourne Muggles Erica Crombie states that the stories and characters "have huge effects on the decisions I make in life."[34] This type of reverence is not unusual for a fan when discussing a favorite text. Nor is *Harry Potter* the first fantasy children's book series to garner a cult-like following. What is significant is the particular formula or combination of various elements that makes the series so appealing to so many fans around the world. However, could the *Harry Potter* books serve more than just a means of emotional catharsis for teens? Given the fantasy and more mystical elements of the stories, can these books function as an aid for teens in the formation of their spiritual identity?

"It is our choices, Harry, that show what we truly are, far more than our abilities": Story and Spiritual Discovery

The development of teenage spiritual identity is a highly debated and controversial subject matter. This topic has been investigated in numerous fields such as psychology, pedagogy, sociology, cultural studies and even psychobiology with the discovery of the "God spot" in the temporal lobe.[35] Any discussion of spirituality inevitably triggers debates over what constitutes "spirituality" and how that differs from "religion."[36] Mindful of these philosophical conundrums, the sole focus of this investigation is to examine what role, if any, the *Harry Potter* series plays in the formation and development of teen spiritual identity. For the purposes of the current analysis, spirituality will be defined as comprising of two distinct yet overlapping components. The first aspect of spirituality is a set of beliefs that forms our understanding of who we are and helps us to make sense of the world around us. This aspect also acts as our moral compass that informs our decisions and choices. The second aspect of spirituality is a connection to a divine source which transcends our daily human life. This divine source is often characterized as a god, goddess, deity or in spiritual terms a "divine energy." However, there are two more important points to consider when discussing spirituality or one's spiritual identity. First, spirituality is a complex concept. Second, spiritual development is a process.[37]

Developing one's spirituality is challenging at any age; however, when a child is also discovering his or her individual identity during those turbulent adolescent years, the spiritual path can be difficult to negotiate. However difficult it may be, the spiritual self is a central part of our individual identity, thus crucial to who we are. Zijderveld argues that "identity construction always contains a spiritual dimension" and that this spiritual dimension "is the metaphysical framework that gives meaning to life and the world."[38] Johnson and Boyatzis regard spiritual development as "an integral part of normal, human cognitive developmental mechanisms and processes."[39] So rather than seeing one's spirituality as separate to one's individual identity, the development of one's *spiritual* identity is in fact a vital component of the development of one's *individual* identity. What is interesting to note is that recent research on teen identity formation and teen health has included spirituality as a core factor in these issues.[40] DeSouza acknowledges that in Australia in the healthcare, education and academic sectors, teen spirituality is being taken very seriously.[41] At the heart of many of these issues and debates is the impact that popular cultural texts, such as the *Harry Potter* series, has on developing hearts and minds during these formative years.

So what exactly is the nature of the relationship between these texts and their teen fans? As previously stated, using characters as a means to explore and work through issues and emotions can be very empowering and liberating. Markell & Markell found the *Harry Potter* series to be a profound therapeutic tool in helping children deal with grief and loss.[42] However, *Harry Potter's* explosive popularity is not just due to its healing and cathartic value. There is something much more powerful at work in this relationship between teen readers and these books. In his seminal book *Textual Poachers*, Jenkins compares the relationship between fan and text to that of a spiritual worshipper and religion.[43] In his discussion on *Star Trek* fans or "Trekkies" Jenkins argues that this "zealous relationship to fictional texts" is a result of the fans' "claims about the mythic possibilities of *Star Trek*."[44] Much of the Trekkie rhetoric frequently adopts the tone of a religious devotee. The same can be said of die-hard *Harry Potter* fans. Their love and adoration for the stories and its characters often takes on the same type of profound religious idolization. Australian *Harry Potter* fan Erica Crombie states that character Albus Dumbledore "...was like a god, he gave advice and moral lessons and life lessons and he is the person in the book you look up to."[45] This type of deep emotional and spiritual connection with these fictitious characters can be explained in part due to the power of story.

Ancient cultures relied on oral narratives as their fundamental form of communication.[46] These oral narratives or stories were an important means of conveying information, explaining natural and supernatural phenomenon, and imparting wisdom. As civilizations developed, the format of stories became more sophisticated, but the function of the story has remained the same. Like ancient myths and legends, sacred texts such as The Bible and The Qu'ran have provided deep spiritual messages that have formed the foundations of religions. In her book *The Story Factor: Inspiration, Influence and Persuasion through the Art of Storytelling*, Simmons argues that stories are extremely powerful.[47] She contends that stories can blend facts, emotions, and the truth to influence listeners in ways that raw facts or information cannot, explaining, "When you tell a story you invoke a power that is greater than the sum of the facts you report. It has emotional content and delivers a contextual framework and a wisdom that reaches past logical rational analysis."[48]

The story has the potential to persuade in ways not found in other mediums. As Simmons so aptly states, "Why do you think religion is full of stories?"[49] The spiritual lessons and teachings of many religions are conveyed in story form because "enormous power resides in the rituals and dramas of religious institutions because of their ability to bring to life the stories on which they are based."[50] Many religions seek to convey principles of how to live to their congregants. However, due to the inherent spiritual nature of religion, these messages also address more complex and abstract philosophies about life and death, good and evil, resurrection and rebirth, faith and nihilism and complicated moral conundrums. It is through the modality of story that these intricate and involved moral lessons can be more readily absorbed and understood.

Like sacred texts, *Harry Potter* is dense with moral conundrums. However, the books also raise more complex and philosophical questions. What separates this series from sacred texts like The Bible is that these profound issues are coupled with more mundane adolescent matters like clashing with teachers, kissing someone for the first time, doing homework, fighting with friends and excelling at sports. The key difference between the two texts is their central purpose. The Bible was written as a set of moral guidelines for life and for many believers it is an unquestionable source of "truth," whereas the *Harry Potter* series was written as children's entertainment and it has never been promoted as anything other than a work of fiction. However, these entertaining stories also deal with deeper moral, ethical and spiritual challenges and issues.

There are two final ingredients that make *Harry Potter* so appealing: the nostalgic recreation of the past and the charm of magic and magical creatures. In order to be influential the story must engage its reader and to do that it must have a realistic or credible premise, setting and characters.[51] Once this everyday type of character and setting are established, the story then can take on more fanciful turns. The function of the everyday type of character and setting gives the story "believability," which allows the reader to engage with and relate to the character and thus become invested.[52] The problem with older sacred texts like The Bible is that they are not believable for many young readers as they are not geared towards winning over a contemporary teen audience. In the first book, *Harry Potter and the Philosopher's Stone*, the central protagonist is an average English boy who lives in an ordinary household and experiences common teen problems such as fighting with his "sibling" and feeling misunderstood and unloved. Beginning the story this way allows readers to identify with him. Provided that these ordinary elements are consistent and believable aspects to the character, plot and setting, the story can then take on more elaborate and fantasy-like qualities.[53]

So given the power of the story in religion and the similarities between *Harry Potter* and other sacred texts, how exactly do these books assist in the formation of teen spirituality? As previously discussed, fictitious characters can function as a means of exploring difficult emotions and issues in a safe and imaginary world. Through the blend of more realistic with more fantastic ones, Rowling has created a realm where teens can both identify with characters and escape their current reality. These fictitious characters and their problems give teens the opportunity to adopt various mental states in order to discover the first aspect of spirituality, which is their set of beliefs or "metaphysical framework." This set of beliefs allows us to understand who we are and make sense of the world around us. For example, Harry's relationship with Professor Snape demonstrates how conflicting emotions, loyalties and fear can play out in complex and ever-changing ways. Via this ongoing tension, teens can "test" their own views of these emotional lessons, with which the books are rich. The use of magic in the books can easily be read as a metaphor for issues surrounding taking control over one's life, the choices one makes and the life path one chooses. How do teens make such decisions without dire consequences? This very question is explored frequently, particularly in one scene from *Harry Potter and the Half Blood Prince* where Harry casts a dark and crippling spell, "Sectumsempra," on Draco with horrible results. These types of lessons challenge readers to "try-on" different mindsets as they engage with the characters. As a consequence of this engagement, readers are confronted with and can explore these deeper issues.

The second aspect of spirituality, the connection to a divine source, is perhaps a little more complex, and the relationship between this aspect and the text is a little less direct. The larger philosophical questions surrounding identity, personal fulfillment and life purpose certainly raise questions about whether such a divine source exists. If one comes to the conclusion that such a divine source does exist, then this raises further questions as to the greater purpose of these profound issues. The presence of ghosts and issues of death and rebirth are frequent themes throughout the *Harry Potter* series. However, it is the characters' use of magic and inclusion of magical creatures that evokes important spiritual questions for teens. These magical elements in the series raises issues of faith, belief in a divine source, miracles, reincarnation and a larger cosmic plan. Australian Potter fan Crombie states that "*Harry Potter* dealt with a lot of things that other children's books didn't. It answered a lot of questions I had in my mind which I didn't know that I had."[54] It is in the guise of entertainment that teens are able to explore more philosophical questions, gauge their belief systems, explore their emotions and test out spiritual issues. The fact that these books fulfill several different needs for teens, but in entertaining ways, is what makes them so successful and an ideal vehicle for exploring their spirituality.

Teen readers who grew up with the series are now finally willing to say goodbye to *Harry Potter*. However, they will always cherish the important life lessons the series gave them. Australian fan Erica Crombie states that the lessons in the books have heavily influenced her life decisions.[55] Crombie dropped out of high school but decided to return and complete her studies so that she can go on to be a social worker. She credits the books for turning her life around: "What I learnt in *Harry Potter* is that if you don't have motivation to do something for yourself, you should do it for the greater good. That's Harry's whole life."[56] This popular fictitious wizard will always bring back fond memories. Australian fan Adam Shelley is ready to put the books down but says, "I can't imagine my life without Harry."[57] He states that for him the stories were about "finding yourself"[58] and that the series had a profound impact on his life.

Conclusion: Harry Potter to the Rescue!

The *Harry Potter* phenomenon has appeared at a time in Australian history where young people are more and more uninterested in their spirituality. Despite the appeal of other similar texts, *Harry Potter* nourishes teen spirituality in ways others do not. As Andrew Futral so aptly states, "*Harry Potter* is about confronting fears, finding inner strength, and doing what is right in the face of adversity. *Twilight* is about how important it is to have a boyfriend."[59] During the release of the final film in 2011 Australian fans conveyed how deeply this text had influenced their lives. The level of devotion expressed by these fans indicated that *Harry Potter* was far more than just good entertainment and that this text performed a number of different meaningful and profound functions. Fans found that they could identify with Harry's plight as a boy growing into a teenager and finally into a young man. The storylines, characters and magical world all provided teen readers with a rich array of spiritual, emotional and philosophical lessons. Certainly on a more superficial level, many fans acknowledge the pleasure in reading such entertaining tales. However, fans expressed that their strong emotional connection to this text was due to its lessons.

Harry Potter combines the plight and angst of a growing teenager with a magical world where characters fight magical creatures, perform magic with their wands, solve mysteries in haunted castles, and count owls, elves, witches and giants amongst their closest friends. It is this blend of relatable everyday events with the more unreal mystical elements that provides the perfect backdrop for profound life lessons. The appealing combination of ensconcing mundane teen problems in a fantasy world gives these everyday issues new life. For example, lying to one's teacher out of devotion to one's best friend is not an original scenario for exploring issues of honesty and loyalty. However, when one throws in a haunted bathroom, an ogre on the loose and magic, then the moral tale becomes a lot more engaging. *Harry Potter* does present more than just simple moral tales: Deeper and more complicated issues such as one's relationship to the self and others, one's connection to the divine and one's choice of life path are presented in these books. The inclusion of these more profound topics only works as well as it does because of the collision of the two worlds: the ordinary human one with the extraordinary magical one. As a result of this collision, readers make choices about what they believe to be "real" and "unreal." This dance between fact and fiction gives them the freedom to explore these more profound and complicated philosophical conundrums in safety.

The timing of the *Harry Potter* books coincides with the advent of the digital technology era. Although not entirely responsible for Australia's teen spiritual listlessness, digital technology has certainly had a massive impact on our daily lives. The overwhelmingly popularity of the *Harry Potter* books and films at this point in our social history certainly suggests that this text is filling more than just an entertainment void. Like previous sacred texts before it, *Harry Potter* could be the antidote to our Australian spiritual crisis. Could it be that fans have discovered the "mythic possibilities" of *Harry Potter*? With seven books, fan clubs, exhibitions, amusement parks, eight films, merchandising and a huge cult following, *Harry Potter* certainly bears all earmarks of a new religion.

Notes

1. Simon Rogers, "Top-Selling 100 Books of All Time," *The Guardian,* January 1st 2011, http://www.guardian.co.uk/news/datablog/2011/jan/01/top-100-books-of-all-time.
2. Macy Halford, "Harry Potter and 'A Dance with Dragons': Breaking Records, Boggling Minds," *The New Yorker,* July 18th, 2011, http://www.newyorker.com/online/blogs/books/2011/07/harry-potter-deathly-hallows-george-rr-martin-dance-with-dragons.html.
3. Casey O'Lear, "Twilight versus Harry Potter: Fantasy Showdown," *The Nevada Sagebrush,* November 18th, 2008, http://nevadasagebrush.com/blog/2008/11/18/twilight-vs-harry-potter-fantasy-showdown.
4. Kara Lyn Andersen, "Harry Potter and the Susceptible Child Audience," *CLCWeb: Comparative Literature and Culture* 7 (2005). http://docs.lib.purdue.edu/clcweb/vol7/iss2/2.
5. Australian Government, "National School Chaplaincy Program Overview," *Department of Education, Employment and Workplace Relations,* 2011, http://www.deewr.gov.au/Schooling/NSCP/Pages/Overview.aspx.
6. Micheal Ostling, "Harry Potter and the Disenchantment of the World," *Journal of Contemporary Religion* 18 (2003): 3.
7. Em McAvan, "The Postmodern Sacred: Popular Culture Spirituality in the Genres of Science Fiction, Fantasy and Fantastic Horror," Phd diss., Murdoch University, 2007, 228.
8. Ibid., 228.
9. Ibid., 228.
10. Orson Scott Card, *Characters and Viewpoint* (Cincinnati: Writer's Digest Books, 2010).
11. Lisa Zunshine, *Why Do We Read Fiction?* (Columbus: The Ohio State University Press, 2006), 17.
12. Ibid., 17.

13. Australian Bureau of Statistics, "1301.0—Yearbook Chapter, 2009–10: Characteristics of the Population," June 4, 2010, http://www.ausstats.abs.gov.au/ausstats/subscriber.nsf/LookupAttach/4102.0Publication29.06.117/$File/41020_Childrendigital_Jun2011.pdf.

14. Philip Hughes, "Is Decline in Religion Inevitable? Religion and Young People: A Global Perspective," *Christian Research Association Bulletin* 18 (2008): 1.

15. Marion Burkimsher, Cited in Philip Hughes, "Is Decline in Religion Inevitable? Religion and Young People: A Global Perspective," *Christian Research Association Bulletin* 18 (2008): 4.

16. Ibid., 4.

17. Ibid., 4.

18. Michael Mason, Andrew Singleton, and Ruth Webber, *The Spirit of Generation Y: Young People's Spirituality in a Changing Australia* (Mulgrave: John Garrett Publishing, 2007), 303.

19. Peter Garrett, "National School Chaplaincy Program," *Minister's Media Centre*, Canberra, 2011, http://ministers.deewr.gov.au/garrett/national-school-chaplaincy-program.

20. Ibid.

21. Christopher Bantick, "Chaplaincy Program Participants Beyond a Prayer," *The Australian*, May 21, 2011, 14.

22. Australian Bureau of Statistics, "1301.0—Yearbook Chapter, 2009–10."

23. Marian De Souza, "The Role of School Education Programmes in Nurturing the Spirituality of Young People," in *At the Heart of Education: School Chaplaincy and Pastoral Care*, ed. James Norman, (Dublin: Veritas, 2004); Judith J. Slater, "Spirituality and the Curriculum," *Taboo: The Journal of Culture and Education* 9 (2005): 59–68; Jacqueline Hodder, "Young People and Spirituality: The Need for a Spiritual Foundation for Australian Schooling," *International Journal of Children's Spirituality* 12 (2007): 179–190; Mary Raftopoulos and Glen Bates, "'It's that Knowing that You Are Not Alone': The Role of Spirituality in Adolescent Resilience," *International Journal of Children's Spirituality* 16 (2011): 151–167.

24. Don Tapscott, *Growing Up Digital: The Rise on the Net Generation* (New York: McGraw Hill, 1998).

25. Nicholas Carr, *The Shallows* (London: Atlantic Books, 2010).

26. Marian DeSouza and Brendan Hyde, "Spirituality of Children and Young People: A Consideration of Some Perspectives and Implications from Research Contextualized by Australia," *International Journal of Children's Spirituality* 12 (2007): 97–104.

27. Ibid.

28. Carr, *The Shallows*.

29. DeSouza and Hyde, "Spirituality of Children and Young People," 101.

30. Ibid., 101.

31. Samantha Landy, "My Life Growing up with Potter," *Herald Sun*, July 17, 2011, 26.

32. Kathy Evans, "Last Train to Hogwarts," *The Age*, June 26, 2011, 21.

33. Ibid., 21.

34. Ibid., 21.

35. David Fontana, *Psychology, Religion and Spirituality* (Oxford: BPS Blackwell, 2003), 80.

36. Zinnbauer et al. "The Emerging Meanings of Religiousness and Spirituality: Problems and Prospects," *Journal of Personality* 67 (1999): 889–919; Cheryl Delgado, "A Discussion of the Concept of Spirituality," *Nursing Science Quarterly* 18 (2005): 157–162.

37. Roehlkepartain et al. "Spiritual Development in Childhood and Adolescence: Moving to the Scientific Mainstream," in *The Handbook of Spiritual Development in Childhood and Adolescence*, ed. Eugene C. Roehlkepartain, Pamela Ebstyne King, Linda Wagener and Peter L. Benson (Thousand Oaks: Sage, 2006), 9.

38. Theo Zijderveld, "Cyberpilgrims: The Construction of Spiritual Identity in Cyberspace," Ma diss., Netherlands: Utrecht University, 2008, 6.

39. Carl N. Johnson and Chris J. Boyatzis, "Cognitive-Cultural Foundations of Spiritual Development," in *The Handbook of Spiritual Development in Childhood and Adolescence*, ed. Eugene C. Roehlkepartain, Pamela Ebstyne King, Linda Wagener and Peter L. Benson (Thousand Oaks: Sage, 2006), 212.

40. DeSouza and Hyde, "Spirituality of Children and Young People" 97–104; John W. Fisher, "It's Time to Wake Up and Stem the Decline in Spiritual Well Being in Victorian Schools," *International Journal of Children's Spirituality* 12 (2007): 165–177; Jacqueline Hodder, "Young People and Spirituality: The Need for a Spiritual Foundation for Australian Schooling," *International Journal of Children's Spirituality* 12 (2007): 179–190; Michael T. Buchanan, "Attending to the Spiritual Dimension to Enhance Curriculum Change," *Journal of Beliefs and Values* 31 (2010): 191–201; Sian Cotton, Meghan E. McGrady and Susan S. Rosenthal, "Measurement of Religiosity/Spirituality in Adolescent Health Outcomes Research: Trends and Recommendations," *Journal of Religion and Health* 49 (2010): 414–444.

41. Marian De Souza, "The Role of School Education Programmes in Nurturing the Spirituality of Young People," in *At the Heart of Education: School Chaplaincy and Pastoral Care*, ed. James Norman (Dublin: Veritas, 2004).

42. Kathryn A. Markell and Marc A. Markell, *The Children Who Lived: Using Harry Potter and Other Fictional Characters to Help Grieving Children and Adolescents* (New York: Routledge, 2008).

43. Henry Jenkins, *Textual Poachers* (London: Routledge, 1992), 12–13.

44. Ibid., 13.

45. Evans, "Last Train to Hogwarts" 21.

46. Joseph Campbell, *The Masks of God: Primitive Mythology* (London: Secker & Warburg, 1960).

47. Annette Simmons, *The Story Factor: Inspiration, Influence and Persuasion through the Art of Storytelling* (New York: Basic Books, 2006).

48. Ibid., 115–116.

49. Ibid., 55.

50. James M. Day, "Speaking Belief: Language, Performance and Narrative in the Psychology of Religion," *The International Journal for the Psychology of Religion* 3, no. 4 (1993): 217.

51. Card, *Characters and Viewpoint*.

52. Simmons, *The Story Factor*.

53. Card, *Characters and Viewpoint*.

54. Kathy Evans, "Last Train to Hogwarts," 21.

55. Ibid., 21.

56. Ibid., 21.

57. Ibid., 21.

58. Ibid., 21.

59. Andrew Futral, "Just Having Fun," *Tumblr*, 2010, http://andrewfutral.tumblr.com/post/141911450/i-am-currently-reading-twilight-because-i-dont.

J.K. Rowling's Innovative and Authoritative Online Presence

Savannah Sharp

In 2011, J. K. Rowling testified for two hours in conjunction with the implosion of *The News of the World* about the paparazzi harassment she has endured. She spoke about her "sense of invasion" at the violating tactics used by photographers and journalists despite being "'highly contactable' through her agent, PR firm and publishers."[1] Successful authors have always had a celebrity status, but today's aggressive paparazzi have created new challenges for author privacy. Popular authors such as J.K. Rowling can solve this issue by donning a mantle of engaged leadership on the Internet to interact with their readers on a more controlled level, both in terms of themselves and in terms of the distribution of their text. Rowling has developed two distinct online resources for her fans: her personal site at jkrowling.com and the growing *Harry Potter* experience-based site at Pottermore.com. At these websites, young readers receive models for how to engage with their identities as readers and how to harness their potential influence in writing online. As students transition from being readers to writers in an Internet age, they must also come to terms with the need for ethical and authoritative control of their textual experiences and their identities. In today's digital society, many teenagers and young adults begin to have a personal and text-centered presence amongst their peers. From texting to Facebook timelines, students understand the need for a carefully self-controlled presence online to moderate social pressures. For them, J.K. Rowling is a positive and cutting-edge role model who is highly aware of her need to communicate most effectively with her various audiences. The continual development of useful and engaging online resources empowers Rowling's status as an author who is aware of the variety of reasons that people have for visiting her different websites, as she provides new material for teachers and students across the world.

J.K. Rowling's personal website, jkrowling.com, is a medium for Rowling to stay in touch with her eager fans while still maintaining a hands-on sense of control over her information. Jkrowling.com has had two major editions, and her newest site is designed to act as a site primarily about Rowling herself and the significant achievements of her career. Rowling used the first edition to interact with her fans, take questions, and release exclusive excerpts from her books. Some features were as simple as little games and puzzles related to *Harry Potter*. Rowling also featured fan sites that she admired and books that inspire her. This first edition of her personal website was mostly centered on Rowling's status as the "keeper of the keys" of the wizarding world.

In addition to the *Harry Potter* resources on jkrowling.com, other parts of her website existed as a means of mediating the fans' interest in her personal life and her public responses to rumors and press stories. In the first edition, jkrowling.com featured several clickable images that led to more information about Rowling. The "News" newspaper, her "Rumors" tabloid, and her "Diary" were used to answer some common and popular questions about Rowling's past, the series, and her plans for the future. Some of Rowling's news stories were very personal, such as an announcement that she was expecting her third child.[2] The audience intended for this announcement was those who might be interested in personal stories but would only wish to hear them from Rowling herself. Other stories were more related to Rowling's craftsmanship as an author. Through her website, she announced publication dates for her final two books, tour dates, and more.[3] This aspect of her website has not changed with the second edition of jkrowling.com, launched in March 2012.

In the second edition of her website, the design has cut out the visual element of looking at Rowling's cluttered desk and replaced it with a very literal timeline. Beginning with the most recent news story, visitors can scroll back through headlines and images that document landmark occasions such as the announcement of her new book, *The Casual Vacancy*; receiving the Order of the British Empire in 2001; Bloomsbury Publishing making an offer on *Harry Potter and the Philosopher's Stone* in 1996; and more. The timeline can also be filtered to show stories about Rowling, *Harry Potter*, "The New Book," and any additional filters that might be added in the future. This interactive but primarily informative design structures the experience of the viewer to help him or her learn about J.K. Rowling and her achievements as a writer and philanthropist. The "insider" information that was originally part of jkrowling.com has been removed to establish a more professional and streamlined experience. Jkrowling.com acknowledges this change, and notes, "Potter fans might have noticed that some of the material about Harry's world is no longer on J.K. Rowling's website. Please note that it will eventually find a home on Pottermore."[4] This redirection of interest to Pottermore, which I will elaborate on, casts a distinct separation between Rowling's two websites and highlights the important different in their purpose. Rowling is continuing to develop different online resources for promoting herself and for sharing her material, and her consistent progression empowers her status as a popular author.

As Rowling empowers herself, she also empowers her fans and readers. When Rowling launched the first edition of jkrowling.com, she began to run polls with three questions to choose among, which she would then answer (in her own cryptic way). A total of 5 polls were available from May 15, 2004 (when the site launched) until February 21, 2006.[5] While Rowling's polls may not have been constant or actively maintained, they did present an opportunity for fans around the world to ask the author for insider knowledge. The act of letting her readers *choose* the question gave them a degree of agency rarely seen from contemporary authors. For readers at the time these polls were published, collective interaction with a best-selling young adult author was new and exciting. Even six years after her last poll closed, this kind of responsive interaction is incredibly rare. When students and young writers are being told in the classroom that collaboration and audience-awareness improve the writing experience, it is encouraging to see a successful author like Rowling engaging with her audience's sense of anticipation and curiosity. Some students have done school projects researching Rowling's life through her website and interviews, seeking to understand the person in a way only possible in today's Internet Age. Others, creating their own websites, blogs, and fan fiction, must decide whether to include personal profiles as part of their writing or on a separate site meant only for friends. As they explore these issues, the young writers discover how the web can help them or undermine their privacy as they establish their all-too-public online identities.

New Privacy Issues Online

Of course, not all fans are passive in their enthusiasm. Another feature of Rowling's website was a mysterious door behind which Rowling revealed new features and news for her series. The door was an unlabeled part of her website when it came online. Its pathway was accessed through a pink eraser labeled with a question mark, and a sign hung around the door handle reading "Do Not Disturb." With Rowling's fans having such diverse skills and interests, it was not long before news broke that the mysterious door had been hacked. In 2004, a skillful fan announced that he had broken through the codes of Rowling's site. Behind the door was an excerpt that *Harry Potter* fans tried to decode: the "lorem ipsum" excerpt from Cicero's *De finibus bonorum et malorum* that is used by publishers and graphic designers as placeholder text. In other words, it was a fruitless effort. After the hacking was made public, the door was basically left alone. Rowling addressed this attempt in the Rumours section of her website, explaining that the discovered Latin text "behind the (ahem) impossible-to-open-door" was only filler text for web developers.[6] Beyond this incident, there were no additional (significant) hackings of Rowling's website. This is actually quite an impressive record, considering the degree of Rowling's popularity. The ability of Rowling's programmers to reinforce her site and prevent further, more serious hacks speaks to the importance of security that Rowling places on her materials. While students certainly do not need to grapple with such skilled and avid fans in relation to protecting their own work, it is worthwhile to note (and perhaps discuss or debate) the principles at stake here. Rowling values her work and uses the necessary technical means of protecting it as she goes about sharing it with others.

J.K. Rowling has truly pioneered the role of an active online author, and the online interactions between her fans and her work have set a precedent that other authors have yet to match. Authors, buried in millennia of pen and ink protocol, are facing new challenges to the security of their work and how audiences interact with new information. Plagiarism is no longer the only threat to an author's livelihood: The leaking of information poses an equally harmful threat to the author's creation of a new and thrilling experience for readers. The final releases of *Harry Potter* novels were riddled with spoiler campaigns from "Snape Kills Dumbledore" spoilers to the first attempt of hacking of J.K. Rowling's website in 2004 to Amazon shipping errors that caused books to arrive early at readers' homes. *Harry Potter* mania demonstrates that authors must legitimize and control their online presence in order to prevent the desire for book piracy.

Other authors have discovered that they must also fiercely protect their interests once they become famous. Stephenie Meyer, the author of the *Twilight* series, had her own run-in with piracy when a leaked copy of her work-in-progress, *Midnight Sun*, went viral on the Internet. *Midnight Sun* was intended to be a re-telling of *Twilight* from the perspective of Edward, the brooding vampire who Bella, the original narrator, loves. In many ways, *Midnight Sun* was a spin-off of *Twilight* and satisfied fans' desire for more material about Edward and Bella without requiring the creation of a new plot and characters. After it leaked online, so many fans had downloaded and read this leaked work-in-progress that Meyer eventually posted it for download on her own website even though she wrote, "I'd rather my fans not read this version of *Midnight Sun*."[7] Meyer also included a very strongly worded testimonial about this violation of her creative process: "I think it is important for everybody to understand that what happened was a huge violation of my rights as an author, not to mention me as a human being... This has been a very upsetting experience for me, but I hope it will at least leave my fans with a better understanding of copyright and the importance of artistic control."[8]

Still, it is better for Meyer to make this half-finished story available through her website instead of leaving it to torrent sites and other unauthorized users. Both Meyer and Rowling achieved phenomenal success through authorship in spite of the intense creative pressure that their fans and the press created. Certainly Dickens did not have to anticipate this brand of kind of aggressive fandom when his works were being published. Fandom is changing, and bestselling authors are beginning to decide how they should best adapt to public demands for additional material.

One of the sources for this demand is the enthusiasm by fans for creating their own *Harry Potter* fiction and other adaptations. In fan fiction, a wide variety of a canon's fans will craft their own stories based on the characters of the chosen original source material. Some fans introduce new original characters, some fans put familiar characters in new situations, and some fans retell established stories from the perspective of a different character. There is an astonishing variety of creativity at play in these stories. When I am working with my students to think about how to compare and contrast the means by which stories are communicated, I turn to fan fiction to illustrate the complexity of the subject. By studying how fans create new work with established characters and storylines (I use *A Very Potter Musical* [This live musical is now available as a series of short movies on YouTube or http://www.teamstarkid.com/avpm.html] to illustrate this point), my students begin to engage with the concept of textual ownership. The issue at hand is not necessarily that of copyright — I explain the copyright complications to prevent confusion — but instead I focus on how fans consider themselves co-owners of the *Harry Potter* reading experience. After investing so much time, energy, and thought into the complex universes that authors create, it is hardly unfair for readers to feel so deeply bonded to the material. These new creators acknowledge the rights and authority of the source material's author, but they also want to gain something for themselves out of this reading relationship. Some fans want to know more of what the author knows as a means of extending their reading experience; J.K. Rowling is a very open author on this count.

Pottermore

After years of anticipation for each of the last several novels, many *Harry Potter* fans grew up in a state of continuously waiting for the next book. When the final *Harry Potter* book was released, fans expressed a communal loss for their enjoyable reading experience. However, in the summer of 2011, as the final movie was released, J.K. Rowling announced the development of Pottermore.com. This was to be Rowling's latest official method of hosting *Harry Potter* fans while sharing new canonical background information, and most notably (and profitably) the eventual sale of ebooks. The "About Pottermore" page describes the site as "a unique online reading experience from J.K. Rowling, built around the Harry Potter books. Share and participate in the stories, showcase your own Potter-related creativity, and discover additional information about the world of Harry Potter from the author herself."[9] Considering the precedent of innovative and engaging interaction available through J.K. Rowling's website, many fans were excited at the prospects of this new website and the 18,000 words of new information that Rowling promised.

After its announcement in June 2011, Pottermore continued to push its way through a myriad of slow developments, or at least it seemed that way to fans. After a round of beta testing, for which only a small segment of contest-winning fans could access the site, the website was promised to be open to the public in October 2011, but remained unavailable for months after. With the *Harry Potter* franchise otherwise completed, fans were easily becoming frustrated with waiting for online material, and many gave up on checking for updates. When J.K. Rowling was writing her books, many fans understood that an author's craftsmanship takes time, and that the years that would go into writing the books would improve the quality of the stories that hit the shelves. A website, on the other hand, is a much more mysterious thing to the common reader, which it makes it all the more difficult for readers to be patient. Many publications had begun to note this frustration, including *The Telegraph*, which published one fan's disappointment: "This is very, very bad advertising for JKR. Is she aware of what is happening? It is frustrating for all the fans, and worst of all there is no satisfactory response."[10] When Pottermore announced in March 2012 its pending opening to the public, the web developers acknowledged the fans' collective exasperation by beginning their announcement: "We know that the extended wait for those wishing to be part of Pottermore has been frustrating, and we'd like to thank you all for your patience so far."[11] This open acknowledgement, accompanied by good news, helped smooth over some of the ire fans had been storing and paved the way for a successful launch.

In April 2012, Pottermore opened to the public, and fans began to sign up and experience the first taste of this extension of the *Harry Potter* books. Even though fans have been appeased by the impressive contents of Pottermore, the frustration with waiting is worth remembering as we begin to wait for the next big development: *The Chamber of Secrets*. As the seven-book wait begins once more on Pottermore, it is important to see the lessons to be learned from Pottermore's fluctuating situation. There are exciting, interesting online experiences being developed for fans, but these interactive sites must be finished and maintained on schedule, or at least relatively close to being on schedule. Authors operate on press and word-of-mouth buzz, and there was certainly eager anticipation for Pottermore. As students, teachers, and scholars produce all sorts of online materials, there is a very real risk of frustrating readers by promising groundbreaking material and then not explaining why goals are not being met.

To date, over two million users have enjoyed the beginnings of Pottermore. At the moment, fans can experience a computer-game style walkthrough of *Harry Potter and the Philosopher's Stone*, brew potions, duel, and buy things at Diagon Alley. A complete experience that includes all seven books will eventually be available. Pottermore is a safe, advertising-free, and adult material-free place to post comments and art as students interact within Harry's world. As such, it's a training space for the larger world of social media with its hazards and pitfalls.

Two substantial services that Pottermore provides are the sale of digital *Harry Potter* materials and a lead-up to the fabled *Harry Potter Encyclopedia*. Both of these elements have long been anticipated by fans and teachers alike. The first service, the sale of downloadable audio books and ebooks, is the more technical aspect of *Harry Potter* publishing available through Pottermore. While ebooks were not as popular in 2007 when *Deathly Hallows* was published, there has been increasing demand for the books to be available for the Kindle, Nook, and other e-readers. Rowling and her publisher had not responded to this call until Rowling announced in the Pottermore welcome video, "[Pottermore] will also be the exclusive place to purchase digital audio books and, for the first time, ebooks of the *Harry Potter* series."[12] In addition to the ebooks, the highly successful, award-winning recordings of Rowling's books by Jim Dale and Stephen Fry will be available for download through Pottermore. (The audio books were available before through iTunes.) Waiting to make these products available on Pottermore was not motivated by Rowling's determination to keep products away from her fans. Instead, by waiting until she had her own platform for releasing her materials, she is maintaining control of her franchise. If she released these products through the traditional vendors, these vendors would take a cut of the profits.

Considering how much Rowling donates to charity, Rowling seems to be making the more ethical decision by taking the time to develop her own distribution platform. Many of the popular intellectual works are distributed through corporations such as Apple that have little to no record of charitable giving. While it is not necessarily the fault of the author to choose to sell through popular means (publication and distribution are difficult enough), Rowling has the means and opportunity to establish her own unique distribution methods. Between Rowling's charitable track record and the ethical troubles plaguing some media giants, it seems that the distribution of electronic materials through Pottermore will be more in touch with Rowling's innovative and socially responsible record. By keeping control of the distribution process for her electronic materials, Rowling is setting an admirable, authoritative, and ultimately unusual precedent for releasing her materials into a new medium that other popular authors might adopt.

The other goal informing the creation of Pottermore is certainly the fabled *Harry Potter Encyclopedia*. This much-discussed publication has a long, complex history. Rowling has always acknowledged that she "hoards" scraps of information about her universe. The publication of such books as *Fantastic Beasts and Where to Find Them* and *Quidditch through the Ages* (2001) proved that Rowling is capable of writing interesting and informative texts that do not center on plot points. After *Deathly Hallows* and *Tales of Beedle the Bard* were published, Rowling remarked that she might eventually write a companion encyclopedia for the series. While this idea for an encyclopedia floated in the ether, the online *Harry Potter Lexicon* assembled the in-text material from Rowling's books and interviews as an online resource. Rowling had spoken of the Lexicon positively; she gave it her official "Fan Site Award" on jkrowling.com. In 2008, RDR Books and Steve Vander Ark began to prepare to print the *Harry Potter Lexicon* and sell it. At this point, Rowling went to court to protect the copyright on her material. The *Lexicon* in its then-current state was blocked, but it was successfully modified and released in 2009 as a companion book to Rowling's books, although it is certainly not an official source.

Pottermore is the beginning of Rowling's response to the interest in additional information while she still maintains her authority as the only source of authentic, unprinted information. With the addition of 18,000 words of new material and information, Pottermore has added fascinating new material to *Harry Potter* canon. Scholars and fan fiction writers alike will be delighted by a new set of facts to discuss and analyze, as they learn the fuller biographies of characters like Minerva McGonagall, Professor Quirrell, and Mr. Ollivander. The developments do not stop with this first release of information through Pottermore. On jkrowling.com, one of the Frequently Asked Questions is "What about the Harry Potter Encyclopaedia?" J.K. Rowling has responded, "For a long time I have been promising an encyclopaedia of Harry's world, and I have started work on this — some of it forms the new content in Pottermore. It is likely to be a time-consuming job, but when finished I shall donate all royalties to charity."[13] No matter how she develops and publishes the contents of all of her background knowledge of the *Harry Potter* universe, the concept of a *Harry Potter Encyclopedia* solidifies J.K. Rowling as a model of an imaginative and determined author. She maintains control over her original materials and demonstrates a thoughtful and ethical awareness of how she can share her ideas with her fans while maintaining her personal integrity as a famous author.

Besides selling ebooks and offering exclusive information, Rowling has made Pottermore an interactive forum, with places for visitors to post comments, duel, and look for online "friends." This step in adapting her books into an online interactive world under the author's creative control marks a new model for writers and literary fans everywhere. For those writers, Pottermore offers a completely new form of storytelling, blending encyclopedia, computer game, and novel into an interactive form. Children picking up the books for the first time can not only accompany their reading with the movies but with the site, immerse themselves in Harry's world and discover compelling new facts about their favorite characters. Even children too young or otherwise unready for chapter books can try the online game for a less complex and perhaps less frightening version of Harry's story.

Final Thoughts

What can students take away from Rowling's experiences and innovations? A high school senior will not have the same innovative resources as one of the most successful authors on the planet, but some of Rowling's influences and goals can help students feel empowered about their own work. As I discuss fan fiction with my students, I encourage them to take a leaf from the book of fan "ownership" and incorporate a sense of ownership over their material into their assignments. With some assignments, students find this is easy; with others, it is more difficult.

J.K. Rowling and her cooperative relationship with her online audience provide a useful model for students trying to find ownership over their writing. What is so innovative about J.K. Rowling's online presence is how unique it is. Rowling thinks about her readers, her fans, and the engaging experiences she can offer them, while successfully establishing that her achievements and her identity are fundamentally her own. Students' confidence in their work, and likely the work itself, can be much improved if students are encouraged to feel the intense ownership over their ideas that J.K. Rowling invests in hers.

NOTES

1. Ben Webster and Paul Sanders, "Even my Children were Targets. I was so Angry, Says J. K. Rowling; Leveson Inquiry," *The Times (London),* November 25, 2011.

2. "HPL: Guide to Jkrowling.com — The Daily Newspaper," *HP-Lexicon.org*, November 1, 2007, http://www.hp-lexicon.org/about/sources/jkr.com/jkr-com-news.html.
 3. Ibid.
 4. "J.K. Rowling," *JKRowling.com*, accessed April 29, 2012, http://www.jkrowling.com/en_GB/#/harry-potter.
 5. "HPL: Guide to Jkrowling.com — FAQ Poll," *HP-Lexicon.org*, last modified April 1, 2007, http://www.hp-lexicon.org/about/sources/jkr.com/jkr-com-poll.html.
 6. Padfoot5, "Harry Potter's Page," *HarryPottersPage.com*, forum, June 26, 2004, http://www.harrypotterspage.com/forums/lofiversion/index.php?t801.html.
 7. Ibid.
 8. Stephenie Meyer, "StephenieMeyer.com / Twilight Series / Midnight Sun," *Stephenie Meyer.com*, August 28, 2008, http://www.stepheniemeyer.com/midnightsun.html.
 9. "Pottermore: About Pottermore," Pottermore.com, accessed March 7, 2012, http://www.pottermore.com/en/about.
 10. "Harry Potter and the Pottermore Web Mystery," *The Telegraph*, March 4, 2012, http://www.telegraph.co.uk/culture/harry-potter/9121868/Harry-Potter-and-the-Pottermore-web-mystery.html.
 11. Pottermore Editor, "Waiting for Pottermore?" *Pottermore Insider*, March 8, 2012, http://insider.pottermore.com/2012/03/waiting-for-pottermore.html.
 12. J.K. Rowling, "J.K. Rowling Announces Pottermore," October 4, 2011, http://www.youtube.com/watch?feature=player_embedded&v=LIApkyunK9Y.
 13. J.K. Rowling, "FAQs," JKRowling.com, accessed April 29, 2012, http://www.jkrowling.com/en_GB/#/about-jk-rowling/faqs-and-rumours.

Exploring eNotes.com: A Grounded Theory of Harry's Place in Language Arts Pedagogy

JAMES B. KELLEY

At the opening of the 21st century, some conservative Christian groups across the United States and beyond argued that *Harry Potter* glamorized witchcraft and thus put children at spiritual risk. Their well-publicized protests frequently ended in school board decisions and occasional court cases about whether or not to restrict access to J.K. Rowling's immensely popular series in school libraries or to forbid its use in the classroom altogether. (Cursory media reports on the *Harry Potter* controversies abound. According to Rob Boston's 2002 account, some early attempts to limit student access to the *Harry Potter* books were defeated by an organized and enlightened citizenry who, although conservative, rallied to oppose extremism, intolerance, and censorship. Coverage of subsequent attempts can be found, for example, in *American Libraries*, the publication of the American Library Association, which offered regular updates on a 2006 school board decision to allow *Harry Potter*'s continued presence in the media centers of downtown Atlanta public schools. See "Harry Potter Faces the Challenge from Georgia"). Despite the media coverage of these controversies, little attention has been given to the views of school teachers who have found themselves on the front line in such disputes. The debates have died down in mainstream media, but teachers can still be heard talking in online forums with students and with one another about these controversies and about what they see as the proper place of the *Harry Potter* books (if indeed they see the books as having a place) in contemporary language arts pedagogy.

This essay examines postings by teachers about the *Harry Potter* series at eNotes.com, a commercial internet service that describes itself as "used daily by thousands of students, teachers, professors, and researchers."[1] (In late October 2011, eNotes.com was ranked by Quantcast.com as the 261st most frequently visited internet site by users within the United States, placing it well ahead of other sites popular among students: sparknotes.com [ranked 534th], shmoop.com [ranked 1,226th], gradesaver.com [ranked 1,711th], and cliffsnotes.com [ranked 1,778th]). Searching for occurrences of the phrase "Harry Potter" at eNotes.com, I located 265 relevant statements by 97 teachers that were posted between March 4, 2007 and January 4, 2012. The average statement is 160 words in length and written by a middle-school or high-school teacher in response to a question posed by a middle-school or high-school student. (The questions themselves are not reviewed here, but it bears mentioning that the students' questions on *Harry Potter* differ from the questions found in the eNotes discussions of such widely taught literary works as Harper Lee's novel *To Kill a Mockingbird*, or Robert Frost's poems "The Road Not Taken" and "Stopping by Woods on a Snowy Evening." Whereas the student-posted questions on more canonical works are often well crafted and end in phrases [e.g. "Explain your response with direct reference to the text" or "Please specify with examples from each text"] that strongly suggest that they were written by teachers for student use as writing prompts or paper topics, the questions posted by students on *Harry Potter* often seem uneven in quality and include very general questions such as, "What do you think about Harry Potter?") I retrieved copies of these teachers' online statements to students and to other teachers, grouped the statements by teacher, and then analyzed the statements using grounded theory.

Grounded theory is a method of qualitative research in the social sciences allowing one to discern meaningful patterns within a large set of qualitative data, such as these collected statements on *Harry Potter*. The goal of this grounded theory project is to generate a nuanced way of talking about these teachers' statements emerging from within the statements themselves rather than imposed by the analyst from outside and from on high. After discussing grounded theory in a little more detail, I will present three sample statements and then discuss the results and implications of the analysis.

Grounded Theory in Practice

Using grounded theory, I read and "coded" (that is, systematically annotated) each statement for significant local items — key phrases and small ideas, often called "incidents" or "events"— and then grouped closely related local items into tentative clusters, often called "categories." Ian Dey explains that in this process of coding and categorizing, "We have to be both attentive and tentative — attentive to the data, and tentative in our conceptualizations of them."[2] In following what is called the constant comparative method, I reconsidered the significance of each incident as I moved back and forth on two levels: just as I read the incidents in the statements by different teachers against one another, I also "move[d] back and forth between the logical construction [my tentative categories] and the actual data [the text of the teachers' statements] in the ongoing search for understanding through description."[3]

Although the language sometimes varies, other experts on grounded theory similarly focus on the importance of a slow, thoughtful approach to the material. According to Robert C. Bogdan and Sari K. Biklen, for example, the analyst develops intimacy with the data through reading and re-reading. They advise that the reader "take long, undisturbed periods and carefully read your data at least twice," "get a sense of the totality of your data," and only then "begin to develop a preliminary list of possible coding categories."[4] To develop these categories, Bogdan and Biklen explain, "You search through your data for regularities and patterns as well as for topics [that] your data cover, and then you write down words or phrases to represent these topics or patterns."[5]

Grounded theory analysis begins with an open-ended question about how to account for what is present in the collected material. I began my analysis of teachers' online statements about the *Harry Potter* series with a general question: What do teachers say when they talk with students and with each other about this popular series? Through repeated, close engagement with the teachers' statements, I developed related questions and identified tentative categories. My questions expanded to include the following: Have the teachers themselves read the *Harry Potter* books, and if so, what have they thought of them? What have been the teachers' experiences with teaching or not teaching the novels, and do these experiences match their wishes? What are the teachers' views on the literary merit of the series? What do teachers see as the proper place of the series, if any, in the language arts classroom? This grounded theory approach required that I revisit the statements until a level of theoretical saturation was achieved, a point at which no new questions or insights emerged. Thus, even when employing a streamlined form of grounded theory (as advocated by Barney Glaser) rather than its more highly structured counterpart (as presented by Anselm Strauss and Juliet Corbin), I found the analysis of the statements to be demanding in terms of time and labor.

Coding Three Sample Statements

Three sample statements by teachers serve here to illustrate the coding process, demonstrating how new categories are created to accommodate newly encountered incidents and how categories, once created, are used to organize related incidents across statements by multiple teachers.

The first statement was posted by a tenth-grade teacher. At 87 words, this short post responds to a middle school student's open-ended question "What do you think about Harry Potter?" The teacher answers:

> I have loved this series of books. I began reading with my youngest son and we finished the whole series. The books demonstrate the fight against good and evil and we discussed the many times that Harry struggled with making good decisions and his unselfish acts to protect those people around him. Another reason I love Harry Potter is that his books encouraged a whole new generation to read. This sparked my son's reading for enjoyment and opened him up to an entirely new appreciation for literature.

This short answer contains a string of incidents that prompt the creation of a number of categories. The teacher's positive personal reaction to the novels, as seen in the repeated use of "love," can be placed in a category tentatively named *Reception* and then made a little more specific by adding the parenthetical details *(personal, positive)*. The second and third sentences attest to the speaker's experience of reading and discussing the books with younger readers, in this case with the teacher's own child rather than with students in the classroom. These sentences thus might be placed in the category *Reading and discussing (with youth, with family, outside of the classroom)*. The third sentence presents a literary theme ("the fight against good and evil") and illustrates the use of the book to instill values in a younger generation of readers ("we discussed the many times that Harry struggled with making good decisions and his unselfish acts to protect those people around him"), two incidents that might be placed in the categories *Theme (good v. evil)* and *Values (making good decisions, acting selflessly)*, respectively. The final two sentences offer three interconnected incidents — "encouraged a whole new generation to read," "sparked my son's reading for enjoyment," and "opened him up to an entirely new appreciation for literature" — that might be placed in the category *Reading (encouraged, for individual, for younger generation)*.

The second statement was contributed by a ninth-grade teacher to a discussion thread on the topic of "cultural illiteracy." The full post measures 182 words, but only the first half relates to Rowling's series:

> It is a truly sad state of affairs when students (and even some parents!) think that Harry Potter is real and that there are witches and wizards among us. I have one student who complained when I referenced Harry Potter when teaching The Hero's Journey, claiming that she doesn't believe in what Harry Potter says he can do ... and her parents brought me into a meeting with the principal about "preaching" magic! When even parents cannot distinguish between fact and fiction, what hope can we hold for their kids?

The teacher speaks to an experience of using *Harry Potter* not as an assigned text but rather as an example in a classroom discussion of the archetype of the hero's journey and reports strongly negative reactions by both a student and the student's parents. The first incident might be placed in the category *Use (classroom, example, hero's journey)*, and the latter two incidents might be placed in the categories *Student reaction (negative, witchcraft)* and *Parental reaction (negative, witchcraft)*.

The third statement comes from a twelfth-grade teacher responding to a question about the advantages and disadvantages of adapting children's stories into films and other media. At 353 words, this statement is well over twice the average length. Although only the second half deals specifically with the *Harry Potter* series, the content is generally relevant and bears quoting at length. The teacher supports "anything that gets kids to read" but sees a problem with translating print works into other media:

> If the child can watch it on TV, on stage, or in the movie theatre instead of reading it, most kids today will opt for that. It is instant gratification and doesn't take as much time as the actual reading. So, they get the story, but they don't get the discipline, the language, the sentence structure, and the overall benefits that reading brings.... Take, for example, the Harry Potter stories. The films are excellent in terms of special effects, etc., however, you cannot effectively mash 300–500 pages of material into a 2-hour film. Something pivotal will be left out, rearranged, or otherwise destroyed or altered. The book allows time for readers to consider what they would do in the character's shoes, and it allows for the character's thoughts and motives to be played out in a way the stage and screen are lacking.

This teacher's support for "anything that gets kids to read" echoes an incident in the first statement and thus might be placed in the pre-existing category *Reading (encouraged, for younger generation)*. Similarly, the observation about books "allow[ing] time for readers to consider what they would do in the character's shoes" may fit alongside an incident in the first statement in the category *Values (making good decisions)*. The second half of the statement (beginning with "Take, for example, ...") similarly echoes an incident in the second statement in the use of *Harry Potter* as an example used to make a larger point and thus can be placed in the category *Use (discussion, example, film adaptation)*.

The exact phrasing of each category is unimportant. What is important is that the categories develop through close engagement with and constant comparison of the teachers' statements; the categories should emerge from within the data rather than be imposed from above. Once the statements were coded, I reviewed and sought to discern the relationships among the most fully populated categories.

Groups of closely related categories that contained a wide range of incidents from a wide range of teachers became candidates for promotion to themes. Themes are the overall patterns and concerns in the teachers' statements; they are the essence of what these teachers have to say about Harry Potter in this online forum. While the teachers express a range of opinions and experiences, their statements can generally be grouped under three interconnected themes: *Teachers as Fans*, which addresses the teachers' personal reactions to the series; *Classroom Applications*, which addresses the teachers' experiences with using the series as instructional material; and *Literacy and Appreciation of Literature*, which addresses the teachers' views on the role that the *Harry Potter* books might play in language arts pedagogy in particular and in promoting literacy in general.

The ways in which teachers talk about Rowling's series often contradict the positions presented in scholarly analyses of the *Harry Potter* phenomenon. Such discussions have generally not examined the experiences of teachers and the place of the *Harry Potter* series within contemporary language arts pedagogy; at most, critics have tended to focus on the significance of the Hogwarts School of Witchcraft and Wizardry within the world of the series itself or on the pedagogical applications of *Harry Potter* at the university level. (For example, Erin A. Pyne's *The Ultimate Guide to the Harry Potter Fandom* surveys the use of *Harry Potter* novels in university courses in the physical sciences, composition, sociology, philosophy, and other disciplines but says nothing about *Harry Potter* in middle school and high school classrooms). Conversely, the teachers' statements make almost no reference to published scholarship, and conflicts between what the teachers and the critics tend to say suggest that teachers arrive at their conclusions independently of published scholarly work. If critics wish for their scholarship to reach beyond academia, this analysis may ultimately suggest that they may need to rethink how they might make their work more accessible to broader audiences.

Theme 1: Teachers as Fans

The theme to emerge first from the teachers' statements is their affection for and detailed knowledge of the *Harry Potter* books. One university professor disparages *Harry Potter* as "an on-going, book-by-book continuation of a simple kid's story about a little boy who goes to magic school" and "a mediocre fantasy series for children about wizards, nothing more." However, most of the statements show strong familiarity with the story lines, and no fewer than nine teachers express unconditional appreciation of the series. For example, one middle school teacher writes, "I can honestly say that I love the Harry Potter series," and two high school teachers write, "I'm a Harry Potter mega-fan" and "I am so big on Harry Potter." A number of these teachers explain in their statements why they are such fans. "I love these books since there is really so much to learn from [them]," writes a twelfth-grade teacher. Similarly, another twelfth-grade teacher explains, "I have never been so drawn into a series of novels.... I read all 7 novels back to back and completely appreciated the growth of the characters and the complexity of the intertwining of plot lines and the novels progressed. I can't recommend these novels more highly for ALL levels of readers."

As other teachers explain, however, being a fan does not always mean that one finds literary merit in *Harry Potter*. A tenth-grade teacher writes: "I happened to like all Harry Potter and Dan Brown books. I suppose because I read them for sheer escapism and not for any literary significance." Similarly, a teacher at the community college level enjoyed reading the series but does not view it as serious literature: "I'm low brow in terms of literature so my only real favorites in that area were the last four Harry Potter books. As far as non-fiction, I'm a bit more refined." Other teachers similarly define *Harry Potter* as popular rather than serious literature. One such teacher writes, "While I encourage my students to read Harry Potter... I do explain to them the joys of what I consider the classics." While discussing the favorite books of middle school students, including Rowling's books, another teacher explains, "I wouldn't call their choices Great American Lit by any means." Being fans is also not the only reason that these teachers might read *Harry Potter*, other statements reveal. A middle-school teacher discusses "[t]rying to keep up with my middle school students" by reading books that are written for them, and a tenth-grade teacher writes, "It's always nice to keep abreast of what our young readers are reading."

For all their familiarity with the series, the teachers participating in the online forum do not seem to view the depictions of the school and teachers in *Harry Potter* as problematic. Some of the teachers adore the series precisely because it is so closely tied to a school. Only one teacher (in answering a student's general question about types of irony) comments briefly on the series' mixed representations of teachers: "A modern example of satire would be the *Harry Potter* series in children's literature, which, among other things, makes mirth at the expense of the British educational system, particularly boarding schools for very young children. This is not the primary intention of the book, but the reader can get some good laughs just the same." Published scholarship on the novels is often far more critical of the representation of the school.

For example, Megan Birch reads *Harry Potter* as marked by anti-intellectualism, stereotyping of teachers, and disdain for institutions of formal education. "In the Harry Potter series," she writes, "real learning occurs outside the classroom and with little influence from a teacher's instructional style or ability or their knowledge."[6] She finds herself most disturbed by "the series' mockery of schools and teachers and the suggestion that teachers have very little power to shape instruction or the institution of schooling," "the limiting idea that being a good teacher is about who you are as a person rather than what you know or what you have the capacity to become," and "the message that who you know is more profoundly valuable than what you know."[7] These criticisms are echoed by Gregory Bassham, who argues that education at Hogwarts suffers from incompetent teachers, limited contact with Dumbledore (Harry is the notable exception), and a formal curriculum that is "too narrow and vocational" to be of value outside of the school.[8] This trend among the critics opposes that of the teachers, who often find the series worth reading and even worth considering as material for inclusion in their classroom in one form or another.

Theme 2: Classroom Applications

The teachers' statements suggest that *Harry Potter* is not generally assigned in the classroom as standard reading or used in read-aloud activities for two reasons. As previously noted, its literary merit is often called into question, but a second, powerful reason is the potential for opposition or controversy. The teachers frequently talk about not being allowed to assign it to their students. A tenth-grade teacher laments: "I can't teach any of the Harry Potter books because they deal with sorcery. The kids gobble them up as soon as they're published, but we don't dare teach them!" Others suggest avoiding the series altogether because, as another teacher puts it, there is "too much debate on that one." Only two teachers report having taught the series as assigned material without incident.

One way that teachers incorporate *Harry Potter* in the classroom with risking controversy is to allow students (with parental permission) to read the books individually rather than to assign them to the class as a whole. A twelfth-grade teacher summarizes this strategy:

> When it comes to books on the [assigned reading] list, any that are also considered "classics" have always gone unchallenged in the schools in which I've taught. *Harry Potter* is one that has come under scrutiny.... I have my students do 2 or 3 independent book projects throughout a semester, and allow them to read ANYTHING, as long as it is on their reading level. Several parents (and some other teachers) have raised objections to *Harry Potter*, but my theory is that it is an independent project, which is completely open. If parents want to censor their children, that is fine. I'm not going to.

Although most teachers participating in the forum do not appear to use *Harry Potter* in the classroom, they do regularly use examples from Rowling's series in their classroom discussions on a variety of literary topics, including theme, symbol, conflict and resolution, character development, and the hero's journey. Similarly, in the online forum itself, teachers often make *Harry Potter* references as they answer students' questions on other subjects, including commonly taught works such as *The Odyssey, Hamlet, 1984*, and *The Crucible*.

Here again, teachers seem to operate without need for critics. A number of teachers report using Harry Potter to illustrate the hero's journey, but beyond occasionally naming Joseph Campbell, they make no reference to publications on this very topic, much less to criticism suggesting that a mythopoeic approach might blind the reader to shortcomings in the storyline. After noting published Campbellian analyses of *Harry Potter* by five scholars, for example, Tison Pugh and David L. Wallace argue that the series' push for the heteronormative development of a young male hero unnecessarily restricts what is possible even within the fantasy setting of the novels.[9]

Responding to a question about whether or not *Star Wars* merits inclusion in the classroom, a ninth-grade teacher mentions four films centering on male characters. The statement represents this second theme even as it points toward the third and final theme: "The Hero's Journey runs throughout myths and legends of all cultures, and students relate more readily to pop culture as an attention grabber. Once they see the pattern for Luke Skywalker, Harry Potter, Indiana Jones, and Will Turner, they are more apt to see it in "Gawain and the Green Knight," *The Odyssey*, and *The Hobbit*."

Theme 3: Literacy and Appreciation of Literature

While teachers may be uncertain about the series' literary merit or about its presence in their classroom, they generally agree that the series both promotes literacy among children and young adults and serves as a gateway to more challenging or canonical literature. A middle-school teacher praises *Harry Potter* for "introduc[ing] young people to allusions," for example, and a tenth-grade teacher likes the series' genre because, "above all, it 'turns on' some types of student far more than other, more traditional novels." A twelfth-grade teacher writes about the series: "I think one of the greatest things about these books is that they get young people reading," and in a discussion thread full of references to *Harry Potter*, a community college teacher writes that canonical literature is often "downright boring and irrelevant for modern readers, especially younger ones" and that sci-fi and fantasy should take precedence over Faulkner or Hemingway: "If we want them to read the classics, get them hooked on sci-fi and fantasy first. Give them werewolves and vampires and ghosts and aliens, and that can whet their appetite for reading mainstream and classic literature."

Few teachers question such valuing of *Harry Potter* and criticize the commercialization of the series in a manner that matches the trend among critical and academic treatments. A twelfth-grade teacher criticizes the books themselves: "One book tells you everything you need to know. The rest of them are just repetitions of the first. Marketing is everything, and Harry Potter branding is almost beyond belief." A community-college teacher is critical of the translation of the books into films: "[T]he only real reason that the Harry Potter books (or any books, really) are made into films is to make money. ... The adaptation encourages kids to consume more products (buy the DVD, buy the action figures, etc) instead of having the books live in their minds. ... one of its effects is to make kids into consumers instead of thinkers."

Scholarly pieces seem more consistently skeptical of the claim that *Harry Potter* fandom promotes literacy and advances young peoples' appreciation of literature. In her introduction to a 2003 collection of essays on *Harry Potter*, Giselle Liza Anatol quotes Jack Zipes, who sees the series as promoting consumption, not reading. Anatol herself writes: "These series are designed not to stimulate readers' imagination and intellectual processes but rather to stimulate customers to 'buy' and 'rebuy' not only books, but also CDs, audio- and videotapes, computer games, sugared cereals, and clothing."[10] This line of criticism is revisited in Elizabeth E. Heilman's introduction to the 2009 essay collection *Critical Perspectives on Harry Potter*, in which Heilman challenges the same claim that the series has created a new generation of readers:

> It has ... been credited for a renaissance in reading for children all over the world — but this is largely a folk legend. Though indeed many children read the Harry Potter series, an extensive analysis of research on reading trends supported by the National Endowment for the Arts shows that most of these children do not go on to read many other books outside of school or become teens and young adults who read. Others will remain reading strictly in fantasy/mystery genres. More than half of American adults won't read a single novel in a year according to the National Endowment for the Arts and, in the last decade, as millions of Harry Potter books have sold, the decline of reading has almost tripled.[11]

Heilman believes that the series can have value in the classroom as a springboard for examining complex issues — including "the construction of identity, the meaning of home, the difference between schooling and learning, and what it means to be a leader" — but she fears that the series often does not receive serious treatment in the classroom: "Without support, teachers developing curriculum around these books sometimes focus on trivia, for example, having students create models of Hogwarts School or invent their own flavor of Every Flavor Bean."[12] Her reservations seem warranted; the lesson plans provided by Scholastic that are regularly referenced in the teachers' statements and throughout eNotes.com often engage in this very type of "trivia," such as creating Hogwarts yearbooks or crafting golden snitches out of ping-pong balls, feathers, glue, and gold spray paint.

Conclusion

The teachers' statements reveal three contradictory trends. These teachers are mostly fans of the series, untroubled by the problematic depiction of teachers in the novels. They do not use the novels as assigned texts but do bring them into the classroom as individual reading projects or, more commonly, as shared points of reference for discussions of literary elements such as symbol, theme, or archetype. Finally, they do not consistently regard *Harry Potter* as serious literature but tend to value the books as a tool for improving literacy and as a gateway for student appreciation of canonical works. Taken as a whole, the teachers' posts more generally demonstrate little to no interest in academic and critical discussions of the series.

These observations are not necessarily disheartening but do have implications for the scholarship of teaching and learning. Scholars publishing in this area (especially those publishing in essay collections marketed toward teachers and school libraries) may wish to find ways to make the results of their work more available in various formats, including online forums and live workshops. Middle school and high school teachers are already engaging students and other teachers in interesting, thoughtful discussions of workplace constraints, literary merit, pedagogical value, and other topics related to *Harry Potter*. Scholars working in these same areas may wish to explore ways to make themselves part of those discussions.

NOTES

1. "About Us," *eNotes.com,* 2011, http://www.enotes.com/help/about.
2. Ian Dey, *Qualitative Data Analysis* (London: Routledge, 1993), 102.
3. Michael Quinn Patton, *Qualitative Evaluation Methods* (Newbury Park, CA: Sage, 1980), 314.
4. Robert C. Bogdan and Sari K. Biklen, *Qualitative Research for Education* (Boston: Allyn & Bacon, 2007), 185.
5. Ibid., 173.
6. Megan Birch, "Schooling Harry Potter: Teachers and Learning, Power and Knowledge," in *Critical Perspectives on Harry Potter*, ed. Elizabeth E. Heilman (New York: Taylor & Francis, 2009), 116–17.
7. Ibid., 119.
8. Gregory Bassham, "A Hogwarts Education: The Good, the Bad, and the Ugly," in *The Ultimate Harry Potter and Philosophy: Hogwarts for Muggles,* ed. Gregory Bassham (Hoboken, NJ: John Wiley & Sons, 2010), 220.

9. Pugh Tison and David L. Wallace, "Heteronormative Heroism and Queering the School Story in J. K. Rowling's *Harry Potter* Series," *Children's Literature Association Quarterly* 31, no. 3 (2006): 261.

10. Giselle Liza Anatol, "Introduction," in *Reading Harry Potter: Critical Essays*, ed. Giselle Liza Anatol (Westport, CT: Greenwood Publishing Group, 2003), xii.

11. Elizabeth E. Heilman, "Introduction," in *Harry Potter's World: Multidisciplinary Critical Perspectives*, ed. Elizabeth E. Heilman (New York: Routledge, 2003), 2.

12. Ibid., 9.

Part III

Meaning in Children's Books Within the University

Legit Lit: Of Spells and Serious Scholarship

J. Steve Lee

"So what is Quidditch?" [Harry asked Hagrid.]
"It's our sport. Wizard sport. It's like — like soccer in the Muggle world — everyone follows Quidditch — played up in the air on broomsticks and there's four balls — sorta hard ter explain the rules" [*SS* 79].

We expect college students to tend toward the uncanny and peculiar. One might see the common college student lounging in the college yard or throwing the Frisbee to pass time before the next class. The peculiar side ranges from toga parties to college pranks (or hacks as they are called at MIT) but if you look closely enough you just might see some Muggle Quidditch.

While Muggle Quidditch is completely earthbound, college students playing Quidditch are found running around an open field with broomsticks between their legs attempting to throw a ball into three hoops for points. At Middlebury College, the students having been playing since 2005. In the July 2007 publication of *The Chronicle of Higher Education*, Alex Benepe (then a junior at Middlebury) revealed that "he answers e-mail messages a couple of times each week from students at other colleges seeking advice on how to start their own clubs."[1] College teams have formed the International Quidditch Association to govern and organize extramural matches between university teams. While this extracurricular activity is growing outside of the classroom, surprisingly another outgrowth of Potter interest in growing inside the classroom: *Harry Potter* courses. From Finger Lakes Community College to Stanford University, *Harry Potter* is becoming a part of the curriculum in colleges and universities across the country.

"Colleges all over the nation are embracing *Harry Potter* mania, and many are offering courses that focus on the books and their characters," reports

Michael Keathley on *Best Colleges Online*.[2] Although the exceptionally popular book saga (selling well over 400 million copies, making it the most successful book series in history) has come to an end in 2007 with the publication of *The Deathly Hallows,* and Hollywood has squeezed every last dollar from the movie-goer with the release of its two-part finale, university classrooms are continuing the interest that students have with *Harry Potter* and the wizarding world.

CNN News reports this continued fascination with J.K. Rowling's books: "The fictional boy wizard lives in college classes across the country where the children's books are embraced as literary and academic texts. Drawing on their expertise in theology, children's literature, globalization studies and even the history of witchcraft, professors have been able to use Harry Potter to attract crowds of students eager to take on a disciplined study of the books."[3] And disciplined studies it has been. Analysis of the books has caused students to grapple with issues such as racism, genetics, bullying, sacrifice, storytelling, mythology, friendship, evil, and propaganda. Anywhere from an examination of *Harry Potter* as a significant contribution to children's literature to the divine themes embedded in the text to the science behind the magic, *Potter* has arrived at college.

The reach of the book series is not limited to literature but has penetrated such disciplines as diverse as science, sociology, education, ethics, philosophy, rhetoric, theology, and international relations. Dr. Alan Reifman, professor of Human Development and Family Studies at Texas Tech University, explains that "beyond being an entertaining and thought-provoking literary series, *Harry Potter* has now become the subject matter of college courses."[4] Dumbledore and his army are not limited to orientation and seminars, but have apparated into fully credited courses. Dr. Reifman concludes his article by playfully predicting that "so rapidly is the Potter franchise expanding its reach into American higher education, I'm sure it's only a matter of time before the candy sections of university bookstores will be selling Chocolate Cauldrons!"[5]

But the expansion of the Potter franchise is not only found in American higher education. Courses that include *Harry Potter* are found across the Atlantic and Pacific Oceans. From Durham, England to Guangzhou, China, the Potter scholarship has extended its spell. Universities are seemingly bewitched with interest in all things Potter.

The following is a sample list of some of the higher educational institutions that incorporate Potter into the curriculum:

Arizona State University (Honors College)
Augustana College
Ball State University
Belmont University
Bridgewater State University
Brown University (Pre-College Program)
Buffalo State University

Cerritos College
Clemson University
Durham University
Eastern Michigan University
Emory University
Finger Lakes Community College
Frostburg University
Gordon College
Georgetown University
James Madison University
Kansas State University
Kent State University
Lawrence University
Lenoir-Rhyne University
Liberty University
Marshall University (Honors College)
Marymount Manhattan College
Middle Tennessee State University
Meredith College
Morehead State University
Northern Arizona University
North Georgia College & State University
Oregon State University
Ohio State University
Oklahoma University
Otterbein University
Pepperdine University
Princeton University
Rivier College
Sun Yat-sen University
Stephen F. Austin St. University
Southern Utah University
Swarthmore College
Stanford University
St. Catherine University
Texas Lutheran University
Texas A & M University
Tufts University
University of California, Irvine
University of California, Davis
University of Iowa (Honor Program)
University of Nebraska
University of Sioux Falls
University of Texas at Dallas
University of Texas at Austin
University of Washington
University of Wisconsin (Marshfield)
Virginia Tech University
Yale University

Seminars, Orientations, Etc. (Non-Credit Classes)

At Augustana College, just outside of Davenport, Illinois, in Rock Island, the Summer Academy offers a summer high school enrichment program titled "A Return to Hogwarts," which gives students "a chance to get out of the sun and spend time analyzing the ... *Harry Potter* series."[6] The course is being offered by Pastor Richard Priggie, chaplain of Augustana College, who also teaches an elective freshman curriculum called *The Soul of Harry Potter*, which reportedly fills up within twenty-four hours of being opened for registration every year.[7] High school students in "A Return to Hogwarts" examine the literary structure of the series, use a Marauder's Map for a scavenger hunt, watch the films, and even play a round or two of Quidditch.[8] Other schools such as Penn State University have developed similar programs for children's summer camps.[9]

The first day on campus is nerve racking for anyone, but Oregon State University has a special potion to overcome the freshman frights. In the fall of 2010, Mamta Accapadi, OSU's dean of students, offered a freshman course titled "Finding Your Patronus." Freshman courses are nothing new. They help students adjust to college life, get oriented to the layout of the campus, and find an immediate community. At Oregon State, however, a familiar wizard provides a ready connection for the freshman. "I'm hoping that I have a lot of Harry Potter fans in the room, so that everyone will start out having something in common," Accapadi said. "I feel like that will minimize barriers and the class will gel way more quickly."[10]

By offering this course, Oregon State provides an avenue to bridge the divide between freshman and the college life with their U-Engage courses. These courses are taught by the faculty and staff of the university and "include important information, including practicing critical analysis, identifying campus resources, developing a sense of belonging and contributing to a diverse community — skills that will help them deal with future college courses and life on campus."[11] Accapadi, herself a Potter fan, is apparating from the administrative office as Dean of Students to the classroom to better assist freshman with the challenges they will face. "You may even encounter a Snape on campus," she said.[12]

Science

One of the earliest courses involving the *Harry Potter* series appeared at Frostburg State University. This school in the panhandle of Maryland provides one of the best known of the Potter courses: "The Science of Harry Potter." This three-credit honors seminar looks at the science behind the magic. Questions covered in the course include: Can antigravity research produce a flying broomstick? Is the three-headed dog, Fluffy, possible by genetic engineering?

Physics professor George R. Plitnik explores these issues with fifteen juniors and seniors. David Dishneau of the *Associated Press*, reporting on the Harry Potter science class, says the "class is not all fun and games, despite his [Plitnik's] penchant for dressing up as Albus Dumbledore, headmaster of Hogwarts School of Witchcraft and Wizardry." Plitnik noted before putting on his wizard's hat and robe for class, "This is not something where you just show up and talk about Harry Potter books and get a grade... This is a college-level class."[13]

The course that Plitnik created is inspired not only by the *Harry Potter* novels, but more directly by science writer Roger Highfield's popular *The Science of Harry Potter: How Magic Really Works*, published in 2002. *Science News* said the book was "far-ranging ... enlightens Harry Potter's magical realm, but also the magic taking place in labs and classrooms in our own world." Highfield, according to the back cover of the book, "explores the fascinating links between magic and science to reveal that much of what strikes us as supremely strange in the Potter books can actually be explained by the conjurings of the scientific mind."[14]

Dishneau reports that the class requirements include a final project along with a Potter themed presentation and "two written exams and daily quizzes." While the class is designed for non-science majors, the amount of work is more than anticipated. "Plitnik tempers the serious approach with sometimes zany teaching methods. The bearded, 61-year-old acoustics expert is renowned on campus for his costumes, props (a rubber chicken is never far away) and other gimmicks."[15]

In an entirely different continent, another science course is using *Harry Potter* to draw students, specifically in the field of genetics. At Sun Yat-sen University in China, the 2012 school year began with an elective course on genetics with Harry Potter in its name. Chen Suquin, the lecturer behind the course, declared that "genetics courses are generally dry, and she hoped to arouse students' interest in this way. She said many scientists in the United States and Europe study medicine and biology using Harry Potter as case, though they are conducting serious research, they can formulate it in an easy and humorous way, and that's where she got the idea for the course."[16] Suquin proclaims that the Potter stories provide an avenue to examine genetics "such as cats of different colors, and people of different colors."[17]

Humanities

While high school summer enrichment programs and freshman seminars offer *Harry Potter* as part of their curriculum, the mainstream academic community is not ambivalent about J. K. Rowling's literary contribution. Henry Jenkins, a professor of literature and comparative media at MIT, said "Rowling's novels could become fodder for serious academic study."[18] Jenkins went on to compare Hawthorne's reception as an author with Rowling's, "Nathaniel Hawthorne's books were potboilers in their time and became part of the literary establishment. No one knows if the Harry Potter books will be part of the literary curriculum 100 years from now, but it's quite possible."[19]

Quite possible, indeed. "The students in Swarthmore College's 'Battling Against Voldemort' class are learning to look at their favorite children's series with adult eyes," notes Jennifer Vineyard of *MTV News*.[20] Professor Melinda Finberg teaches *Harry Potter* (along with the *Lord of the Rings* and the *His Dark Materials* series) as a bridge to get students to grasp basic concepts of literary theory and step up their own writing skills. "I thought, 'What are the kids reading this summer? *Harry Potter*!'" Finberg said. "This group of students is the *Harry Potter* generation."[21] While "Battling Against Voldemort" course is a serious academic endeavor into the *Potter* world at Swarthmore College, it does not change the fact that it's the students' favorite course: "This is by far my coolest class. I'm reading *Harry Potter*, and [a fellow student] is reading Plato's *Republic*. It felt a little unfair," one related.[22]

The students for the class's twelve seats are determined by a lottery. Once it begins, they take a serious look at the books as a real contribution of literature examining themes, metaphors, Jungian archetypes, good, evil, and philosophy's ambiguities. The class makes continued references to such works as *Crime and Punishment* and *1984*, as well as allusions to Nazi Germany, fascist Italy and the French Revolution.

Several companion books have been published examining the literary inspiration and historical background of the *Harry Potter* books: *Harry Potter's Bookshelf: The Great Books Behind the Hogwarts Adventures* by John Granger[23] and *Harry Potter and History* by Nancy R. Reagin.[24] The content of such books reinforce the academic value of *Harry Potter* as worthwhile scholarly endeavor.

Harry Potter's Bookshelf by the Potter Pundit John Granger examines the literary background that Rowling was inspired by and drew from to create the *Harry Potter* series. He examines the influences on Rowling such as Dante Alighieri, Jane Austen, Bram Stoker, Dorothy Sayers, Charles Dickens, Charlotte Bronte, William Shakespeare, Jonathan Swift, Geoffrey Chaucer, and C. S. Lewis. The book description states that it, "Explores the literary landscape of themes and genres J.K. Rowling artfully wove throughout her novels — and the influential authors and stories that inspired her."[25] The author John Granger shares his motivation in writing *Harry Potter's Bookshelf*:

> A common ambition of the books I have written is answering the question, "Why are the *Harry Potter* books so popular?" and my response is always a variation on "It's the literary artistry that engages and transforms readers that is the real magic of the books." That answer involves discussing the usual English literature topics like narratological voice and setting, as well as the more bizarre and less well-known devices and story scaffolding that Ms. Rowling uses, like literary alchemy and vision symbolism.[26]

Rowling's reliance on these literary giants indicates the seriousness of the series for thoughtful readers.

Nancy R. Reagin, professor of history and women's and gender studies at Pace University, provides a guide to the history behind the magic of *Harry Potter*. The back cover of *Harry Potter and History* pledges that the reader will discover answers to many questions: "Were Voldemort and the Death Eaters similar to the Nazis? How did Muggles use mandrakes, bezoars, cauldrons, and love potions? Would a woman have more rights as a witch or a Muggle?

How do the Malfoys compare to Muggle English aristocrats? Who was the real Nicolas Flamel?"[27] Reagin promises, "You'll find the answers and more inside this book, the first to explore the real history behind the world of Harry Potter. From Dementors to the Dark Mark, from Hogwarts to house-elves, *Harry Potter and History* takes a revealing look at the historical backdrop of J. K. Rowling's novels."[28]

At St. Catherine University in the Twin Cities of Minnesota, the student-run English club responded to the question, "If you could have a class on anything, what would it be?" by requesting a *Harry Potter* course in 2009. The winter semester of 2010 saw the creation of "Six Degrees of Harry Potter," a 200-level literature course taught by Professor Cecilia Knochar Farr. The workload of the course involved reading all seven books of *Harry Potter* as well as one scholarly book along with a collection of essays. The students discussed topics in class and in small groups as well as complete a final research paper.

Evan Gaydos, graduate of St. Kate's (as the student tend to call their alma mater) in 2012, served as the teaching assistant to the course. Gaydos reports, "I've talked with people who really want to take the class and I tell them, 'You're going to be doing a ton of reading in this class, in an extremely short period of time.... And they say, 'That's fine.' They're totally willing to do it."[29]

Professor Farr understands the appeal of *Harry Potter*, "These novels were very meaningful to my children, in the same way they are to my students," she says. "For this generation, this was a huge phenomenon. They grew up with the Harry Potter novels."[30] Developing a love for reading and literature is her passion. Author of *Reading Oprah: How Oprah's Book Club Changed the Way America Reads*, Professor Farr comments that "I'm always trying to meet my students where they are and show them how making literature a part of their life is a valuable experience. It's a part of our liberal arts learning at St. Kate's."[31]

Early in the release of the *Harry Potter* series, many religious attacks were made against the books, claiming that it led children away from God and even into witchcraft. Ironically, one of the most prolific courses on *Harry Potter* is coming from a Yale Divinity School graduate student. Danielle Tummino, instructor of Yale's "Christian Theology and Harry Potter," informs that her dual interest in literature and theology motivated her to create the course.

Covering themes ranging from sin to the resurrection, she tells the undergraduates in her class, "I know that *Harry Potter* is what brought you here, but I hope theology is what keeps you here. Because regardless of your religious tradition, the questions theology asks — how do we love people? What does it mean to live a good life? Why does evil occur?— are questions of deep meaning that we should all take time to ask."[32]

On her website she reveals how the course came about. She "first designed the Christian Theology and Harry Potter course in the attic apartment of two professors during the summer of her final year as a graduate student at Yale because she wanted to forge a new way of teaching theology that made a topic close to her heart more accessible and exciting for students."[33] The first course was offered on a cold afternoon in January of 2009. Seventy-nine students showed up to enroll for the class with only eighteen spots available.[34] It quickly became one of the most popular courses on campus, repeating at Yale as well as arriving at Tufts University.

Meanwhile, in England, Durham University is using *Harry Potter* to explore prejudice, civic duty and societal behavior. "Harry Potter and the Age of Illusion" is part of the university's degree program in Educational Studies.[35] Dr. Martin Richardson, head of the Department of Education, states, "A number of themes will be explored, including the world of rituals, prejudice and intolerance in the classroom, bullying, friendship and solidarity and the ideals of and good citizenship [sic]."[36]

Harry as a cultural phenomenon is the focus of Emory University's course in American Studies entitled "Harry Potter in America." Starting in the spring of 2012 the "course will put an emphasis on the books' impact on children across the nation."[37] Its instructor, Professor Catherine Ross Nickerson of the Institute of Liberal Arts, commented that "students often talk about the experiences of reading books and seeing the films as something that shaped their childhood."[38] Chelsea Hermond, who reported on the class in the school newspaper *The Emory Wheel*, indicated that the course syllabus will be reading and writing intensive and "will examine ... the censorship based on religious objections, fan fiction, the Orlando theme park and Muggle Quidditch."[39] If the course goes well, Nickerson hopes to repeat it in the future.

The following is only a small sample of *Harry Potter's* legitimacy as a worthwhile academic endeavor as indicated by the varied interest Rowling's book has conjured in so many uses in the classroom:

James Madison University had one of the earliest courses on *Harry Potter*: "The World of Harry Potter: A Critical Cross-Disciplinary Examination." One of the course's projects for Education majors required "students to create a lesson plan based on the books that could be used to teach math, science, and English to grade school students."[40] "Harry Potter's Library" at Kansas State University compares and contrasts the series with readings from Roald Dahl, C. S. Lewis, and E. Nesbit. Georgetown University's "Knights of Old and Harry Potter," examines the relationship of *Harry Potter* with medieval literature as well as themes of heroism and coming of age. An analysis of mystery in Ohio State University's "Harry Potter: Mystery and English Comedy," demonstrates how answers to mysteries are usually contrary to initial impressions. *Harry Potter* has also broken into philosophy courses at Bridgewater State College in Massachusetts, where "The Ethics of Harry Potter" provides the opportunity to compare the ethics of Aristotle with the book series.[41] Edmund Kern, author of *The Wisdom of Harry Potter* and history professor at Lawrence University, has taught a course in the history department called "Thinking about Harry Potter." Its prerequisite requires a "'copious knowledge' of all 4,000-plus pages of the seven-book series. Rather than the books themselves, the course will focus on the ever-increasing academic interest in Potter as cultural and literary icon."[42] Stanford University's "Harry Potter: The Meaning behind the Magic" focuses on a deep analysis of Rowling's form and theme as well as the series' impact on British and American literature. Finally, the University of Texas evaluates the use of persuasive language in the *Potter* books in its class titled "Rhetoric of Harry Potter." The course description has students taking "a look at some of the most effective uses of rhetoric in the novels and the political and social implications it may have. Additionally, students will examine major issues like race, violence, and propaganda in the books and write essays and final projects on a theme they've selected from the course."[43]

Lasting Impact

Is the use of *Harry Potter* in colleges and universities just a passing fad or will Rowling's books have a staying power that outlasts their critics? Dr. Martin Richardson of Durham University states, "You just need to read the academic writing which started to emerge four or five years ago to see that Harry Potter is worthy of serious study."[44] Not only has the academic writing (listed in the Appendix) of *Harry Potter* been prolific, but the use of the books in higher education classes is obvious. We need to recall the words of MIT professor Henry Jenkins who uttered back in 2005 that "Rowling's novels could become fodder for serious academic study."[45] That much has certainly come to pass. Will it last? How will Rowling's books be remembered in the next generation? Unfortunately, we don't have Professor Sybill Trelawney's divination skills, but James W. Thomas, a professor of literature for over thirty years at Pepperdine University, is much more confident about its impact, naming it "legit lit." "For my entire adult life, I've studied serious literature and read great books. I *feel* like I've read a *million* books, so I ought to know when I come across a great one — which brings me to J. K. Rowling and the *Harry Potter* books.... I believe ... that Rowling's Potter story is a great book, is legitimate literature, legit lit."[46]

NOTES

1. Sierra Millman, "Generation Hex," *The Chronicle of Higher Education* 53, no. 46 (2007): A4.
2. Michael Keathley, "15 Fascinating College Courses for the Ultimate Potter Scholar," *Best Colleges Online*, July 18, 2011, http://www.bestcollegesonline.com/blog/2011/07/18/15-fascinating-college-courses-for-the-ultimate-potter-scholar.
3. Patrick Lee, "Pottermania Lives on in College Classrooms," *CNN News*, March 25, 2008, http://articles.cnn.com/2008-03-25/entertainment/cnnu.potter_1_potter-books-harry-potter-luna-lovegood?_s=PM:SHOWBIZ.
4. Alan Reifman, *Psychology Today: On the Campus*, "Harry Potter, Quidditch, and the American University," June 1, 2011, http://www.psychologytoday.com/blog/the-campus/201106/harry-potter-quidditch-and-the-american-university.
5. Ibid.
6. Keathley, "15 Fascinating College Courses."
7. "Summer Academy at Augustana College," http://www.augustana.edu/x18387.xml.
8. Ibid.
9. David Dishneau, "Harry Potter Goes to College," *CBSNews.com*, September 23, 2003, http://www.cbsnews.com/stories/2003/11/19/national/main584456.shtml.
10. Theresa Hogue, "Special Freshmen Classes Feature Harry Potter, Avatar," *LIFE@ OSU*, Sept 27, 2010, http://oregonstate.edu/dept/ncs/lifeatosu/2010/special-freshmen-classes-feature-harry-potter-avatar.
11. Ibid.
12. Ibid.
13. Dishneau, "Harry Potter Goes to College."
14. Roger Highfield, *The Science of Harry Potter: How Magic Really Works* (New York: Penguin Books, 2002), back cover.
15. Dishneau, "Harry Potter Goes to College."
16. Huang Yuli, "A Spellbinding Course for Potter Putterers," *China Daily*, January 6, 2012, http://www.chinadaily.com.cn/usa/china/2012-01/06/content_14391662.htm.
17. Ibid.
18. Lisa Poole, "Harry Potter Fans Create Makeshift College," *USATODAY.com*, Associate Press, October 10, 2005, http://www.usatoday.com/life/lifestyle/2005-10-10-potter-univ_x.htm.
19. Ibid.
20. Jennifer Vineyard, "'Harry Potter' Goes to College: Students Study the Books in New Courses," *MTV News*, September 25, 2008, http://www.mtv.com/news/articles/1595623/harry-potter-goes-college.jhtml.
21. Ibid.
22. Ibid.
23. John Granger, *Harry Potter's Bookshelf: The Great Books Behind the Hogwarts Adventures* (New York: Berkley Publishing Group, 2009).
24. Nancy R. Reagin, *Harry Potter and History* (Hoboken, New Jersey: John Wiley & Sons, 2011).
25. "Penguin Publisher's Website Book Description," *Harry Potter's Bookshelf*, Penguin.com, 2012, http://us.penguingroup.com/nf/Book/BookDisplay/0,,9780425229798,00.html?Harry_Potter%27s_Bookshelf_John_Granger.
26. John Granger, *Harry Potter's Bookshelf: The Great Books Behind the Hogwarts Adventures*, ebook (New York: Berkley Publishing Group, 2009), 6.
27. Nancy R. Reagin, *Harry Potter and History* (Hoboken, New Jersey: John Wiley & Sons, 2011), back cover.
28. Ibid.

29. Melissa Rohs and Pauline Oo, "Harry Potter Topic of New Course at St. Catherine University," *St. Kate's News*, February 22, 2010, http://minerva.stkate.edu/news_events.nsf/stories/harry_potter.
30. Ibid.
31. Ibid.
32. Danielle Tumminio, "About Danielle," *Danielle Tumminio*, 2011, http://danielletumminio.com/?page_id=2.
33. Danielle Tumminio, "Theology & Harry Potter," *Danielle* Tumminio, 2011, http://danielletumminio.com/?page_id=9.
34. Lee, "Pottermania Lives On in College Classrooms."
35. "Durham University Students Offered Harry Potter Course," *BBC News*, August 18, 2010, http://www.bbc.co.uk/news/uk-england-wear-11011279.
36. Ibid.
37. Chelsea Hermond, "New Course in American Studies to Focus on 'Harry Potter' Books and Movies," *The Emory Wheel*, October 27, 2011, http://www.emorywheel.com/detail.php?n=30318.
38. Ibid.
39. Ibid.
40. Keathley, "15 Fascinating College Courses."
41. Ibid.
42. "December 2007 Faculty Profile: Edmund Kern," *Lawrence University*, http://www.lawrence.edu/news/facprofiles/kern.shtml.
43. Ibid.
44. "Durham University Students Offered Harry Potter Course."
45. Poole, "Harry Potter Fans Create Makeshift College."
46. James W. Thomas, "Repotting Harry Potter: Popular Lit Made Legit," *Hog's Head Conversations: Essays on Harry Potter* ed. Travis Prinzi (Allentown, PA: Zossima Press, 2009).

Scribere Paedegogia: The Magical Art of Teaching Composition

CYNTHIA K. O'MALLEY

Harry Potter is amazing not only because he is a boy magician, savior of the wizarding world, and the spitting image of his father (except for his eyes), but also because he is an icon in both his world and ours. When J.K. Rowling started writing Harry's story, she opened a doorway that revealed the magical world to those who had only dreamed of it. The series lends itself easily to many types of education, but it is well-suited to freshman composition courses for several reasons, both mechanical and literary. The *Harry Potter* books are well-written in a manner that appeals to adults while still being accessible to a ten-year-old's reading level. The grammar and punctuation are accurate, the sentence structure sound, and the flow of ideas smooth. These are excellent examples to show writing students. There are also many academic works about the series, providing well written and thought-provoking essays for the students to further explore critical thinking and composition development with their favorite Hogwarts student.

Literarily, *Harry Potter* is a virtual gold mine for any teacher hoping to inspire her students toward personal development and moral betterment. Harry is "a terrific role model, if somewhat imperfect, just like the kids who are devouring the books."[1] Harry, Ron, and Hermione are three close friends who follow their hearts and do what they know to be morally right despite the repercussions of their choices. These may include getting in trouble, being teased, or even putting themselves in danger. When dealing with a classroom full of freshmen who are just finding out who they really are away from their families and delving into their own inner selves, what better examples could we have than Harry or Ron, who are strong young men who show respect to others, and Hermione, a determined young woman who stands up for and can take care of herself? *The New York Times Book Review* says "the characters are impressively three-dimensional ... and move along seamlessly through the narrative," which are important things for students to notice and understand.[2] Well-rounded characters may not seem important in teaching composition, but the standard Freshman Composition class offers the chance to teach much more than pre-determined, formulaic essays. Harry, his friends, his enemies, and his journey fit nicely to aid the instructor in taking advantage of those opportunities.

Using *Harry Potter* in these classes provides an accessible text and allows students to explore their own capabilities in the development of both their writing and their lives. In my experience, most students are amused when they first learn we'll be reading *The Sorcerer's Stone*. Those who have never had an interest in reading it are then resigned to the fact, while others are excited to be returning to an old favorite. The majority of students seem engaged in the story and the resulting class discussions, and most of them share their inner thoughts about the issues that arise in the book.

Harry's influence around the world is unquestionable. His influence in the writing classroom should be as well. *Harry Potter* also shows how the things learned in the classroom can affect students outside of class. The Hogwarts students apply their knowledge to their interactions with others and the battles they face in the real world just as our students can use their writing skills in other classes, daily lives, and future careers. Simply put: The benefits of *Harry Potter* in Developmental Writing and Freshman Composition are magical, and though the students aren't at Hogwarts, they easily learn along with Harry.

I was a *Harry Potter* fan before I was a scholar or a teacher, reading the books and the fan fiction, going to the movies, and talking to other fans long before I was assigning *Harry Potter and the Sorcerer's Stone* to my Developmental Writing and Freshman Composition students. I later realized that's what allowed me to see what value the Potter books could have in my classrooms. Finding a new method to teach an old subject is a challenge faced by every teacher from preschool to post-graduate. We want our students to be engaged in the work, to see and understand the relevance of each lesson, and ultimately, to learn more than we are actually teaching.

I began to realize my favorite books, TV series, songs, and movies have helped me reach a deeper understanding of the literature I studied in graduate school and even taught me life lessons. In retrospect, I can see that television and stories from so many types of media have helped me earlier in school as well. Those characters I came to know were able to give me a new insight or understanding of history, science, social interactions, and more. *Harry Potter* has the impressive ability to be applied to a wide variety of life and academic lessons from many fields in nearly any manner and at any age. For these reasons, and simply because I enjoy the topic, I developed a lesson plan to teach Developmental Writing with *Harry Potter* to my first class of college freshmen.

Throughout the first book, we see Harry leaving behind the only family he has ever known and entering a new world that is completely alien to him. As he adjusts to his new environment, he learns things about himself, which opens the pathway to self-discovery. This coincides nicely with the typical experience of a new college student who has just left home and entered the world of higher education, meeting new people and attending new classes that can make even the most confident students feel inadequate. Even for non-traditional students, Harry's experiences strike a chord of familiarity. College life is new and different for both the eighteen-year-olds fresh out of high school and the older students seeking a fresh start after caring for family or spending years in the workforce.

The parallels between Harry's first year at Hogwarts and the students' first year in college offer something for them to draw upon in their writing exercises, making it more personal. By connecting with the character on this level, the students can easily respond to the "Why did you do that?" question as Steven Lynn suggests in *Texts and Contexts*. This question is the purpose of psychological criticism and brings "to consciousness the hidden fears and desires that disturb and control our lives."[3] Giving our students the tools to address those hidden fears and desires can affect both the content of their writing and the way they deal with the world around them. This is just one more way they can learn from Harry. Despite his youth in the first novel, "Harry's resolution in the face of adversity is the result of conscious choice and attention to what is and is not within his control.... Harry worries about who he *is*, but realizes that what he *does* matters most."[4] Most freshmen, especially those fresh from high school, are still learning how to prioritize their lives and how to determine which events they truly can and cannot control. Assignments can be designed to encourage those thought processes and develop important thinking, coping, and critical analysis skills that will help them throughout college and into the workforce.

The assignments I used are fairly simple, but I tried to keep them varied enough to allow everyone to access the material and the writing from a range of approaches. While the difficulty level of assignments may need changing, the variety is appropriate to any undergraduate class because it allows different types of learners more opportunity to see something of themselves in the book and their own writings.

Over the years (and as the rest of the *Harry Potter* series was released), I have come up with more assignment ideas than I could possibly use in one semester, many of which I share below. I invite interested teachers to pick and choose from these as appropriate for their classes, their teaching style, and their lesson plans. Much of my lesson plan has a focus on diversity and tolerance because I feel very strongly that acceptance can benefit everyone. I encourage students to explore what diversity really means and how there is more to it than race. The entire *Harry Potter* series demonstrates prejudice of varying sorts, and the wizarding world's challenges can easily be seen as a metaphor for things in our "Muggle" history. They echo the Nazis, Civil Rights, Suffrage, class differences (especially as highlighted by the Occupy movement), racial profiling, LGBT Rights, and more, allowing for broad discussions that span historical topics and current events. Even in just the first book, these prevalent themes are presented in a way that even a tween can comprehend. The college freshman can therefore relate and understand it while also learning to engage higher cognitive skills and thought processes.

Just as the Dursleys made snap judgments about wizards, most people make snap judgments about things they don't understand. The remedy (which sadly, the Dursleys never attempt) is to recognize that this is happening and make an attempt to learn the truth. Through exposure, education, and discussion, students develop a deeper understanding about the world around them, which leads to a stronger sense of self-awareness. Critical analysis of the book, other writings, or other people is useful and will be required of them in other courses, but the ability to critically analyze oneself is key to fighting mindless prejudice as well as an important aspect of personal growth. I also bring up every type of diversity I can think of, both in the real world and in *The Sorcerer's Stone*. Discussion on the stereotypes assigned to the houses, or the presumptions about Muggleborns, the stigma of squibs, even the class differences between the Malfoys and Weasleys has always proven interesting. There's a certain pleasure in watching students make the connections between those prejudices in Harry's world and the similar ones in our own.

I often set aside an entire day for guest speakers who represent different races, nationalities, religions, educational backgrounds, eating preferences, sexual orientations, family structures, career paths, and more. I create a list of labels and ask the students to guess which speaker fits which label(s). The students are surprised when they guess wrong, and their feedback on that class regularly mentions learning things they didn't know and challenging their preconceptions. Just as there are diverse cultures in *Harry Potter* (Muggles and Wizards) which reflect race and ethnicity in our world, there are status differences (the wealthy families like the Malfoys versus the poorer families like the Weasleys) and even the diverse collection of beings in Harry's world. Afterward, I ask the students to consider how many labels they can apply to themselves, which creates a new way of thinking and encourages development of self-reflection and assessment skills. The goal with this assignment should be to explore varied views on multiple topics. This is not to suggest that these labels or the people to whom they apply are "right" or "wrong." As Freire says in *Pedagogy of the Oppressed*, "It is not our role to speak to the people about our own view of the world ... but rather to dialogue with the people about their view and ours."[5] Diversity is out there, and learning to recognize it and understand it through dialogue is the first step to stopping or preventing prejudice.

Most students easily recognize some of the bigotry and prejudice seen in *Harry Potter*, but sometimes they have difficulty recognizing both sides of it, and seeing the reflections in their own lives. So many people seem to forget that prejudice goes in every direction, but *Sorcerer's Stone* shows that early on. The Dursleys' feelings about anything outside of the norm are made quite clear from the first paragraph. They are "proud to say that they were perfectly normal, thank you very much. They were the last people you'd expect to be involved in anything strange or mysterious, because they just didn't hold with such nonsense" (*SS* 1). Their judgments, closed-mindedness, and determined beliefs that their way is the only right way lead them to cruel behavior that would easily be classified as child abuse if the authorities knew. The psychological damage Harry suffers during his childhood with the Dursleys will likely stay with him just as long as the trauma of fighting a war at such a young age would. On the flip side, Harry has barely entered the wizarding world when both he and the reader are introduced to the wizard-supremacist way of thinking with Draco's comments about "the other sort" and keeping magic only in the "old wizarding families" (*SS* 78). To encourage broader thinking, I created assignments that require the students to consider both literary and real-life stereotypes and prejudices. Slytherins are evil; African-Americans are criminals; Hufflepuffs are scared; blondes are stupid; Muggles are not as evolved as wizards; gays are wrong and shouldn't marry; wizards are freaks; Republicans are rich jerks — some of these are broad-sweeping hatred against a specific group of people based solely on one defining aspect, while others are unfair generalizations of the group based on the actions of a few. Students consider these and more throughout the following assignments.

Journaling Assignments

I use journal entries to provide the students with frequent but small and low-risk writing assignments that continue throughout the semester to allow for ample writing practice. My policy is to mark these on a complete/incomplete basis without evaluating them on format, grammar, sentence structure, etc. These exercises are more helpful to the students if they are allowed the knowledge that the content is most important. This releases them from the pressure of being "right" and allows them to simply put words on the page. While I have them do most of their entries in response to the sections they've read or whatever might be on their minds at the time, I do use some specific assignments to prod them into thinking in different ways.

- A Whole New World — This is an excellent journal assignment for the beginning of the semester, especially with a Fall semester Freshman Composition class for which most of the students are fresh out of high school. I have the students write a narrative of their first day/weekend/week at school focusing specifically on the new experiences and anything that was unexpected or seemed unusual to them. Some students will write something much like Harry's first experiences at Hogwarts, seeing similarity between their own dorm assignments and Harry's sorting ceremony, or marveling at the technology available to them if they didn't have much at their high school. Some students, whether because they took some time off between high school and college, or this isn't their first semester on campus, or they have parents or older siblings in college, or they live nearby and aren't staying in a dorm room, or they are not as easily phased as others, will see fewer new and different things, which I liken to the purebloods' experience when contrasted with Harry's, Hermione's, or any other Muggle-raised students at Hogwarts. A particularly fun part of this exercise is asking the students to go back and re-evaluate it after they've started the book and read about Harry's experiences. This, if teachers are lucky, is where the students will really start to identify with the book, and that's precisely what we're going for here.
- Bullying and Belittling — Draco Malfoy is introduced in chapter five and immediately presented as a snob. Harry is reminded of his horrid cousin Dudley and is happy to get away from the then-unnamed boy (*SS* 77–79). Chapter six finally brings about the actual introduction, along with Draco's statement that "some wizarding families are much better than others" and "you don't want to go making friends with the wrong sort" (*SS* 108). Draco's negativity continues throughout the series, and he plays heavily in the class sessions I spend on diversity and tolerance, but in these small journal entries, I like to mention his bullying ways. He threatens Harry on the train, tricks him into a duel to try and get him expelled, bullishly snatches items away from both Harry and Neville, and more. I ask the students to consider these behaviors and write about a time when they experienced this kind of heartless teasing and bullying. Even those who were the most popular and well-loved in high school can usually pinpoint a time or two when they were subject to cruel words, vague threats, and name-calling. It's my hope that bringing those

things to the students' attention will make them think about it the next time they feel like carelessly belittling someone else (which I think we're all guilty of from time to time).

- Mirror of Erised — One of my favorite journal assignments was to have students write one to two pages about their deepest desires. After reading the chapter on the Mirror of Erised, each student was to imagine what he or she would see in the mirror. I supply a series of questions to help the students delve deeper into these thoughts, asking them to describe their physical appearance in the mirror, how the reflection differs from the room they imagine themselves standing in, who else is in this reflection with them, what those people are doing, and more. This allows for a more personal connection to Harry and practice in writing descriptive narrative as they attempt to make the mental image clear to the reader. One former student wrote about a dream birthday trip to Paris, spelling "Paris" and "surprise" backwards to imitate "Erised," while others wrote more personal things like a visit with a late parent or the culmination of a major personal goal.

Technical Aspects of Writing

Clearly, the purpose of a college-level Freshman Composition course is to teach students how to write at an acceptable college level and how to use academic voice and proper attributions in their work. Developmental Writing must start a bit below that as it forms a bridge for students who have completed high school or earned a GED but are not yet ready for the beginning assignments of Freshman Composition. Regardless of the class level, I often include quick assignments to aid with their essay construction, grammar and punctuation, as well as non-essay writing skills.

- Grammar and Punctuation Quidditch — While officially taught in elementary school, grammar and punctuation skills are often still a problem for college writers. Though it is currently untested, I have included rules and instructions for a Quidditch game to engage the students in better learning to use standard grammar and punctuation (available in the Appendix).
- Fan Fiction Proofreading — Proofreading assignments can easily use any sample writing instead of a *Potter* related selection, but the students seem more engaged when the grammar and punctuation drills relate to their reading and previous discussions and journal writing. It seems to make the process less tedious when incorporated into the fun of the *Potter* world and can have a direct correlation to how much they get from the exercise. Fan fiction offers a way to combine the *Harry Potter* theme of the class with grammar lessons

and provides students with the opportunity to practice finding and fixing grammatical and punctuation errors without the usual practice of correcting their own work or the work of their peers. While there are some excellent fan fiction writers, much of the work is amateur and roughly done with little or no proofreading. The students' assignment is to carefully proofread a story and correct all grammar and punctuation problems they find. I assign this at the beginning of the semester, and instruct the class to correct it, but do not return it to them. This will allow me to determine which grammar problems require the most attention and review those grammar lessons as part of the editing process. At midterms or later, I assign them to proofread the same story again so I can judge their progress. Assigning a story to proofread that doesn't originate from the class relieves the worry of upsetting a classmate, and my students felt it was a nice break from reading each other's essays. The story I select can also trigger their imaginations, which helps to broaden thinking processes and serve to make their writing better. A quick online search for *Harry Potter* fan fiction will provide ample choices.

- Spotting Disorganized Thoughts — The workshop style of teaching writing requires students to peer review each other's papers, a task which is sometimes embarrassing or daunting for many of them. Unfortunately, it is also pointless if the students in question do not first know how to find the big problems in their peers' papers. To help them develop this skill, I find an amateur book review or essay about *Harry Potter* online and have the entire class read it. It should be one with poor organization, incomplete logic, and weak or inadequate support for the claims it makes (this likely won't take long to find—I just search a few blogs and *Harry Potter* forums, especially older ones from the late '90s or early '00s). Individually, in small groups, as a whole class, or ideally some combination of the three, the students then work to identify what is wrong with the essay and how they would fix it. I like to offer a well-written essay as well to provide an example of the preferred results. The possible discussions about why the argument falls flat or how the poor organizational structure causes problems are invaluable.

Full Essays

The primary goal of English 101 (or the equivalent expository composition class at any university) is to have the students write essays. In my experience, the expectation is four essays throughout the semester, averaging about 1,000 words each. I was also expected to do at least one in-class diagnostic essay at the beginning of the semester and I often repeat that for finals so I can see how far they've come. The smaller assignments, journal entries, and technical exercises aid in the overall quality of the students' writing, and many of them can easily turn into content for a full polished essay. I try to include something to open new thinking pathways in each assignment, though this can send students into a panic. They are comfortable with churning out the things they already know, but tend to be terrified of being asked to reveal and think about the things they don't know. This fear is necessary "if we are to lead students from knowing to thinking"[6] which will eventually circle back around to knowing new things and allowing them to further think about even more.

- Personal Narratives — A popular choice for these early writing classes, the personal narrative can both challenge the students and allow them to relate easier if they are asked to connect their narrative to the reading. The journaling assignment comparing their experiences coming to college with Harry's experience attending Hogwarts is an excellent example of this. Drawing it out into a full length essay requires them to really pay attention to their environment and what things are new to them. The students must question everything they encounter at school and whether or not it will fit into their essays. Throughout this process and the necessary reviewing of Harry's early experiences with Diagon Alley and Hogwarts, they begin to understand that everyone has those moments of fear and insecurity and learn how they can overcome them. Previous students have talked about relating to Harry's fear that he would suddenly be sent back home, or that he would do something horribly wrong and be ridiculed or ostracized.

- Internal Exploration — Harry spends hours watching himself in the Mirror of Erised, looking at the reflections of his silent and long-gone parents, grandparents and other family, and this shows the observant reader so much about Harry's desires. His final experience with the Mirror, when he finds the Sorcerer's Stone in his pocket, reveals Harry's inner character in a way that has yet to be revealed. Despite the fact he obviously still misses his parents, his deepest desire is to find that stone and protect the wizarding world from Voldemort (*SS* 291). When asked to write about their deepest desires, some students will skate by with something light-hearted like the previously mentioned birthday trip to Paris, but most will explore their future career goals, their desires for a happy marriage, or even, as in Harry's case, their longing for another conversation with a lost loved one. The process of taking that simple journal exercise and turning it into a full essay allows students to delve deeper into their own desires, often discovering things about themselves that they previously had not known. The personal development then comes with the writing development, allowing students to emerge with a deeper understanding of both their inner thoughts and the best ways to express those thoughts clearly.

- Cultural Exploration — The discussions and journal assignments that come from the prejudicial attitudes seen in *Harry Potter and the Sorcerer's Stone* as well as the class period with guest speakers lend themselves well to further exploration. Many students have never been asked to examine or define their own culture, and in fact "students whose ethnicity is unmarked in the United States — i.e., students who are white" often fail to see themselves as even having a culture.[7] Until Hagrid shows up on his birthday, Harry probably thinks of himself that way as well. He is suddenly plunged into a completely unfamiliar culture and is frequently seen feeling unsure of himself and out of place, despite the fact he is clearly a part of it. Acclimating himself to the wizarding culture allows Harry to also see that the Muggles, even middle-class white Muggles, have their own culture, too. For this essay option, I ask students to deeply consider their own lives and the cultures to which they belong and explore their origins, whether because of their heritage, their religion, the region in which they grew up, or a connection to any number of sub-cultures in our society. Then I ask students to select an unfamiliar culture to explore through ethnographic research (interviews, attendance of cultural events, and other studies of the cultural group). A compare and contrast essay will allow them to share their learned understanding of the new culture while delving deeper into their own and learning new things about themselves in the process, thereby planting the seeds for a growing cultural fluency. Such fluency will encourage them to see situations, problems, and people from multiple points of view, deepening their analytical thinking skills to serve them well in any discipline.

Conclusion

Over the years, I have enjoyed the *Potter* series in many ways: reading it myself; watching the movies; writing about it; studying it; sharing it with my daughter as she grew up with Harry; seeing the other, younger, children in my community develop a love for it; and teaching with it in my college writing classes. I have found that Harry and his friends are always changing, growing, and learning. Even in subsequent readings, I continually find new angles and new opportunities to learn from it and teach with it. The series presents "a philosophy that offers comfort to readers, both kids and adults, as they try to work their way through the instability and uncertainty of the world."[8] We are drawn to stories we can connect with, and people of all ages find something in *Harry Potter* that strikes a chord of familiarity, allowing those connections. My students have told me they find it easier to write about things they understand or things that make them care, and Harry allows for both. I was thrilled to see statements in their journals about the enjoyment of reading, which many of them had never before experienced.

The Hogwarts instructors have taught many young witches and wizards, but they also teach college students, graduate students, and for that matter, students of life itself. Ultimately, it was my love for *Harry Potter* that led me to that first assignment. I was seeking an opportunity to garner some validation for my pop culture interests; I believed it was an important and useful tool, and I was searching for a way to make use of that. The ultimate truth is that *Harry Potter* has not only proven beneficial in these writing classes, but also demonstrated the ability to allow students of all areas, levels and ages to develop perhaps the most important and magical skill: that of thinking for themselves.

Notes

1. Edmund M. Kern, *The Wisdom of Harry Potter: What Our Favorite Hero Teaches Us about Moral Choices* (New York: Prometheus Books, 2003), 18.
2. J.K. Rowling, *Harry Potter and the Sorcerer's Stone* (New York: Scholastic, 1997), i.
3. Steven Lynn, *Texts and Contexts: Writing About Literature with Critical Theory*, 3rd ed. (New York: Longman, 2001), 171.
4. Kern, *The Wisdom of Harry Potter,* 19.
5. Paulo Friere, *Pedagogy of the Oppressed* (New York: The Continuum Publishing Corporation, 1970), 85.
6. Kristin Dombek and Scott Herndon, *Critical Passages: Teaching the Transition to College Composition* (New York: Teachers College Press, 2004), 13.
7. Dombek and Herndon, *Critical Passages,* 90.
8. Kern, *The Wisdom of Harry Potter,* 20.

Getting Medieval in the Classroom

RENEÉ WARD

J. K. Rowling's *Harry Potter* series is one of the most significant literary works of the twentieth and twenty-first centuries. Widely read, debated, and viewed by children, adults, and scholars alike, it is a global cultural reference. Rowling's series also reflects the modern era's fascination with the Middle Ages. Like J. R. R. Tolkien's *Lord of the Rings* or C. S. Lewis's *The Chronicles of Narnia* (with which it is often compared), the *Harry Potter* series epitomizes modern medievalism in fantasy literature, the "impulse to rework or recreate a gesture towards the Middle Ages, sometimes in a careful and precise way but mostly making use of some standard images and motifs that evoke the medieval."[1] Indeed, the series consistently evokes the Middle Ages, from the architecture of Hogwarts and the space of the Forbidden Forest to the structure of the novels themselves, which draw heavily upon medieval romance patterns and motifs.

A number of critics, however, lambaste Rowling's medievalism as inaccurate or mediocre. Jack Zipes, for instance, argues that Rowling's description of the Dursley family's attitude towards magic as "very medieval" (*POA* 2–3) actually "misinterprets history."[2] People in the medieval period, he continues, believed in magic, while the Dursleys do not. Such careless use of sources, in Zipes's opinion, reveals mediocrity.[3] Similarly, Allesandra Petrina, while discussing references in the series to the European witch-hunts, suggests that Rowling's "handling of pointedly medieval material may appear lame."[4] Unlike Zipes, however, Petrina recognizes that Rowling "does not strive for historical accuracy," and she concludes that her reworking of medieval myths and legends contributes to the success of the series.[5]

Indeed, as Edmund M. Kern explains, the *Harry Potter* series is an historical fantasy[6]; it is not intended to be historically accurate. More importantly, the books adapt and interlace motifs, themes, or characters from medieval sources in order to explore contemporary concerns. Their medievalism has purpose. "Rowling," Kern writes, "takes up big issues rooted in the past and explores them in the present.... She takes elements of very old tales, which have never really gone away, and reshapes them for a present day audience that is eager (if only unconsciously) to encounter them in new and contemporary contexts."[7]

These "big issues"—which range from race, identity, and gender to faith, history, and social hegemonies—were of no less concern to medieval writers and audiences than they are to those of the modern period. Such issues appear in a range of medieval texts, from romances (Arthurian and non–Arthurian) to crusade accounts. Rowling develops her trio of protagonists directly in response to conflicts involving issues such as class, gender, and race. Harry, for instance, spends the first decade of his life impoverished, despite the relative comfort in which the Dursley family lives, and Harry, Ron, and Hermione are all, at some point, discriminated against, either for personal conditions or traits, or for befriending and aiding disadvantaged groups. From a pedagogical perspective, then, *Harry Potter* provides an entry point for teaching themes important in Western culture. Additionally, Rowling's medievalism is a useful tool for introducing students to the Middle Ages, as well as for challenging them to explore issues relevant to both the medieval period and the twenty-first century.

The discussions below highlight a number of key topics that relate easily to medieval and modern contexts, that easily overlap with each other, and that provide opportunity for creative and traditional approaches. They are by no means exhaustive, and can easily be combined with other topics or pedagogies. Many of the discussions have been previously employed in a university setting, but they could easily be adapted for other environments, and upper year or advanced students should be expected to engage more thoroughly with secondary readings or theoretical texts. The Appendix includes a list of useful resources for each topic.

Manuscripts and Books

Manuscripts and books were a significant part of medieval culture, initially within centers of learning such as monasteries and universities, and, later, within wealthy household libraries. Today, illuminated manuscripts are the most easily recognized medieval artifacts. The mention of the word "manuscript" often brings to mind images such as the *Lindisfarne Gospels* or the *Book of Kells*. These manuscripts demonstrate the complexity and artistry of manuscript production, a lengthy and costly process, especially if folios contained illuminations. Frequently, compilers would collect and bind a variety of manuscript folios, sometimes grouping together apparently unrelated items (into collections now identified as miscellanies) or items with related content, often by genre — religious texts, for instance — or by topic — monstrous beings, for instance — (the *Beowulf* manuscript, for example, has contents collected together because of a concern for monstrous races or beings. For a discussion of this aspect of the collection and the tales within, see Andy Orchard, *Pride and Prodigies: Studies in the Monsters of the Beowulf Manuscript*). These bound collections — folios organized, trimmed, and sewn into coverboards of various materials — constitute some of the earliest books in Western culture.

Rowling repeatedly emphasizes the importance of books and learning in the series, especially through Hermione and her reputation as the brightest witch of her age, which arises from her voracious appetite for knowledge and her willingness to research and read regularly. (Andrew Blake suggests that "Harry becomes a willing reader as soon as he is introduced into a world in which books and reading are important" in *The Irresistible Rise of Harry Potter*, page 31.) However, while Harry does read, it is often out of necessity. Hermione is the character with the voracious appetite for knowledge and reading. Harry and Ron read when forced to do so for school assignments or to find an answer to their latest mystery, but this is also usually at Hermione's insistence). Rowling also highlights books and manuscripts as important cultural objects. The Hogwarts Library keeps its collection of older, advanced magic, and dark magic volumes under heavy surveillance in its Restricted section; students use parchments and quills — which is highly evocative of medieval practice — to take notes in class and to complete written assignments; and books themselves become formidable characters, such as Edwardus Lima's *The Monster Book of Monsters*, which Hagrid assigns for his Care of Magical Creatures class.

Students can explore the use of manuscripts and books in *Harry Potter* alongside a study of medieval production techniques. A range of smaller projects are possible, such as the making of quill pens and ink, or the learning of calligraphy and the related field of palaeography, with an emphasis on different medieval hands. These smaller projects can expand into larger individual or collaborative projects that emphasize codicology. For instance, students can make their own manuscript pages or bound books; they can experiment with vellum, with set-up techniques such as pricking, or with illumination, including the application of gold leaf. (Such assignments can be costly, although the cost will be high only if one employs more authentic ingredients and materials, such as vellum and gold leaf). This type of assignment easily extends to other art forms such as painting and tapestry. Hogwarts is replete with both, and tapestries appear elsewhere, such as in the Black family house, which serves briefly as headquarters for the Order of the Phoenix. Students can study and experiment with materials and techniques in order to emulate the original style and practices of medieval art forms. They can also explore medieval art and hands (whether in paintings or illuminated manuscripts) through a blended media project. They can adapt a section of the series — or, indeed, of a related medieval text — into graphic novel form. This medium lends itself well to experimentation, in image and text, and students can emulate medieval forms in their own creations. Whenever possible, students should research and experiment with authentic techniques and materials.

Bestiaries

The medieval bestiary — a book or manuscript that presents images of birds, animals, or other creatures (actual or imagined) along with interpretive and moralizing narratives — was a highly popular vernacular genre in the late Middle Ages. Many of the narratives and images within medieval bestiaries derive from the Latin prose *Physiologus*, "a Greek work believed to have been composed in Alexandria as early as the second century."[8] Medieval monastic communities preserved copies of the *Physiologus* because they were useful educational tools: animals functioned as "human exemplars" for the members of the religious order or for the church community at large.[9] In the twelfth century, earlier versions of the *Physiologus* were expanded through the inclusion of new chapters on various birds and animals, as well as through the integration of material from Isidore of Seville's *Etymologies*. These expanded versions (which became known specifically as bestiaries) had a greater popularity than their predecessors, and versions began to appear outside of the monastic realm in vernacular languages, especially in French and English.

Rowling draws heavily upon the bestiary tradition and demonstrates a keen interest in the related fields of mythology and folklore. The series overflows with mythical and magical beings, whether in the form of scholarly enterprise — the students study hinkypunks and Cornish pixies, for example, in Defense Against the Dark Arts — or in the form of secondary characters who befriend and aid Harry and his companions — such as the centaur Firenze or the werewolf Remus Lupin. Moreover, Rowling emulates the bestiary genre in her short companion text *Fantastic Beasts and Where to Find Them*. *Fantastic Beasts*, written under the pseudonym Newt Scamander and designed to look like one of Harry's school books, includes an introduction which unpacks the history of the wizarding world's difficulty in dealing with non-human races. Specifically, it addresses whether a species should be classified as "Beast" or "Being," the latter category being the only one which grants "legal rights and a voice in the governance of the magical world."[10]

Students can thus examine the plethora of magical and mythical beings within the series and within *Fantastic Beasts* in relation to the medieval bestiary. They can compare Beasts and Beings within the series and *Fantastic Beasts* to renowned bestiaries such as the mid-twelfth century Bodleian *Bestiary* (MS Bodley 764) or the *Aberdeen Bestiary* (Aberdeen MS 24). Students can also compile a bestiary of Rowling's magical and mythical beings, one modeled upon the medieval genre. Further, a focus on non-human beings within the series presents an opportunity to study medieval cartography. Medieval maps — which typically depict Jerusalem as the center of the known world — are peopled by monstrous beings and races, many of which appear in a literally marginalized environment: on the edges or circumference of the world. Students can examine medieval maps (the Hereford *Mappa Mundi* is the pinnacle example) and map-making techniques in order to create their own cartographic representation of the wizarding world. Students can design a map which represents Harry's world, with Hogwarts Castle as the central point from which all else radiates. The map should similarly include key spaces and places within the magical realm, as well as non-human species. These projects easily overlap with the manuscripts topics in the study of the manuscripts and maps and, should students choose, in the methods and materials employed in their own creations.

Language and Names

Mythical and monstrous beings such as those found in bestiaries and maps also demonstrate Rowling's medievalism from a linguistic perspective. As John Block Friedman notes, "Antique and medieval writers sought the meanings of objects in the etymologies of their names, for they believed that the name of a thing, far from being arbitrary, was the key to its nature."[11] In his *History of Animals*, for instance, Aristotle goes to great lengths to categorize and stratify all living beings, whether plant, animal, or human. (In Aristotle's system, plant life occupies the lowest place and human life occupies the highest place in the hierarchy. See books 7–10, *The History of Animals*.) In a different work, he argues that each item's essence has a teleological purpose, whether intrinsic or extrinsic. (See Aristotle's discussion on the axe for an example of this theory, in 2.1.412b of *On the Soul*.) Certain types of things have certain types of souls specific to both their bodies and to their purpose of being. Medieval thinkers such as Isidore of Seville similarly believed in the relationship between the thing named and the thing itself. In Book 12 of his *Etymologies*, Isidore explores the etymology of the Latin word "lupus" and explains that the cognate Greek word, "λύκος," evokes the wolf's desire to slaughter "whatever it finds in a frenzy of violence."[12] For Isidore, the wolf is a bloodthirsty creature precisely because its name marks it as "a violent beast, eager for gore."[13]

Many characters within *Harry Potter* have names that imply something about their natures, whether physical features or personality traits. Rowling draws heavily upon words which have Celtic, Germanic, or Latin origins, and plays upon their etymologies. She admits that she has a penchant for names, and that many of the names in her series have specific meanings. In an interview with Larry King in 2000, Rowling confessed: "I am a bit of a name freak. A lot of the names that I didn't invent come from maps. Snape is a place name in Britain. Dumbledore means — dumbledore is an old English dialect word for bumblebee, because he is a musical person. And I imagine him humming to himself all the time."[14] Rowling's choice of a name for her headmaster, and the behavior with which she identifies him suggests that, within her series, names imply an already extant meaning (or meanings) firmly associated with the individual named. For instance, as Eliza T. Dresang suggests in her essay, "Hermione Granger and the Heritage of Gender," found in *The Ivory Tower and Harry Potter*, Rowling's Hermione is a multi-faceted character whose name draws upon existing meanings from contexts in Greek myth, a famous Shakespearean play, and novels by two twentieth-century writers. Rowling's use of the name evokes all previous uses and contexts in myths and/or narratives by other writers. Dresang identifies several significant Hermiones: the daughter of Helen and Menelaeus from Greek mythology, Shakespeare's character in *The Winter's Tale*, the title character from H. D.'s *HERmione*, and one of D. H. Lawrence's characters in *Women in Love*.

Students can explore Rowling's use of language in a variety of ways. They can examine the relationship between etymologies and the objects or people that they signify, and can contrast them to medieval accounts in ethnographic texts. They can also explore associations with significant people and events in England's past, such as those evoked by the Percy family name. This name, which Rowling uses for a member of the Weasley family, evokes Henry "Hotspur" Percy (made famous by Shakespeare in *1 Henry IV*) and a period of civil unrest and political turmoil in English history not unlike the strife caused by Voldemort and his followers in the wizarding world. Additionally, students interested in classical languages can examine Rowling's use of Latin, especially in magical spells. Advanced students can read and translate the Latin edition of *Philosopher's Stone* (*Harrius Potter et Philosophi Lapis*), which presents something of a conundrum for language scholars. The translation of the volume into Latin resulted in the creation of a large number of new words in the language precisely because much of Rowling's vocabulary lacks equivalent words in the classical language.

Architecture

The monastic revival (c. 1000) launched by Cluny, in south-eastern France, triggered a parallel boom in medieval architecture, and many extant structures in western Europe demonstrate striking features of Romanesque architecture — such as round arches, pillars, stone barrel and groin vaults, sculpted lintels and tympanums — and Gothic architecture — such as pointed arches, ribbed pillars, flying buttresses, and stained glass. Britain's Norman period gave rise to magnificent stone structures — such as castles, churches, and, later, cathedrals — although, due to repeated expansion and repair, many instances exhibit more than one architectural style.

While these architectural developments resonate within the novels through descriptions of Hogwarts Castle, the film franchise brings them to life through its selection of set locations. The eight films include scenes shot at a variety of well-known English sites. For instance, the fourteenth-century Gloucester Cathedral Cloisters features in the first film, while the Great Hall at Christ Church College, Oxford, serves as the model for the dining hall at Hogwarts. Other locations used for filming include the thirteenth-century Lacock Abbey, Alnwick Castle in Northumberland, and Durham Cathedral. Students can research medieval Romanesque and Gothic architectural features and their influence on the structures described in the books and evident in the sites used for the films. They should explore the architectural features themselves, as well as the social and cultural forces which led to such innovations, particularly in the Gothic period. If proximity and funds permit, fieldtrips to specific locations such as the Gloucester Cloisters or Durham Cathedral are advised. The newly-opened Warner Bros. Studio Tour presents another possible fieldtrip opportunity, especially as it includes access to sets such as the Hogwarts dining hall and a 1:24 scale model of Hogwarts Castle. Scholars not within proximity to such sites can take advantage of any local examples of Romanesque and Gothic architecture (whether medieval or from a later period).

Sites with specific links to the film franchise also provide an opportunity for students to explore the histories associated with the architecture and how

Rowling thus evokes the past through names and places. Many of the film sites have links to significant people or events in England's medieval past. Gloucester Cathedral has links to William the Conqueror and the creation of the Domesday Book, and is also the burial site of Edward II. Alnwick Castle has more intrinsic connections to the series: it is and has been owned, for the past seven hundred years, by the Percy family, and thus overlaps with Rowling's use of names.

Medicine and Magic

Medieval manuscripts often include recipes for medical treatments such as liniments and poultices. Recent scholarship suggests that such medical recipes have strong connections to female authors and readers despite the fact that women represent "only a very small proportion of the total number of practitioners whose names are recorded." Siraisi points out that while rare examples of famous female healers exist — such as Trotula of Salerno or Hildegard of Bingen — female participation in the healing profession was increasingly limited in the Middle Ages, especially after the university system established professional schools, from which women were excluded.[15] James Weldon, for instance, argues that the fifteenth-century anthology, *Biblioteca Nazionale*, Naples, MS XIII.B.29., which includes a range of texts, from medical prescriptions to a version of Chaucer's "The Clerk's Tale," was compiled for a secular female audience. He identifies the nature of the recipes — which include treatments for common colds, poor complexion, and healthy pregnancy and childbirth — as of particular interest to women.[16]

Medieval manuscripts also often include or are comprised entirely of alchemical recipes. As Peggy A. Knapp explains: "Alchemical treatises share a few basic ideas: that alchemy speeds up the process already at work in Nature, that gold represents the perfect balance between the elements of earth, water, air, and fire toward which Nature is heading, and that alchemy could hurry the lower metals toward gold through 'projections' involving mercury, sulfur, and furnaces."[17]

The study of alchemy became increasingly popular in the late medieval and early modern periods, and numerous alchemists earned fame through their writings and experiments (purported or real), including Michael Scot (c. 1175–1234), Elias of Cortona (d. 1253), Albertus Magnus (Albert the Great; 1200–1280), Nicolas Flamel (1330–1418), and John Dee (1527–1608). A number of medieval and early modern authors likewise included references to alchemy in their texts, including Chaucer, whose "Canon's Yeoman's Tale" (in the *Canterbury Tales*) concerns alchemy, and Ben Johnson, whose comedy

The Alchemist explores the practice of alchemy and, among other things, the legend of the philosopher's stone.

As readers discover, while magic abounds in the wizarding world, medicine (albeit the magical kind) remains a necessary field. Harry, Ron, and Hermione all experience the ministrations of Madam Pomfrey while at Hogwarts. The treatments they receive vary, from simple chocolate to Skele-Grow, but are usually administered by a trained professional. Hogwarts is not the only institution in which health care occurs. Harry and his companions visit St. Mungo's Hospital for Magical Maladies and Injuries, and there discover that even the best magical care is unable to reverse or remedy some conditions. While visiting Arthur Weasley at St. Mungo's, Harry learns of the permanent mental incapacitation of the Aurors Alice and Frank Longbottom, both of whom were tortured with the Cruciatus Curse, and of Gilderoy Lockheart, on whom a memory charm backfired. While the presence of an infirmary at Hogwarts and a full-scale wizard hospital in London parallels health care systems in the modern world, many of the materials employed by witches and wizards, especially in the healing arts, evoke medieval practices and beliefs. The mandrake plant (or mandragora), about which Hogwarts' students learn in Professor Sprout's Herbology class, and which is an ingredient in a potion used to heal those petrified by a basilisk, appears in several late medieval manuscripts. While the manuscripts identify mandrake as a useful garden plant with medicinal properties, they also draw attention to its shape, which evokes the human form, and the associated belief in its deadly shrieks and groans. The *Oxford English Dictionary* identifies mandrake, "Mandragora officinarum (family Soanaceae)" as "a poisonous and narcotic Mediterranean plant ... with a very short stem and solitary purple or whitish flowers. It was formerly credited with magical and medicinal properties." It also identifies a number of medieval sources which reference mandrake, including British Library, Harley MS 2253 (*The Harley Lyrics*, c. 1325), and British Library MS Add. 33996 (*Medical Recipes*, c. 1450). Likewise, two of the known ingredients for Polyjuice Potion—fluxweed and knotgrass—appear in late medieval and early modern books concerned with herbology and health. The *OED* identifies knotgrass (Polygonum aviculare) as "a common weed in waste ground" which could be used to make an infusion "formerly supposed to stunt the growth," and flux-weed (Sisymbrium sophia) as "a supposed remedy for the flux or dysentery." References to knotgrass appear in texts such as William Turner's *Libellus de Re Herbaria Novus* (1538), while references to flux-weed appear in others, such as Henry Lyte's *A Nieuwe Herball* (1578), an English translation of an earlier Flemish herbal.

Rowling draws heavily upon lore related to healing practices from medieval and early modern sources such as herbals, recipe collections, and gardening books. Kern identifies, among many examples, "the seventeenth-century guide to medicinal plants," *Culpeper's Complete Herbal*—a post-medieval source derived from medieval lore and texts concerning health and healing—as one of Rowling's sources for the names of "magical plants [and] ingredients."[18] Students can use *Culpeper's Complete Herbal* as a starting point for research on the correlations between health care within the wizarding world and medieval culture, with an emphasis on plant-based ingredients such as mandrake, fluxweed, or knotgrass. They can also experiment with some of the medical recipes found within late medieval or early modern sources and contrast the results to modern plant-based pharmaceuticals. Additionally, students can examine Rowling's use of medieval alchemical lore. Most obviously, the title and focus of her first book explicitly connects Harry Potter to the medieval alchemist Nicolas Flamel and to the legend of the philosopher's stone, which is believed to provide everlasting life and relief from all illnesses. Students can readily explore these connections, or they can extend their study to other manuscripts, some of which provide an opportunity to work with classical languages. Students can examine, for instance, a range of the extant alchemical treatises, from the Latin *Ars alchemie*, "one of the most ancient Latin alchemical texts that is not translated directly from Arabic,"[19] to later English texts such as George Ripley's *Compend of Alchemy* (1470–71) and Thomas Norton's *Ordinal of Alchemy* (1477). They may also wish to contrast Rowling's use of alchemy to that of medieval and early modern writers such as Chaucer and Johnson, or experiment with and record the results of some of the processes or recipes outlined in the manuscripts.

Disease: Regulated Bodies

The topic of disease lets students explore medieval social structures through a *Harry Potter* lens. Specifically, the series demonstrates the regulation—even oppression and extermination—of bodies differentiated or marked by disease or other anomalies. Medieval perceptions of and responses to leprosy and the plague provide useful models for comparative analyses of the social regulation of bodies within the wizarding world. Medieval society regulated diseased bodies through a system of separation and segregation: it labeled and exiled those afflicted with disease. Michel Foucault notes on page 198 of *Discipline and Punish: The Birth of the Prison* that in the medieval period, the leper "was caught up in the practice of rejection, of exile-enclosure; he was left to his doom in a mass among which it was useless to differentiate." He also identifies systems of segregation as "ways of exercising power over men, of controlling their relations, of separating out their dangerous mixtures." As Michel Foucault explains, in order to control the threat that lepers presented, communities exiled individuals suffering from leprosy into enclosed environments. Within these environments, individual identity was lost; one was known only as a part of the larger colony, as part of the larger diseased body. Foucault also notes that plague-stricken towns underwent a similar process of "strict spatial portioning: the closing of the town and its outlying districts, a prohibition to leave the town on pain of death, the killing of all stray animals; the division of the town into district quarters, each governed by an intendant."[20] The plague-stricken town was, he observes, "a segmented, immobile, frozen space," and movement from one's given place, particularly during times of plague, was to risk one's "life, contagion or punishment."[21]

In the novels, wizarding society's hierarchies, whether under the Ministry or Voldemort, evoke Foucault's discussion of separation and segregation through their compartmentalization of society's inhabitants and their behaviors. As mentioned in the section on bestiaries, all species in the wizarding world receive categorization as either "Beast" or "Being"; further, many species (beasts and beings alike) are classified, registered, monitored, controlled, and, in some cases, exterminated. Students can research medieval responses and approaches to disease in relation to the treatment of unusual or non-normative bodies within the wizarding world, with an eye to the class structures inherent in such regulation. The regulatory systems of the Ministry of Magic are, essentially, systems of power and control that contribute to the wizarding world's construction and stratification of identity. The treatment of werewolves, for instance, parallels the medieval regulation and containment of lepers. Despite the intelligence of the werewolf's human form, the potential threat of his lupine form prevents him from being categorized as a Being. Instead, he is aligned with magical creatures such as Acromantulas and Manticores, creatures that are "highly intelligent" but are "classified as 'beasts' because they are incapable of overcoming their own brutal natures" (*FB* xiii). Consequently, werewolves are shunned from mainstream society, forced into an impoverished, marginalized existence.

Such studies can also easily extend to the regulation of witches and wizards themselves. For instance, the Ministry closely monitors transfiguration, and all Animagi must register with the Ministry. The strict regulation of such activities, like the regulation of disease, relates to medieval culture. In particular, the medieval identification and regulation of ethnic groups such as the Jews—who were confined to specific urban locations, forced to identify visually, and prohibited from participating in many trades—resonates with the Ministry's identification and regulation of all species within the magical community.

Feasts and Food

Feasts feature prominently in medieval culture, often as markers for the secular and sacred calendars. They accompanied specific celebratory events, from coronations to saints' days. Feasts are also prevalent in medieval literature, especially in the romance genre, and, in many medieval texts, the celebratory nature of food accompanies games or entertainments. For instance, in the fourteenth-century Middle English romance *Sir Gawain and the Green Knight*, King Arthur refuses to begin his New Year's feast until he has seen or heard of some marvelous adventure. Similarly, in the *Gest of Robyn Hode*, a late-medieval ballad, Robin refuses to dine until he has been entertained by a marvel or is joined by a distinguished guest.

Rowling highlights feasts and food from the outset. Although students and teachers at Hogwarts partake of modern fare, the number and types of culinary celebrations in the series evoke medieval practices, from the setting of the dining hall to the socially ordered and hierarchical seating arrangements. Students enjoy feasts on various occasions, such as on Halloween and Christmas, and during the Tri-Wizard Tournament; they also sit in a socially divided and hierarchal pattern, at tables with the rest of their house members, while Dumbledore and the other teachers sit at the head table. Individuals with a penchant for culinary delights can examine feasts and food within Rowling's novels in relation to their counterparts in medieval culture and literature. Students can research the occasions for and functions of feasts, the social implications of seating within the hall, and the common types of foods consumed daily or at such elaborate events. Additionally, students can experiment with medieval recipes for culinary items as basic as bread and butter or as elaborate as a full meal with roasted hare. This topic overlaps with manuscripts and books, as many medieval miscellanies include recipes. Students can examine the production, use, and readership of manuscripts in which recipes appear, and can contrast them to modern production and use of recipe books.

The economic and social aspects of food also provide opportunities for research-based projects on medieval culture. Literary depictions of feasts do not always correspond to actual practice or to the realities which the working class faced, including famine, harsh working conditions, and heavy tithes on food production. Explorations of food in relation to class, then, provide students with insight into the medieval feudal system — its ideology, practice, effectiveness, and decline — and resonate greatly with Rowling's concern for issues linked to class in *Harry Potter*. In the opening chapters of the first book, for instance, she contrasts Harry's lack of food and his underprivileged position within the Dursley household to Dudley's excessive appetite and consumption (of all things, not just food). She reinforces associations between food and class on the Hogwarts Express, when Harry meets Ron. Harry, who delightfully plunders the food trolley with his new-found wealth, immediately shares it all with Ron, who cannot afford such treats and faces, instead, a grim, economic lunch of homemade (and much disliked) corned beef sandwiches. At Hogwarts, though, all students have access to substantial nourishment, so much so that food appears to be a social equalizer. Yet, as readers discover, this is not the case. The subplot concerning House Elves and their position within the magical world as a type of enslaved peasant class becomes a major concern for Rowling's protagonists, especially for Hermione, and for Harry, who befriends and frees Dobby, the house-elf enslaved and mistreated by the Malfoy family.

Medieval Romance

Medieval romance — ubiquitous in the high and late Middle Ages — is a diverse and complex literary genre. Nonetheless, most romances employ a narrative structure (departure-adventure-return, or separation-initiation-return) based upon a quest motif which ultimately transforms the protagonist of a story into a hero, or, in rare instances, a heroine. On page 30, Joseph Campbell identifies this ritualized sequence as "The standard path of the mythological adventure of the hero." In this pattern, which he calls the monomyth, "[a] hero ventures forth from the world of common day into a region of supernatural wonder: fabulous forces are there encountered and a decisive victory is won: the hero comes back from this mysterious adventure with the power to bestow boons on his fellow man." Many romances employ similar motifs, although not always in the same manner. Some of the most prominent motifs in medieval romance include feasts/food and mythical/magical beings, both of which are discussed above, and forests and tournaments.

In medieval romance, the forest represents the wilderness or uncivilized space. Inhabited by social outcasts, nature's beasts, and supernatural beings, it is a liminal space, one that elides and calls into question the boundaries between the human, civilized world, the untamed wilderness, and the other world or the supernatural realm. The forest also serves as a testing ground for knights; while in the forest they prove their prowess against each other, the natural world, and magical or mythical beings. More importantly, as acceptable courtly behavior does not actually include acts of physical aggression, the forest becomes the space in which it is permissible, even necessary, for the knight to access his capacity for wild or uncivilized — that is, churlish and violent — behavior.

The tournament likewise connects to the knight's capacity for violence and his martial success. In historical practice, knights proved their prowess through participation in local wars or the crusades. Inexperienced or unemployed knights, however, required a forum for martial practice. This need led to the development of tournaments. Initially, tournaments operated as a training tool for inexperienced knights. However, as the Middle Ages progressed, they became more elaborate, and melées, the earlier staged battles between groups, evolved into ritualized duels, typically in the form of a joust.[22]

As a number of critics demonstrate, the *Harry Potter* series draws heavily upon the structure typical of most medieval romances. (Heather Arden and Kathryn Lorenz discuss the structural similarities between the *Harry Potter* volumes and French medieval romances such as Chrétien de Troyes' *Le Conte du Graal* [*The Story of the Grail*] and Marie de France's lay *Guigemar*. See their co-written articles, "The Ambiguity of the Outsider in the Harry Potter Stories and Beyond," and "The Harry Potter Stories and French Arthurian Romance.") Each volume includes some type of challenge, whether physical, emotional, or intellectual, and the first three books employ the departure-adventure-return structure in their depiction of Harry's departure for Hogwarts, time at the school, and return to the Dursley household. Rowling's series also draws upon the forest and tournament motifs. Students can thus explore a range of pedagogical possibilities. They can pursue traditional research projects on the function, regulation, and habitation of medieval forests in contrast to spaces within *Harry Potter*. The Forbidden Forest, for instance, houses terrifying and mythical creatures such as Acromantulas and Centaurs, and a number of Harry's challenges or significant encounters take place within the forest. Students can also pursue creative comparative projects, such as the development of a board game which focuses on different aspects of the forest (regulation, dangers, inhabitants, functions), or they can examine specific characters associated with the forest, such as Hagrid, who, as Gamekeeper, evokes medieval foresters, and who represents two common inhabitants of the forest in medieval romance, the giant and the wild-man. Students can similarly examine tournaments in medieval texts and historical practice with an eye to how Rowling deploys the motif in her series. Harry's challenges frequently evoke the martial traditions of quests and tournaments, the most obvious parallel being the Tri-Wizard Tournament in *Goblet of Fire*. Students can use their research to experiment with reenactment, of martial challenges or events both in medieval accounts and in *Harry Potter*. They can also expand this line of inquiry to include examinations of the modern-day activities of the Society for Creative Anachronism or recent adaptations of Quidditch.

As with the scope of this article, this list of motifs is not exhaustive. Other medieval motifs resonate in *Harry Potter*, such as confraternities and torture. For instance, direct parallels exist between medieval knightly orders — fictional (the Knights of the Round Table) or real (the Order of the Garter) — and a number of selective and hierarchical societies within the series (Voldemort's Death Eaters, the Order of the Phoenix, and Dumbledore's Army). Dolores Umbridge's pedagogical practices — including her desire to employ the unforgivable curses — evoke medieval torture. Overall, however, the discussions presented here provide a starting point for both traditional and creative approaches to Rowling's medievalism and the relationship between *Harry Potter* and the medieval period.

Notes

1. M. J. Toswell, "The Tropes of Medievalism," in *Defining Medievalism(s)*, ed Karl Fugelso, Studies in Medievalism 17 (Cambridge: D. S. Brewer, 2009), 69.

2. Jack Zipes, *Sticks and Stones: The Troublesome Success of Children's Literature from Slovenly Peter to Harry Potter* (New York and London: Routledge, 2001), 178.

3. Ibid.,178.

4. Alessandra Petrina, "Forbidden Forest, Enchanted Castle: Arthurian Spaces in the Harry Potter Novels," *Mythlore* 24, no. 3–4 (2006): 98.

5. Ibid., 98.

6. Edmund M. Kern, *The Wisdom of Harry Potter: What Our Favourite Hero Teaches Us about Moral Choices* (Amherst: Prometheus Books, 2003), 180.

7. Ibid., 189.

8. Debra Hassig, *Medieval Bestiaries: Text, Image, Ideology*, Res Monographs on Anthropology and Aesthetics (Cambridge: Cambridge University Press, 1995), 5–6.

9. Joyce Salisbury, *The Beast Within: Animals in the Middle Ages* (London and New York: Routledge, 1994), 114.

10. Newt Scamander (J.K. Rowling), *Fantastic Beasts and Where to Find Them* (New York: Scholastic, 2001), x.

11. John Block Friedman, *The Monstrous Races in Medieval Art and Thought* (Syracuse, NY: Syracuse University Press, 2000), 109–10.

12. Isidore of Seville, *The Etymologies of Isidore of Seville*, trans. Stephen A. Barney, W. J. Lewis, J. A. Beach, and Oliver Berghof (Cambridge: Cambridge University Press, 2006), 12.2.23.

13. Ibid., 12.2.24.

14. J.K. Rowling, "The Surprising Success of Harry Potter," Interview with Larry King, *Larry King Live!* Cable News Network, October 20, 2000, *Accio Quote*, http://www.accio-quote.org/articles/2000/1000-cnn-larryking.htm.

15. Nancy Siraisi, *Medieval and Early Renaissance Medicine: An Introduction to Knowledge and Practice* (Chicago: Chicago University Press, 1990), 27.

16. James Weldon, "The Naples Manuscript and the Case for a Female Readership," *Neophilologus* 93, no. 2 (2009): 703.

17. Peggy A. Knapp, "The Work of Alchemy," *Journal of Medieval and Early Modern Studies* 30, no. 3 (Fall 2000): 575.
18. Kern, *Wisdom*, 181.
19. Antony Vinciguerra, "The *Ars Alchemie*: The First Latin Text on Practical Alchemy," *Ambix* 56, no. 1 (March 2009): 57.
20. Michael Foucault, *Discipline and Punish: The Birth of the Prison*, trans. Alan Sheridan (New York: Vintage Books, 1995), 195.
21. Ibid., 195.
22. *Oxford Encyclopedia of the Middle Ages*, online ed., s.v. "Tournaments." http://www.oxford-middleages.com.

To Grow Up Blake in a Potter World: Teaching *Songs of Innocence and of Experience*

WHITNEY E. JONES FRANCIS

When asked, students of the senior-level children's literature course I co-teach give unanimously identical reasons for their interest in the class: *Harry Potter*. They also candidly admit that their least favorite work on the syllabus is early Romantic poet William Blake's *Songs of Innocence and of Experience: Shewing the Two Contrary States of the Human Soul*. While the opportunity to talk *Potter* in an academic environment is a siren call no true fan can resist, originary works of children's literature from the Romantic period such as Blake's *Songs* do not elicit the same sort of excitement. Rather, reading Blake seems to cause confusion and frustration. Blake's seemingly simplistic treatment of the states of innocence and experience evokes the nursery rhymes of infancy, yet Blake's *Songs* are far from simple. Blake's complex and partially defined transcendent state of higher innocence and his refusal to adhere to traditional characterizations of oppositions asks students to set aside their fairy tale concepts of a world divided into good and bad, beautiful and ugly, innocence and experience. Essentially, Blake is difficult. However, his position as an important figure in the origins of children's literature makes his presence on the syllabus essential. (Nursery rhymes and hymns for children existed before Blake. However, Blake's *Songs*, along with the emphasis the Romantics placed on everyday, figures like the child have been identified by major critics — U.C. Knoepflmacher, James Holt McGavran, Jr., and Roderick McGillis to name a few — as central shaping influences on our own contemporary perceptions of childhood). So how do we convince the students of children's literature to put down their *Potter* and pick up their Blake?

By *not* putting down *Potter*.

Susan Groenke and Lisa Scherff suggest, "Adolescents like young adult novels because, unlike classical, canonical works, these novels have been written *about* adolescents, *with adolescent readers in mind*."[1] Adolescents view YA novels, including the *Harry Potter* series, "as relevant to their lives and experiences," whereas a work like William Blake's *Songs* feels alien and, unfortunate to say, boring.[2] Likewise, Catherine L. Belcher and Becky Herr Stephenson note the usefulness of "popular culture — and the *Harry Potter* series in particular — in facilitating student engagement ... for making connections to high-level concepts, and maintaining student engagement over an extended period of time."[3] The relevance that the college student attaches to a young adult or popular work like *Harry Potter* becomes a useful means of introducing students to Blake's *Songs* in such a way that excites rather than intimidates them.

In this essay, I suggest that investigating the Blakean cycle of higher innocence — an individual's development from innocence through experience to a transcendent state which combines the two previous states — within the *Harry Potter* series can clarify the process as it is found at its source, in Blake's *Songs*. William Blake's *Songs of Innocence and Songs of Experience's* influence on children's literature is immense. The pattern of development explored in *Songs* reverberates in various forms throughout children's literature of the nineteenth and twentieth centuries. By exploring the movement from innocence to experience for both *Potter* and *Songs,* the students discover, in a work they are by and large resistant to — Blake's poems — a pattern of growth and maturation already familiar to them through their favorite childhood text: *Harry Potter*. I use a close reading of Blake's and Rowling's texts, along with practical suggestions for in-class exercises and discussions to reveal the connection between a collection of eighteenth-century poems written by a possible madman and a popular series of books written by a young mother in a coffee shop. By making these connections, I hope to clarify for my students the trajectory of children's literature from its origins to its current manifestations and to emphasize its coherency around the essential theme of children's literature — growth and maturation. (Though this essay seeks particularly to explore the connections with *Potter* and Blake, other Romantic texts, characters, and themes remain particularly relevant: the Byronic hero, Wordsworth's "spots of time" from *The Prelude*, Coleridge's fascination with dreams, and the gothic novel's concern with space, identity, and the supernatural.)

Growing Up, Blake Style

Before discussing *Harry Potter*, I will outline the pattern of development that leads to higher innocence in Blake's *Song* to stress the importance of "growing up" to Blake's poetry. *Innocence* and *Experience* oppose each other in landscape and in tone, both of which represent a particular, internal state of mind — innocence and experience. Whereas the speakers of the pastoral poems of *Innocence* trust social institutions and feel no fear of the mysterious world around them, the speakers of the urban poems of *Experience* fear and distrust not only God and the natural world, but also those institutions that manipulate the divine and the natural for power or profit.

Blake insists on the importance and goodness of both states of innocence and experience, despite their disparities. These states of development are, as D.G. Gillham notes, stages through which individuals naturally progresses during human development: "Innocence trembles always on the brink of extinction and the wrongs of Experience create, immediately, an experienced being to cope with them. The avidity of Innocence to embrace all that may be enjoyed ensures, indeed, that it will find the means of its own destruction," a natural and inevitable progression.[4] Though both stages are necessary to progress, they are also subordinate to a third, transcendent state — higher, or organized, innocence. This third state combines what is best from innocence and experience and results in a fuller, more comprehensive understanding of the natural and manmade worlds.[5]

One of the difficulties of teaching Blake's cycle of higher innocence is that the poems in *Songs* do not quite ever illustrate the final stage of development — higher innocence. Alfred Kazin argues that the difficulty of reading Blake "lies in his refusal to concede a distance between what is real and what is ideal; in his desperate need to claim them as one."[6] The "Introduction" to *Innocence* perhaps comes closest to exploring the necessary synthesis of the other two opposing states, of the real and the ideal. However, there is no third part of *Songs*, no *Songs of Higher Innocence*, so the synthesis of the real and ideal that leads to a transcendent state beyond innocence and experience remains mostly undefined, causing students to doubt and distrust Blake and his work. Students initially understand Blake's cycle as hierarchical, with innocence as a safer, purer, brighter state superior to experience, which is dark, frightening, and hostile. They often feel that Blake insists on a return to the initial state of innocence and have difficulty conceptualizing a cycle in which experience is just as necessary as innocence, and in which innocence is just as harmful as experience.

The *Harry Potter* series helps abolish this notion of a hierarchy that places innocence above experience by utilizing a Blakean cycle and playing with Blakean opposites like pastoral and urban, fear and naiveté, trust and disillusionment. *Potter* also goes where Blake himself, in *Songs*, does not: fully into the transcendent realm of higher innocence. To clarify Blake's cycle for students, I ask them to investigate ways in which Rowling's world is, as

Blake's is, composed of contrary settings and internal states of mind, explore Rowling's understanding of fear and social institutions in comparison to Blake's, and, most importantly, to chart Harry's movement beyond simple opposing states of being, beyond fear, and beyond the physical world to a Blakean state of higher innocence. For the Potter-centered college student, whose Hogwarts letter came with the acceptance letter to their university of choice, seeing Blake's cycle play out in a world familiar to them through not only years of re-reading, but through film, fan fiction, and fan culture as well, translates an abstract concept of development into a narrative they know and love.

Showing the Two Contrary States of Harry Potter

In *Harry Potter and the Sorcerer's Stone,* Rowling relies on contraries to build her dual muggle and wizarding worlds. Her use of oppositions differs drastically between *Sorcerer's Stone* and *Deathly Hallows,* which I consider, respectively, a book of innocence and a book of experience. The oppositions of *Sorcerer's Stone* suggest that Harry's world can be neatly categorized into good and evil, magical and muggle. These oppositions grow more complicated as the series progresses until, finally, all boundaries have dissolved; the lines between good and evil blur and the muggle and magical worlds collide. This synthesizing of oppositions is exactly what Blake attempts to accomplish in *Songs.*[7]

Sorcerer's Stone is a book of innocence. In its "simple" explanation of the muggle and wizarding worlds, it expresses a view of the world that contains "a clearly defined morality as the powers of good and evil line up against one another."[8] Students are astutely aware of this delineation and view the rift between good and evil as the central theme of the series, making the discussion of contraries an excellent place to begin a discussion of Blake and Rowling together. Rowling divides the world and its inhabitants into straightforward, non-breachable oppositional categories that reflect the basic way in which Blake's innocent also understands the surrounding world. The muggle Dursleys are "perfectly normal ... the last people you'd expect to be involved in anything strange or mysterious, because they just didn't hold with such nonsense" (*SS* 1). The easy language suggests this world is composed of two states: normal and strange, sense and nonsense. The emphasis on contraries continues; Mr. Dursley is a "big, beefy man with hardly any neck," while his wife is "thin and blonde and ha[s] nearly twice the usual amount of neck" (*SS* 1). The amusingly contradictory images evoke an innocent fairy tale atmosphere of oppositions: good and bad, beautiful and ugly, male and female, rich and poor. These obvious oppositions make the first installment of Rowling's series a work of Blakean innocence formed from the innocent child's perception of an adult world: "[l]ittle children do not see shades of gray or ambivalence in behavior; instead, they separate the world into good and evil: Albus Dumbledore versus Voldemort, Harry Potter versus Draco Malfoy, the sacrificial James and Lily Potter versus the selfish Vernon and Petunia Dursley."[9]

Juxtaposing *Sorcerer's Stone* and *Deathly Hallows* highlights the more innocent treatment of oppositions in the first book when compared to the last. As Roberta Seelinger Trites notes, the books grow darker, more "adolescent" with each new installment, ending in a novel whose fictional world is frighteningly overcast by death.[10] Trites notes that the essential difference between the innocent *Sorcerer's Stone* and the experienced *Deathly Hallows* provokes confusion and even outrage from some students. Having signed up for a course entitled "Children's Literature," they do not expect to see darker, more mature works like *Deathly Hallows* on the syllabus. These reactions assist a discussion of Blake and Rowling as students debate the necessity of pain, violence, and brutality in children's literature. Not only are fairy tales often our first introduction to cruelty and violence, but this same cruelty and violence is mirrored in both *Potter* and *Songs*, and revealed in these works to be necessary if painful parts of the state of experience, a state that is essential to the story of growing up.

The pervasion of death in even the title of the seventh book immediately signals the series' fall from innocence to experience. The difference in Harry's attitude towards Dumbledore in *Sorcerer's Stone* and in *Deathly Hallows* most clearly illuminates the loss of innocence that occurs throughout the series, the loss of belief in an easily categorized and defined world of good and evil, and reflects the students' own sense of betrayal and confusion over Dumbledore's role in Harry's life. In *Sorcerer's Stone*, Harry sees his mentor as an omniscient supreme being: "I think he knows more or less everything that goes on here, you know" and Ron views Dumbledore as a "crazy" "hero" (302). By *Deathly Hallows*, however, Harry has come to question and even distrust Dumbledore: "Some inner certainty had crashed down inside him... He had trusted Dumbledore, believed him the embodiment of goodness and wisdom. All was ashes" (360). Harry's disillusionment grows more pronounced throughout the series as the clearly defined boundaries between good and evil found in *Sorcerer's Stone* fade into ambiguity, and a world of innocence gives way to a world of experience.

The elements that Blake uses to characterize the state of experience— fear of the natural world and distrust of social institutions—are present in *Harry Potter* from the very beginning and grow more prominent as the series progresses. Fear of Voldemort and the Ministry of Magic's ineptitude and corruption are familiar subjects to the Potter fan. Just as Blake distrusts a "repressive social system" that reinforces "the mandates of institutional power," so too does Harry come to realize that the bodies of power in the wizarding world that should be working to protect him are often working against him.[11] Using Harry's distrust of institutions that on the surface seem built to aid society but in reality hinder or, even worse, harm it helps our students understand Blake's criticism in *Song of Experience*. The poem "London" from *Songs of Experience* best expresses the urban corruption of nature and the mental anguish institutional corruption and control enacts on the terrified and confused experienced mind. Emphasizing "charter'd street[s]" and "mind-forg'd manacles" most effectively evokes the sort of control that the powerful inhabitants of "black'nd church[es]" and bloody "Palace walls" impose through fear on their weak and woeful citizens. This same corruption exists in *Harry Potter* on multiple levels, from the Ministry to Azkaban and eventually to Hogwarts itself. Students readily identify moments of social injustice in the series and are often concerned with the treatment of house elves, the law that denies wands to any creature except magical humans, and Voldemort's easy infiltration of the Ministry of Magic.

I encourage students to explore the moments of corruption they have identified in Blake and *Potter* through two already familiar images from the *Potter* series that illustrate respectively the innocent mind's ignorance of a corrupt world, and the experienced mind's recognition of a fallen, experienced world. The first image depicts the statue Harry encounters in the Ministry of Magic in *The Order of the Phoenix*: "A group of golden statues, larger than life-size, stood in the middle of a circular pool. Tallest of them all was a noble-looking wizard with his wand pointing straight up in the air. Grouped around him were a beautiful witch, a centaur, a goblin, and a house elf. The last three were all looking adoringly up at the witch and wizard" (*OOTP* 127).

For a naïve, younger Harry, the statue is a symbol of the goodness, equality, and justice of the wizarding world.[12] However, the statue is a lie. Students point to injustices within the wizarding world quite easily and note, as Hermione does, that the statue hides the true hierarchical structure of the wizarding society that positions human wizards at the top and delegates creatures like house elves to servitude and slavery. The original statue, which sanitizes the true social situation of the wizarding world, embodies the state of innocence in its rose-colored, utopian view of an actually corrupt society.

The original statue is destroyed during the fight between Harry, Voldemort, and Dumbledore at the end of *The Order of the Phoenix,* and is replaced in *Deathly Hallows* with a much more insidious, yet candid, statue reflecting not only Voldemort's control of the Ministry, but also the fall of Rowling's world into a state of experience:

> It was rather frightening, this vast sculpture of a witch and a wizard sitting on ornately carved thrones... Engraved in foot high letters at the base of the statue were the words MAGIC IS MIGHT ... what [Harry] had thought were decoratively carved thrones were actually mounds of carved humans: hundreds and hundreds of naked bodies ... all with rather stupid, ugly faces, twisted and pressed together to support the weight of the handsomely robed wizards [*DH* 241–42].

The new statue illustrates the Blakean movement from an innocent perception of the world to an experienced one. The original, peaceful statue's destruction represents the destruction of this idealized perspective. Though the new statue is brutal, its open recognition of hierarchical social structures points to the experienced mind's more realistic understanding of social, political, and religious corruptions.

Asking students to analyze these two statues as representations of Harry's understanding of the world promotes various responses. Many students feel that the second statue encapsulates the moment in which they realized the true danger of Harry's situation, when they realized how far the wizarding world had fallen. Others feel that the original statue foreshadows the fall, and in some ways, is more sinister than the second statue. They are right. The first statue hides what the second statue says outright, suggesting that the utopian alliance of all magical creatures proposed by the first statue is only a ruse, covering something as ugly as the second statue itself.

Directing students' attention to the statues in the Ministry of Magic helps them understand Blake's increasing disillusionment with social institutions from *Innocence* to *Experience*. The experienced mind's greater understanding of social institutions ultimately leads to a sense of disillusionment that is, for both Blake and Rowling, heightened by fear. The child, the innocent, realizing that the world is not as good as he had formerly thought, fears those institutional powers that have betrayed him to misery and death. Despite his greater experience and knowledge of this new world, his faith in his own understanding of people deteriorates and even the most familiar images become foreign. Everything that surrounds the experienced mind is terrifyingly unknown. Exploring images of fear in the works of Rowling and Blake reveals a vital roadblock to maturation.

Fear of the unknown best characterizes the experienced mind and that keeps it from seeing the beauty of a contradictory world. The speaker's expression of fear in the song of *Experience*—"The Tyger"—emphasizes how the new knowledge of experience is, in its own way, as ignorant as its opposite state, innocence. In these rhythmically pounding lines, Blake presents a horrified litany of questions: "What immortal hand or eye?" "In what distant deeps or skies," "what wings," "What the hand," "Did he who made the lamb make thee?" The speaker doubts the benevolence of a God who creates both tiger and lamb, but to reveal the ignorance of the terrified speaker, Blake counters the text with an illuminated image of a tiger that is more kitten than killer. Fear preys upon the experienced mind, emphasizing the tiger's violent ferocity and obscuring the view of the tiger as a thing of beauty, a creature more scared of man than, if man were wise, he would be of it.

Many students have read this oft-anthologized poem repeatedly in high school and after, and are "over it." Though their reluctant familiarity with the poem often leads to an outright dismissal of its relevance, the poem and its concern with fear take on new interest when discussed alongside *Potter* and Rowling's use of institutionalized fear as a weapon. Many fans and students can adeptly discuss the various ways in which Voldemort exploits fear of the unknown to further his hold on the wizarding world. He creates around himself a mythos by establishing a taboo on the use of his very name. Ron's explanation of the taboo reveals Voldemort's deft manipulation of fear: "The name's been jinxed, Harry, that's how they track people! Using his name breaks protective enchantments, it causes some kind of magical disturbance.... You've got to give them credit, it makes sense. It was only people who were serious about standing up to him, like Dumbledore, who ever dared use it. Now they've put a Taboo on it, anyone who says it is trackable..." (*DH* 389–90).

The Taboo makes the protection impossible; a name, a word, the utterance of a few syllables, under Voldemort's reign, means death. The imprecise language Ron uses to describe the Taboo's protection-destroying enchantment — "it causes *some kind* of magical disturbance" — suggests the unknown origin and nature of this sort of power and of Voldemort's magic.

Those who refuse to give into fear, who refuse to call Voldemort "He-Who-Must-Not-Be-Named" or "You-Know-Who," are those who are not afraid to stand up to him. As Dumbledore constantly reminds Harry, "Always use the proper name for things. Fear of a name increases fear of the thing itself" (*SS* 298). For many students, Dumbledore's words have resonated in their own lives, and his reassuring advice gives not only Harry power over fear, but gave many of my students the power to see how fear blinds Blake's terrified speaker of "The Tyger," hindering him from true knowledge of the terrible, but beautiful, beast.

Higher Innocence at King's Cross Station

The individual who can view the tiger without fear has the ability to move beyond experience, to attain a more sophisticated state of innocence often referred to as higher innocence and coined "organized innocence" by Blake.[13] By banishing the fear that corrupts experience, Harry can transcend experience itself, moving into this organized innocence. Dependent upon the successful movement through both states — innocence and experience — organized innocence synthesizes two seemingly contradictory states. Judith Plotz identifies higher/organized innocence as "larger, freer, and more empowered" than either innocence or experience on its own.[14] The "Introduction" to *Songs of Innocence* illustrates the eventual synthesis of innocence and experience that is central to Blake's cycle. The traveler through life achieves higher innocence through the combination of the two supposedly contrary states, joining the natural with the manmade and innocence with knowledge unhindered by fear. Only obtainable through the combination of contrary states, higher innocence is characterized by the desirable traits of innocence — imagination, love, trust, and joy — as well as the desirable traits of experience — knowledge, wisdom, and shrewd curiosity. The individual who achieves this transcendent state rises above the dangerous naiveté of innocence as well as the imprisoning fear of experience to understand the oppositions of the world as necessary, good, and compatible.[15]

Both Blake and Rowling insist on the necessity of synthesizing the contraries of innocence and experience, ignorance and knowledge. Harry's willingness to interact with evil, experience, corruption, power, arrogance, and ambition in all of its darker forms shows a Blakean ability to admit to the necessity of opposites. The dreams and visions "that he both feared and ... prized" join his mind to Voldemort's, a dangerous voyeuristic glimpse that leaves Harry desirous of more and "disconcerted" when the images "become blurred," leaving him afraid that "the connection between himself and Voldemort had been damaged" (*DH* 436). Despite Dumbledore, Hermione, and Ron's attempts to convince Harry to close off his mind from Voldemort's influence, Harry refuses, finding power in the intimate connection he shares with the dark wizard. Ultimately, Harry's ability to represent good and yet understand evil moves him past the solitary states of innocence and experience to the almost impossible state of higher innocence that "transcend[s] the condition of antithesis."[16]

The chapter "King's Cross" embodies Harry's transcendence into higher innocence. Harry surrenders his life to Voldemort, who attacks Harry with the same killing curse of "green light" that, seventeen years ago, killed Harry's parents (*DH* 704). Harry "wakes up" to find himself in a hazy mist that solidifies into an abandoned King's Cross station, an important meeting point between the muggle and wizarding worlds, one especially important to Harry, who is redefined by his ability to cross through the brick barrier at Platform 9¾. The station has become a meeting point of oppositions, between life and death, memory and present, mundanity and magic. That Harry's death brings him to an indistinct divide, a place in which barriers blur, suggests the abolishment of oppositions. At the same time, Voldemort's killing curse severs Harry's connection to him, suggesting the reaffirmation of the strict boundaries found in book one. However, this is not the case. What Harry's sacrificial death has purged from his body is not his ability to understand, to access, both "good" and "evil," but the fear and corruption Voldemort embodies. The "small, naked child" that occupies the misty, abandoned King's Cross station of Harry's mind "flail[s] and struggle[s]," a terrified and angry infant beyond Harry's help.

Harry who escapes fear, or rather transcends it through his love for family, friends, and community, embraces Dumbledore's statement from book one that "to the well-organized mind, death is but the next great adventure" (*SS* 297). Because Harry purges from his body the embodiment of fear and corruption, because he embraces experience rather than fearing it or attempting to control it, he is able to rise above it, to attain a well-organized mind as well as organized innocence. Voldemort, who has spent his life in the pursuit of immortality, fails where Harry succeeds because his pursuit is motivated by the fear of death, and fear for both Blake and Rowling is a snare that inhibits growth and shadows true knowledge, destroying the terrified mind to which it clings.

Reading *Potter* demolishes student fear of Blake and replaces academic terror with understanding and intellectual growth. Though I was a devoted acolyte of Blake's poetry before I became a frenzied *Potter* fan, I can understand my current students' reluctance towards *Songs of Innocence and of Experience*. They probably embraced *Potter* at a playground insider's recommendation; it was a series of books uniquely their own, its popularity passed by word of mouth rather than from the teacher's hand to theirs.[17] Blake comes to them, not through their peers, but from that teacher's hand. While the text can be deceptively simplistic and maddeningly difficult, after discussing the relationship between *Potter* and Blake's *Songs*, students were more willing to look for cycles of innocence and experience in other texts, handing in final projects that explored the Blakean cycle within works like *Alice in Wonderland, The Golden Compass, Treasure Island, The Secret Garden,* and *Twilight.* They often brought class discussion around to issues of innocence and experience, and if a student used one of the contraries in a hierarchical manner, positioning innocence as superior to experience, one or more of the other students would jump in to correct them. Belcher and Stephenson believe that "students use what they know to build a bridge to knowing more."[18] I agree. The familiar story, characters, and issues of *Harry Potter* can help students understand and appreciate Blake as something more than a canonized, assigned text, explaining *Songs* in such a way that not only illuminates difficult notions of higher innocence, but that also turns in on itself, revealing the deeper importance, meaning, and value of the Potter series itself.

Notes

1. Susan L. Groenke and Lisa Scherff. *Teaching YA Lit through Differentiated Instruction* (Urbana: National Council of Teachers of English, 2010), 2.
2. Ibid.
3. Catherine L. Belcher and Becky Herr Stephenson, *Teaching Harry Potter: The Power of Imagination in Multicultural Classrooms* (New York: Palgrave Macmillan, 2011), 66.
4. D.G. Gillham, *Blake's Contrary States: The 'Songs of Innocence and of Experience' as Dramatic Poems* (Cambridge: Cambridge University Press, 1966), 121–22.
5. Alfred Kazin, "Introduction," in *The Portable Blake* (New York: Penguin, 1976), 40.
6. Ibid, 23.
7. Harold Bloom, *The Visionary Company* (Garden City: Doubleday, 1961), 29.
8. Julia Eccleshare, "The Changing Writer: From Philosopher's Stone to Goblet of Fire," in *A Guide to the Harry Potter Novels*, ed. Julia Eccleshare (London: Continuum, 2002), 20.
9. Katherine M. Grimes, "Harry Potter: Fairy Tale Prince, Real Boy, and Archetypal Hero," in *The Ivory Tower and Harry Potter*, ed. Lana A. Whited (Columbia: University of Missouri Press, 2002), 91.
10. Roberta Seelinger Trites, "The Harry Potter Novels as a Test Case for Adolescent Literature," *Style* 35, no. 3 (2001): 472.
11. Nicholas M. Williams, *Ideology and Utopia in the Poetry of William Blake* (Cambridge: Cambridge University Press, 1998), 45.
12. Ken Jacobsen, "Harry Potter and the Secular City: The Dialectical Religious Vision of J.K. Rowling," *Animus* 9 (2004): 96.
13. William Blake, *The Four Zoas* in *The Portable Blake* (New York: Penguin, 1976), 400.
14. Judith Plotz, *Romanticism and the Vocation of Childhood* (New York: Palgrave, 2001), xv.
15. Bloom, *The Visionary Company*, 29.
16. Jacobsen, "Harry Potter and the Secular City," 80.
17. Andrew Blake, *The Irresistible Rise of Harry Potter* (London: Verso, 2002), 66.
18. Belcher and Stephenson, *Teaching Harry Potter*, 7.

Casting *Lumos* on Critical Cultural Studies: Gender, Hegemony and Other Social Stereotypes

AMANDA FIRESTONE

Consider the word *pedagogy*. It invokes images of stuffy rooms filled with older, affluent instructors who wax poetic about times when teaching was simpler, when the banking system worked, and students were well-behaved and knew their place. Even the way it rolls off the tongue, there's something elitist about it. Ped-uh-Gō-Gey. It sounds freakishly similar to Hermione's teaching moment with the overly-exaggerated "Wing-*gar*-dium Levi-*o*-sa!" (*SS* 171). But, as David Buckingham reminds us, "To discuss pedagogy is to focus ... on the *social relationships* between teachers and students"[1] (author's emphasis). And while theories abound, there are few instructions for *how* to make classroom strategies for fostering those relationships a reality.

The best I've been able to do in my communication classes is attempt to find common ground with my students. Popular culture references from my adolescence largely are obsolete at this point. Students' eyes cross when I say, "As you wish," "Bueller ... Bueller ... Bueller," or "Hey you guys!" (These are all references from 80's movies: *The Princess Bride* [1987], *Ferris Bueller's Day Off* [1986], and *The Goonies* [1985]). My almost-world-famous Wookiee yelp elicits smirks and occasionally boos. Can you imagine? But the moment I slip in a Potter reference — "*Accio* dry erase marker!" — and they jump to life. Some students' faces become happily animated while others, who clearly understand the reference but are *so over it*, roll their eyes. They get it, and in that moment I've simultaneously broken the lull in the classroom and engaged their attention.

I teach upper level Communication courses, specifically those connected to women, gender, and identity in terms of communication tactics and discourses that construct our cultural ideas and beliefs about these categories.

The students that take these courses generally fall into two types: students fulfilling requirements for the Communication degree and students fulfilling other requirements — like the writing quotient or exit standards — to graduate. In short, I teach juniors and seniors who are stressed out by finishing university with full course loads while simultaneously navigating the ever encroaching "real world." Telling these students that I can help them better understand concepts connected to the course objectives through media texts like *Harry Potter* produces grumbles, snickers, and muffled cheers. It's always a mixed bag of responses, but I persist, telling them that I will try to make the class's readings and themes relevant through popular culture examples. After all, we all watch television, go to the movies, surf the web, and go shopping.

Introducing Critical Cultural Studies

In a nutshell, my stake in Communication is critical cultural studies and the way media shapes our lives. Cultural studies as a discipline grew from traditional literary criticism and sought to step away from *high art* in favor of exploring "the everyday and the ordinary."[2] As Graeme Turner writes, cultural studies concerns itself with "those aspects of our lives that exert so powerful and unquestioned an influence on our existence that we take them for granted."[3] Everything can become a site of inquiry for cultural studies, from dance fads to summer blockbuster movies to food preferences. Through methods like textual analysis, cultural studies seeks to analyze not only artifacts for structures and aesthetic values but to also examine "the wider structures that produced them — those of culture itself."[4] And perhaps more importantly, as a discipline it allows us to engage those seemingly benign and boring aspects of our lives to discover the critical issues — matters of gender, sexuality, race, and class for instance — that reveal the distribution and inequities of power in our society.

Stuart Hall, considered one of the pioneers of the field, talks about the entrance of feminist scholarship to cultural studies during the 1970's in his retrospective piece "Cultural Studies and Its Theoretical Legacies." Hall describes how feminism, "as the thief in the night ... interrupted, made an unseemly noise, seized the time, [and] crapped on the table of cultural studies."[5] Feminist scholars forced cultural studies scholars to re-evaluate everything they thought they knew and understood about power dynamics. While Hall and many of his (male) colleagues insisted that the field was open and available to all kinds of investigation, when it came time to examine the core reading list — largely consisting of theorists like Marx, Gramsci, Richard Hoggart, and Raymond Williams — it became abundantly clear who was given prestige and precedence. Hall reflects: "Now that's where I really discovered about the gendered nature of power."[6]

My stake in this as an academic pursuit is always bound to questions of gender and sexuality. Texts such as fictional narratives like *Harry Potter* are the representations of culture in a specific context, like a candid snapshot of a fleeting moment. We can examine and interpret these texts to provide insights to larger societal issues, particularly those concerning hegemony and power structures. Kenneth Burke, who is not strictly considered a member of the cultural studies club, theorized in the 1930s that literature functions as "proverbs writ large."[7] Media texts are imbued with prescriptions that subtextually engage readers to think about specific values or lessons.[8] The *Harry Potter* books are no exception. So what does Rowling's series teach us about what it means to be a girl or a woman? Which gendered behaviors are normalized and which ones are signified as unusual or abnormal?

Call it what you will — media literacy, critical engagement, consciousness raising — I envision my job as providing students with tools that allow them to look below the surface of the culture we daily navigate to find the hidden meanings, motivations, and interpretations that reside there. Hall insists that a scholar "cannot absolve himself or herself from the responsibility of transmitting those ideas, that knowledge ... to those who do not belong, professionally, in the intellectual class."[9] It's up to us as teachers to share what we observe, learn, and "know" with our students as means of fostering their critical engagement with media. This is the core of my teaching philosophy. No matter how theoretical or abstract concepts may seem to students, I find ways to solidify them in the mediated world they know so well, and then go the next step forward: show them that there is *more* to consider.

Exploring Sexuality and Gender

Frequently, the Potter series is a prime example in my classroom for talking about constructions of gender and even sexuality. Challenging my students to sit with discomfort as Ms. Frizzle would say, "Take chances, make mistakes, get messy!" (*The Magic Schoolbus*) is an integral part of my classroom. We read Judith Butler and discuss what it means to separate sex from gender and the practicalities or realities of doing so. The students begin to understand that body and performance are not the same thing, nor does one fully indicate the other. I ask them: "How do we know that Albus Dumbledore is gay?"

Some students immediately protest, "There's no way he's gay!" and "That would be weird." Other students, perhaps those with a bit more textual savviness,[10] say, "J.K. Rowling said he's gay; he must be." A simple question opens a frank and I daresay honest conversation about how we differentiate between what or who is gay, straight, and any other label in between. They begin to interrogate ideas about stereotypes and what that means in terms of judging people at face value. Those students who are fans of the books cite things like Dumbledore's penchant for ultra-colorful robes and accessories like socks. I push them further. Do his choice of robes and socks somehow mark him as homosexual?

The conversation begins to move swiftly, switching from the *Harry Potter* example to real world or lived experience examples. In my classroom, students work through concepts by melding media examples with their experiences. Some of the students make the leap from Dumbledore's wardrobe to societal stereotypes about gendered clothing, insisting that the color pink *can* signify whether a man identifies as gay. Inevitably, someone disagrees, citing a friend who regularly wears a pink shirt who is not gay. We've moved into conversation about the correct performances of masculinity through clothing and color choices. The students understand that there are definitely unwritten rules about what men should and should not wear. Disobeying these rules means a potential for miscommunication in terms of sexual identity, which could lead to uncomfortable confrontations where personal and private decisions are questioned. By the end of the class period, I encourage the students to make conscious changes to their wardrobe or grooming routine that might change how other people perceive them, and when we next meet, I ask students who have taken the challenge to share their experiences.

While many of them don't go so far as to believe that other people's ideas about their sexual orientation have changed, many of my female students do encounter differing perceptions from others when they choose not to wear makeup. We talk at length about advertising, so-called beauty products and the hazardous chemicals of which many are comprised. We talk about the reactions women receive when they change their beauty routine. Frequently, women who stop wearing makeup are asked if they're tired, if they've been super busy, or if they had a rushed morning. Conversely, for those who don't usually wear makeup daily, people ask what the special occasion is, whether they have someone they want to impress, and that they look prettier than usual — something a little extra about them. Many of these women are shocked by the marked change in the way they're treated. I entreat them to go back to the text. How does *Harry Potter* handle this same, very real, situation?

Hermione arrives to the Yule Ball on the arm of Victor Krum and it takes Harry several minutes to recognize her; he simply calls her a "pretty girl" when she first enters his line of sight (*GOF* 413). Upon recognizing that it's Hermione, Harry notes the changes to her normal appearance: "sleek and shiny" hair versus her usual curly chaos, "floaty, periwinkle-blue" robes contrasted with her house uniform and standard black robe, a nervous smile with noticeably smaller teeth than before (*GOF* 414). In the filmed adaptation of this scene, Hermione first peeks her head around a pillar before descending the staircase to meet Victor. Parvati Patil is the first person to notice her arrival and exclaims, "She looks beautiful!" Alone on the stairs, Hermione has a grand entrance in a satin rose-colored dress rather than wizarding robes, highlighting her new performance of femininity. In both the book and film, Ron picks a fight with Hermione after seeing her "transformation" and chosen date as his way of coping with his emotional discomfort with her clear change from bookworm to desirable partner.

When I remind my students of this moment, I can see the light bulbs come on above their heads. It's as though they never considered that scene as a representation of a common experience for women. They may not be at a formal dance or on a date, but somehow they recognize that the added effort to perform "beautiful" often gets them praise. Once again, I push them further in their thinking. If Burke believes that novels are didactic texts, what does this scene teach us? Or rather, what does this scene, combined with situations we have specifically experienced, tell us about culture and society? Inevitably, they come back to one answer: women are valued first by how they appear and any other characteristics are secondary.

Representations of Hegemony

It's not enough to examine identity traits like sexuality and gender as stand-alone characteristics. No, we must think in terms of multiplicity, or as Kimberle Crenshaw calls it, intersectionality. In her influential piece, "Mapping the Margins," Crenshaw reminds us that "[t]he problem with identity politics is ... that it frequently conflates or ignores intragroup differences."[11] When I explain the term hegemony to my classes, I talk about the power of the big five: gender, race, class (affluence), sexuality, and religion. In the Western world, the ideal representation of hegemony is a straight white man who ascribes to Christianity and who was born into or achieves upper-middle class or high class status. If just one of those five variables is changed, then the innate privilege that individual engenders is lessened. Additionally, while the big five are tried and true tells of where a person lands on the proverbial hegemonic totem pole, other factors such as education level, able-bodiedness, job status, and more also dictate the potential for privilege levels.

At this point, my students' faces are blank stares. "But what does that mean?" they ask. Back to the Potterverse I go for my prime examples. Hegemony looks like Lucius Malfoy. Some of the students look confused, unfamiliar with the character. I use the classroom technology to Google a photo of Jason Isaacs; the first few images returned are of him in character as Malfoy senior. I hear a few muffled "ohs" and "ahs" signaling recognition. When Lucius and Draco, his son, meet Harry and the Weasley family in Flourish and Blotts, Lucius makes his privilege clear by deriding the Weasleys' necessity to buy second-hand items like Ginny's transfiguration textbook. While Arthur Weasley, patriarch to the brood, defends his family, there is distinct recognition that Lucius Malfoy has greater privilege because he has exponentially more money. Even as a child, Draco understands his father's — and by proxy his own — position in the wizarding world. When he first meets Harry on the train, he also notices Ron in the compartment. He says: "No need to ask who you are. My father told me all the Weasleys have red hair, freckles, and more children than they can afford" (*SS* 108).

So, what does this mean for hegemony and more importantly ideas of intersectionality? Hands tentatively peek into the air, and I can practically see the wheels working inside of their heads. By changing just one component of the big five, affluence, the power dynamic between Lucius and Arthur has shifted dramatically: though both of these characters are Caucasian wizards of a similar age who are married with children, their separation in class status prevents them from participating in the same societal circles. This positions Lucius as better than Arthur. The Potter fans in the class argue and disagree from their seats. "But Malfoy is the *bad* guy! He can't be better!" Ah! Now we have an opportunity to start new dialogue to potentially allow us, as a class, to ferret out the twisty-turny complexities of identity and power structures.

Those students who have protested are thinking in terms of character archetypes. Lucius is a class-one antagonist, and in the end he will receive his punishment for crimes against the wizarding world. I agree with them that he's "the bad guy." But of course, ideas about goodness or badness are highly subjective, as are ideas about what is influential, powerful, and dangerous. I talk through these concepts using Lucius to help clarify some of the confusion. Malfoy is a politician, and it's only because we know the story through Harry's first person limited perspective that we understand the private details about Lucius's life. In the world of the tale, any witch or wizard who recognizes Lucius by his public persona, rather than his private exploits, sees someone who comes from an ancient and well-respected wizarding family, who has a tremendous amount of wealth, who has the privilege of knowing the Minister of Magic personally, and who appears invested in the youth of that world as a school board member. When all of this is added together, Lucius Malfoy doesn't seem so bad. Further, when compared to Arthur Weasley, who does have a similar family lineage but can't otherwise begin to claim the same attributes, hegemonically speaking Lucius is higher on the totem pole.

Before the students are aware of it, we're doing basic compare and contrast work for the Malfoy family and the Weasley family. Obviously, the Malfoys are upper class. Lucius is on the Hogwarts Board of Governors and "donates" heaps of galleons to strategic Ministry of Magic departments and politicians. Arthur works for the Ministry in the Misuse of Muggle Artifacts Department, which is posited as a low level white-collar (white robe?) job. Neither matriarch works at a job as such. We know that Narcissa Malfoy runs the sprawling Malfoy Manner with the aid of house-elves, while Molly Weasley is in charge of every domestic duty at the tiny Burrow, which includes raising her seven children. Molly can't seem to remember that Ron dislikes corned beef sandwiches or that she *always* gives him a maroon sweater for Christmas, indicating that she has more children than she can keep track of. Narcissa has only her son, Draco, to consider, and she appears to focus all of her attention on him, making the Unbreakable Vow with Severus Snape and physically pulling him out of the way during the skirmish at Malfoy Manner. The comparisons appear endless between these two families, but again, it's not enough to talk about fictional characters. I need to make this tangible for my students.

"How many of you pay your own tuition in full?" I ask. A few hands go into the air. The students who haven't raised their hands look around, their eyes darting nervously from classmate to classmate. "Now, how many of you pay some of your tuition?" There are more hands than there were before. And finally, "How many pay no tuition?" This time there are fewer hands than before but more than the students who foot the full bill themselves. Those simple questions begin to reveal the disparities and intersectionalities of the students. It's not an accident that students who have multiple siblings are not likely to have tuition paid in part or full for them, while students who are only children have significant financial support. It's not an accident that students whose parents or guardians work in professional positions or jobs that require higher education have considerable financial support, whereas students with blue-collar or low level white collar working parents or guardians have less support.

For some of these students, it's the first time they have considered how they fit into the hegemonic hierarchy of things. Their initial assumptions are that they are "just another college student." But, when we begin class discussions about who we are as individuals — where we grew up, what our family structures resemble, which cultures we were exposed to as children and adolescents — things begin to crystallize. Suddenly the students are recognizing that those experiences and fixed variables, like parentage, contribute to their self-identity as well as the privilege that they receive as a result of it. It is impossible to separate our individual threads of our identities from the whole. In theory we can analyze, interpret, and critique those individualities: gender, sexuality, affluence, and so on, but we must always come back to the understanding that these are fluid categories melding with and drifting from one another.

Conclusion

Like most popular culture references, I assume that *Harry Potter* will run its course and eventually lose capital in the classroom. My inner fan has begun screaming at me. "No! It can't be true. *Harry Potter* will live in our hearts *forever* as a story that asks us to believe in loyalty, hope, friendship, and the power of goodness!" Perhaps more accurately, it will live in my heart that way. While I continue to get older, many of the students will remain in a specific age cluster, from around eighteen to twenty-three, and culture refuses to stand still so that my references remain current and prescient. In a few short years, I will need to adapt, but for now, *Harry Potter* remains one of the key ways that I relate to my students.

The series provides me a way to introduce cultural studies and concepts concerning sexuality, gender, hegemony, and intersectionality to students who come to my classroom from wide-ranging majors. In terms of gender lessons, much of how we live and function in a gendered world is bound in how we are meant to dress. For men, choosing bright colors and accessories causes questions about sexual identity. Dumbledore's fashion choices are a potential semiotic clue to his identity as gay and are consistently used as evidence to draw that conclusion, which ultimately is a matter of interpretation. We learn that the most important worth of a woman is her beauty and the performance of femininity regardless of her abilities or talents. Hermione is just "one of the guys" until the Yule Ball when her change in clothes effectively *outs* her as a young woman. And finally, when we begin to examine how separate parts of identity interact, we begin to see how power is distributed among people who have inherently more privilege than others. Lucius, while cast as an antagonist, has far more privilege than Arthur, who is a "good guy" but can't seem to provide adequately for his family. There's a conversation here about how affluence allows for greater access to all sorts of things, from material objects to potential healthcare options, including birth control.

My pedagogy practices, my tactics and techniques for building social relationships with my students, are highly invested in popular culture. It's a common ground where we can meet and where we can share and exchange power in ways that a standard classroom environment does not allow for. When I have a student that clearly knows more about a pop culture text than I do, I let him or her teach through that example. He or she becomes an expert, and I become a student. Like some of the professors at Hogwarts, I ask my students to demonstrate their burgeoning knowledge for their classmates, giving them the opportunity to gain confidence in their speaking skills and argumentation. I know that in the coming years the classroom capital of *Harry Potter* will fade, but for the moment, my students and I stand together on the figurative Platform 9¾, waiting for the train to school. Mischief Managed.

NOTES

1. David Buckingham, "Introduction: Fantasies of Empowerment? Radical Pedagogy and Popular Culture," in *Teaching Popular Culture: Beyond Radical Pedagogy,* ed. David Buckingham (London: UCL Press, 1998), 3.

2. Graeme Turner, *British Cultural Studies: An Introduction,* 3rd ed. (Hoboken: Routledge, 2002), 2.

3. Ibid., 2.

4. Ibid., 16.

5. Stuart Hall, "Cultural Studies and Its Theoretical Legacies," *Stuart Hall: Critical Dialogues in Cultural Studies,* ed. David Morley and Kuang-Hsing Chen (London: Routledge, 1996), 268.

6. Ibid., 268–269.

7. Kenneth Burke, *The Philosophy of Literary Form* (Berkeley: University of California Press, 1973), 294.

8. Ibid., 294.

9. Hall, "Cultural Studies and Its Theoretical Legacies," 267.

10. Henry Jenkins, *Textual Poachers: Television Fans and Participatory Culture* (New York: Routledge, 1992), 19, 87.

11. Kimberle Crenshaw, "Mapping the Margins: Intersectionality, Identity Politics, and Violence against Women of Color," *Stanford Law Review* 43, no. 6 (July 1991): 1242.

Introducing English Literature in Pakistan

Asma Mansoor

Introduction

In the contemporary world of technical gymnastics, spontaneous entertainment has become the trademark of life. The youth of today disdain wasting time on anything that requires an extended assimilation of information and the gradual absorption of knowledge. Therefore, classical literature generally appears a frightening subject for almost all students owing to the complex variety of ideas, diction and styles along with the fact that it appears to be almost alien. However, for those students who are dealing with English as a second language and yet are undertaking English Literary Studies, the task of coping with English literary works becomes rather daunting, particularly if they take up the course at the university level. A number of undergraduate students in an L2 context fare poorly owing to the austere dimensions of literature that is accredited as "Classic." On the other hand, a number of these second language students revel in reading the latest bestsellers. Although the votaries of belletristic literature frown upon Popular Fiction, it does have its advantages among second language learners, as I discovered teaching in a Pakistani university. Since what the academics perceive as classical literature is difficult for the students of literature to digest at a stage when their interest in the subject is undergoing a slow, meiotic development, popular literature may be used to initiate them into the world of the "Classics" without making them lose interest in their field of study. This essay suggests how the teaching of the *Harry Potter* books as a sample of Popular Fiction in an L2 undergraduate English Literature program may enable the students to develop a foundational understanding of the ingredients that go into making "Literature." It also endeavours to show how pulp fiction can catapult them into appreciating the factors that are involved in the creation of literary monuments. It is however, pertinent to mention here that the activities described in this essay are based on my personal experience and have been designed on the basis of a hands-on experience of teaching both Popular Fiction as well as other literary genres to Pakistani undergraduate students.

Problems Encountered While Studying and Teaching

In post-colonial Pakistan, English Language and Literature are considered to be powerful periapts, catalysing social amelioration. With English playing the role of the "Wand of Destiny" (*DH* 415) in Pakistani society, many students elect to study English Literature at the undergraduate and graduate levels in Pakistani universities. Owing to the fact that Pakistan's school system is markedly stratified along class lines, the quality of education received by all is not equal. Many students take up the subject owing to social requirements instead of choosing it on the basis of any intimacy with the subject. This factor is supplemented by the fact that a number of students who take up this discipline at the university level have a rather weak foundation in the English language due to a number of weaknesses in the Pakistani school system. Moreover, there is a generally held erroneous perception amongst most Pakistani students of English Literature that they can acquire fluency in both spoken and written English through studying English Literature. However, despite all the wrong reasons for entering this rather trying domain, this does not mean that these students are not motivated in developing a strong understanding of literary studies. A majority of them determinedly pursue the subject and do manage to specialise in this discipline at post-graduate levels as well. However, they have to overcome a number of obstacles along the way, such as a weak grip on the English language, a very rudimentary background in the subject coupled with cultural differences and a lack of exposure to English in a practical context. This tends to inhibit their rapid adjustment to the rigorous demands of English literary studies. However, it is the teachers who have an even more difficult time than the students. Not only do the teachers have to initiate these novice L2 students of English Literature to the basics of the subject, they also have to assist them in overcoming the above-mentioned hindrances through various techniques and devices. A number of universities in Pakistan, which offer specialization in English Literature at the undergraduate level, have devised modules that function on the premise of introducing major literary works and stylistic patterns that the students will encounter at the very onset of their degree programs. While this kind of a module does help the students in developing a base in the discipline, most of the students complain of its being a rather dry, banal as well as an intensely demanding subject owing to their lack of familiarity as well as comfort level in dealing with works written in complex or archaic English.

Apart from that, a direct contact with "Classical English Literature" becomes a retarding factor in enabling some students to comfortably navigate through the course. With writers like Milton, Shakespeare, Chaucer, Henry Fielding, etc. being introduced at the very onset of studies in English Literature, most of the sophomore L2 students in Pakistani universities have to encounter an entire fuselage of complex styles, archaisms, references to ancient writers, difficult terminology, etc. As a result, a few of the students drop out of the degree program, while a number of other students continue to fare poorly.

Despite this ground reality, the situation is not insoluble. What is required is a modulation in the succession of the literature courses that are taught at the beginning of the degree program. In addition, one of the resources that can be utilized in developing literary acumen in novice English Literature students is to use Popular Fiction, which some of the students have already read independently, as a means of developing an understanding of English Literature and its varying paradigms. While this proclivity towards reading popular writers may be looked down upon by numerous literary scholars and scholars, as a teacher of Popular Fiction, I found this subject to be of great help in establishing a foundation in English literary studies amongst university level L2 students.

The pragmatic utilization of Popular Fiction in preparing second language students of English Literature may counter the opinions of the connoisseurs of English literature who frown upon Popular Fiction and state that it is inferior to Literature that has been canonized. However, there are multiple arguments both for and against this argument. Ken Gelder represents this reality in the following words: "Literature and Popular Fiction exist in a constant state of mutual repulsion or repudiation."[1]

This mutual repulsion or repudiation might be a bone of contention between the two categories of literature; however, what has to be kept in mind is that in all forms of literature, language functions along a hierarchy of literariness.[2] It begins its ascent from the merely semantic purpose, soaring through the figurative horizons of language, accruing connotative complexity as it finally escalades to the pinnacle of "what may be termed the universal imaginary."[3] Language, then, in any literary text has "varying and increasing levels of signification and resonance."[4] One notices that language functions along this continuum of literariness in Popular Fiction as well. Keeping this idea in mind, I chose the *Harry Potter* series as the core text for initiating L2 students, who were at the initial stages of their undergraduate degree in English Literature, into the stylistic, thematic and generic topography of English Literature. The *Harry Potter* meta-narrative is a mélange of various literary patterns and genres. It is a blend of the elements contained in fairy tales (both European and Asian), children's fiction, detective mystery novels, multiple plot lines, myths, realism, fantastic elements that are reminiscent of the realm of the Faerie, and numerous other ingredients which may be utilized not merely in second language environments, but also in classes composed of students whose first language is English. Since this work displays not only a resplendent multigenerity, its stylistic diversity and narrative technique may be constructively exploited as a pedagogical device for introducing English literature to its sophomore students.

Identifying Literary Conventions

One of the primary obstacles that a teacher of English Literature encounters while introducing English literary conventions to neophytic students is explaining how literary works imbibe traditions from other works and literatures from across the globe. While introducing such conventions through drawing parallels between different works is useful, it takes an investment of a greater amount of time and effort in tracing the relevant materials. Moreover, the introduction of a plethoric variety of reading material at the very onset of their degree program tends to create apprehensions amongst novice L2 students. Using a text that they enjoy and find relatively easy tends to dilute their trepidation about how to study the subject at the alpha stage of their academic quest. The need at this hour is to initiate the maximum number of L2 students into the literary characteristics of their discipline and then to prepare them for pursuing the subject both extensively and intensively through canonized literary works.

As highlighted earlier, the *Harry Potter* novels are a unique blend of various literary conventions. Intertextuality tends to grant this narrative with an expansive literary range and play, as Harry's quest becomes utilized to incorporate the quest of Everyman. Myths and fairytales form the substratum of the *Harry Potter* series establishing the magical element of the narrative. In order to elucidate how these elements have been incorporated in other literary works, one of the assignments that may be given to the learners is to read another fairy tale or myth from any region and time of the world about a heroic quest. They should then be tasked with tracing the basic outline of the story and also to enlist the trials faced by the hero. Subsequently, the students should be asked to write a simple outline of at least one book of the *Harry Potter* series of their own choice and highlight the tests that the protagonist undergoes. Once they have done that, the similar points between the two outlines may be compared. What comes to the fore are the "mythemes"[5] which, according to Claude Levi Strauss, are the constituent components of myths and by extension of multiple literary compositions. In doing so, the students are initiated into the conventions of structuralism and also bring to the fore the various stages of the monomyth[6] as defined by Northrop Frye. This activity may be further refined to bring many other literary conventions to the fore as the "Genre and Literary Conventions Quiz" given in the Appendix elucidates. It is noteworthy to mention here that the prescribed texts of the *Harry Potter* series ought to have been read by the students in advance before they proceed with the sample activities.

Moreover, the worksheets in the appendix are merely samples and may be modified and improved in accordance with the course outline of the institution where literature courses are taught to second language students of English Literature. The factors which were kept under consideration by the author of this essay were the introduction to literary conventions incorporated in various literary works. Moreover, the rationale behind making the students explore the fairy tale and mythological elements suffused within the structure of the novel was that the students paid a close attention to the structure of the novel at hand. In addition, by extensive reading and comparisons, they acquired an understanding of the basic elements that went into the ordering of a literary text. This activity also gave them the freedom to choose any myth and fairy tale of their own choice. While the students traced the similarities between the *Harry Potter* novels and their own selected texts, ensuing discussions enabled them to comprehend the notion of how a number of recurring motifs and themes contribute in universalizing the message and import of a given text. The extra reading and research through encyclopedias and other resources, albeit of a simple nature, enabled the L2 students to rise out of their passivity and to actively learn and apply literary concepts regarding a text that they found rather easy to understand at the preliminary stages of their learning. In most L2 environments, particularly in Third World and developing countries, students are generally seen to be passive listeners in English Literature classes, relying on rote learning to pass their exams. Through this methodology, they discarded this passivity as they applied the relevant literary terms and notions in a practical context and in an interactive environment. However, in this setting it was mandatory that the tasks set in such worksheets were supplemented by class discussions in which the teacher acted as a facilitator and not merely as the fountain of knowledge.

In addition, by comprehending the basic terms like "bildungsroman" and "monomyth," the students were enabled to identify these elements in advanced level Classical Literature. For instance, in the International Islamic University of Islamabad in Pakistan, Popular Fiction is taught in the third semester of the Bachelor Studies program in English Literature. In the fourth semester, subjects like Classical and Romantic Poetry as well as Classical Fiction are incorporated in the course. It came to be seen that the students who had studied the various stylistic and thematic dimensions in the *Harry Potter* series as a part of their Popular Fiction course were able to delineate the mythemes and the elements of fairy tales and the monomyth present in texts like *Great Expectations, Pride and Prejudice*, etc. In addition, they could identify magical elements and their significance as well as the model of the heroic quest in a text like *The Faerie Queene*, which, owing to its archaic speech patterns and heavy indebtedness to myths becomes extremely difficult for sophomore L2 students of English Literature to decode at the onset of their literary studies. The most positive results were evinced when the students identified the monomyth and bildungsroman patterns of Wordsworth's *Prelude*.

Identifying Stylistic Terms and Patterns

The *Harry Potter* novels are a rich reservoir of various stylistic patterns employed by Rowling with consummate skill. Techniques like neologism, intertextuality, multigenerity, etc. all coalesce to grant this meta-narrative a unique status as a pedagogical tool for introducing English Literature in an L2 context. Moreover, with a wide array of characters extending across an expansive socio-political, cultural and fantastic canvas, her art of characterization may be used as a beginning point to introduce sophomore L2 students of English Literature to the various techniques of characterization that the author has employed in the *Harry Potter* novels. One of the traditionally used techniques is the employment of the flow chart technique to define characters. However, this technique could be used in a worksheet incorporating a multiple variety of short questions as well.

While the "The Art of Characterization Worksheet" (available in the Appendix) brings to the fore the various aspects of character and helps the students to absorb the conventions of analyzing literary characters, it also encourages them to consult other books, develop and utilize appropriate vocabulary and also to analyze within multiple thematic contexts. While beginning with such simple outlines, the L2 students gradually learn how to organize and arrange information in literary essays, a task in which a number of L2 students of English Literature in Pakistan face enormous difficulties.

Since all literary works are interwoven in a myriad of ways, sharing and exchanging linguistic, stylistic and semantic genomes, an intertextual study of a work implies a comparison in stylistic terms such as allusions, borrowing, etc. According to Graham Allen:

> Works of literature ... are built from systems, codes and traditions established by previous works of literature. The systems, codes and traditions of other art forms and of culture in general are also crucial to the meaning of a work of literature. Texts, whether they be literary or non-literary, are viewed by modern theorists as lacking in any kind of independent meaning. They are what theorists now call intertextual. The act of reading, theorists claim, plunges us into a network of textual relations. To interpret a text, to discover its meaning, or meanings, is to trace those relations. Reading thus becomes a process of moving between texts. Meaning becomes something which exists between a text and all the other texts to which it refers and relates, moving out from the independent text into a network of textual relations. The text becomes the intertext.[7]

In the context of teaching the students to develop an intertextual approach while reading a literary text, the *Harry Potter* novels function as an important pedagogical tool. This is owing to the fact that the *Harry Potter* novels are replete with neological innovations, literary allusions, etymological clues and display a unique blend of multiple genres; activities may be devised to bring these aspects to the fore. For instance, since the *Harry Potter* novels display intertextual richness, the students may be asked to investigate allusions to various literary compositions as a part of their assignment. This would aid them in developing the skills for a comparative analysis of literary texts. Sample Activity Three, available in the appendix, may be of some help.

Identifying Multiple Thematic Paradigms

The literary canvas of English literature is not merely connected through a stylistic and linguistic circuitry, it also displays a thematic plexus in which many perennial themes and debates are constantly recycled and re-explored. Since literary studies do not merely require a stylistic evaluation of a written composition, its thematic structure has to be explored, both as a discrete unit as well as through its thematic juxtaposition with other texts. As is highlighted in the "Allusions in the Harry Potter Series Worksheet" (given in the Appendix), the *Harry Potter* novels enjoy a stylistic kinship with other literary works through J.K Rowling's employment of the techniques of allusion and neologism. This stylistic allusion creates a thematic collation within various texts as well. For instance, if one were to take the theme of the heroic quest, Harry's quest from Book 1 through Book 7 may be compared with the heroic quest of the Red Cross Knight in the *Faerie Queene* by Edmund Spenser. Moreover, Harry's travails in the world of witchcraft and wizardry bear a thematic resemblance with those of Pip in *Great Expectations*. As discussed earlier, once the L2 students are able to identify various thematic patterns in the *Harry Potter* novels, they are able to identify similar or different thematic paradigms in different texts. This hones the students' techniques of comparative analysis, which is of vital importance in writing literary essays. The literary essays that the questions in the "Thematic Comparison and Contrast Worksheet" demand are based on this premise and are primarily designed for students who have studied Popular Fiction as a part of their course work.

In the "Thematic Comparison and Contrast Worksheet," the questions do not merely focus on a thematic analysis but are also based upon the notion that the students should gradually be introduced to various literary eras and theories. For example, question 2 in the worksheet indirectly alludes to a literary theory, while question 3 refers to Victorian fiction. The stress, however, is on the word *gradually* since it would not be advisable to bombard these students with extensive knowledge. The aim is to introduce various concepts related to English Literary Studies at the initial stages of their undergraduate degree in English Literature, so that their academic base in the subject develops smoothly.

To conclude, what this essay has set out to highlight are some of the means through which the *Harry Potter* novels may be used for introducing English Literature in L2 environments. As a pedagogical tool, the *Harry Potter* series can provide anchorage to the L2 students in English Literary Studies. The inclusion of Popular Fiction as a part of the BS (Bachelor of Studies) English course work in Pakistani universities like the International Islamic University in Islamabad enables the students to develop the necessary skills. At a later stage, it also aids them in analyzing different literary works as well as in comprehending literary terms and devices through a text that they find to be commensurate with their language proficiency.

NOTES

1. Ken Gelder, *Popular Fiction: The Logics and Practices of a Literary Field* (London and New York: Routledge, 2004), 11.
2. F. Abiola Irele, "Sounds of a Tradition: The Souls of Black Folk," in *The Cambridge History of African American Literature*, ed. Maryemma Graham & Jerry W. Ward Jr. (Cambridge: Cambridge University Press, 2011), 21–38.
3. Ibid., 23.
4. Ibid., 25.
5. Charles E. Bressler, *Literary Criticism: An Introduction to Theory and Practice*, 4th ed. (New Jersey: Pearson Prentice Hall, 2007).
6. Ibid., 153.
7. Graham Allen, *Intertextuality* (London and New York: Routledge, 2000), 1.

Portkey to the Scholarly Disciplines

ELISABETH C. GUMNIOR

In *Harry Potter and the Goblet of Fire*, J. K. Rowling introduces yet another one of the wizarding world's public transportation systems. As Harry, Hermione, and the Weasleys are on their way to the secret location of the Quidditch World Cup, Mr. Weasley explains:

> For those who don't want to apparate or can't, we use Portkeys." They're objects that are used to transport wizards from one spot to another at a prearranged time. (...)
> "What sort of objects?" said Harry curiously.
> "Well, they can be anything," said Mr. Weasley. "Unobtrusive things, obviously, so Muggles don't go picking them up and play with them ... stuff they think is just litter.... You just need to touch the Portkey, that's all, a finger will do —"

A finger will do, indeed. Despite the dire warnings and expressions of disgust from their more cautious compatriots, some academic Muggles have begun to play with a specific piece of litter that has transported them to new places. Harry Potter the character, the series of books, the marketing phenomenon, the cultural icon that many of their colleagues deride has become their means of transport to new dimensions of inquiry within and across the universe of academic disciplines. The traces left by those who have employed this portkey have created an intricate network of scholarly discussions that is gaining not only strength and momentum, but also richness and maturity.

According to Cornelia Rémi's (aka Viola Eulenfeder, aka Viola Owlfeather) comprehensive international bibliography of *Harry Potter* literature,[1] academic investigations of the Potter books and cultural phenomenon began appearing only two years after the first *Harry Potter* book had been published in the UK. Rémi's bibliography is in itself an intriguing piece of scholarship that deserves further analysis, but even at a cursory glance the growing volume of this inventory proves that many scholars are not afraid to touch what their colleagues might consider the litter of popular culture. In doing so, they generate intriguing new discussions beyond the books themselves, beyond the marketing hype, and beyond the confines of their own communities. I will argue here that, in fact, academic engagement with everything Potter has become an integral part of the fan phenomenon and that a thorough examination of that body of academic literature can serve Potter scholars in a variety of ways. An assessment of the depth and substance of the ongoing discussions for instance may be the most potent way to gauge the often disputed merit of the series. Moreover, such an analysis can provide insights into just how the magic of this portkey works by revealing how scholars from a variety of disciplines relate to *Harry Potter* and how, in turn, their contributions can serve as very effective entry points to their disciplines for their students and colleagues.

I will begin this meta-analysis with what I consider to be a representative as well as convenient sampling of critical *Harry Potter* research and scholarship, made available in the form of eleven collections of critical essays published in the U.S between 2002 and 2011:

Harry Potter and the Literary and Cultural Critics:
> *The Ivory Tower and Harry Potter: Perspectives on a Literary Phenomenon*, edited by Lana Whited, 2002
> *Reading Harry Potter: Critical Essays*, edited by Giselle Liza Anatol, 2003
> *Harry Potter's World: Multidisciplinary Critical Perspectives*, edited by Elizabeth E. Heilman, 2003
> *Critical Perspectives on Harry Potter* (2nd ed.) edited by Elizabeth E. Heilman, 2008
> *Reading Harry Potter Again: New Critical Essays*, edited by Giselle Liza Anatol, 2009

Scholarly Wizardry Across the Disciplines
> *Harry Potter and Philosophy: If Aristotle Ran Hogwarts*, edited by David Baggett and Shawn E. Klein, 2004
> *The Psychology of Harry Potter: An Unauthorized Examination of the Boy Who Lived*, edited by Neil Mulholland, 2005
> *Harry Potter and International Relations*, edited by Daniel H. Nexon and Ivar B. Neumann, 2006
> *The Law and Harry Potter*, edited by Jeffrey E. Thomas and Franklin G. Snyder, 2010
> *The Ultimate Harry Potter and Philosophy: Hogwarts for Muggles*, edited by Gregory Bassham, 2010
> *Harry Potter and History*, edited by Nancy R. Reagin, 2011

These collections represent only the tip of a still growing iceberg. Yet, these are no mere scribblings of besotted fans; the inquiries undertaken are as often motivated by serious and well-considered skepticism as by enthusiastic appreciation of the novels, films and commercial phenomenon. Moreover, the editors all have very clear visions of the transportive or portkey function of their collections. Because the scope of my analysis of these books is somewhat constrained in the context of the present volume, I will focus on the way each editor articulates this vision in their introductions and through the organization of the content.

Harry Potter, the Literary Scholars, and the Cultural Critics

While the academic and/or literary elite may dismiss *Harry Potter* as an object of serious critical analysis — literary criticism icon Harold Bloom famously argued that 35 million readers can indeed be wrong about the literary value of Rowling's books[2] — for many academic worker-ants in English, Communication and Cultural Studies, and Education, Rowling's books have become the shared cultural artifact or portkey that allows them to enter into a variety of new discussions with their students and with each other.

Lana Whited, Giselle Liza Anatol, and Elisabeth E. Heilman, the editors of the first three collections published in the U.S., all make more or less direct references to Potter critics, and all three present cogent arguments for why the books should not be dismissed as just so much litter on the cultural landscape of our time.

In her introduction to *The Ivory Tower and Harry Potter*, Lana Whited takes on Jack Zipes's assertion that the popularity and commercial success of the books have obscured the criteria by which even children's literature should be judged, if it is to be taken seriously. While admitting that "the serious discussion we ought to be having about the literary merits of J. K. Rowling's Harry Potter novels is threatened by the clouds of commercialism encircling the books,"[3] Whited is nonetheless convinced that the criteria for what makes a literary classic are not so easily covered up. "[L]iterary scholars," she writes, "can see past the distraction of the books' commodification to accomplish the sort of thorough analysis the series begs."[4] Whited organizes her collection to further illustrate her point. The essays in the volume engage readers not only in discussions of how specific criteria of literary analysis and criticism can be applied to Rowling's novels, but also in critical discussions of these very criteria. Even at their most critical and skeptical Whited's contributors show that the novels could already rightfully claim their place in a classic literary canon because they

- follow familiar forms and genres without being merely derivative
- use language in ways that call "the readers' attention to the language itself and to how language reflects culture and cultural values"[5]

- engage readers by invoking their real world experiences in intriguing ways
- reflect the values of the places and times that produce them

Giselle Liza Anatol responds to criticism by William Safire, who argued in a *New York Times* article that the only way to arrest the infantilization of adult culture is to recognize the Potter novels' limitations as children's books.[6] In the introduction to *Reading Harry Potter*, she points out, rather sharply, that because the Potter series could become the millennial generation's defining narrative "[n]eglecting the potency of the novels and relegating them to the category of childhood trivia can result in the dangerously mistaken conclusion that the books do not reflect and/or comment upon the cultural assumptions and ideological tensions of contemporary society, and that they have no effect on the intellectual and social development of today's children and tomorrow's adults."[7]

To illustrate that point in particular, Anatol's collection begins with a section of essays exploring the *Harry Potter* novels through theories of child development before moving on to sections discussing literary influences and socio-cultural values.

Anatol's main concerns are "the tendency among some scholars to under-theorize children's fiction"[8] and their more generally held assumption that "conversations produced within university settings cannot be shared, understood, interpreted, or answered from outside the academy."[9] There is an undertone of frustration with literary scholars' and cultural critics' attitudes towards children's and young adult literature in Anatol's remarks that will be familiar to anyone who takes a serious scholarly approach to works written for children and young readers only to see that such critical engagement is treated dismissively. "This body of literature is a powerful tool for inculcating social roles and behaviors, moral guides, desires, and fears," she points out. Hence the purpose of her collection is to interrogate the internal and external mechanisms—the messages within and about those works—by which this inculcation is accomplished and, furthermore, to show how such interrogations can bridge the gap between the pursuits of intellectual engagement and of pleasure, between academia and society at large.

Elizabeth Heilman, too, sees the series' commercialization and admits that "[in] the postmodern context in which we live, cultural products promoted by multinational corporations can serve as a powerful form of authority promoting unequal relations of power and a dreary aesthetic,"[10] but rather than snubbing the books, Heilman suggests, academics should draw on the inquiry paradigms, theoretical lenses, and methodological perspectives of their disciplines to engage critically with the books, to "talk back to Harry Potter,"[11] and to teach their students to do so as well.

In fact, what distinguishes Heilman's *Harry Potter's World* is the deliberate manner in which she introduces the critical and analytical ways of thinking of her discipline in order to provide teachers with the curricular support that allows them to engage their students in meaningful explorations of *Harry Potter*, explorations that are grounded in both or either cultural studies and literary theories. In addition, Heilman constructs a framework that makes it possible for students to engage meaningfully with the secondary literature about the series and thereby to become more familiar and comfortable with academic discourses.

In the introductory chapter, "Fostering Critical Insight through Multidisciplinary Perspectives," Heilman presents four critical perspectives and theoretical lenses, each represented by its own selection of essays: cultural studies, reader response, literary studies, and social/ideological critique. As much as possible, she draws clear lines between them, explaining, for instance, that the cultural studies perspective looks at ways in which the Potter books in particular and the Potter phenomenon in general fit into contemporary culture, while ideological critique examines how contemporary cultural values and norms are reflected and represented in the books and films. At the same time, she is careful to show that critical perspectives can overlap and complement each other to the benefit of the reader's experience with the text. Heilman posits that the purpose of her collection is to help teachers do what much of the critical pedagogical literature asks them to do: "use powerful critical themes, address popular culture, and make meaningful connections to students' interests" and do so "on a range of levels, examining the relationship among cultural products and power at the macro level of political and economic structures — but also at the micro level, considering cultural and aesthetic nuances in language, texts, and personal responses."[12]

The primary purpose of all these essay collections "is to take a rigorous critical view of the books."[13] The assembled sets of scholars are deeply rooted in a wide array of postmodern literary and critical theories. Literary analyses, for instance, trace the vast network of intertextual connections in Rowling's books, or they demonstrate the multi-layered literary heritage of the series through detailed comparisons to folktales, British public school stories, and fantasy fiction. In doing so, they refute many of the critics who have accused Rowling of simply creating an amalgam of familiar literary motifs and themes at best, or plagiarizing at worst. Cultural studies approaches, on the other hand, explore issues such as racism and sexism, materialism and classism, xenophobia and oppression in order to uncover the ways in which Rowling might try to undermine or perpetuate conventional ideology and determine how successful she is at her project.

Competing and opposing views are easily illustrated in critical anthologies like these, which makes them very useful instructional tools. In each of the collections there is at least one pair of essays that demonstrates that even though authors might look at the same material, they often come to very different conclusions based on both their academic and their personal biases. In addition, the essays illustrate a variety of inquiry paradigms that help novice scholars construct and refine their own research projects (on this and other series).

Both Anatol and Heilman have recently presented second editions of their books. Anatol's *Reading Harry Potter Again* and Heilman's *Critical Perspectives on Harry Potter* demonstrate that the scholarship is maturing, and that the scholars' own experiences with the text undergo reconsiderations and revisions. Both editors speak to the continued appeal of the series and the expanding body of critical literature as an opportunity to engage with the "increasingly wide array of theory,"[14] the community of writers producing it, and "our writing Selves of the past five years."[15]

Anatol brings back six contributors to the earlier collection, all of whom pick up where they left off "readdressing and revising arguments made [in their earlier essays] in light of the completion of Rowling's series."[16] Eight new authors bring new perspectives on previously discussed concepts and new topic areas to the table. For her own collection, Heilman changed not only the title; she also significantly revised the structure and content of the book. It is still divided into four sections, but the focus of these is slightly different from the first edition: Perspectives on Identity and Morality, Critical and Sociological Perspectives, Literary Elements and Interpretations, and Cultural Studies and Media Perspectives. Heilman's introduction again offers in-depth explanations of the theoretical underpinnings of the various critical perspectives. In fact, I would argue that her introductory remarks are even more helpful to both teachers and students and thus make the book even more interesting as a textbook introduction to literary and cultural studies. Each of the sections contains at least one revised and updated essay from the first edition in addition to a total of thirteen new essays, including two by returning writers. Both collections provide important insights into the progress of Potter scholarship now that all the books of the series have been published.

Employing a cultural/literary artifact that is already familiar to most readers, the essays in each of these collections serve as portkeys especially for academic novices by illustrating how scholars in literary and cultural studies think and argue. Moreover, because the authors are usually upfront about the nature and the extent of their passion for, or objections against the series, their essays provide much food for thought and material for further discussions. As a result of the magic of meaningful engagement they engender, *Harry Potter* has become the portkey to the once-forbidding Ivory Tower. In addition, the study of literary and cultural artifacts is proving its relevance beyond the walls of that tower.

S.W.A.D.—Scholarly Wizardry Across the Disciplines

In the introduction to his book, *Popular Culture Studies Across the Curriculum*, Ray Browne argues that "the popular culture of a country is the voice of the people—for better or worse, their likes and dislikes, the lifeblood of their daily existence, their individual and national way of life"[17]; "[it] is the basic, unvarnished democratic culture that makes us, at the same time, similar and fundamentally human."[18] Therefore, cultural studies, the examination, interrogation, and analysis of popular culture in general, and specific popular culture artifacts in particular, have become a powerful and indispensable tool for academics. Popular culture is "a kind of daily world currency,"[19] Brown contends, and cultural studies, which "interpenetrates all disciplines,"[20] provides scholars, educators, and students with the tools to understand the value and uses of that currency.

In philosophy, scholars are beginning to see the study of popular culture as a way to break down traditional perceptions of the discipline both in academia and in mainstream culture. In a chapter in Browne's book Raymond Ruble points out that "...philosophy is not seen by our culture as having anything meaningful to contribute to the discussion [of culturally important topics]. Philosophy is not even on the radarscope, so to speak. Philosophy, the love of wisdom, has a minimized cultural status in America. Even our existence as an academic discipline is seldom acknowledged by our culture, and to the extent that it is 'acknowledged' it is treated as a quintessential ivory tower subject having no relevance to the 'real world.'"[21] He concludes: "Popular culture ignores [philosophy] because [philosophers] ignore it."[22] Ruble sees serious engagement with popular culture as essential if the discipline wants to successfully argue its relevance and engender more interest, especially among students, in philosophical thought. This kind of engagement is already demonstrated by works such as William Irwin's *Popular Culture and Philosophy Series* which aims to bridge the gap between "high" and "common" culture, redefine the philosophical canon, and reinvigorate philosophy's connection with its existential environment.[23]

With *Harry Potter and Philosophy: If Aristotle Ran Hogwarts* David Baggett and Shawn E. Klein take an approach similar to Elizabeth Heilman's but from a different disciplinary vantage point. Theirs is the first collection of critical essays from outside literary studies published in the U.S. and another installment in Irwin's series. Like Heilman, the editors create a framework that offers support for readers and turns them into students of philosophy. *Harry Potter and Philosophy* is also divided into four sections, titled after the names of the four houses of Hogwarts, each exploring a different area, from moral philosophy and value theory to metaphysics. The various chapters connect even the most casual reader with philosophical thought from Plato and Aristotle to Descartes, Nietzsche, and Hegel. In their introduction Baggett and Klein acknowledge that while Rowling obviously did not intend to write the books as philosophical treatises, the complexity of her stories makes them "a useful roadmap for navigating readers through one terrain of philosophical landscape after another."[24]

The tenor of their introduction indicates that Baggett and Klein clearly see their book as a way to introduce philosophy and philosophical reflection, analysis, and synthesis as both an academic discipline and a human pursuit; they want their readers to become "philosophically literate." The essays in this collection are written primarily with fans and academic novices in mind. They are not strictly speaking about the Potter novels, nor are they explicitly critical discussions of the Potter phenomenon; rather, they are introductory lectures in philosophy that use the books as a starting or reference point.

The second Potter volume in Irwin's series, and according to editor Gregory Bassham "ultimate," is *Harry Potter and Philosophy: Hogwarts for Muggles*, published in 2010. It picks up where the previous collection left off, covering now the entire seven books. In his introduction Bassham reaffirms the connections between popular culture and philosophy: "Philosophy, as Plato said, begins with wonder."[25] Wonder, in turn, nourishes the mind, which is why Rowling doesn't shy away from complex issues, even if her readers might not be able to grasp all of the implied subtleties. Books like his, Bassham obliquely argues here, provide the digestive aids that help to get the most nourishment for the mind not only out of Rowling's books but also out of the works of great philosophical thinkers. "Like others involved in the popular culture and philosophy movement, our hope is to bring philosophy out of the ivied halls of academia and make its methods, resources, and critical spirit available to all."[26]

The success of the *Blackwell Popular Culture and Philosophy* series (both volumes are in the list of top 100 bestselling books on Amazon; Baggett and Klein's are currently at #65, Bassham's is at #18 [information retrieved 4/15/2012])—over thirty volumes on everything from *Metallica and Philosophy* to *Hunger Games and Philosophy*—makes a compelling argument for the value of popular culture studies as a way to connect the world of academia with the world at large. By applying, as Bassham suggests, the methods, resources, and critical spirit of various academic disciplines to popular culture artifacts and issues, our vision and understanding of their relationships to each other changes. In addition, passive consumers are encouraged and enabled to become active and critical thinkers.

In the same spirit that produced the above collections, Daniel H. Nexon and Ivar B. Neumann have basically assembled an introductory casebook to the study of international affairs. The essays in *Harry Potter and International Relations* are organized thematically — the four sections of the book cover globalization, conflict and warfare, geography and myth, and pedagogy — and illustrate different ways in which international relations scholars engage with popular culture. Far from considering popular culture in general and the *Harry Potter* series in particular as cultural litter not worthy of scholarly examination, the editors point to the emerging body of critical commentary and argue that "Harry Potter provides particularly fertile ground for evaluating and illuminating the engagement between popular culture and international politics. The international and political dimensions of the Harry Potter phenomenon, we believe, make it uniquely suitable for analysis by scholars of international relations."[27]

In the introductory chapter to their book, Nexon and Neumann follow Heilman's example and explain the various critical lenses that the study of popular culture offers to scholars of international affairs:

- Politics and popular culture which seeks to understand the cause-effect relationship between popular culture and international relations.
- Popular culture as mirror which stresses the usefulness of popular culture in explaining or elucidating issues in world politics.
- Popular culture as data which studies popular culture as evidence of norms, beliefs, identities, etc.
- Popular culture as constitutive which seeks to determine how popular culture shapes other representational systems and thus plays an active rather than a passive role in the conduct of world politics.[28]

As the tone and the scholarly depth of the essays in this collection indicate, *Harry Potter and International Relations* is not only intended as an engaging introduction to international relations theories for students, but first and foremost as an invitation to international relations scholars to explore the intersections between the studies of popular culture and global politics. Nexon and Neumann reason that as popular culture increasingly becomes the medium for the communication of ideas, concepts, and theories of politics, international relations scholars will have to (1) become more thoughtful about both the potential and the limitations of popular culture as a teaching tool and (2) more clearly define what new insights and approaches they can bring to the analysis of popular culture that are not already covered by disciplines such as cultural studies, communications, anthropology, literature, and cultural sociology.[29] Two chapters of the book in the section on globalization provide indications of both how difficult it can be to carve out disciplinary territory in an essentially interdisciplinary field and what the nature of the international studies scholars' contributions to cultural studies can be.

Harry Potter and the Law, introduced by Jeffrey E. Thomas and Franklin G. Snyder, is probably the most surprising entry to the multidisciplinary body of Potter scholarship ... at least until one realizes, as I did, that law and literature collaborate in various ways. (For more information on this collaboration, readers can go to the Law and Layers in Popular Culture Collection at the University of Texas Tarlton Law Library, http://tarlton.law.utexas.edu/exhibits/lpop/index.html, or consult one of the many introductory textbooks on law and literature, such as Richard Posner's *Law and Literature*, 3rd ed.) Laws and legal institutions are an important part of Rowling's narratives, Thomas points out in the preface to his collection, and the depictions of these resonate with readers. "This may suggest that the depictions are either consistent with readers' values or opinions. Alternatively, if the depictions are not reflective, they may influence the development of values and opinions."[30] Like his colleagues in Philosophy and Political Science, Thomas points to the important connection between his discipline/profession and popular culture: "Our popular culture is the context within which our legal system operates and is reformed."[31]

The collection grew out of a conference on, *The Power of Stories: Intersections of Law, Culture, and Literature*, co-sponsored by Texas Wesleyan University Law School and the University of Gloucestershire. Thomas's collection brings together the Potter scholarship presented there and elsewhere into a coherent introduction to legal terms, concepts, methods, and resources in order to bring the critical spirit of the discipline to audiences outside of the law school classroom, the law office, or the courtroom.

The book is divided into five sections that discuss (1) legal traditions and institutions in the wizarding world, (2) crimes and punishments, (3) issues of identity such as family relationships and racial and gender differences, (4) economic issues, and (5) the narratives' role as archetypes to illustrate legal principles in legal education and beyond. While all the essays clearly reflect the discursive patterns of legal scholarship — for instance the penchant for almost epic amounts of footnotes and extremely detailed definitions of terms and concepts — they are clearly written for lay readers. Thus they provide the portkey for those readers to more informed perspectives on law and legal matters.

Harry Potter and History, edited by Nancy R. Reagin and published in 2011, is the most recent addition to the set of books I have chosen to discuss here. Reagin is not only the editor of this volume but also the series editor of the new *Wiley Pop Culture and History Series* and the editor of *Twilight and History*. This new series is one more indication how important the study of popular culture and its artifacts has become to academic disciplines across the curriculum. In the introduction to *Twilight and History*, Reagin argues that "if we place [the novels' characters] against the backdrop of their original historical cultures [they] stand out in sharp relief, and many details are freshly illuminated. The sparkle and glitter when we shine this new light [of historical inquiry] upon them, and ... we understand them better."[32] This applies equally to *Harry Potter*.

Reagin and her contributors shine their new light on the series by constructing the history of British wizarding society in relationship to the known history of European muggle societies. The benefit for Rowling's readers is threefold:

1. The collection presents the subject of history in engaging ways and proves that its study does not need to be boring.

2. It shows how knowledge of history can enhance the reading pleasure of a literary text, which, in turn, can increase knowledge and understanding of history.

3. It implicitly teaches readers something about the process of writing history, demonstrating that history and our perception of it are constructed and thus can be reconstructed on the basis of new insights or perspectives.

The portkey function of *Harry Potter*—as well as of this collection—is explicitly stated in the concluding essay, Anne Rubenstein's "Hermione Raised Her Hand Again: Wizards Writing History." "The world of Harry Potter books and movies," Rubenstein points out, "shows us how Ron, Harry, and Hermione turn into historians. It offers fans the chance to think like historians, too" and to discover that "doing history" can be a lot of fun.[33] What it means to have fun doing history is amply illustrated by the contributors to this collection.

Leviosa or the Way Forward in Scholarship

As Rémi's bibliography demonstrates, the body of critical examinations of *Harry Potter* is growing at a rapid pace. An analysis of that body can, of course, give a detailed picture of who contributes to it, what scholars are interested in, and how they approach and articulate those interests. However, it can also provide insights into what areas of study are not yet included. Notably absent from this collection of sources are any articles examining the place of the series in the college classroom, especially outside of literary studies, or the use of the critical secondary literature on *Harry Potter* as a teaching tool. While in both Europe and the U.S. the number of Potter-related college and university courses is steadily increasing, there is little evidence that those teachers report or reflect on their experiences. Their silence on the issue may have something to do with the general skepticism and occasional derision they face from the public as well as their colleagues. It is therefore to be hoped that the present collection will fill a rather large gap in the critical literature.

In the university of the 21st century, the study of popular culture in all disciplines will become more rather than less important because our popular culture, to lean on a remark I quoted earlier, is the context within which our societies operate and continuously change. The way forward then is to lift up the work we and our students do with popular culture to a new level, to showcase and highlight it as true scholarship. In my classes, I use the critical secondary literature rather than the primary sources — Rowling's series — as the starting point for discussions. Students who come to my courses as fans of the books leave as well-informed contributors to the already ongoing discussions of *Harry Potter* in all disciplines. We examine disciplinary inquiry patterns and discourses in order to better understand — and here I am leaning a bit again — the methods, the resources, and the critical spirit of these disciplines. Moreover, we gain a clearer understanding of the role popular culture plays in shaping, rather than merely reflecting, our society and all its institutions, including the university. We throw the doors of the Ivory Tower wide open, no passwords required.

For this discussion I have left out a lot of very valuable material: single-authored books, published theses, the blogosphere, and much more. For those interested in exploring this material further, I'd like to point one more time to Cornelia Remi's outstanding bibliography, or, for a less voluminous starting point, J. Steve Lee's partial bibliography in this volume's Appendix. But regardless of the limitations of my source material, the collections of critical considerations of the *Harry Potter* texts and phenomenon I have discussed here establish the fact that the critical gaze on Harry is expanding and deepening. Those who still persist in arguing that the series has nothing to offer but infantile entertainment and rubbish to be rejected are missing the opportunity to engage in an inter-, intra-, multi-, and cross-disciplinary and cross-generational conversation that can help us reconsider what it means to learn and to know. Not only the *Harry Potter* novels, but also *Harry Potter* scholarship have become crucial portkeys to academia and academic disciplines in the 21st century.

Notes

1. Cornelia Rémi, Harry Potter Bibliography, April 29, 2012, http://www.eulenfeder.de/hpliteratur.html.
2. Harold Bloom, "Can 35 Million Book Buyers Be Wrong? Yes," *Wall Street Journal*, July 11, 2000, A26.
3. Lana Whited, "Introduction," in *The Ivory Tower and Harry Potter*, ed. Lana Whited (Columbia: University of Missouri Press, 2002), 12.
4. Ibid., 9.
5. Ibid., 9.
6. William Safire, "Besotted with Potter," *New York Times*, January 27, 2000, A27.
7. Giselle Liza Anatol, "Introduction," in *Reading Harry Potter*, ed. Giselle Liza Anatol (Westport, CT: Praeger, 2003), xv.
8. Ibid., xiv
9. Ibid., xiv.
10. Elizabeth E. Heilman, "Introduction," in *Harry Potter's World: Multidisciplinary Critical Perspectives*, ed. Elizabeth E. Heilman (New York: Routledge Falmer, 2003), 9.
11. Ibid., 9.
12. Heilman, *Harry Potter's World*, 10.
13. Anatol, *Reading Harry Potter*, xv.
14. Elizabeth E. Heilman, "Introduction," in *Critical Perspectives on Harry Potter*, ed. Elizabeth E. Heilman (New York: Routledge, 2009), 1.
15. Giselle Liza Anatol, "Introduction," in *Reading Harry Potter Again: New Critical Essays*, ed. Giselle Liza Anatol (Santa Barbara, CA: Praeger, 2009), xii.
16. Ibid.
17. Ray B. Browne, "Introduction," in *Popular Culture Studies Across the Curriculum*, ed. Ray B. Browne (Jefferson, NC: McFarland, 2005), 11.
18. Ibid., 12.
19. Ibid., 3.
20. Ibid., 5.
21. Raymond Ruble, "Popular Culture and Philosophy," in *Popular Culture Across the Curriculum*, ed. Ray B. Browne (Jefferson, NC: McFarland, 2005), 69.
22. Ibid., 74.
23. Ibid., 73.
24. George Bassham, "Introduction," in *The Ultimate Harry Potter and Philosophy: Hogwarts for Muggles*, ed. George Bassham, Blackwell Philosophy and Popular Culture Series (Hoboken, NJ, Wiley, 2010), 3.
25. Ibid., 1.
26. Ibid., 2.
27. Daniel H. Nexon and Iver B. Neumann, "Introduction," in *Harry Potter and International Relations*, ed. Daniel H. Nexon and Iver B. Neumann (Boulder, CO: Rowman & Littlefield, 2006), 4.
28. Ibid., 3–4
29. Ibid., 9.
30. Jeffrey E. Thomas and Franklin G. Snyder, *The Law and Harry Potter* (Durham, NC: Carolina Academic Press, 2010), vii.
31. Ibid., viii.
32. Nancy R. Reagin, *Twilight and History*, Wiley Pop Culture and History Series (Hoboken, NJ: Wiley, 2010), 3.
33. Anne Rubenstein, "Hermione Raised her Hand Again: Wizards Writing History," in *Harry Potter and History*, ed. Nancy R. Reagin (Hoboken, NJ: Wiley, 2011), 320.

The Queen City Muggles:
Town and Gown Go to Hogwarts

SUSAN JOHNSTON

> [I]f the field is left to a bunch of intellectual Muggles who believe the traditional novel is dead, they'll kill the damn thing.[1]
> — Stephen King

> The public does not like bad literature. The public likes a certain kind of literature and likes that kind of literature even when it is bad better than another kind of literature even when it is good. Nor is this unreasonable, for the line between different types of literature is as real as the line between tears and laughter; and to tell people who can only get bad comedy that you have some first-class tragedy is as irrational as to offer a man who is shivering over some weak warm coffee a really superior sort of ice.[2]
> — G.K. Chesterton

The Book That Lived

July 21, 2007. There seem, rather suddenly, "to be a lot of strangely dressed people about. People in cloaks" (*SS* 3). There is nothing about these mall parking lots, ordinarily colorless and deserted on a summer night, "to suggest that strange and mysterious things would soon be happening all over the country" (*SS* 2), but they are happening nonetheless. For today is the release of *Harry Potter and the Deathly Hallows*, the last volume in J.K. Rowling's phenomenally successful series, the Book that Lived, and even Muggles like ourselves are celebrating, "this happy, happy day!" (*SS* 5).

May 10, 2008. And again, there seem to be rather a lot of strangely dressed people about. There is little about the staid grounds of this old college campus to suggest strange and mysterious things will soon be happening, but as the doors are thrown open, it seems that the city's college professors are behaving very strangely indeed. Donning their convocation gowns! Welcoming children! And *is that a broomstick?* For today, town and gown meet to celebrate all things Harry, the world-wide phenomenon of the Boy who Lived.

It is ten months after the publication of *Harry Potter and the Deathly Hallows,* and the University of Regina, in Regina, Saskatchewan, is hosting *Harry Potter and the Queen City Muggles,* an all-ages convention somewhere between a conference and a block party, at its old downtown campus. In Darke Hall, the beautiful, if somewhat dilapidated theater, a range of academic papers from a variety of disciplines is capped, in the afternoon, with an address by the Canada Research Chair in the Culture of Childhood, Mavis Reimer, on "A World Apart? Mapping the Harry Potter Series." The historic lecture theater on the second floor features astronomy professor Martin Beech's "Reading the Stars," and in an old laboratory on the third floor a doctoral candidate in chemistry from the University of British Columbia, Erin Lindenberg, demonstrates Muggle potions. Undergraduates Christine Moleski and Lauren Perchuk, just down the hall, are leading children's sessions on drawing magical creatures and making their own marauder's map. Out on the lawn, Education student Callista Szachury referees Quidditch for Muggles. The first floor hallway is crowded with exhibit tables from the local Comic Readers' Bookshop, and nearby local writers are reading aloud their favorite passages from the series. Truly the old campus, long the sleepy locus of Continuing Education and spring break children's camps, has roused from its slumber.

It happened nearly by accident, this strange collaboration of faculty and fans, librarians and local writers. Everywhere I'd been that summer, I had seen something itself stranger than owls by day, more mysterious than people in cloaks, odder in its way than a cat reading a map (*SS* 2–3). I'd seen readers. On the beach, at the cottages, in the parks, on the buses and at the festivals: everywhere I'd been, I'd seen readers reading. Odder still, they were all reading the same book. I felt as if I was part of something that had not been seen under the sun since the glory days when universal literacy was in its infancy and the latest numbers of Charles Dickens' stories were selling a hundred thousand at a time; I felt as New Yorkers must have done, waiting on the piers that legendary autumn of 1841, as they cried out to the vessel incoming from London with the last number of Charles Dickens' *The Old Curiosity Shop* and the news of little Nell's death[3]; I felt as if I had emerged from my refuge in libraries grown ever more silent to discover that the whole world was a library.

Reading in Decline

To make sense of this brave new world I felt I'd found, I should say that my career as an academic has been marked from its beginning by a sense of decline. I began my master's degree in 1987, the year Allan Bloom published his famous jeremiad on the decay of the humanities, *The Closing of the American Mind*; defended my doctoral dissertation only months before Bill Readings' seminal *The University in Ruins*; and am now raising my children in the midst of what Mark Bauerlein terms *The Dumbest Generation*[4]; from the outset, I have sensed, as many of my generation of academics do, that after us will come the deluge, and it was cold comfort to discover, as I have done in my comparatively settled middle age, that this crisis is chronic rather than emergent.[5]

The fact is, however perennially complaints about the decline of the humanities have bloomed on academic greens, there is good reason to believe that the long-awaited decline is now upon us, in the form of shrinking faculty lines and burgeoning class sizes[6]; what is more, there is every reason to believe, with Bauerlein, that literacy skills are at last declining, precisely as teachers have prophesied for so long. In 2007, for example, the same year as the publication of *Deathly Hallows*, the Pan-Canadian Assessment Program (PCAP) found the number of Saskatchewan thirteen-year-olds achieving proficiency in reading to be 9 percent, rather than the 22 percent which is the average nationwide.[7] Yet between 25 and 30 percent of these students will crowd first-year classes at the University of Regina every fall, though if the indicators were to be believed, by Fall 2012, fewer than half of those first-year students would be reading at college level.

Nor is the problem unique to Saskatchewan. In 2008, a leading composition scholar responded to the growing chorus of voices bemoaning declining literacy amongst post-secondary students by repeating the famous 1988 Connors and Lunsford comparative study of formal error in college writing.[8] While, in 2008, it seemed the rate of formal error had remained remarkably stable since at least 1917,[9] Lunsford and Lunsford also found that kinds of error were shifting dramatically, and shifting in ways that point to the same decline in reading skills that is appearing in national testing. In particular, while sentence-level writing challenges such as comma splices and sentence fragments have declined, error patterns related to reading challenges, such as wrong word and homonym errors, have increased; indeed, where the 1988 study found 2,217 wrong word errors in 3000 papers, by 2008 Lunsford and Lunsford found 3080 wrong word errors in just 877 papers, fully 14 percent of all errors in their nationwide sample.[10] (Moreover, the authors note that spelling errors, which in 1988 outnumbered all other errors by three to one, in 2008 accounted for only 6.5 percent of all errors found, an improvement they quite rightly attribute to the widespread use of word processor spell checking. However, while students have come to rely on these spellcheckers, such tools do not flag correctly spelled wrong words, and indeed may suggest a wrong word as correction [796]).

This is not, of course, to say that Johnny can't read. But as teachers and parents who have observed the remarkable rise in the use of social technologies over the past decade are most of them aware, the pressing difficulty is that Johnny *won't* read: in 2002, only 52 percent of Americans aged 18–24 reported reading a book for pleasure over the preceding year.[11] The news is not all bad, of course; as a major NEA report recently noted, elementary schools have lately noted genuine progress in reading ability, but, alarmingly, "all progress appears to halt as children enter their teenage years."[12] While the number of nine-year-olds who read almost every day for fun has remained consistent over the past twenty years, and actually shows marginal growth from 53 percent to 54 percent, thirteen-year-olds have seen a five percentage point decline over the same period — and seventeen-year-old leisure readers have declined by nine percentage points over the same period, so that in 2004 only 22 percent of this age group reported voluntary reading.[13] So Johnny won't read, and neither will Jane, and soon enough, *won't* becomes *can't*: while reading test scores for nine-year-olds, who have shown no declines in the rate of voluntary reading, are higher than ever, scores for seventeen-year-olds have been trending slowly downward since 1992, and the rate of decline increases as we enter the first decade of the 21st century and the Web 2.0 generation.[14] Dana Gioia notes on pages 13–14 of *To Read or Not to Read: A Question of National Consequence* that reading proficiency rates, stagnant among women, are declining amongst men, such that the gender gap in reading achievement is widening without women showing measurable gains.

I'm arguing two things here: first, that the crisis in the humanities, so often prophesied, is in fact real, and, second, that the roots of this crisis lie in the gradual decline of reading. For whatever else they may be, including a call to the examined and examining life, the humanities are fundamentally about books. I do not mean by this a lament for the loss of a "Great Tradition," though I think we are, indeed, losing it and that this loss is to be lamented; I concur in fact with Martha Nussbaum, who notes that calls, such as Allan Bloom's, to return to such a tradition, by "focusing only on what can be made to look extreme or absurd ... in practice feed the popular disdain for the humanities that has led to curtailment of departments and programs and to the rise of narrow preprofessional studies."[15] Rather, I propose that not just the great heritage of western literature but the heritage of all literatures is at risk in the decline of reading, and with them the robust and engaged life of the citizen. Not for nothing does the National Endowment for the Arts, in 2007's *To Read or Not to Read*, describe itself "not [as] an elegy for the bygone days of print culture, but instead ... a call to action"[16]; for indeed more than reading is at risk.[17] Literary readers are not only three times more likely to participate in other forms of art and culture, including attending jazz and classical concerts, plays, musicals, and art museums, they are also much more likely than non-readers to play sports, attend sporting events, exercise, or engage in outdoor activities[18]; what is more, across age groups, gender, education levels, census regions — that is, *universally*— literary readers are far more likely to volunteer or do other kinds of charity work,[19] to vote,[20] and to follow current and public affairs through a whole variety of media.[21]

This broad pattern of civic engagement is both a corollary and a consequence of the call to freedom books declare. Nussbaum distinguishes between the traditional "liberal studies" of ancient Rome, that is, that education "suited for the freeborn gentleman," and that "which makes its pupils free, able to take charge of their own thought and to conduct a critical examination of their society's norms and traditions."[22] To this task of freedom, not just books but literary experience is critical. As C.S. Lewis notes, and the NEA quotes: "Literary experience heals the wound, without undermining the privilege, of individuality. There are mass emotions which heal the wound; but they destroy the privilege.... But in reading great literature I become a thousand men and yet remain myself.... Here, as in worship, in love, in moral action, and in knowing, I transcend myself; and am never more myself than when I do."[23]

This is to say, as Nussbaum does, that "the artistic form makes its spectator perceive, for a time, the invisible people of their world"[24]; it is to say that those crowds, waiting on the piers of New York for news of little Nell's death and in the bookstore parking lots for the latest news of Harry Potter's life, have been called out of themselves and into a mode of life in which they are both irreproachably themselves and themselves *with others*. For

> [i]n reading a realist novel with active participation, readers do all that tragic spectators do — and something more. They embrace the ordinary. They care not only about kings and children of kings, but about David Copperfield, painfully working in a factory, or walking the twenty-six miles from London to Canterbury without food. Such concrete realities of a life of poverty are brought home to them with a textured vividness unavailable in tragic poetry.[25]

This "textured vividness," I suggest, does more for the reader than reveal the ordinary; it reveals it *as real* at the same time as it embraces it as *extraordinary*. *David Copperfield*, *The Old Curiosity Shop*, *Hard Times*— such novels bare indeed the "concrete realities" of life, but they do so in part by asserting the extraordinary power of the ordinary to bring us into contact with others no longer alien but familiar. Not for nothing does Dickens call "fancy"—that capacious power of the imagination—"the one thing needful."[26]

In this sense, J.K. Rowling's Muggle world reminds us of the poverty of a life lived without books, without the imaginative sympathy that books help to call into being. It is worth recalling here the hermetic sterility of Number Four, Privet Drive, where Dudley's second bedroom, with its "shelves ... full of books" are "the only things in the room that looked as though they'd never been touched" (*SS* 37–38). In the barren wasteland of Dursleydom, everything is "perfectly normal, thank you very much" (*SS* 1), and the astonishing magical world all around them is "dangerous nonsense" that must be "stamp[ed] out" (*SS* 36). Vernon Dursley is, we may say, the younger cousin of those enemies of fancy, Dickens' immortal Messrs. M'Choakumchild and Gradgrind, for whom "[f]act, fact, fact, [was] everywhere in the material aspect of the town; fact, fact, fact, everywhere in the immaterial ... and everything was fact between the lying-in hospital and the cemetery, and what you couldn't state in figures, or show to be purchasable in the cheapest market and saleable in the dearest, was not, and never should be, world without end."[27] This is not to say that the Dursleys eschew leisure—those untouched books of Dudley's "second bedroom" stand next to the broken televisions, cine-cameras, air-rifles, the wreckage of Dudley's ephemeral amusements (*SS* 37)—but that in these amusements they find nothing but self and self-interest. Even as Mr. Sleary of the traveling circus in *Hard Times* asserts that "[p]eople mutht be amuthed," he notes too that "there ith a love in the world, not all Thelf-interetht after all"[28]; indeed, for Sleary as for Dickens that imaginative sympathy which is "the wisdom of the Heart"[29] is nourished in the soil of fancy and fairy-tales. Dangerous nonsense, indeed, these books may be, books which call us out of ourselves and into a robust engagement with the concrete and extraordinary lives of the once-alien other, but more dangerous still is the self-absorption of a world without readers. "By every measure captured by the Survey of Public Participation in the Arts, literary readers lead more robust lifestyles than non-readers. These findings contradict commonly held assumptions that readers and arts participants are passive, isolated, or self-absorbed."[30]

Magic for Muggles

And so it was that in the summer of 2007, knowing as I did that reading was everywhere declining and seeing in that decline something of the barren wasteland, the "great wilderness" the Gradgrindian system makes and will make,[31] I emerged from what Milton called "beholding the bright countenance of truth in the quiet and still air of delightful study"[32] to find readers blossoming everywhere. Young and old they were, from the seven-year-old still painstakingly sounding out "Di ... a ... gon ... all ... ey!" to the medievalist delighting in Rowling's Latinisms, from harried mothers with one eye on the hot dogs and the other on Harry to shamefaced businessmen with their copies of *Deathly Hallows* peeking out of their briefcases. Back on campus the experience was the same. From modernists to Miltonists, physicists to philosophers, those for whom books live were absorbed in the Boy Who Lived.

It was Marcel DeCoste, my colleague and co-organizer, and also, not coincidentally, my husband, he who had read each of the first six novels aloud to our children, who first saw in this curious conjunction of readers like and unlike the germ of a conference, and the following May, in *Harry Potter and the Queen City Muggles*, we sought to give this shared passion "a local habitation and a name."[33] From its inception we imagined it as a space of community, a moment when the academy answered the love of all things Harry by enacting a love of its own. We would have papers, yes, for dust-dry as our scholarship may sometimes seem to the world outside our walls it is in that scholarship that the humanities, and indeed the academy as a whole, articulates the call to freedom and inquiry we profess, but we would also have games, stories, science, art — all those modes of performance and of play through which, from childhood on, we articulate a passionate engagement with the world and the world of the book. We would charge nothing; we would turn no one away; we would tear open the veil between the university and the community, between the wizarding world and our ordinary, extraordinary lives.

Remarkably, perhaps, money was found.[34] Still more remarkably, a team came together; Marcel and I were joined by Warren James, Young Adult Librarian of Regina Public Libraries, by our colleague Noel Chevalier and by Barbara McNeil and Meredith Cherland, from the Faculty of Education, by an administrative assistant, Loanne Myrah, apparently capable of leaping tall bureaucracies in a single bound, by a tireless team of undergraduates spearheaded by Lauren Perchuk and our free elf, Blaise Boehmer; everywhere we turned for help we found comrades. And on May 10, 2008, we put on our robes and wizard hats and flung open the doors of the old downtown campus to find it transformed, a Hogwarts, a home for magic and mystery and ideas that, like Harry, live.

We found, in fact — and this is what made the conference not just possible but a success, a success which itself gave rise to Queen City Comics (organized by Sylvain Rheault of the Department of French, University of Regina), again an all-ages event, the following year — not just readers but the robust engagement that readers bring and that we thought was vanishing. High school students wrote essays for our contest; children came with their parents and grandparents; wizards large and small congregated on the lawn for our barbecue; academics turned to children and children to academics, rather as Alice and the unicorn turn to each other, discovering to their delight that both are real and that both are part of Wonderland:

> Alice could not help her lips curling up into a smile as she began: "Do you know, I always thought Unicorns were fabulous monsters, too! I never saw one alive before!"
> "Well, now that we *have* seen each other," said the Unicorn, "if you'll believe in me, I'll believe in you. Is that a bargain?"[35]

We learned, in other words, that to believe in reading is to believe in unicorns, and to share our love of reading with the world outside our walls is to share the unicorns with them. Nor is this a glib example. Martha Nussbaum remarks:

> Narrative play does teach children to view a personlike shape as a house for hope and fear and love and anger, all of which they have known themselves. But the wonder involved in storytelling also makes evident the limits of each person's access to every other.... The habits of wonder promoted by storytelling thus define the other person as spacious and deep, with qualitative differences from oneself and hidden places worthy of respect.[36]

If the humanities are to survive, they must call out in each person such habits of wonder. Charles Dickens did this once, for crowds on the pier; J.K. Rowling does it now. If the road to the capacious imagination which is the inheritance of free citizen and free elf alike can no longer begin with Dickens, this does not mean that the road is closed. It may be, as I think I have shown, that without readers these habits of wonder and the free life of the citizen they forge are endangered, but we in the academy suppose to our own peril that we are not part of the danger. We mourned the vanishing culture of books, of the stories that we love, but we forgot, as Chesterton says, that the public, too, has books and stories that they love. If we want them to join us, we must first join them; the road that begins with *Harry Potter* leads also to Tolkien's *The Hobbit* and from there to Dickens, to Defoe, to Shakespeare; it leads, after all, both there and back again.

Notes

1. Stephen King, "J.K. Rowling's Ministry of Magic," *Entertainment Weekly*, August 17, 2007, 34.
2. G.K. Chesterton, *Charles Dickens* (Ware: Wordsworth Editions, 2007), 53.
3. Edgar Johnson, *Charles Dickens: His Tragedy and Triumph*, vol. 1 (New York: Simon and Schuster, 1952), 304.
4. Allan Bloom, *The Closing of the American Mind* (New York: Simon and Schuster,

1987); Bill Readings, *The University in Ruins* (Cambridge, MA: Harvard University Press, 1996); Mark Bauerlein, *The Dumbest Generation: How the Digital Age Stupefies Young Americans and Jeopardizes Our Future (Or, Don't Trust Anyone Under 30)* (New York: Tarcher/Penguin Group, 2008).

5. Gary Burns, "Television and the Crisis in the Humanities," in *Rejuvenating the Humanities*, ed. Ray B. Browne and Marshall W. Fishwick (Bowling Green: Bowling Green State University Press, 1992), 153.

6. Ibid.

7. Government of Saskatchewan, Ministry of Education, *2009 Saskatchewan Education Indicators Report: Prekindergarten to Grade 12* (Regina, SK: Saskatchewan Ministry of Education, 2009), 46–7.

8. Andrea A. Lunsford and Karen J. Lunsford, "'Mistakes Are a Fact of Life': A National Comparative Study," *College Composition and Communication* 59, no. 4 (2008): 781–2; Robert Connors and Andrea A. Lunsford, "Frequency of Formal Error in Current College Writing, or Ma and Pa Kettle Do Research," *College Composition and Communication* 39, no. 4 (1988).

9. Lunsford and Lunsford, "'Mistakes Are a Fact of Life," 800.

10. Ibid., 784, 795–796.

11. Dana Gioia, ed. *To Read or Not to Read: A Question of National Consequence*, Research Report 47 (Washington, DC: National Endowment for the Arts, 2007), 7.

12. Ibid., 5.

13. Ibid., 8.

14. Ibid., 12.

15. Martha C. Nussbaum, *Cultivating Humanity: A Classical Defense of Reform in Liberal Education* (Cambridge, MA: Harvard University Press, 1997), 298.

16. Gioia, *To Read or Not to Read*, 6.

17. Ibid., 77.

18. Ibid., 87.

19. Ibid., 88.

20. Ibid., 89.

21. Ibid., 89.

22. Nussbaum, *Cultivating Humanity*, 30.

23. C.S. Lewis, *An Experiment in Criticism* (Cambridge: Cambridge University Press, 1995), 140–1; qtd. in Gioia, *To Read or Not to Read*, 90.

24. Nussbaum, *Cultivating Humanity*, 94.

25. Ibid., 95.

26. Charles Dickens, *Hard Times; For These Times* (Peterborough, ON: Broadview Press, 1996), 41, 245.

27. Ibid., 61.

28. Ibid., 310.

29. Ibid., 248.

30. Dana Gioia, *The Arts and Civic Engagement: Involved in Arts, Involved in Life*, Research Brochure (Washington, DC: National Endowment for the Arts, 2006): 4.

31. Dickens, *Hard Times*, 241.

32. John Milton, "The Reason of Church Government Urged Against Prelaty," *Complete Poems and Major Prose*, ed. Merritt Y. Hughes (New York: Macmillan Publishing Company, 1957), 671.

33. William Shakespeare, *A Midsummer Night's Dream*, in *The Riverside Shakespeare*, ed. G. Blakemore Evans (Boston: Houghton Mifflin Company, 1974), V.i.17.

34. *Harry Potter and the Queen City Muggles* was made possible by grants from the University of Regina President's Conference Fund, the Humanities Research Institute, the Faculty of Arts, the Faculty of Education, the Faculty of Graduate Studies and Research,

the Department of English, the Department of Chemistry, the University of Regina Students' Union, and the Centre for Continuing Education, whose unflagging support, under the direction of Harvey King, included the generous donation of administrative assistant Loanne Myrah's time and talent. I must also thank Steve Hahn, Michelle James, Jamie Paris, Janet Moleski, Gabrielle Patterson, Drew Richardson, Jessica Sinclair, and Coby Stephenson, and a number of other volunteers too numerous to mention, as well as the students and scholars whose papers enriched the academic stream.

35. Lewis Carroll, *Through the Looking-Glass and What Alice Found There*, in *The Penguin Complete Lewis Carroll*, intro. Alexander Woolcott (Harmondsworth: Penguin, 1982), 210–1.

36. Nussbaum, *Cultivating Humanity*, 89–90.

Appendix: Worksheets and Supplemental Materials

Hogwarts Academy Core Subjects (Whited)

Subject	Professor(s)	Textbook	Equipment
1. Flying	Madam Hooch	None (practical instruction only)	Broomstick
2.			
3.			
4.			
5.			
6.			
7.			
8.			

Ministry of Magic
Wand Registration (Whited)

Witch/Wizard (Name) _____

Specifications Concerning Wand

Date created _____

Wood _____

Length _____

Core magical ingredient* _____

Quality of motion† _____

Drawing of the wand

*Dragon heart string, unicorn hair, phoenix feather, or other
†Springy or bendy, rigid or inflexible, swishy, etc. (Use an adjective.)

Hogwarts Academy
Dragon Trivia (Whited)

1. What is the name of the dragon Hagrid hatches from an egg in *Harry Potter and the Sorcerer's Stone*?

2. What type of dragon does Hagrid hatch in *Harry Potter and the Sorcerer's Stone*?

3. Which member of the Weasley family works with dragons?

4. In what country does the Weasley family member work with dragons?

5. Harry is able to win the dragon task in the Triwizard Tournament with what type of charm?

6. What object does Harry summon to himself, in order to win the dragon task in the Triwizard Tournament?

7. What character in the Harry Potter series has a first name that means "dragon"?

8. Translate the Hogwarts motto: "Draco dormiens nunquam titillandus"?

9. What core magical ingredient in some wands comes from dragons?

10. Name a type of dragon mentioned in the Harry Potter series other than the type hatched by Hagrid in the first book.

Study Sheet for Novels (Whited)

Title:

Author:

Author's dates:

Publisher:

Date of publication:

Period:

Genre:

Major characters:

Point of view/Narrator:

Tone:

Setting (time and place):

Major conflict(s): (On the other side of this sheet, summarize the plot.)

Themes:

Motifs:

Symbols:

Foreshadowing:

Other notes:

Child with Autism Chart (D'Errico)

Theme	*Description*	*Example in Harry Potter*	*Example in Modern Culture*	*Example in my Life*
Friendship	Value of Friendship	*Harry has good friends, Hermione and Ron who help him.*	*"You're My Best Friend" song by Queen*	*My good friends are named John, Paul, and George.*
Bullying	Bullying is Wrong			
Prejudice	Pre-judging, though prevalent, is wrong			
Choices	Importance of making good choices			
Help	Ask for help			
Uniqueness	You are unique			
Abilities	You have special talents			
Community	You can contribute to your community			
Society	You have a place in this world			
Faith	Believe in yourself			

List of Autism Resources (D'Errico)

Baron-Cohen, Simon. *Autism and Asperger Syndrome.* Oxford University Press, 2008.

DeMars, Teresa. *ASD & Me.* Charity Press Books, http://charitypressbooks.com.

Elder, Jennifer. *Different Like Me: My Book of Autism Heroes.* USA: Jessica Kingsley Publishers, 2005.

Hall, Kenneth. *Asperger Syndrome, the Universe and Everything.* USA: Jessica Kingsley Publishers, 2000.

Hoopmann, Kathy. *Blue Bottle Mystery: An Asperger Adventure.* USA: Jessica Kingsley Publishers, 2001.

_____. *Lisa and the Lacemaker: An Asperger Adventure.* USA: Jessica Kingsley Publishers, 2002.

_____. *Of Mice and Aliens: An Asperger Adventure.* USA: Jessica Kingsley Publishers, 2001.

Kluth, Paula and Patrick Schwarz. *Just Give Him the Whale! 20 Ways to Use Fascinations, Areas of Expertise, and Strengths to Support Students with Autism.* USA: Brookes, 2010.

Larson, Elaine Marie. *I Am Utterly Unique.* USA: Autism Asperger Publishing Company, 2006.

Levy, Jonathan. *What You Can Do Right Now to Help Your Child with Autism.* USA: Sourcebooks, 2007.

Madrigal, Stephanie and Michelle Garcia Winner. *Superflex(r): A Superhero Social Thinking Curriculum Package.* USA: Think Social Publishing, 2008. http://socialthinking.com.

Masters, Lisa. *The Funny Side of Autism.* USA: Inkwell Productions, 2010.

Miller, Susan Martins. *Reading Too Soon: How to Understand and Help the Hyperlexic Child.* USA: Center for Speech and Language, 1993.

Notbohm, Ellen. *10 Things Every Child with Autism Wishes You Knew.* USA: World Future Horizons, 2005.

Pike, Rachel. *Talking Together About an Autism Diagnosis.* London: National Autistic Society, 2008.

Shore, Stephen M. and Linda G. Rastelli. *Understanding Autism for Dummies,.* Wiley Publishing, 2006.

Learning Word Parts: Vol and Mort (Frankel)

J.K. Rowling's *Harry Potter and the Sorcerer's Stone* introduces us to many characters and spells with word parts related to their meanings. Bellatrix, the female warrior star, contains the root "bel," warlike, also seen in "belligerent" and "bellicose." Likewise, the name Voldemort begins with "vol"—meaning to will or to wish—and ends with "mort": death. The name should tell you this is quite a sinister character!

VOL: Volunteer, voluntary, involuntary, volition, benevolent, malevolent.

MORT: mortal, immortal, mortuary, mortify, mortician, post-mortem, rigor-mortis

Complete these sentences with the vol or mort word that fits.

(Other Latin roots here include ben/bene: good, mal: bad, post: after, and im/in: not)

1. Voldemort is a very _____ character who likes to see bad things happen to people.

2. A _____ showed that the man had died of natural causes.

3. Joining the Reading Club is _____ , so only join if you really want to read.

4. Cary was _____ when the entire school learned about his secret crush.

5. Is there a _____ who would be willing to go pick up our pizza?

6. Even though Shakespeare died, people consider his plays and poems to be _____ .

7. Cassie went to school to learn how to become a _____ , and then got a job at a mortuary.

8. He's a _____ man who is always looking for ways to help people.

Spellbook of Latin Roots (Frankel)

Amortentia *A love potion.* Am, amor (friendship, love): amiable, amatory, amorous

Animagus *A wizard or witch who can transform into an animal.* Anim (living, breath): animated, animation, Anime, animal, equanimity, unanimous

Aguamenti *Charm that conjures a fountain or jet of clear water from the caster's wand.* Aqua (water): aquatic, aquarium, aqueduct, aqueous, aquarelle; Ment/mens (mind): Mensa, mental, mention, mentation

Avis *Conjures a flock of small, twittering birds.* Avi (bird, flying): aviary, aviation, aviator, avionics, avian

Conjunctivitis Curse *A spell that affects the eyes and vision of the target.* Co/com/con (with, together): co-pilot, company, companion, conspiracy, convivial, conjunction; Junct (join): junction, adjunct, conjugal, joint

Crucio *One of the "Unforgiveable Curses," this spell causes the victim to suffer almost intolerable pain.* Cruc (torture): crush, excruciating, crucify, crucible, crucial, crusade

Densaugeo *Curse which causes the victim's teeth to enlarge grotesquely.* Dens/dent/dont (teeth): dentistry, dentures, orthodontist, endodontia, dentifrice; Aug/auct (grow, become greater): augment, auction, augur, august

Expecto Patronum *"Patronus Charm."* Patr (father, protector): patronize, patronage, patron, paternal, paternity, patriot, expatriate

Expelliarmus *Causes opponent's weapon to fly away.* Ex (out): exit, expel, expulsion, excavate, exhale, extract; Pel/pul (push): expel, expulsion, repel, dispel, propeller, propulsion, compulsion, impulse; Arm (weapon): armaments, armature, armor

Fidelius Charm *"Secret Keeper Charm."* Fid (trust, faith): confide, confidence, infidelity, fidelity, perfidy, perfidious

Finite Incantatum *Stops currently operating spell effects.* Fin (end, stop): finite, finish, fine, indefinite definite, definition, final, affinity, infinitesimal

Homorphus Charm *Werewolf Charm. Its exact effects aren't given.* Homo (same): homosexual, homogenize, homonym, homophone, homeopathy; Homo (man): Homo Sapiens, homicide, homunculus; Morph (shape, change): metamorphosis, morphology, dimorphic, biomorphic, amorphous

Imperio *"Imperius Curse." One of the "Unforgiveable Curses," this spell causes the victim to be completely under the command of the caster, who can command anything she wishes.* Imper/emper (command, order, rule): imperial, empire, emperor, imperative

Langlock *A jinx that glues the target's tongue to the roof of his or her mouth.* Ling/lang (tongue, language) language, bilingual, linguist, linguistics

Locomotor Mortis *"Leg-Locker Curse." Locks together the legs of the victim, making him unable to walk.* Loc (place): location, locale, allocate, dislocate, locus; Mot/mov (move, motion): motor, emotion, promote, demote, remote, motivate, removable; Mort (death): mortification, mortal, immortality, post-mortem, mortuary

Lumos Solarum *Generates a brilliant blast of light, as bright as the sun.* Lum/luc (light, clarify, understanding): lumen, illuminate, elucidate, pellucid, Lucifer; Sol (sun): solarium, solar system, parasol, solstice

Mobilicorpus *Moves a body.* Mob (move): mobile, mobilize, immobilize; Corp/corps (body or unit): corpse, corporation, incorporate, discorporate, corporeal

Portus *Creates a Portkey of instant transportation.* Port (carry): port, portal, porthole, portable, portage, export, import, report

Protego *"Shield Charm." Protects from harm.* Prot (protect, defend): protégé, protectorate, protectant, protective

Sectumsempra *Covers victim with cuts.* Sec (cut): section, dissect, bisect, vivisect, intersection, secateurs

Veritaserum *A powerful truth potion. It is used to make the drinker answer any questions put truthfully.* Ver (truth): verify, veracity, version, aver, verisimilitude

Wingardium Leviosa *Allows the user to make an object levitate.* Lev (rise, up): lever, elevator, levitate, elevate, relieve, alleviate, levity, leverage

Greek and Roman Gods and their Vocabulary (Frankel)

Major Gods	Known for	Related Words
Ceres	Goddess of grain and growing	cereal
Chronos	Titan; ruler of the universe; represented time	chronic, chronology
Hermes / Mercury	Speedy messenger god, guided souls to judgment	hermetic, mercurial
Mars	God of war	martial
Juno	Queen of the gods	June, Junoesque
Jove	King of the gods	jovial
Pluto	God of wealth	plutonium, plutocracy
Saturn	Gloomy sacrificed titan	saturnine, saturnalia
Venus	Goddess of love	venerate
Vesta	Goddess of the hearth	vestal, vestibule
Vulcan	God of fire; blacksmith for the gods	vulcanize, volcanology

Minor Gods		
Arachne	Greek weaver changed into a spider	arachnid, arachnophobia
Atlas	The titan who held up the sky	atlas
Atropos	The fate that cut the thread of life	atrophy
Aurora	Roman goddess of the dawn	aurora borealis
Calypso	Island nymph	calypso
Cerberus	Three-headed dog	cerebral, cerebellum
Chaos	The beginning of creation	chaos, chasm
Clotho	The Fate that spun the thread of life	cloth, clothe, clothing
Echo	Forced to repeat others' words	echo, echolocation
Flora	Goddess of spring and flowers	florid, floral
Fortuna	Goddess of luck	fortune, fortunate
Furies	Spirits of revenge	fury, furious, infuriate
Helios	Titan of the sun	heliotrope, helium
Hercules	Performed 12 very difficult labors	herculean
Hydra	Many-headed water serpent	hydrophobia, hydraulics
Hypnos	God of sleep and dreams	hypnotize, hypnosis, hypnobate
Mnemosyne	Goddess of memory, mother of Muses	mnemonics, mnemenic, mneme
Morpheus	Many-formed god of dreams	anthropomorphism, morpheme
The Muses	Nine Goddesses of the arts	music, museum, amuse, mosaic
Narcissus	He fell in love with his own reflection	narcissism
Nemesis	The goddess of revenge and balance	nemesis
Nike	Winged goddess of victory	Nike

Minor Gods	Known for	Related Words
Odysseus	Mariner known for his ten-year journey	odyssey
Pan	Satyr known for his wild cry	panic, pandemonium
Phobos	Son of Ares; god of fear	agoraphobia, claustrophobia
Prometheus	Taught humanity arts and skills	promethean
Proteus	Shape-changing sea-god	protean
Psyche	Princess who represents the soul or mind	psychology, psychosis
Python	A monstrous serpent killed by Apollo	python
Satyr	Man-goat hybrid known for rude behavior	satyr
Sibyls	Prophetesses of Apollo	sibyl, sibylline
Sirens	Nymphs who captured sailors by singing	siren, sirenian, siren call
Somnos	A god of sleep	somnambulist, insomnia
Stentor	Herald of the gods noted for his loud voice	stentorian
Tantalus	Punished in Hades by constant temptation	tantalize
Terpsichore	Muse of dance	terpsichorean
Titans	Gigantic parents of the gods	titanic, titan
Typhon	Titan of the oceans	typhoon
Zephyrus	Gentle west wind	zephyr

Other

Aegis	Medusa-headed breastplate	aegis
Akademos	Greek hero for whom Plato named his teaching grove	academy, academic
Amazon	Fearless warrior women	amazons, Amazonian
Ambrosia	Heavenly food of the gods	ambrosia
Chimera	Fire-breathing three part monster	chimera, chimerical
Chorus	Group narrators of traditional Greek theater	chorus, choral, choir
Draco	An Athenian legislator known for severity	draconian
Epicurus	Philosopher who believed in pleasure.	epicure, epicurean
Hellenes	The Greeks	Hellenic
Hippocrates	Famous Greek physician	Hippocratic oath
Labyrinth	Impossible maze that contained the Minotaur	labyrinth, labyrinthine
Lethe	River of forgetfulness	lethargy, lethargic, lethal
Mentor	Faithful adviser to Odysseus	mentor
Museum	Temple of the Muses	museum
Nectar	Sweet beverage of the gods	nectar, nectarine

Other	Known for	Related Words
Olympus	Mountain where the gods dwelt	Olympiad, Olympics
Oracle	Foreteller	oracle, oracular, oraculum
Pandora's Box	Source of all evil in the world	Pandora's box
Phaeton	Famous sun charioteer	phaeton
Spartans	Warriors who lived in simple conditions	spartan
Stygian Witches	Crones living in a gloomy cave	stygian
Stoics	School of philosophy believing in avoiding passion	stoic, stoical
Therma	Greek city known for hot springs	thermometer, thermonuclear
Thespis	The Father of Greek tragedy	thespian

Grown Up Books like Harry Potter (Frankel)

These are all adult fantasy novels, but ones not too graphic for older kids and young teens. For those looking for a more challenging read but not disturbingly explicit writing, these are good choices to consider.

Classics

Bulfinch's Mythology by Thomas Bulfinch
Sherlock Holmes by Sir Arthur Conan Doyle (not fantasy, but it has the mystery element and is great for kids and teens)
Le Morte D'Arthur by Thomas Malory
The Scarlet Pimpernel by Baroness Orczy
Ivanhoe by Sir Walter Scott
The Hobbit and *The Lord of the Rings* by JRR Tolkien
The Once and Future King and *The Book of Merlyn* by T. H. White
A Thousand and One Nights
Beowulf
Folklore and myth from around the world

Fantasy Humor

Myth Adventures and *Phule's Company* books by Robert Asprin
Thursday Next and *Nursery Crimes* books by Jasper Fforde
The Discworld Series by Terry Pratchett

Hero's/Heroine's Journey Fantasy for Teen through Adult

The Magic Kingdom of Landover series by Terry Brooks
The Ender Saga and *The Tales of Alvin Maker* by Orson Scott Card
The Dragon and the George series by Gordon R. Dickson
The Princess Bride by William Goldman
The Farseer Trilogy by Robin Hobb
Wildwood Dancing and *Cybele's Secret* by Juliet Marillier
Elantris and the *Mistborn* series by Brandon Sanderson
Tailchaser's Song by Tad Williams
The Chronicles of Amber by Roger Zelazny
Star Trek, Star Wars, D&D, and similar franchise novels
Almost everything by Peter S. Beagle, Charles de Lint, Neil Gaiman, Robert Heinlein, Mercedes Lackey, and Robin McKinley

Grammar Quidditch (O'Malley)

- Prepare your Quaffle Passes, Bludgers, Quaffle Goals, and Snitches
  - Quaffle Passes will be handled by the Chasers and should be simple sentences with basic grammatical or punctuation errors typed out on white slips of paper all cut to the same size and folded. Place them in a dark cloth bag or some container where students cannot see them. Examples include the following:
    - Proper nouns not capitalized
    - Missing commas
    - Superfluous commas
    - Lack of final punctuation in a sentence
    - Common, but not difficult, misspelled words
  - Bludgers are meant to knock a player off his or her broom, so they need to be more difficult. Create a list, 1–2 sentences per item, which you will read aloud for the Beaters. Beaters are required to write the entire thing on the board using correct punctuation and spelling. Examples include the following:
    - Sentences with questionable meaning, such as Let's eat Grandma! versus Let's eat, Grandma!
    - Two independent clauses that could either be written as separate sentences or a compound sentence.
    - Complex sentences.
    - Sentences using homonyms that are frequently misused
  - Quaffle Goals should be complex or compound sentences with intermediate errors. Put these on slips of paper in a separate container. They will not be used as often as the Quaffle Passes. Examples include the following:
    - A complex sentence missing all punctuation
    - Sentence fragments
    - Incorrect verb use
    - Pronoun-antecedent disagreement
    - Misplaced modifiers
  - Snitches are rare and elusive, so you only need a few of them for the whole game. They should be printed out on yellow or golden paper and cut to the same size as the Quaffle Passes. Place them in the same container as the Quaffle Passes and mix them in well. They're also worth the most points, so make them count! Examples include the following:
    - Complex-compound sentences with no punctuation and a misspelled word or two

- Complex sentences with multiple punctuation errors
- Complex or compound sentences with poor grammatical structure
- Divide the class in half, and let each team select their positions (depending on the size of the class)
  - One or two people should be the Keeper(s) and will be responsible for answering the Quaffle Goal questions.
  - One or two people should be the Seeker(s) and will be responsible for answering the Snitch questions.
  - The remainder should be split between the Beaters who will be responsible for fielding Bludger questions and the Chasers who will be responsible for answering the Quaffle Pass questions.
- Scoring
  - A correct Quaffle Pass earns 1 point, and it means that team retains control; an incorrect answer means the other team takes control.
  - After five correct Quaffle Passes, the team can attempt a Quaffle Goal question.
  - A correct Quaffle Goal will score the team 10 points; an incorrect answer means no score and the other team takes control.
  - The opposing team can play Bludgers in an attempt to gain control. A correct answer to a Bludger earns 5 points, and means the team can immediately take a Quaffle Goal question in an attempt to score; an incorrect answer means that player is knocked out of the game and the opposing team takes control.
  - A correct Snitch answer will score the team 50 points (or 150 if you want to keep to the book scoring). An incorrect Snitch answer means the opposing team's Seeker has the opportunity to try.
  - All members of the winning team earn whatever prize fits your grading scale: bonus points on an essay, extra points for this activity, a boost on their final grade, etc.
- Game Play
  - Select the starting team (rock paper scissors, flip a coin, etc.).
  - The Chaser from starting team (Team A) selects a slip from the bag of Quaffle Passes and Snitches.
  - If it's a Quaffle Pass, the same Chaser provides the correction (on the board or on an overhead projector so the class can see it) and names another Chaser on the same team to "pass" to.
  - Chasers continue to pass to each other with new Quaffle Pass questions until they miss one, complete five successful ones, or the other team interrupts with a Bludger.
  - Once a team has five successful passes, the Keeper takes a Quaffle Goal question.

- When Team B wants to interfere, their Beater calls for a Bludger. Team A's Beater then comes to the board to write out the verbally delivered problem.
- If the Beater successfully writes the problem correctly, he or she has dodged the Bludger and game continues. If not, he or she must sit out until the next Snitch is drawn, thereby giving the team more of a challenge.
- When drawing from the bag, if a Chaser pulls out a golden slip of paper, the Snitch has been sighted! The Seeker from the same team must respond with the corrections needed within a time limit (60 seconds should be plenty of time). If one team's Seeker fails to "catch" the snitch, the other team's Seeker has a chance. If both Seekers fail, the game resumes but control changes teams. If one Seeker succeeds, you can either end the game and start a new one as time permits, or just continue to play if you prefer.

Genre and Literary Conventions Quiz (Mansoor)

1. Consult an encyclopedia and briefly define the following literary terms:
   a. Myth

   b. Fairy tale

   c. Folk tale

   d. Bildungsroman

   e. Monomyth

2. Choose any myth or fairy tale from any authentic source, containing the motif of a hero's quest. In simple terms, delineate the outline of the tale and also enumerate the obstacles that the hero faces while endeavoring to complete his quest. Compare the outline and the trials of this hero with the outline of any one of the *Harry Potter* novels that you have read as well as the tribulations endured by Harry Potter himself.

3. Based on the comparison drawn above, is it correct to assume that the *Harry Potter* novels are a blend of fairy tale and mythological elements?

4. Explain briefly how the *Harry Potter* series fulfills the criterion of a bildungsroman and also that of a monomyth.

5. Look up the following terms in an encyclopedia and specify their characteristics.
   a. Detective mystery novels

   b. Children's fiction

   c. Fantasy fiction

   d. Realistic fiction

Identify the characteristics of these genres in any one of the *Harry Potter* novels.

6. In which genre would you place the *Harry Potter* series and why? Give a detailed answer.

The Art of Characterization Worksheet (Mansoor)

Name of the character: _____

1. Is it a major character or a minor character?

2. Is it round or flat and why? Give a brief explanation.

3. Is the character stock or stereotype?

4. Is the character static or dynamic?

5. Fill in the following table highlighting the character traits of the nominated character. Fill in the blanks with evidence from the text.

Name: Hermione Granger	Evidence from Text
Personality Attributes:	
Age Group	_____
Social Background	_____
Role Definition:	
Antagonist/Protagonist	_____
Gender	_____
Relationship with Hero	_____
Behavior/Ethics	_____
Growth/Change	_____
Opinions about the Character:	
Author's Description of the Character	_____
Other Characters' Opinions of the Character	_____
Your Opinion of the Character	_____

6. Using the flow sheet that you have filled, write an essay on Hermione Granger's character elucidating the complexities in her personality and her role as Harry's friend.

7. Concentrate on the adjectives given in the following list. List each one below the appropriate name.

Harry Potter		Draco Malfoy
	Stubborn	
	Resourceful	
	Trustworthy	
	Malicious	
	Conniving	
	Privileged fairy tale prince	
	Impulsive	
	Pure blood	
	Pompous	
	Resilient	
	Arrogant	
	Brave	

8. The following chart elucidates Harry Potter's role as a fairy tale hero and a real boy living in the real world. In the boxes below both categories, place evidence from the text of *Harry Potter* that support both of these categories.[1]

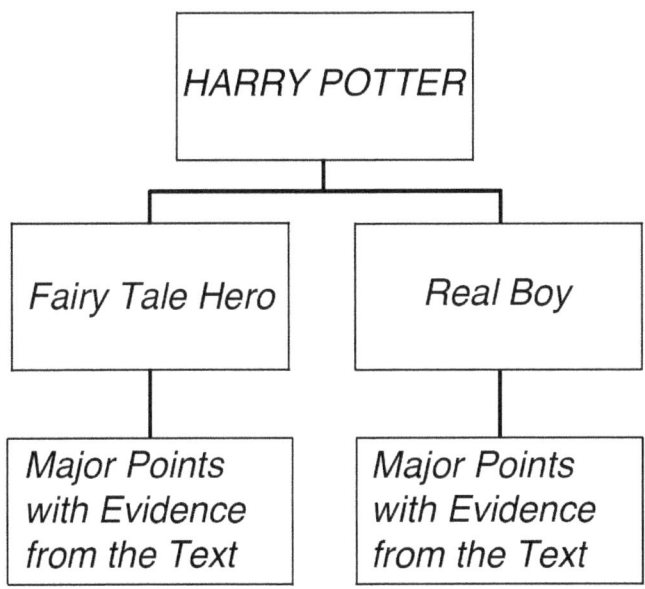

9. Using the above flow sheet, discuss Harry Potter's role as a fairy tale hero and a real boy and the obstacles that he has to encounter. Refer to Katherine Grimes' essay "Harry Potter: Fairy Tale Prince, Real Boy and Archetypal Hero" to support your answer.[2] In addition, consult online research articles and reference books to supplement your arguments.

Notes

1. Activity modified from Joanne Collie & Stephen Slater, *Literature in the Language Classroom: A Resource Book of Ideas and Activities* (New Delhi: Cambridge University Press, 2009), 96–97.

2. Katherine Grimes, "Harry Potter: Fairy Tale Prince, Real Boy and Archetypal Hero" in *The Ivory Tower and Harry Potter: Perspectives on a Literary Phenomenon,* ed. Lana A. Whited, 89–122 (Columbia and London: University of Missouri Press, 2002).

Allusions in the Harry Potter Series Worksheet (Mansoor)

1. Explore why the following characters have been named so. What are the origins of their names? Do you find similar names in other literary compositions? If so, briefly write about the original sources of those names.

   a. Draco Malfoy

   b. Hagrid

   c. Argus Filch

   d. Minerva McGonagall

   e. Albus Dumbledore

   f. Professor Quirrell

   g. Sirius Black

   h. Remus Lupin

   i. Daedalus Diggle

   j. Hermione Granger

2. Do you find any references to the *Arabian Nights* and fairy tales of various regions in the world? If so, give at least five examples and briefly elucidate their sources.

3. Do you find any allusions to the Bible in the *Harry Potter* series? Give examples.

4. Write a full-length essay on the allusive texture of the *Harry Potter* series. Refer to critical essays in various books and research journals. Give quotations from these sources as well as from the text to support your answer.

Thematic Comparison and Contrast Worksheet (Mansoor)

1. Friends are of vital importance in enabling someone to attain emotional and mental equilibrium as well as in providing succour in times of trouble. How would you analyze the treatment of friendship in the novels *Frankenstein* and *Harry Potter and the Deathly Hallows*?

2. "An over-cute *woman's no better nor a long-tailed sheep*—she'll fetch none the bigger price for that," says Mr. Tulliver about Maggie in *The Mill on the Floss*. Is he justified in this statement? How would you compare Maggie with any other intelligent female character, Hermione Granger, for instance, that you have studied? How do both women defy gender stereotypes?

3. *Harry Potter and the Philosopher's Stone* highlights the multiple forms of child abuse and the importance of the family unit. This is a theme that has been extensively canvassed in Victorian literature. Choose any one Victorian novel that deals with the theme of child abuse and family unity and give a detailed comparison and contrast of the treatment of these two themes in both texts.

4. Voldemort is a tangible manifestation of evil while Milton's Satan is presented as the author of evil. How would you compare both these characters? How has the eternal conflict between good and evil been brought to light through these characters?

Medieval Prompts and Projects (Ward)

Included below are a variety of creative pedagogical approaches or prompts that can be adapted for use in classrooms concerned with Rowling's medievalism (or for any similar course on medieval or modern topics). Feel free to pilfer and edit/adapt these ideas at will.

Note to Students

Think of this assignment more as a portfolio than anything else. The challenge is to present, in a limited amount of time, space, and words, the relationship between an element of *Harry Potter* and one or more medieval counterparts. You will want to consider various connections or themes between the series and the medieval topic, as well as Rowling's innovations in her reworking of the medieval material. You should make it clear to your audience (which will first be me, and then the class at large) what cultural and sociological forces influence the items under discussion, whether medieval or modern.

Possible Projects

- Recipe Experiment
    - Experiment with a recipe of some sort from a medieval manuscript or book.
    - The recipe can be for medicinal, magical (alchemical), or cookery items.
    - Share the experiment results (in whatever form) with the class.
- Re-creation 1
    - Emulate one of the art forms found in *Harry Potter* that derives specifically from a medieval form (manuscripts and books, tapestry, painting, calligraphy, architecture, sculpture, and so on).
    - Research the original techniques and materials and recreate them as best as possible in your own project, whether it is something inspired by or a copy of an already existing artifact.
- Re-creation 2
    - Emulate one of the cultural practices found in medieval culture and literature and emulated in *Harry Potter*, such as feasts and tournaments.
    - Research, plan, and execute the re-creation as an event in which the entire class participates.
    - Research the original techniques and materials, and replicate them as best as possible in your own project.

- Board Game
  - If you are ambitious enough, you could develop a board game, in the tradition of extant games such as *Dungeons and Dragons*, *The Settlers of Catan*, and so on.
  - Draw on one of the medieval sources or themes for your game; focus either entirely on this medieval source or blend it with *Harry Potter* material.

However, keep in mind that we will want to PLAY the game in class at some point! Thus, you may wish to have a "good" version and then some mock-up versions so that the class can break out into smaller groups.

- Graphic Novel
  - Adapt a segment of medieval material to convey its relationship to *Harry Potter* or to emulate Rowling's adaption of medieval sources.
  - Create a minimum of 6 illustrated frames to convey the contents of your text selection.
  - Include brief liner notes at the base of each frame that indicate basic plot elements and use dialogue in the frames as necessary.
  - Medium is entirely up to you: charcoal, watercolor, acrylic, pastel, oil, pencil crayon, crayon, or even cut and paste images, computer graphics or animation.
- Slide presentation
  - If you select this option, keep in mind that you do not want the content to be text heavy. Limit the number of words used in your presentation (the maximum should be 50 words).
  - You should also limit the number of slides. No more than 5 slides are permitted. Both of these limitations will force you to be efficient and creative with your time and space.
- Poster Presentation
  - Here, again, you should keep text balanced with image. You may wish to consider variations on the poster idea. If you have one that you would like to try, outline it in a proposal first.
  - Typically, poster presentations are limited to a single sheet of poster board or to one of the tri-fold presentation boards.
- Collage

The Collage follows the same basic principles of the Poster Presentation but without text. Quite simply, it is a purely visual medium. However, you are not limited to just a physical poster. You may wish to create a slideshow presentation that is entirely visual, a small movie/video, or a book-style collection (it could even overlap with the short movie option below).

- Dramatic Adaptation and Performance
    - Prepare an outline of how you would adapt and arrange the performance of a selected portion of non-dramatic medieval text.
    - You should choose a section of the text (i.e. a single scene or a specific episode within a piece of poetry or fiction) rather than an entire text to stage.
    - Consider all of the following as you prepare your adaptation: setting, stage, costumes, props, lighting, script, blocking, and performance cues.
    - Prepare and perform the adaptation.
- Short Movie
    - Youtube.com has hundreds of homemade videos that serve as possible models. You could look at some of the Silly Histories clips, or some of the historical events and figures clips. Here are a few (wonderful) examples:
        - Silly Histories' Charles II Song: http://www.youtube.com/watch?v=War-7M9Nv3A
        - The Bayeux Tapestry, Justin Timberlake Style: http://www.youtube.com/watch?v=bQ8A5gRe_Dw
        - Joan of Arc ("Seven Nation Army" by the White Stripes): http://www.youtube.com/watch?v=wQydMhY9OpI&feature=related

A List of Medieval Resources (Ward)

http://bestiary.ca   Link for *The Medieval Bestiary: Animals in the Middle Ages*, a searchable site compiled by independent scholar David Badke. The site is comprehensive, and includes information on different beasts, as well as the manuscripts in which entries on them exist.

http://www.lib.rochester.edu/camelot/cphome.stm   Link for *The Camelot Project* at the University of Rochester, New York. The *Camelot Project* is the largest online database of texts and resources on Arthurian literature and traditions. It also includes minor projects on other medieval topics and figures such as Robin Hood and the Crusades.

http://www.oxford-middleages.com   The login page for the Oxford Encyclopedia of the Middle Ages. Most post-secondary institutions likely subscribe to this electronic resource, which is searchable and a highly valuable starting place for researching all things medieval. The resource holds over 3000 entries on a range of interdisciplinary topics.

http://www.evellum.com   The Australian based *Evellum* project, which specializes in digital facsimiles and editions of medieval manuscripts, also offers a plethora of pedagogical tools. *Evellum's* website has pages for manuscript and book projects, including a "Resource Warehouse," which offers, among other things, photographic images, print resources (essays and books), DVDs, short film clips (for topics ranging from how to make a quill pen to ink recipes and attaching coverboards to a book), all at reasonable prices.

http://illuminations.ca/index.html   Website of Kathryn Finter, an Ottawa-based artist and illumination expert. Finter includes a how-to guide and a bibliography (print and electronic sources) on her website, along with an entire alphabet of illuminated letter samples and a variety of manuscript page and image facsimiles. For teachers with access to departmental, program, or faculty funds, the prospect of actual artist-led workshops also exist.

http://www.nottingham.ac.uk/ins/index.aspx   Website for the Institute of Name Studies at the University of Nottingham, which houses major research projects on place names in England, including an online searchable key for place names.

Print Resources

Adamson, Melitta Weiss, ed. *Food in the Middle Ages: A Book of Essays*. New York; London: Garland, 1995.

Arden, Heather, and Kathryn Lorenz. "The Ambiguity of the Outsider in the Harry Potter Stories and Beyond." In *The Image of the Outsider in Lit-*

erature, Media and Society, edited by Will Wright and Steven Kaplan, 430–34. Pueblo: University of Southern Colorado, 2002.

_____. "The Harry Potter Stories and French Arthurian Romance." *Arthuriana* 13 (2003): 54–68.

Barber, Richard, and Juliet Barker. *Tournaments: Jousts, Chivalry and Pageants in the Middle Ages.* Woodbridge: Boydell, 1989.

Barker, Juliet R. V. *The Tournament in England, 1100–1400.* 1986. Woodbridge: Boydell, 2003.

Baxter, Ron. *Bestiaries and their Users in the Middle Ages,* Stroud: Sutton, 1998.

Bice, Deborah. "From Merlin to Muggles: The Magic of Harry Potter, The First Book." In *Elsewhere: Selected Essays from the "20th Century Fantasy Literature: From Beatrix to Harry" International Literary Conference,* edited by Deborah Bice. New York: University Press of America, 2003. 29–37.

Briggs, Katharine M. *A Dictionary of Fairies: Hobgoblins, Brownies, Bogies and Other Supernatural Creatures.* London: Allen Lane, 1976.

Clark, William W. *Medieval Cathedrals.* London: Greenwood, 2006.

Clark, Willene B., and Meradith T. McMunn, eds. *Beasts and Birds of the Middle Ages: The Bestiary and Its Legacy.* Philadelphia: University of Pennsylvania Press, 1989.

Classen, Albrecht, ed. *Handbook of Medieval Studies: Terms, Methods, Trends.* Berlin: de Gruyter, 2010. 3 vols.

Cockrell, Amanda. "Harry Potter and the Secret Password: Finding Our Way in the Magical Genre." In *The Ivory Tower and Harry Potter: Perspectives on a Literary Phenomenon,* edited by Lana A. Whited, 15–26. Columbia and London: University of Missouri Press, 2002.

Cohen, Jeffrey Jerome, ed. *Monster Theory: Reading Culture.* Minneapolis: University of Minnesota Press, 1996.

Colbert, David. *The Hidden Myths in Harry Potter.* New York: St. Martin's Griffin, 2005.

_____. *The Magical Worlds of Harry Potter: A Treasury of Myths, Legends, and Fascinating Facts.* Toronto: McArthur, 2001.

Cosman, Madeleine Pelner. *Fabulous Feasts: Medieval Cookery and Ceremony.* New York: G. Braziller, 1976.

Culpepper, Nicholas. *Culpeper's English Physician and Complete Herbal, Arranged for Use as a First Aid Herbal by Mrs. C. F. Leyel.* Hollywood: Wilshire Book Company, 1971.

Curley, Michael J., trans. *Physiologus.* Austin and London: University Press of Texas, 1979.

Eco, Umberto. "The Return of the Middle Ages." In *Travels in Hyperreality,* translated by William Weaver, 59–86. San Diego, New York and London: Harcourt Brace Jovanovich, 1990.

Fiero, Gloria K. *The Humanistic Tradition: Book 2—Medieval Europe and the World Beyond.* 5th Edition. Boston, McGraw Hill, 2006.

Flores, Nona C., ed. *Animals in the Middle Ages: A Book of Essays.* New York: Garland Publishing, Inc., 1996

Friedman, John Block. *The Monstrous Races in Medieval Art and Thought.* Syracuse, NY: Syracuse University Press, 2000.

Fugelso, Karl, ed. *Defining Medievalism(s).* Studies in Medievalism 17. Cambridge: D. S. Brewer, 2009.

_____. *Defining Medievalism(s) II.* Studies in Medievalism 18. Cambridge: D. S. Brewer, 2009.

_____. *Defining Neomedievalism(s).* Studies in Medievalism 19. Cambridge: D. S. Brewer, 2010.

George, Wilma and Brunsdon Yapp. *The Naming of the Beasts: Natural History in the Medieval Bestiary.* London: Duckwork, 1991.

Hard, Robin. *The Routledge Handbook of Greek Mythology.* London and New York: Routledge, 2004.

Hassig, Debra. *Medieval Bestiaries: Text, Image, Ideology.* Cambridge: Cambridge University Press, 1995.

Hassig, Debra, ed. *Mark of the Beast: The Medieval Bestiary in Art, Life, and Literature.* New York: Garland Publishing, 2000.

Hieatt, Constance B., Brenda Hosington, and Sharon Butler. *Pleyn Delit: Medieval Cookery for Modern Cooks.* Toronto: University of Toronto Press, 1976.

James, Montague Rhodes, ed. *The Bestiary: Being A Reproduction in Full of Ms. Ii 4. 26 in the University Library, Cambridge, with Supplementary Plates from Other Manuscripts of English Origin, and a Preliminary Study of the Latin Bestiary as Current in England.* Oxford: Roxburghe Club, 1928.

Jones, Peter Murray. *Medieval Medicine in Illuminated Manuscripts.* London: British Library, 1998.

Kaeuper, Richard W. *Chivalry and Violence in Medieval Europe.* Oxford: Oxford University Press, 1999.

Keen, Maurice. *Chivalry.* New Haven and London: Yale University Press, 1984.

Kieckhefer, Richard. *Magic in the Middle Ages.* Cambridge: Cambridge University Press, 1989.

Knapp, Peggy A. "The Work of Alchemy." *Journal of Medieval and Early Modern Studies* 30.3 (Fall 2000): 575–99.

Kronzek, Allan Zola, and Elizabeth Kronzek. *The Sorcerer's Companion: A Guide to the Magical World of Harry Potter.* New York: Broadway Books, 2001.

Le Goff, Jacques. "The Wilderness in the Medieval West." In *The Medieval*

Imagination, translated by Arthur Goldhammer. 47–59. Chicago and London: University of Chicago Press, 1988.

Lindow, John. *Handbook of Norse Mythology*. Santa Barbara: ABC-CLIO, 2001.

McCulloch, Florence. *Medieval Latin and French Bestiaries*. Revised ed. Chapel Hill: University of North Carolina Press, 1962.

Mittman, Asa Simon. *Maps and Monsters in Medieval England*. New York; London: Routledge, 2006.

Mittman, Asa Simon, ed., with Peter J. Dendle. *The Ashgate Research Companion to Monsters and the Monstrous*. Farnham, Surrey: Ashgate, 2012.

Murgatroyd, Paul. *Mythical Monsters in Classical Literature*. London: Duckworth, 2007.

Orchard, Andy. *Dictionary of Norse Myth and Legend*. London: Cassell, 1997.

_____. *Pride and Prodigies: Studies in the Monsters of the Beowulf Manuscript*. Cambridge and Rochester, NY: D. S. Brewer, 1995.

Orgelfinger, Gail. "J. K. Rowling's Medieval Bestiary." In *Defining Medievalism*, edited by Karl Fugelso, 141–60. Studies in Medievalism 17. Cambridge and Rochester, NY: D. S. Brewer, 2009.

Petrina, Alessandra. "Forbidden Forest, Enchanted Castle: Arthurian Spaces in the Harry Potter Novels." *Mythlore* 24, no. 3–4 (2006): 95–110.

Porter, J. R., and W. M. S. Russell, eds. *Animals in Folklore*. Cambridge: D. S. Brewer, 1978.

Radding, Charles M., and William W. Clark. *Medieval Architecture, Medieval Learning: Builders and Masters in the Age of Romanesque and Gothic*. New Haven; London: Yale University Press, 1992.

Saunders, Corinne. *The Forest of Medieval Romance: Avernus, Broceliande, Arden*. Cambridge and Rochester, NY: D. S. Brewer, 1993.

Schleissner, Margaret R, ed. *Manuscript Sources of Medieval Medicine: A Book of Essays*. Garland Medieval Casebooks 8. New York; London: Garland, 1995.

Sciacca, Christine. *Building the Medieval World*. London: British Library, 2010.

Scully, Terence. *The Art of Cookery in the Middle Ages*. Woodbridge: Boydell, 1995.

Siraisi, Nancy. *Medieval and Early Renaissance Medicine: An Introduction to Knowledge and Practice*. Chicago: Chicago University Press, 1990.

Stevens, John. *Medieval Romance: Themes and Approaches*. Hutchison University Library. London: Hutchison, 1973.

Theobaldus Episcopus. *Physiologus: Theobaldi Episcopi de naturis duodecim animalium*. Translated by Willis Barnstone. Bloomington: Indiana University Press, 1964.

Vinciguerra, Antony. "The *Ars alchemie*: The First Latin Text on Practical Alchemy." *Ambix* 56, no. 1 (March 2009): 57–67.

Weldon, James. "The Naples Manuscript and the Case for a Female Readership." *Neophilologus* 93, no. 2 (2009): 703–22.

Williams, David. *Deformed Discourse: The Function of the Monster in Mediaeval Thought and Literature.* Montreal and Kingston: McGill-Queen's University Press, 1996.

Prisoner of Azkaban
Writing Assignment (Firestone)

For your final paper, you will be doing what we call feminist textual analysis. The idea is to take a "text" (in this case the novel) and apply scholarship to it to reveal something. The idea is that the general narrative is subtextually telling us something about communication and gender, gender performance, relationships, race, class, and identity. Your mission (should you choose to accept it) is to choose one of the sections from the class — Women and one of the following: media, romance, education, sex, body, motherhood/pregnancy and fandom — and apply the scholarship from that week to a brief excerpt from the book.

I recommend that you choose a very specific moment to focus on in your work: no more than a few pages. (A whole chapter would be a stretch; you want to be as specific as you can so you can dig deeply into the subtext.) You can of course supplement with other examples from the book, but you should use those as support for your particular excerpt.

Your paper will consist of five sections: Introduction, Literature Review, Excerpt Recap, Analysis, and Discussion/Conclusion. Remember, introductions require particular things that will help make your paper more interesting, organized, and clear. Thus, you will need a compelling introductory statement, a sentence or two explaining that statement, a thesis, a purpose statement, and a preview statement.

To begin, I want the "punch in the face." Readers need a "hook" (a left or a right will do) to get them interested and invested in reading your piece. Starting a paper with "This paper is about *The Prisoner of Azkaban* and how it relates to readings from the week about Women and Romance" is frankly boring and gives me no incentive to keep reading. Begin with a startling statistic, a relevant quote by the author, a philosophical rhetorical question (not something that has a yes, no, or blatant answer), or a compelling fact.

Then I need a thesis statement and a purpose statement. REMEMBER! These two sentences do TWO different things. A thesis statement tells me what the paper argues. It uses argument-related action verbs: "I argue, I assert, I show, I contend" and so on. EXAMPLE: "I argue that the Dementors, guards to Azkaban Prison, are representations of patriarchy." A purpose statement explains WHY you're doing it and ultimately what the work DOES. EXAMPLE: "This paper seeks to explore the potential connections between the Dementors' behaviors in the text and the ways that patriarchy oppresses women."

Finally, I need a preview statement(s) that provides a blueprint for how the rest of the paper will look. It gives the signposts that the following sections will cover. EXAMPLE: "I will do this by first examining patriarchy, as defined by Teresa Ebert in her article 'The Romance of Patriarchy,' as a social institution that fundamentally oppresses women through relevant scholarship. Next, I will summarize a moment from the chapter 'The Dementor's Kiss' that provides an opening for the following analysis that links patriarchy to the dementors. A discussion of the analysis and its findings will further the support the connection between the representation of patriarchy through the dementor characters."

Over the next two or three pages, you will relate the key points of the scholarship you have chosen as they relate to your example. This is NOT where your analysis begins. You are reviewing what has been published on your related topic in order to show me that you've done adequate reading, understand the scholarship/theory, and can make a plausible argument/claim. After you've done that, give me the overview of your chosen except. This should cover a paragraph, two at the most. I've read the book; I'm looking for concise and clear summaries.

Now you can begin to analyze. The rule of thought here is "Show me, don't tell me." That means, instead of glossing details from the book with paraphrasing, quote the book to add weight to your argument. Use Rowling's words to make your case. Think of it this way. If someone says, "I don't believe this claim you're making." You can respond with, "Oh, yeah? Well Rowling says on page such and such, 'X,' therefore this interpretation is credible." Generally, you want to work the analysis this way: 1. Present the claim, 2. Show it with the text, 3. Apply your scholarship, 4. Explain why this makes your claim plausible. You'll repeat these four steps each time you examine and explain a detail that furthers your overall argument.

In the discussion section and subsequent conclusion, recap the general paper for me and reformulate your thesis and purpose to say the same thing with new words. REMEMBER, your thesis/purpose may have changed after your started researching and writing. That's okay; it happens all the time. Maybe you discovered something contrary to what you believed was happening. That's what the discussion section is for. Tell me about this journey and, more importantly, tell me about how you arrived at your findings. When you're ready to conclude, make the completed circle, draw the connections back to your introduction. Further explain that statistic so that the reader has an "Ah-Ha" moment since reading your piece. Do the same for rhetorical questions, quotes, and compelling statements.

Now for the specs:

- 6 sources minimum for citation (12 if you're looking for an A)
- Count *Prisoner of Azkaban* as one of the 6
- Works cited should be formatted with MLA (DO NOT USE A CITE GENERATOR!)
- 5 to 7 pages long, does NOT include the works cited or cover page

Good Luck!

A Bibliography of Significant Works on Harry Potter (Lee)

This bibliography is not an exhaustive list by any means. I have tried to provide a representative selection of scholarly as well as significant popular books of secondary literature around the *Harry Potter* series. Some of the best discussions on *Harry Potter* have been found on the internet, but given the hit-or-miss nature of web content, I wanted to focus on published texts.

The parameters I followed are somewhat arbitrary. It is difficult to establish clear and consistent criteria given that the discussion and exploration of Rowling's works is still developing. That being the case, it will be fascinating to see where the conversation on *Potter* will go over the next few decades. I tried to focus on published works that came out *after* the completion of the *Harry Potter* series. There are a few on this list that are before the completion of the series and they are included because of the *scholarly* or *significant contribution* they have made to the exploration of the series. In short, the focus of this bibliography is *academic* in nature. Inevitably, a book, or more likely, several books have been left off this list that certainly fit this ad hoc criteria. That is the nature of list making I suppose.

Fortunately, there is a website that is keeping a running list of publications on *Harry Potter*: http://www.eulenfeder.de/hpliteratur.html. This site is quite exhaustive. It includes not only books, but articles, symposiums, and dissertations (some of which are linked). It also includes foreign languages such as German and French. The list there is well into the hundreds of publications.

Hopefully the bibliography here will be a starting point for readers to delve more deeply into the academic works and research that is truly just now emerging on the most well-received series in the history of publication.

Bibliography

Anatol, Giselle Liza, ed. *Reading Harry Potter: Critical Essays.* (Contributions to the Study of Popular Culture 78) Westport, Conn./London: Praeger, 2003.

_____. *Reading Harry Potter Again: New Critical Essays.* Westport, CT: Greenwood, 2009.

Anelli, Melissa. *Harry, A History: The True Story of a Boy Wizard, His Fans, and Life Inside the Harry Potter Phenomenon.* New York: Simon & Schuster, 2008.

Bassham, Gregory, ed. *The Ultimate Harry Potter and Philosophy: Hogwarts for Muggles.* (The Blackwell Philosophy and Pop Culture Series 20) Hoboken, NJ: John Wiley & Sons, 2010.

Belcher, Catherine L. and Becky Herr Stephenson. *Teaching Harry Potter: The*

Power of Imagination in Multicultural Classrooms. New York: Palgrave Macmillan, 2011.

Berndt, Katrin and Lena Steveker, eds. *Heroism in the Harry Potter Series.* Aldershot: Ashgate, 2011.

Bryfonski, Dedria, ed. *Political Issues in J. K. Rowling's Harry Potter Series.* Detroit: Greenhaven Press, 2009

Colbert, David. *The Magical Worlds of Harry Potter. A Treasury of Myths, Legends, and Fascinating Facts.* Updated and Revised. New York: Berkley Books, 2008.

Duriez, Colin. *Field Guide to Harry Potter.* Downers Grove: IVP Books, 2007.

Garrett, Greg. *One Fine Potion: The Literary Magic of Harry Potter.* Waco: Baylor University Press, 2010.

Granger, John. *Harry Potter's Bookshelf: The Great Books Behind the Hogwarts Adventure.* New York: Berkley Books, 2009.

_____. *How Harry Cast His Spell: The Meaning Behind the Mania for J. K. Rowling's Bestselling Books.* Carol Stream: Tyndale House Publishers, 2008.

_____. *Unlocking Harry Potter: Five Keys for the Serious Reader.* Allentown, PA: Zossima Press, 2007.

Gupta, Suman. *Re-Reading Harry Potter.* 2nd Edition, Basingstoke: Palgrave Macmillan 2009.

Hallett, Cynthia Whitney and Debbie Mynott, eds. *Scholarly Studies in Harry Potter: Applying Academic Methods to a Popular Text.* Lewiston: Edwin Mellen Press, 2005.

Heilman, Elizabeth E., ed. *Critical Perspectives on Harry Potter.* 2nd ed. New York: Routledge, 2008.

Highfield, Roger. *The Science of Harry Potter: How Magic Really Works.* New York: Viking, 2002.

Kern, Edmund M. *The Wisdom of Harry Potter: What Our Favorite Hero Teaches Us about Moral Choices.* Amherst, N.Y.: Prometheus Books, 2003.

Killinger, John. *Life, Death, and Resurrection of Harry Potter.* Macon, GA: Mercer University Press, 2009.

Kronzek, Allan Zola and Elizabeth Kronzek. *The Sorcerer's Companion: A Guide to the Magical World of Harry Potter.* 3rd ed. New York: Broadway Books, 2010.

Lackey, Mercedes and Leah Wilson, eds. *Mapping the World of Harry Potter: Science Fiction and Fantasy Writers Explore the Best Selling Fantasy Series of All Time.* Dallas, TX: BenBella Books, 2006.

Lee, Vera G. *On the Trail of Harry Potter.* New Town: Pitapat Press, 2011.

Manlove, Colin N. *The Order of Harry Potter: Literary Skill in the Hogwarts Epic.* Cheshire: Winged Lion Press, 2011.

Morris, Thomas V. *If Harry Potter Ran General Electric: Leadership Wisdom from the World of the Wizards.* New York: Doubleday, 2006.

Mulholland, Neil, ed. *The Psychology of Harry Potter: An Unauthorized Examination of the Boy Who Lived.* Dallas, TX: BenBella Books, 2007.

Neal, Connie. *The Gospel according to Harry Potter: The Spiritual Journey of the World's Greatest Seeker.* Revised and expanded edition: Louisville: Westminster John Know Press, 2008.

Nexon, Daniel H. and Iver B. Neumann, eds. *Harry Potter and International Relations.* Lanham, MD: Rowman and Littlefield, 2006.

Patterson, Diana, ed. *Harry Potter's World-Wide Influence.* Newcastle: Cambridge Scholars Publishing, 2009.

Prinzi, Travis. *Harry Potter & Imagination: The Way Between Two Worlds.* Allentown, PA: Zossima Press, 2008.

Prinzi, Travis, ed. *Harry Potter for Nerds: Essays for Fans, Academics, and Lit Geeks.* USA: Unlocking Press, 2011.

_____. *Hog's Head Conversations: Essays on Harry Potter. Vol. 1.* Allentown, PA: Zossima Press, 2009.

Reagin, Nancy, ed. *Harry Potter and History.* New York: Wiley, 2011.

Saxena, Vandana. *The Subversive Harry Potter: Adolescent Rebellion and Containment in the J.K. Rowling Novels.* Jefferson, NC: McFarland, 2012.

Thomas, James W. *Repotting Harry Potter.* Allentown, PA: Zossima Press, 2009.

_____. *Rowling Revisited: Return Trips to Harry, Fantastic Beasts, Quidditch, & Beedle the Bard.* Allentown, PA: Zossima Press, 2010.

Thomas, Jeffrey E. and Franklin G. Snyder, eds. *The Law and Harry Potter.* Durham, NC: Carolina Academic Press, 2010.

Tumminio, Danielle Elizabeth. *God and Harry Potter at Yale: Teaching Faith and Fantasy Fiction in an Ivy League Classroom.* USA: Unlocking Press, 2010.

Weiss, Shira Wolosky. *The Riddles of Harry Potter: Secret Passages and Interpretative Quests.* New York: Palgrave Macmillan, 2010.

Whited, Lana A., ed. *The Ivory Tower and Harry Potter: Perspectives on a Literary Phenomenon.* Columbia, Mo.: University of Missouri Press, 2002.

Bibliography

Primary Sources

Arabian Nights. Translated by Sir Richard Burton. Digireads.com Publishing, 2008.

Aristotle, *The History of Animals, Books 7–10.* Edited and translated by D. M. Balme. Loeb Classical Library. Cambridge, MA: Harvard University Press, 1991.

———. *On the Soul.* In *On the Soul, Parva Naturalia, On Breath,* edited by T. E. Page, et al., translated by W. S. Hett. 1936. Loeb Classical Library, 2–203. London: William Heinemann, 1964.

Austen, Jane. *Pride and Prejudice.* 1813. Edited by Tony Tanner. Great Britain: Penguin Books, 2007.

Blake, William. *Songs of Innocence and of Experience.* 1794. London: Tate, 2006. Bloomsbury, 2003.

Blyton, Enid. *The Magic Faraway Tree*, London: Egmont, 2002.

Carroll, Lewis. *Through the Looking-Glass and What Alice Found There.* In *The Penguin Complete Lewis Carroll,* introduced by Alexander Woollcott, 121–249. Harmondsworth: Penguin, 1982.

Chaucer, Geoffrey. "The Canon's Yeoman's Prologue and Tale." In *The Riverside Chaucer,* edited by Larry D. Benson, 282–86. Oxford: Oxford University Press, 1988.

Culpepper, Nicholas. *Culpeper's English Physician and Complete Herbal, Arranged for Use as a First Aid Herbal by Mrs. C. F. Leyel.* Hollywood: Wilshire Book Company, 1971.

Dickens, Charles. *Great Expectations.* Ed. Angus Calder. Great Britain: Penguin Books, 1979.

———. *Hard Times; For These Times.* Edited by Graham Law. Peterborough: Broadview Press, 1996.

Eliot, George. *The Mill on the Floss.* Project Gutenberg. http://www.gutenberg.org/files/6688/6688-h/6688-h.htm.

Ferris Bueller's Day Off. Directed by John Hughes. Performed by Matthew Broderick, Alan Ruck, and Mia Sara. Paramount, 1986. DVD.

Gest of Robyn Hode, A. In *Robin Hood and Other Outlaw Tales,* edited by Stephen Knight and Thomas H. Ohlgren, 80–168. Kalamazoo, Michigan: Medieval Institute Publications, 1997.

The Goonies. Directed by Richard Donner. Performed by Sean Astin, Josh Brolin, and Corey Feldman. Warner Bros., 1985. DVD.

H. D. [Hilda Doolittle] *HERmione.* New York: New Directions, 1981.

Harry Potter and the Deathly Hallows Part 2. Directed by David Yates. Performed by Daniel Radcliffe, Emma Watson, and Rupert Grint. Warner Bros., 2011. Film.

Harry Potter and the Goblet of Fire. Directed by Mike Newell. Performed by Daniel Radcliffe, Emma Watson, and Rupert Grint. Warner Bros., 2005. DVD.

Isidore of Seville. *The Etymologies of Isidore of Seville.* Translated by Stephen A. Barney, W. J. Lewis, J. A. Beach, and Oliver Berghof. Cambridge: Cambridge University Press, 2006.

"J.K. Rowling." JKRowling.com. Accessed March 7, 2012. http://www.jkrowling.com. 1997.

Johnson, Ben. *The Alchemist.* Edited by

Brian Woolland. Cambridge Series Literature. Cambridge: Cambridge University Press, 1997.
Larson, J. "Talking with Rick Riordan." *Book Links* 18, no. 5 (May 2009): 18–20.
Lawrence, D. H. *Women in Love, with a Foreword by the Author*. The Modern Library of the World's Best Books. New York: Modern Library, 1950.
Le Guin, Ursula. *A Wizard of Earthsea*, Harmondsworth, Middlesex: Penguin, 1971.
Lewis, C. S. *The Chronicles of Narnia*. 7 vols. London: Bodley Head, 1950–1956.
Madrigal, Stephanie and Michelle Garcia Winner. *Superflex Takes on Glassman and the Team of Unthinkables*. USA: Thinking Social Publishing, 2009
The Magic School Bus. Directed by Bruce Degen and Joanna Cole. Performed by Lily Tomlin. The Magic School Bus. PBS. 11 Sept. 1994.
Meyer, Stephenie. "StephenieMeyer.com × Twilight Series × Midnight Sun." StephenieMeyer.com. August 28, 2008. http://www.stepheniemeyer.com/midnightsun.html.
Milton, John. *Complete Poems*. Bartleby.com. 1667. http://www.bartleby.com/4/401.html
———. "The Reason of Church Government Urged Against Prelaty." In *Complete Poems and Major Prose*, edited by Merritt Y. Hughes, 640–89. New York: Macmillan Publishing Company, 1957.
Norton, Thomas. *Ordinal of Alchemy*. 1477. Edited by John Reidy. Early English Text Society Series 272. Oxford: Oxford University Press, 1975.
"Pottermore: About Pottermore." Pottermore.com. Accessed March 7, 2009. http://www.pottermore.com/en/about.
Pottermore Editor. "Waiting for Pottermore?" *Pottermore Insider*. March 8, 2012. http://insider.pottermore.com/2012/03/waiting-for-pottermore.html.
The Princess Bride. Directed by Rob Reiner. Performed by Cary Elwes, Robin Wright, and Mandy Patinkin. Columbia Tristar, 1987.
Ripley, George. *The Compend of Alchemy*. 1470–71. Unpublished edition by J. Reidy, 1983.

Rothfuss, Patrick. *The Name of the Wind*. USA: DAW, 2007.
Rowling, J.K. "FAQs." JKRowling.com. Accessed April 29, 2012. http://www.jkrowling.com/en_GB/#/about-jk-rowling/faqs-and-rumours.
———. *Harrius Potter et Philosophi Lapis*. Translated by Peter Needham. London: Bloomsbury, 2003.
———. *Harry Potter and the Chamber of Secrets*. New York: Scholastic, 1999.
———. *Harry Potter and the Deathly Hallows*. New York: Scholastic, 2007.
———. *Harry Potter and the Goblet of Fire*. New York: Scholastic, 2000.
———. *Harry Potter and the Half Blood Prince*. New York: Scholastic, 2005.
———. *Harry Potter and the Order of the Phoenix*. New York: Scholastic, 2003.
———. *Harry Potter and the Prisoner of Azkaban*. New York: Scholastic, 1999.
———. *Harry Potter and the Sorcerer's Stone*. New York: Scholastic, 1998.
———. "J.K. Rowling Announces Pottermore." October 4, 2011. http://www.youtube.com/watch?feature=player_embedded&v=LIApkyunK9Y.
———. "The Surprising Success of Harry Potter." Interview by Larry King. *Larry King Live!* Cable News Network. October 20, 2000. Accio Quote. <http://www.accio-quote.org/articles/2000/1000-cnn-larryking.htm>.
———. "World Book Day Chat." Accio-Quote. Last modified 2006. http://www.accio-quote.org/articles/2004/0304-wbd.htm.
Scamander, Newt (J.K. Rowling). *Fantastic Beasts and Where to Find Them*. New York: Scholastic, 2001.
Shakespeare, William. *1 Henry IV: A Norton Critical Edition*. 3rd ed. Edited by Gordon McMullan. New York and London: W. W. Norton, 2003.
———. *A Midsummer Night's Dream*. In *The Riverside Shakespeare*, edited by G. Blakemore Evans, introduced by Harry Levin, 222–49. Boston: Houghton Mifflin Company, 1974.
———. *The Winter's Tale*. In *The Norton Shakespeare, Based on the Oxford Edition: Romances and Poems*, edited by Stephen

Greenblatt, 191–272. London: W.W. Norton & Co. 1997.

Shelley, Mary. *Frankenstein or the Modern Prometheus.* London: Bradbury and Evans, 1823.

Sir Gawain and the Green Knight, Pearl, Cleanness, Patience. Edited by J. J. Anderson. London: Everyman, 1996.

Spenser, Edmund. *Faerie Queene.* Project Gutenberg. http://www.gutenberg.org/cache/epub/6930/pg6930.html.

Theobaldus Episcopus. *Physiologus: Theobaldi Episcopi de Naturis Duodecim Animalium.* Translated by Willis Barnstone. Bloomington: Indiana University Press, 1964.

Tolkien, J. R. R. *The Hobbit.* London: HarperCollins Publishers, 2007.

_____. *The Lord of the Rings.* London: George Allen and Unwin, 1988.

Manuscripts

Aberdeen Bestiary. Aberdeen, University Library, MS 24.

Ars alchemie. Palermo, Biblioteca comunale, Qq A 10. Fols. 357r–363v.

_____. Oxford, Corpus Christi College, 125. Fols. 97r–100v.

_____. Cambridge, Gonville and Gaius College, 181. 19–32.

_____. Göttingen, Universitätsbibliothek, Hist. Nat. 75. Fols. 18r–18v.

The Beowulf Manuscript. London, British Library, Cotton MS Vitellius A XV. Ff 94–209.

Bodley Bestiary. Oxford, Bodleian Library, MS Bodley 764.

The Book of Kells. Dublin, Trinity College Dublin MS 58.

The Harley Lyrics. London, British Library, Harley MS 2253.

The Lindisfarne Gospels. London, British Library Cotton MS Nero D.IV.

Medical Recipes. London, British Library MS Add. 33996.

The Naples Manuscript. Naples, Biblioteca Nazionale, MS XIII.B.29.

Richard of Haldingham or Lafford. *Mappa Mundi.* Hereford, Hereford Cathedral.

Secondary Sources

Abanes, Richard. *Harry Potter and the Bible: The Menace Behind the Magick.* USA: Horizon Books: 2001

"About Us." *eNotes.com,* 2011. Web. 21 Feb. 2012.

Agee, J. "What is Effective Literature Instruction? A Study of Experienced High School English Teachers in Differing Grade- and Ability-Level Classes." *Journal of Literacy Research* 32, no. 3 (2000): 303–348.

Allen, Richard Hinkley. *Star Names: Their Lore and Meaning.* New York: Dover, 1963.

Anatol, Giselle Liza, ed. *Reading Harry Potter Again: New Critical Essays.* Santa Barbara, CA: 2009.

_____. *Reading Harry Potter: Critical Essays.* Westport, CT: Praeger, 2003.

Andersen, Kara Lyn. "Harry Potter and the Susceptible Child Audience." *CLCWeb: Comparative Literature and Culture* 7 (2005) http://docs.lib.purdue.edu/clcweb/vol7/iss2/2.

Arden, Heather, and Kathryn Lorenz. "The Harry Potter Stories and French Arthurian Romance." *Arthuriana* 13 (2003): 54–68.

_____. "The Ambiguity of the Outsider in the Harry Potter Stories and Beyond." In *The Image of the Outsider in Literature, Media and Society,* edited by Will Wright and Steven Kaplan, 430–34. Pueblo, University of Southern Colorado, 2002.

Atsma, Aaron J., ed. *The Theoi Project: Greek Mythology,* 2011. http://www.theoi.com.

Australian Bureau of Statistics. "1301.0—Yearbook Chapter, 2009–10: Characteristics of the Population." June 4, 2010. http://www.abs.gov.au/AUSSTATS/abs@.nsf/Lookup/1301.0Feature+Article7012009%E2%80%9310.

_____. "Australian Social Trends June 2011: Children of the Digital Revolution." June 29, 2011. Web.http://www.ausstats.abs.gov.au/ausstats/subscriber.nsf/Lookup Attach/4102.0Publication29.06.117/$File/41020_Childrendigital_Jun2011.pdf.

Australian Government. "National School Chaplaincy Program Overview." Department of Education, Employment and

Workplace Relations. 2011. http://www.deewr.gov.au/Schooling/NSCP/Pages/Overview.aspx.

"Autism Spectrum Disorders (ASDs)." *Centers for Disease Control and Prevention.* March 29, 2012. http://www.cdc.gov/ncbddd/autism/data.html.

Bae, Yupin, Susan Choy, Claire Geddes, Jennifer Sable, and Thomas Snyder. *Trends in Educational Equity of Girls and Women.* Washington, DC: National Center for Education Statistics, 2000. http://nces.ed.gov/pubs2000/2000030.pdf.

Baggett, David, and Shawn E. Klein, eds. *Harry Potter and Philosophy: If Aristotle Ran Hogwarts.* Chicago and La Salle: Open Court, 2004.

Bantick, Christopher. "Chaplaincy Program Participants beyond a Prayer." *The Australian,* May 21, 2011, 14.

Barman, Charles R. "Students' Views of Scientists and Science: Results from a National Study." *Science and Children* 35, no. 1 (1997): 18–23.

Barnett, Michael and Alan Kafka. "Using Science Fiction Movie Sciences to Support Critical Analysis of Science." *Journal of College Science Teaching* 36, no. 4 (2006): 31–35.

Baron-Cohen, Simon. *Autism and Asperger Syndrome.* Oxford: Oxford University Press, 2008.

Bassham, George, ed. *The Ultimate Harry Potter and Philosophy: Hogwarts for Muggles.* Hoboken, NJ: John Wiley & Sons, 2010.

Bauerlein, Mark. *The Dumbest Generation: How the Digital Age Stupefies Young Americans and Jeopardizes Our Future (Or, Don't Trust Anyone Under 30).* New York: Tarcher/Penguin Group, 2008.

Baurley, Thomas. "American Mandrake." *Naturally Science and Lore.* Nov. 7, 2010. http://www.technogypsie.com/science/?cat=22.

Bean, Thomas W. & Karen Moni. "Developing Students' Critical Literacy: Exploring Identity Construction in Young Adult Fiction." *Journal of Adolescent and Adult Literacy* 46, no. 8 (2003): 638–648.

Beaufort, Anne. *College Writing and Beyond: A New Framework for University Writing Instruction.* Logan: Utah State University Press, 2007.

Belcher, Catherine L. and Becky Herr Stephenson. *Teaching Harry Potter: The Power of Imagination in Multicultural Classrooms.* New York: Palgrave Macmillan, 2011.

Bettelheim, Bruno. *The Uses of Enchantment.* New York: Random, 1976.

Black, Rebecca W. *Adolescents and Online Fan Fiction.* New York: Peter Lang, 2008.

Blake, Andrew. *The Irresistible Rise of Harry Potter.* London and New York: Verso, 2002.

Blickenstaff, Jacob Clark. "Muggle or Wizard? Science in Harry Potter and the Deathly Hallows (Part 1)." *NSTA Reports* 22, no. 5 (2011): 20–21.

Bloom, Allan. *The Closing of the American Mind.* New York: Simon and Schuster, 1987.

Bloom, Harold. "Can 35 Million Book Buyers be Wrong? Yes." *Wall Street Journal,* July 11, 2000, national edition, A26.

———. *The Visionary Company.* Garden City: Doubleday, 1961.

Bogdan, Robert C. and Sari K. Biklen. *Qualitative Research for Education: An Introduction to Theories and Methods.* 5th ed. Boston: Allyn & Bacon, 2007.

Booth, David, Susan Elliott-Johns, and Fiona Bruce. *Boys' Literacy Attainment: Research and Related Practice.* North Bay, Canada: Centre for Literacy, Nipissing University, 2009. http://www.edu.gov.on.ca/eng/research/boys_literacy.pdf.

Borror, Donald J. *Dictionary of Word Roots and Combining Forms.* Palo Alto, CA: Mayfield Publishing Company, 1971.

Boston, Rob. "Witch Hunt: Why the Religious Right is Crusading to Exorcise Harry Potter Books from Public Schools and Libraries." *Church & State,* March 2002, 8–10, 12.

Bradshaw, Tom & Bonnie Nichols. *Reading at Risk: A Survey of Literary Reading in America* (Research Division Report No. 46). Washington, D.C.: National Endowment for the Arts, 2004.

Bressler, Charles E. *Literary Criticism: An Introduction to Theory and Practice.* 4th ed. New Jersey: Pearson Prentice Hall, 2007.

Browne, Ray B., ed. *Popular Culture Studies Across the Curriculum*. Jefferson, NC: McFarland, 2005.

Buchanan, Michael T. "Attending to the Spiritual Dimension to Enhance Curriculum Change." *Journal of Beliefs and Values* 31 (2010): 191–201.

Buckingham, David. "Introduction: Fantasies of Empowerment? Radical Pedagogy and Popular Culture." In *Teaching Popular Culture: Beyond Radical Pedagogy*, edited by David Buckingham, 1–17. London: UCL Press, 1998. EBook.

Bunker, Lisa. "Wizards, Witches, and Beings: S." *The Harry Potter Lexicon*, August 2, 2011. http://www.hp-lexicon.org/wizards/a-z/s.html.

Burke, Kenneth. *The Philosophy of Literary Form*. Berkeley: University of California Press, 1973.

Burns, Gary. "Television and the Crisis in the Humanities." In *Rejuvenating the Humanities*, edited by Ray B. Browne and Marshall W. Fishwick, 149–62. Bowling Green: Bowling Green State University Press, 1992.

Calkins, Lucy. *The Art of Teaching Writing*. Portsmouth, NH: Heinemann, 1994.

Campbell, Joseph. *The Hero With a Thousand Faces*. 2nd ed. Bollingen Series 17. Princeton: Princeton University Press, 1968.

_____. *The Masks of God: Primitive Mythology*. London: Secker & Warburg, 1960.

Card, Orson Scott. *Characters and Viewpoint*. Cincinnati: Writer's Digest Books, 2010.

Cavanagh, Sean. "Educators Revisit Girls' Loss of Math, Science Interest." *Education Week* 24, no. 34 (2005): 6.

Chandler-Olcott, Kelly., and Donna Mahar, "Adolescents' Anime-Inspired 'Fan fictions': An Exploration of Multiliteracies." *Journal of Adolescent and Adult Literacy* 46, no. 7 (2003): 556–566.

Chesterton, G.K. *Charles Dickens*. Ware: Wordsworth Editions, 2007.

Chorzempa, Barbara Fink, and Laurie Lapidus. "To Find Yourself, Think for Yourself." *Teaching Exceptional Children* 41, no. 3 (January 2009): 54–59. *Academic Search Complete*, EBSCO*host*.

Collie, Joanne & Stephen Slater. *Literature in the Language Classroom: A Resource Book of Ideas and Activities (1987)*. New Delhi: Cambridge University Press, (2009).

Connors, Robert, and Andrea A. Lunsford. "Frequency of Formal Error in Current College Writing, or Ma and Pa Kettle Do Research." *College Composition and Communication* 39, no. 4 (1988): 395–409.

Cooperative Children's Book Center. *Thoughts on Publishing in 2010*. 2011. http://www.education.wisc.edu/ccbc/books/choiceintro11.asp.

Cotton, Sian, Meghan E. McGrady, and Susan R. Rosenthal. "Measurement of Religiosity/Spirituality in Adolescent Health Outcomes Research: Trends and Recommendations." *Journal of Religion and Health* 49(2010): 414–444.

Crenshaw, Kimberle. "Mapping the Margins: Intersectionality, Identity Politics, and Violence against Women of Color." *Stanford Law Review* 43, no. 6 (Jul. 1991): 1241–1299.

Curwood, Jen Scott & Damiana Gibbons. "'Just Like I Have Felt': Multimodal Counternarratives in Youth-Produced Digital Media." *International Journal of Learning and Media* 1, no. 4 (2009): 59–77.

Curwood, Jen Scott & Laura Lee H. Cowell. "iPoetry: Creating Space for New Literacies in the English Curriculum." *Journal of Adolescent and Adult Literacy* 55, no. 2 (2011): 107–117.

Day, James M. "Speaking Belief: Language, Performance and Narrative in the Psychology of Religion." *The International Journal for the Psychology of Religion* 3, no. 4 (1993): 213–229.

Delgado, Cheryl. "A Discussion of the Concept of Spirituality." *Nursing Science Quarterly* 18 (2005): 157–162.

DeSouza, Marian and Brendan Hyde. "Spirituality of Children and Young People: A Consideration of Some Perspectives and Implications from Research Contextualized by Australia." *International Journal of Children's Spirituality* 12 (2007): 97–104.

DeSouza, Marian. "The Role of School Education Programmes in Nurturing the Spirituality of Young People." In *At the Heart of Education: School Chaplaincy and Pastoral Care*, edited by James Norman, 122–133. Dublin: Veritas, 2004.

Dey, Ian. *Qualitative Data Analysis: A User Friendly Guide for Social Scientists*. London: Routledge, 1993.

Dierking, Lynn D. and John H. Falk. "Optimizing Out-of-School Time: The Role of Free-choice Learning." *New Directions for Youth Development* 97 (2003): 75–88.

Dishneau, David. *CBSNews.com*. "Harry Potter Goes to College," September 23, 2003. http://www.cbsnews.com/stories/2003/11/19/national/main584456.shtml

Dombek, Kristin and Scott Herndon. *Critical Passages: Teaching the Transition to College Composition*. New York: Teachers College Press, 2004.

Dubeck, Leroy W. and Rose Tatlow. "Using *Star Trek: The Next Generation* Television Episodes to Teach Science." *Journal of College Science Teaching* 27, no. 5 (1998): 319–23.

"Durham University Students Offered Harry Potter Course." *BBC News*, August 18, 2010. http://www.bbc.co.uk/news/uk-england-wear-11011279.

Eccleshare, Julia. "'Most Popular Ever': The Launching of Harry Potter." In *Popular Children's Literature in Britain*, edited by Julia Briggs, Dennis Butts, and M.O. Grenby, 287–300. Aldershot: Ashgate, 2008.

Elliot, Belinda. "Harry Potter: Harmless Christian Novel or Doorway to the Occult? Interview with Richard Abanes." *Christian Broadcasting Network.com*, October 2007. http://www.cbn.com/spirituallife/onlinediscipleship/harrypottercontroversy/elliott_richardabanes.aspx.

"Enotes.com Traffic and Demographic Statistics by Quantcast.com." *Quantcast.com*, 2011. Oct. 30, 2011.

Evans, Kathy. "Last Train to Hogwarts." *The Age*, June 26, 2011, 21.

Fisher, John W. "It's Time to Wake Up and Stem the Decline in Spiritual Well_Being in Victorian Schools." *International Journal of Children's Spirituality* 12 (2007): 165–177.

Fontana, David, *Psychology, Religion and Spirituality*. Oxford: BPS Blackwell, 2003.

Foucault, Michel. *Discipline and Punish: The Birth of the Prison*. 1977. Translated by Alan Sheridan. New York: Vintage Books, 1995.

Freire, Paulo. *Pedagogy of the Oppressed*. New York: The Continuum Publishing Corporation, 1987.

Friedman, John Block. *The Monstrous Races in Medieval Art and Thought*. Syracuse, NY: Syracuse University Press, 2000.

Futral, Andrew, Just Having Fun, Tumblr blog, 2010. http://andrewfutral.tumblr.com/post/141911450/i-am-currently-reading-twilight-because-i-dont

Garrett, Peter. "National School Chaplaincy Program." Canberra: Minister's Media Centre, 2011. http://ministers.deewr.gov.au/garrett/national-school-chaplaincy-program.

Gee, James Paul. *Situated Language and Learning: A Critique of Traditional Schooling*. New York: Routledge, 2004.

Gelder, Ken. *Popular Fiction: The Logics and Practices of a Literary Field*. London and New York: Routledge, 2004.

Gillham, D.G. *Blake's Contrary States: The "Songs of Innocence and of Experience" as Dramatic Poems*. Cambridge: Cambridge University Press, 1966.

Gioia, Dana. *The Arts and Civic Engagement: Involved in Arts, Involved in Life*, Research Brochure. Washington, D.C.: National Endowment for the Arts, 2006.

Gioia, Dana, ed. *To Read or Not to Read: A Question of National Consequence*, Research Report 47. Washington, D.C.: National Endowment for the Arts, 2007.

Glaser, Barney G. *The Grounded Theory Perspective: Conceptualization Contrasted with Description*. Mill Valley, CA: Sociology Press, 2001.

Glaser, Barney G. and Anselm L. Strauss. *The Discovery of Grounded Theory: Strategies for Qualitative Research*. Chicago: Aldine, 1967.

Gomez, M.L., M.B. Schieble, J.S. Curwood, & D.D. Hassett. "Technology, Learning, and Instruction: Distributed Cognition

in the Secondary English Classroom." *Literacy* 44, no. 1 (2010): 20–27.
Government of Saskatchewan, Ministry of Education. *2009 Saskatchewan Education Indicators Report: Prekindergarten to Grade 12*. Regina: Saskatchewan Ministry of Education, 2009.
Graham Allen. *Intertextuality*. London and New York: Routledge, 2000.
Granger, John. "Harry Potter is Here to Stay." *Christianity Today* 55, no. 7 (July 13, 2011): 50. http://www.christianitytoday.com/ct/2011/july/harryherestay.html.
_____. *Harry Potter's Bookshelf: The Great Books Behind the Hogwarts Adventures*. New York: Berkley Publishing Group, 2009.
_____. *Looking for God in Harry Potter*. USA: Tyndale/Zondervan Publishing, 2004.
Groenke, Susan L. and Lisa Scherff. *Teaching YA Lit through Differentiated Instruction*. Urbana: National Council of Teachers of English, 2010.
Grotta, Daniel. *J.R.R. Tolkien: Architect of Middle Earth*. USA: Running Press, 1992
Gupta, Suman. *Re-Reading Harry Potter*. New York: Palgrave MacMillan, 2003.
Halford, Macy. "Harry Potter and A Dance with Dragons: Breaking Records, Boggling Minds." *The New Yorker*, July 18, 2011. http://www.newyorker.com/online/blogs/books/2011/07/harry-potter-deathly-hallows-george-rr-martin-dance-with-dragons.html
Hall, Stuart. "Cultural Studies and Its Theoretical Legacies." In *Stuart Hall: Critical Dialogues in Cultural Studies*, edited by David Morley and Kuang-Hsing Chen, 261–274. London: Routledge, 1996. Ebook.
Hallett, Vicky. "The Power of Potter." *U.S. News and World Report* 139, no. 3, 2005: 44–51.
Handler, Daniel. "Frightening News." *New York Times*, October 30, 2001, 17.
"Harry Potter and the Pottermore Web Mystery." *The Telegraph*, March 4, 2012. http://www.telegraph.co.uk/culture/harry-potter/9121868/Harry-Potter-and-the-Pottermore-web-mystery.html.
"Harry Potter Faces the Challenge from Georgia." *American Libraries*, June/July 2006, 21.
Hassig, Debra. *Medieval Bestiaries: Text, Image, Ideology*. Res Monographs on Anthropology and Aesthetics. Cambridge: Cambridge University Press, 1995.
Heilman, Elizabeth E., ed. *Critical Perspectives on Harry Potter*. 2nd ed. New York: Routledge, 2009.
_____. *Harry Potter's World: Multidisciplinary Critical Perspectives*. New York, NY: Routledge Falmer, 2003.
Hermond, Chelsea. *The Emory Wheel*. "New Course in American Studies to Focus on 'Harry Potter' Books and Movies," October 27, 2011. http://www.emorywheel.com/detail.php?n=30318.
Highfield, Roger. *The Science of Harry Potter: How Magic Really Works*. New York: Penguin, 2002.
Hodder, Jacqueline. "Young People and Spirituality: The Need for a Spiritual Foundation for Australian Schooling." *International Journal of Children's Spirituality* 12 (2007): 179–190.
Hogue, Theresa. "Special Freshmen Classes Feature Harry Potter, Avatar." *LIFE@OSU*, Sept. 27, 2010. http://oregonstate.edu/dept/ncs/lifeatosu/2010/special-freshmen-classes-feature-harry-potter-avatar.
Hove, Megan. "The Magic Above." *Mercury* 36, no. 4 (2007): 24.
"HPL: Guide to jkrowling.com — FAQ Poll." *HP-Lexicon.org*. April 1, 2007. http://www.hp-lexicon.org/about/sources/jkr.com/jkr-com-poll.html.
"HPL: Guide to jkrowling.com — The Daily Newspaper." *HP-Lexicon.org*. November 1, 2007. http://www.hp-lexicon.org/about/sources/jkr.com/jkr-com-news.html.
Hughes, Philip. "Is Decline in Religion Inevitable? Religion and Young People: A Global Perspective" *Christian Research Association Bulletin* 18 (2008): 1–6.
Irele, F. Abiola. "Sounds of a Tradition: The Souls of Black Folk." In *The Cambridge History of African American Literature*, edited by Maryemma Graham & Jerry W. Ward Jr., 21–38. Cambridge: Cambridge University Press, 2011.
Irvine, Chris. "Harry Potter's Daniel Rad-

cliffe has Dyspraxia." *The Telegraph*, August 17, 2008. http://www.telegraph.co.uk/news/celebritynews/2573230/Harry-Potters-Daniel-Radcliffe-has-dyspraxia.html.

Ivie, Rachel and Kim Nies Ray. *Women in Physics and Astronomy 2005*. College Park, MD: American Institute of Physics, 2005.

Jacobsen, Ken. "Harry Potter and the Secular City: The Dialectical Religious Vision of J.K. Rowling." *Animus* 9 (2004): 79–104.

James, C. Renee. "The Real Stars of Harry Potter." *Mercury* 36, no. 4 (2007): 19–27.

James, Ken. "Is 'Harry Potter ...' Series Truly Harmless?" *Christian Answers.Net*, November 2007. http://www.christiananswers.net/q-eden/harrypotter.html.

Jenkins, Henry. *Convergence Culture: Where Old and New Media Collide*. New York: New York University Press, 2006.

_____. *Textual Poachers: Television Fans and Participatory Culture*. New York: Routledge, 1992.

Johnson, Carl N. and Chris J. Boyatzis. "Cognitive—Cultural Foundations of Spiritual Development." In *The Handbook of Spiritual Development in Childhood and Adolescence*, edited by Eugene C. Roehlkepartain, Pamela Ebstyne King, Linda Wagener and Peter L. Benson, 211–223. Thousand Oaks: Sage, 2006.

Johnson, Edgar. *Charles Dickens: His Tragedy and Triumph*, vol. 1. New York: Simon and Schuster, 1952.

Jones, Jane Houston and Caroline Sagaguchi Kunioka. "The Harry Potter Objects—A Year-round Literary Stargazing Project," July 2011. http://jane.whiteoaks.com/2009/07/09/the-harry-potter-objects-a-year-round-literary-stargazing-project.

Jones, Mary. "The Celtic Tree Calendar." *Jones' Celtic Encyclopedia*. 2004. http://www.maryjones.us/jce/celtictreecalendar.html.

Kazin, Alfred. "Introduction." In *The Portable Blake*, 1–60. New York: Penguin, 1976.

Keathley, Michael. *Best Colleges Online*. "15 Fascinating College Courses for the Ultimate Potter Scholar," July 18, 2011. http://www.bestcollegesonline.com/blog/2011/07/18/15-fascinating-college-courses-for-the-ultimate-potter-scholar.

Kern, Edmund M. *The Wisdom of Harry Potter: What Our Favorite Hero Teaches Us about Moral Choices*. New York: Prometheus, 2003.

Kimbrough, Carey. "The Hero's Journey and *Eragon*." Unpublished paper, Ferrum College, 2011.

King, Stephen. "J.K. Rowling's Ministry of Magic." *Entertainment Weekly*, August 17, 2007, 30–4.

Knapp, Peggy A. "The Work of Alchemy." *Journal of Medieval and Early Modern Studies* 30, no. 3 (Fall 2000): 575–99.

Kress, Gunther R. *Literacy in the New Media Age*. New York: Routledge, 2003.

Krisciunas, Kevin. "Rowling Gets it Right." *Sky and Telescope* 106, no. 6 (2003): 12.

Kurtz, Holly. "Harry Potter Expelled from School." *Denver Rocky Mountain News*, November 6, 1999. http://www.cesnur.org/recens/potter_06.htm.

Lammers, Jayne. C. "'Is the Hangout ... the Hangout?' Exploring Tensions in an Online Gaming-Related Fan Site." In *Videogames, Affinity Spaces, and New Media Literacies*, edited by S.C. Duncan & E.R. Hayes, 23–50. New York: Peter Lang, 2012.

Lammers, Jayne C., Jen Scott Curwood, & Alecia Marie Magnifico. "Toward an Affinity Space Methodology: Considerations for Literacy Research." *English Teaching: Practice and Critique* 11, no. 2 (2012): 44–58.

Landy, Samantha. "My Life Growing up with Potter." *Herald Sun*, July 17, 2011, 26.

Lankshear, Collin & Michelle Knobel. *New Literacies: Everyday Practices and Classroom Learning*. New York: Open University Press, 2006.

Larsen, Kristine. "The Astronomy of Middle-Earth: Teaching Astronomy through Tolkien." In *Cosmos in the Classroom 2004*, edited by Andrew Fraknoi and William Waller, 237–45. San Francisco: Astronomical Society of the Pacific, 2004.

_____. "Harry Potter and the Upcoming

Venus-Jupiter Conjunction: A Unique Outreach Opportunity." *Communicating Astronomy to the Public Journal* no. 4 (2008): 16–17.

———. "Hobbits, Hogwarts, and the Heavens: The Use of Fantasy Literature and Films in Astronomy Education and Outreach." In *Proceedings of IAU-UNESCO Symposium 260*, edited by D. Valls-Gabaud and A. Bokensberg, 306–10. Cambridge: Cambridge University Press, 2011.

———. "Zombies Are Are My Science Homework: Enticing Reluctant Science Students With the Undead." *Connecticut Journal of Science Education* 48, no. 2 (2011): 11–13.

Larsen, Kristine and Marsha Bednarski. "Muggles, Meteoritic Armor, and Menelmacar: Using Fantasy Series in Astronomy Education and Outreach." In *Preparing for the 2009 International Year of Astronomy*, edited by M.G. Gibbs, J. Barnes, J.G. Manning, and B. Partridge, 82–90. San Francisco: Astronomical Society of the Pacific Press, 2008.

Latimer, Matt. *Speech-Less: Tales of a White House Survivor.* New York: Crown, 2009.

Lee, Patrick. "Pottermania Lives on in College Classrooms." *CNN News.* March 25, 2008. http://articles.cnn.com/2008-03-25/entertainment/cnnu.potter_1_potter-books-harry-potter-luna-lovegood?_s=PM:SHOWBIZ.

Lenhart, A., K. Purcell, A. Smith, & K. Zickuhr. "Social Media and Young Adults." *Pew Internet and American Life Project.* Washington D.C.: Pew Charitable Trusts, 2010. http://www.pewinternet.org/Reports/2010/Social-Media-and-Young-Adults.aspx.

Lenhart, A., M. Madden, A. Smith, & A.R. Macgill. "Teens and Social Media." *Pew Internet and American Life Project.* Washington D.C.: Pew Charitable Trusts, 2007. http://www.pewinternet.org/Reports/2007/Teens-and-Social-Media.aspx.

Lessig, L. "Creative Commons." Presented at the Annual ITU Conference: Network for IT-Research and Competence in Education, University of Oslo, Norway, 2005.

Lewis, C.S. *An Experiment in Criticism.* Cambridge: Cambridge University Press, 1995.

———. *Mere Christianity.* San Francisco: Harper San Francisco, 2001.

Lunsford, Andrea A., and Karen Lunsford. "'Mistakes Are a Fact of Life': A National Comparative Study." *College Composition and Communication* 59, no. 4 (2008): 781–806.

Lynn, Steven. *Texts and Contexts: Writing About Literature with Critical Theory.* 3rd ed. New York: Longman, 2001.

Magnifico, Alecia Marie. "The Game of Neopian Writing." In *Learning in Video Game Affinity Spaces*, edited by S.C. Duncan & E.R. Hayes, 212–234. New York: Peter Lang, 2012.

———. "Writing for Whom: Cognition, Motivation, and a Writer's Audience." *Educational Psychologist* 45, no. 3 (2010): 167–184.

Magre, Maurice. "Nicolas Flamel et la Pierre Philosophale." In *Magiciens et Illuminés (Magicians, Seers, and Mystics)*, translated by Reginald Merton, 1930. "Nicholas Flamel," *Alchemylab.com*, accessed May 22, 2012, http://www.alchemylab.com/flamel.htm.

Markell, Kathryn A. and Marc A. Markell. *The Children Who Lived: Using Harry Potter and Other Fictional Characters to Help Grieving Children and Adolescents.* New York: Routledge, 2008.

Mason, Michael, Andrew Singleton, and Ruth Webber. *The Spirit of Generation Y: Young People's Spirituality in a Changing Australia.* Mulgrave: John Garrett Publishing, 2007.

Masters, Lisa. *The Funny Side of Autism.* USA: Inkwell Productions, 2010.

Mayes-Elman, Ruthann. *Females and Harry Potter: Not All That Empowering.* Lanham, MD: Rowman and Littlefield, 2006.

McAvan, Em. "The Postmodern Sacred: Popular Culture Spirituality in the Genres of Science Fiction, Fantasy and Fantastic Horror." Phd diss., Murdoch University, 2007.

McCrum, Robert, William Cran, & Robert MacNeil, *The Story of English.* New York: Penguin, 1992.

Miller, Susan Martins. *Reading Too Soon: How to Understand and Help the Hyperlexic Child*. USA: Center for Speech and Language, 1993.

Millman, Sierra. "Generation Hex." *The Chronicle of Higher Education* 53, no. 46 (2007). http://chronicle.com/article/Generation-Hex/16722.

Mudhar, Raju. "Outing Dumbledore as Gay." *The Toronto Star*, October 23, 2007. http://www.thestar.com/entertainment/Books/article/269449.

Mulholland, Neil, ed. *The Psychology of Harry Potter: An Unauthorized Examination of the Boy Who Lived*. Dallas, TX: Benbella, 2006.

Nash, Robert J. *Liberating Scholarly Writing: The Power of Personal Narrative*. New York: Teachers College Press, 2004.

New London Group. "A Pedagogy of Multiliteracies: Designing Social Futures." *Harvard Educational Review* 66, no. 1 (1996): 60–92.

Nexon, Daniel H. and Iver B. Neumann, eds. *Harry Potter and International Relations*. Boulder, CO: Rowman & Littlefield, 2006.

Noctor, Colman. "Putting Harry Potter on the Couch." *Clinical Child Psychology and Psychiatry* 11, no. 4 (2006): 579–589.

NSTA Board of Directors. "Informal Science Education." *Journal of College Science Teaching* 28, no.1 (1998): 17–18.

Nussbaum, Martha. *Cultivating Humanity: A Classical Defense of Reform in Liberal Education*. Cambridge, MA: Harvard University Press, 1997.

O'Lear, Casey. "Twilight versus Harry Potter: Fantasy Showdown." *The Nevada Sagebrush*, November 18th, 2008. http://nevadasagebrush.com/blog/2008/11/18/twilight-vs-harry-potter-fantasy-showdown.

Orchard, Andy. *Pride and Prodigies: Studies in the Monsters of the Beowulf Manuscript*. Cambridge and Rochester, NY: D. S. Brewer, 1995.

Ostling, Micheal. "Harry Potter and the Disenchantment of the World." *Journal of Contemporary Religion* 18 (2003): 3–23.

Padfoot5. "Harry Potter's Page." HarryPottersPage.com, June 26, 2004. http://www.harrypotterspage.com/forums/lofiversion/index.php?t801.html.

Patton, Michael Quinn. *Qualitative Evaluation Methods*. Newbury Park, CA: Sage, 1980.

Petre, Jonathan. "J.K. Rowling: Christianity Inspired Harry Potter." *The Telegraph*, October 20, 2007. http://www.telegraph.co.uk/culture/books/fictionreviews/3668658/J-K-Rowling-Christianity-inspired-Harry-Potter.

Petridis, A.S. "Jung's Individuation Process." *Soul Therapy Now*, December 5, 2008. http://soultherapynow.com/articles/individuation.html.

Petrina, Alessandra. "Forbidden Forest, Enchanted Castle: Arthurian Spaces in the Harry Potter Novels." *Mythlore* 24, no. 3–4 (2006): 95–110.

Pike, Rachel. *Talking Together About an Autism Diagnosis*. London: National Autistic Society, 2008.

Plotz, Judith. *Romanticism and the Vocation of Childhood*. New York: Palgrave, 2001.

Poole, Lisa. "Harry Potter Fans Create Makeshift College." *USA Today*, October 10, 2005. http://www.usatoday.com/life/lifestyle/2005-10-10-potter-univ_x.htm.

Prinzi, Travis, ed. *Hog's Head Conversations: Essays on Harry Potter*. Allentown, PA: Zossima Press, 2009.

Pugh, Sheenagh. *The Democratic Genre: Fan Fiction in a Literary Context*. Bridgend: Seren, 2006.

Pugh, Tison, and David L. Wallace. "Heteronormative Heroism and Queering the School Story in J. K. Rowling's *Harry Potter* Series." *Children's Literature Association Quarterly* 31, no. 3 (2006): 260–81.

_____. "A Postscript to 'Heteronormative Heroism and Queering the School Story in J. K. Rowling's Harry Potter Series.'" *Children's Literature Association Quarterly* 33, no. 2 (2008): 188–192.

Pyne, Erin A. *The Ultimate Guide to the Harry Potter Fandom*. Winter Park, FL: What the Flux Comics Publishing, 2010.

Raftopoulos, Mary and Glen Bates. "'It's that Knowing that You Are Not Alone': The Role of Spirituality in Adolescent

Resilience." *International Journal of Children's Spirituality* 16 (2011): 151–167.
Rauser, Randel. "'Is J.K. Rowling a Witch?' and other Vile Fundamentalist Christian Gossip." *The Christian Post-The Tentative Apologist*, July 19, 2011. http://blogs.christianpost.com/tentativeapologist/is-jk-rowling-a-witch-and-other-vile-fundamentalist-christian-gossip.
Ray, Katie Wood. *Wondrous Words: Writers and Writing in the Elementary Classroom*. Urbana, IL: National Council of Teachers of English, 1999.
Readings, Bill. *The University in Ruins*. Cambridge, MA: Harvard University Press, 1996.
Reagin, Nancy R. *Harry Potter and History*. Wiley Pop Culture and History Series. Hoboken, New Jersey: John Wiley & Sons, 2011.
Reagin, Nancy, ed. *Twilight and History*. Wiley Pop Culture and History Series. Hoboken, NJ: Wiley, 2010.
"Real Life 'Invisibility Cloak' Makes Objects Vanish." *International Business Times*. Oct. 5, 2011. http://au.ibtimes.com/articles/225375/20111005/invisibility-cloak-refaction-mirage-effect.htm.
Reifman, Alan. *Psychology Today: On the Campus*. "Harry Potter, Quidditch, and the American University," June 1, 2011. http://www.psychologytoday.com/blog/the-campus/201106/harry-potter-quidditch-and-the-american-university. http://minerva.stkate.edu/news_events.nsf/stories/harry_potter.
Rémi, Cornelia. *Harry Potter Bibliography*, April 29, 2012. http://www.eulenfeder.de/hpliteratur.html.
Roach, Ronald. "Survey: American Girls Aren't Interested in STEM Careers." *Diverse: Issues in Higher Education* 23, no. 4 (2006): 54.
Roehlkepartain et al. "Spiritual Development in Childhood and Adolescence: Moving to the Scientific Mainstream." In *The Handbook of Spiritual Development in Childhood and Adolescence*, edited by Eugene C. Roehlkepartain, Pamela Ebstyne King, Linda Wagener and Peter L. Benson, 1–15. Thousand Oaks: Sage, 2006.

Rogers, Simon. "Top-Selling 100 Books of All Time." *The Guardian*, January 1, 2011. http://www.guardian.co.uk/news/datablog/2011/jan/01/top-100-books-of-all-time.
Rohs, Melissa and Pauline Oo, "Harry Potter Topic of New Course at St. Catherine University." *St. Kate's News*, February 22, 2010.
Ruble, Raymond. "Popular Culture and Philosophy." In *Popular Culture Across the Curriculum*, edited by Ray B. Browne, 69–76. Jefferson, NC: McFarland, 2005.
Safire, William. "Besotted with Potter." *New York Times*, January 27, 2000, national edition, A27.
Salisbury, Joyce. *The Beast Within: Animals in the Middle Ages*. London and New York: Routledge, 1994.
Sarna, Nahum M. *Explaining Exodus: The Origins of Biblical Israel*. New York: Schoken Books, 1996.
Sawyer, Jenny. "Missing from 'Harry Potter'—a Real Moral Struggle." *The Christian Science Monitor*, July 25, 2007. http://www.csmonitor.com/2007/0725/p09s02-coop.
Scholastic and Yankelovich. *2008 Kids and Family Reading Report: Reading in the 21st Century: Turning the Page with Technology*. New York: Scholastic, 2008.
Shea, Mike. "Rick Riordan." *Texas Monthly* 35, no. 6 (2007): 60.
Shore, Stephen M. and Linda G. Rastelli. *Understanding Autism for Dummies*. USA: Wiley Publishing, 2006.
Simmons, Annette. *The Story Factor: Inspiration, Influence and Persuasion through the Art of Storytelling*. New York: Basic Books, 2006.
Siraisi, Nancy. *Medieval and Early Renaissance Medicine: An Introduction to Knowledge and Practice*. Chicago: Chicago University Press, 1990.
Slater, Judith. "Spirituality and the Curriculum." *Taboo: The Journal of Culture and Education* 9 (2005): 59–68.
Sneider, Cary. "Reversing the Swing from Science: Implications from a Century of Research." Paper presented at ITEST Convening on *Advancing Research on Youth Motivation in STEM*, Boston Col-

lege, Boston, Massachusetts, September 9–11, 2011. http://www.noycefdn.org/documents/Sneider-The%20Swing%20from%20Science.pdf.

Stein, L. E. "'This Dratted Thing': Fannish Storytelling through New Media." In *Fan Fiction and Fan Communities in the Age of the Internet,* edited by Karen Hellekson, & Kristina Busse, 245–260. Jefferson, N.C.: McFarland, 2006.

Strauss, Anselm, and Juliet Corbin. *Basics of Qualitative Research: Grounded Theory Procedures and Techniques.* Newbury Park, CA: Sage, 1990.

Sykley, Julie-Anne. *Harry Potter Power.* USA: Glass House Books, 2009.

Tapscott, Don. *Growing Up Digital: The Rise on the Net Generation.* New York: McGraw Hill, 1998.

Thomas, Angela. *Youth Online: Identity and Literacy in the Digital Age.* New York: Peter Lang, 2007.

Thomas, James W. *Repotting Harry Potter.* Allentown, PA: Zossima Press, 2009.

———. *Rowling Revisited: Return Trips to Harry, Fantastic Beasts, Quidditch, & Beedle the Bard.* Allentown, PA: Zossima Press, 2010.

Thomas, Jeffrey E. and Franklin G. Snyder, eds. *The Law and Harry Potter.* Durham, NC: Carolina Academic Press, 2010.

Toswell, M. J. "The Tropes of Medievalism." In *Defining Medievalism(s),* edited by Karl Fugelso, 68–76. Studies in Medievalism 17. Cambridge: D. S. Brewer, 2009.

Trites, Roberta Seelinger. "The Harry Potter Novels as a Test Case for Adolescent Literature." *Style* 35, no. 3 (2001): 472–85.

Tucker, Sheryl A. Deborah L. Hanuscin and Constance J. Bearnes. "Igniting Girls' Interest in Science." *Science* 319, no. 5870 (2008): 1621–22.

Tumminio, Danielle. *Danielle Tumminio.* 2011. http://danielletumminio.com.

Turner, Graeme. *British Cultural Studies: An Introduction,* 3rd ed. Hoboken: Routledge, 2002. Ebook.

Vinciguerra, Antony. "The *Ars alchemie*: The First Latin Text on Practical Alchemy." *Ambix* 56, no. 1 (March 2009): 57–67.

Vineyard, Jennifer. "'Harry Potter' Goes to College: Students Study the Books in New Courses." *MTV News,* September 25, 2008. http://www.mtv.com/news/articles/1595623/harry-potter-goes-college.jhtml.

Vogler, Christopher. "Hero's Journey." *Storytech Literary Consulting.* http://www.thewritersjourney.com/hero's_journey.htm#Heroine.

Webster, Ben and Paul Sanders. "Even my Children were Targets. I was so Angry, says J. K. Rowling; Leveson Inquiry." *The Times* (London), November 25, 2011.

Weinstein, Mike. "Astronomy in the Harry Potter Series." *The Harry Potter Lexicon.* July 6, 2011. http://www.hp-lexicon.org/essays/essay-astronomy.html.

Weldon, James. "The Naples Manuscript and the Case for a Female Readership." *Neophilologus* 93, no. 2 (2009): 703–22.

Whited, Lana A., ed. *The Ivory Tower and Harry Potter: Perspectives on a Literary Phenomenon.* Columbia: University of Missouri Press, 2002.

Williams, James. "Harry Potter and the Chamber of Autism." *JamesMW.com,* 2005. http://www.jamesmw.com/harry.htm.

Williams, Nicholas M. *Ideology and Utopia in the Poetry of William Blake.* Cambridge: Cambridge University Press, 1998.

Yuli, Huang. "A Spellbinding Course for Potter Putterers." *China Daily,* January 6, 2012. http://www.chinadaily.com.cn/usa/china/2012-01/06/content_1439 1662.htm

Zijderveld, Theo. "Cyberpilgrims: The Construction of Spiritual Identity in Cyberspace." Ma diss., Utrecht University, 2008.

Zinnbauer et al. "The Emerging Meanings of Religiousness and Spirituality: Problems and Prospects." *Journal of Personality* 67 (1999): 889–919.

Zipes, Jack. *Sticks and Stones: The Troublesome Success of Children's Literature from Slovenly Peter to Harry Potter.* New York and London: Routledge, 2001.

Zunshine, Lisa. *Why Do We Read Fiction?* Columbus: The Ohio State University Press, 2006.

About the Contributors

Jen Scott **Curwood** is a lecturer in secondary English and media studies at the University of Sydney, Australia. Her research focuses on adolescent literacy, technology, and teacher professional development. Her work has appeared in *English in Australia*, the *International Journal of Learning and Media*, and the *Journal of Adolescent and Adult Literacy*.

Denise Dwyer **D'Errico** holds a BA degree in religious studies from St. Mary's College of California, and an MA in pastoral ministries: liturgical music from Santa Clara University. She speaks to audiences on the topics of parenting and autism awareness. Denise has over twenty years' experience as a liturgical musician and musical instructor.

Clare **Diviny** holds a BA degree in broadcast television and an MA in cultural studies. Now a PhD student at Monash University, her research focuses on the relationship between the consumption of supernatural television and the spiritual identity of young adults in Australia.

Amanda **Firestone** is a PhD candidate in the Department of Communication at the University of South Florida. She received her MA degree from Sussex University in Brighton, England, where she focused on gender studies and media. She earned a BA in film and video at Penn State University. Her dissertation focuses on *The Twilight Saga*.

Whitney E. Jones **Francis** is in pursuit of her PhD in literature at the University of Tennessee, Knoxville. Her critical interests lie in 19th-century British literature and children's literature. As a teaching assistant, Whitney co-teaches a children's literature course that begins with the Romantics and ends with *Harry Potter*.

Valerie Estelle **Frankel** has won a Dream Realm Award, an Indie Excellence Award, and a *USA Book News* National Best Book Award for her *Henry Potty and the Pet Rock* parody series. She taught English for several years at San Jose State University and is the author of four books on pop culture: *From Girl to Goddess*, *Katniss the Cattail*, *Buffy and the Heroine's Journey*, and *Harry Potter: Still Recruiting*.

Elisabeth C. **Gumnior** is an associate professor of writing, rhetoric, and technical communication at James Madison University. She has taught *Harry Potter* related courses since 2004. Research interests include exploring *Harry Potter* as a multimodal, multi-media, and multi-authored text and theorizing the role *Harry Potter* plays in the rise of nerd culture and geekdom.

Susan **Johnston** is an associate professor of English at the University of Regina, where she has taught J.K. Rowling and Dickens to senior students and organized undergraduate conferences, including a town-and-gown conference on *Harry Potter*. Her article on the epilogue in *Deathly Hallows*, "Harry Potter, Eucatastrophe, and Christian Hope," appeared in *Logos* in January 2011.

James B. **Kelley** coordinates the English BA program at Mississippi State University–Meridian. His research and teaching interests include 20th century American literature, popular culture and the internet, gender and sexuality, and literary theory. Publications include essays in *The Robert Frost Review* and *Teaching American Literature: A Journal of Theory and Practice*.

Kristine **Larsen** is a professor of physics and astronomy at Central Connecticut State University. The author of *Stephen Hawking: A Biography* and *Cosmology 101*, and co-editor of *The Mythological Dimensions of Doctor Who*, her work focuses on the intersections between science and society. She has taught a number of interdisciplinary university-level courses, including Science and Science Fiction, The Science of Middle-earth, and Zombies and Modern Western Culture.

J. Steve **Lee** is an instructor of theology and philosophy and director of the Lions Scholar Program at Prestonwood Christian Academy, as well as adjunct professor of philosophy and world religions at Mountain View College. His chapter on the literary structure of the series appeared in *Harry Potter for Nerds: Essays for Fans, Academics, and Lit Geeks* (2011). He holds an MA in philosophy of religion and is a PhD student at the University of Texas at Dallas.

Asma **Mansoor** is a lecturer in the Department of English at the International Islamic University, Islamabad, Pakistan. She is pursuing an MPhil degree in English literature and has taught classical poetry and Pakistani literature in English. Her work has been published in *New Writing: The International Journal for the Theory and Practice of Creative Writing*, *South Asian Review*, and *Pakistaniaat*.

Tenille **Nowak** holds a PhD in British literature from Marquette University. She is a senior lecturer at the University of Wisconsin–Marathon County, where she teaches freshman composition and British literature. Her freshman composition courses often involve *Harry Potter* novels. Other publications include pieces in *Studies in Gothic Fiction On-Line* and *Persuasions*.

Cynthia K. **O'Malley** earned an MA degree in English from Middle Tennessee State University in Murfreesboro. Her research interests include pop culture, television, spirituality and philosophy in pop culture, psychological connections in texts, and queer/gender studies.

Savannah **Sharp** earned a BA in English literature from Agnes Scott College and an MA in English literature from Boston College, where she was a teaching fellow and taught two semesters of the freshmen writing seminar, including lessons on using the *Harry Potter* series to create new material.

J. Malcolm **Stewart** is a Bay Area author, journalist and public relations professional with degrees in political science, ministry and comparative religion. He writes a semi-regular blog for the entertainment website www.criticstudio.com, dealing with television and pop-culture. His novel *The Eyes of the Stars* (Double-Dragon Publishing) was released in 2012.

Reneé **Ward** (PhD, University of Alberta) teaches at Wilfrid Laurier University. Her research focuses on narratives featuring shape-shifters, knights and violence. She has published articles on the Middle English *Lybeaus Desconus*, the Middle English romance *Octavian Imperator*, and the *Harry Potter* series; and wrote on classical and medieval bestiary and aviary traditions for the *Handbook of Medieval Studies*.

Lana A. **Whited**, PhD, is a professor of English and director of the Boone Honors Program at Ferrum College (Virginia), where she teaches a course called Harry Potter and the Hero Myth. She is the editor of *The Ivory Tower and Harry Potter: Perspectives on a Literary Phenomenon* (Missouri, 2002), and has published works on the true-crime novel and Appalachian studies.

Index

ADHD 74
adolescence 15, 17, 54, 179
affinity spaces 81, 82, 83, 84, 85, 89, 90
African-Americans 13, 65, 145
age-appropriate 18, 21, 33, 35
alchemy 1, 8, 49, 135, 159–161
The Alchemyst 15
Alice in Wonderland 1–2, 177, 216
allusions 125, 135, 193–194
American Idol 33
Anatol, Giselle Liza (critic) 126, 128, 197, 198, 199, 201, 208
Ancient Runes 12
anime 83
apparition 12
Apples to Apples 76
archetypes 1, 135, 184, 205
architecture 152, 158–159
Aristotle 138, 156, 197, 202–203
Arithmancy 12
art 2, 9, 63, 66, 77, 81, 83, 113, 155, 180, 194, 210, 213, 215; *see also* crafts
Arthur, King 1, 15, 78, 153, 163, 165
Asperger's Syndrome 33
astrology 12, 47
astronomy 2, 12, 57–68, 210
attention span 42
Attribute 76
audience 11, 60, 81–90, 94, 108, 109, 115, 153, 159
Austen, Jane 135
Australia 81, 93–105
authors 17–19, 40, 55, 63, 83, 88, 94, 107, 109–111, 114–115, 135, 159, 160, 190, 201, 210; *see also* children's authors; creative writing; writers
Avada Kedavra 71

banning the series *see* censorship, libraries
Beedle the Bard 10, 114
Bella Swan 48, 78, 110
Bellatrix Lestrange 39, 58, 60
Beowulf 154
Bettelheim, Bruno (critic) 22, 31
Bible 43, 44, 45, 47, 49, 53, 54, 94, 100, 101; *see also* Christianity; God; Jesus; spirituality; Sunday school
bildungsroman 192–193; *see also* coming of age
Blake, William 1, 154, 168–178
blogs 57, 97, 109, 148
Bloom, Harold (critic) 178, 198, 208
Bloom's Taxonomy 17
Bloomsbury Publishing 108
Blyton, Enid (children's author) 94
board games 7, 165
boarding school 8, 95, 123, 200
bookstores 1, 61, 76, 131
Britain 8, 13, 14, 56, 59, 61, 70, 95, 108, 123, 131, 137–138, 157, 159–160, 200, 206, 210
broomsticks 12, 24, 25, 130, 133, 210
Brown, Dan (author) 79, 123
Buffy the Vampire Slayer 47–48
bullying 24, 25, 37, 131, 137, 146
butterbeer 11, 19
Byronic hero 169

calligraphy 154
Campbell, Joseph 1, 4, 15, 16, 17, 20, 38, 106, 125, 164
Canada 81, 96, 210, 211
canon 85, 90, 111, 114, 198, 202
Care of Magical Creatures 9, 12, 154
The Casual Vacancy 2, 108
cellphones 95, 97
Celtic myth and lore 6, 15, 70, 157
censorship 47, 50, 117, 124, 137
Chamber of Secrets 15, 20, 26–29, 38, 112
charades 75
Charms Class 12
Chaucer, Geoffrey 84, 135, 159–161, 190
chemistry 2, 12, 210
chess 36
Chesterton, G.K. (critic) 209, 216
children 1–57, 64, 78, 79, 94, 96–98, 100–102, 115, 117, 121–126, 131, 132, 134, 136, 137, 150, 152, 168, 169, 172, 184, 185, 191, 198–199, 210–216
children's authors *see* Blyton, Enid; Dahl, Roald; Jones, Diana Wynne; LeGuin, Ur-

271

sula K.; Lewis, C.S.; Meyer, Stephenie; Nesbit, E.; Paolini, Christopher; Pierce, Tamora; Pullman, Philip; Riordan, Rick; Snicket, Lemony
children's books 131, 168, 169; *see also Alice in Wonderland*; choose-your-own-adventure; *Chrestomanci* series; comic books; Disney; *Eragon*; fairy tales; folklore; *Golden Compass*; *Groosham Grange*; *Hobbit*; *Hunger Games*; Nancy Drew; *Nicholas Flamel* series; *Percy Jackson*; *Peter Pan*; *Redwall*; *Treasure Island*;*Twilight*; *Uglies*; *Wise Child*; *Wizard of Oz*; *Worst Witch*; young adult literature
China 2, 131, 134
choose-your-own-adventure 82, 86–87
chosen one *see* hero's journey
Chrestomanci series 8
Christian publishers 42
Christianity 42–54, 96, 98, 117, 136, 137; *see also* Bible; God; Jesus; spirituality; Sunday school
Cinderella 9; *see also* fairytales; folklore
civic engagement 137, 213
civil rights 144
class/social status issues 48, 144, 153, 163, 164, 183, 185, 189, 200, 205
classes *see* school subjects
classics *see* Aristotle; Arthur, King; Austen, Jane; *Beowulf*; Blake, William; Chaucer, Geoffrey; Coleridge, Samuel; Dante; Dickens, Charles; *Dracula*; *Faerie Queene*; fairy tales; folklore; Frost, Robert; *Gawain and the Green Knight*; *Gilgamesh*; Gothic; Hawthorne, Nathaniel; Hemingway, Ernest; *Hercules*; medieval romances; Milton, John; *Odyssey*; Plato; *Pride and Prejudice*; Robin Hood; Romantic Movement; *Romeo and Juliet*; Shakespeare, William; *Sherlock Holmes*; *Sundiata*; *Sword in the Stone*; *To Kill a Mockingbird*; *Treasure Island*; Victorian Era; Wordsworth, William
Coleridge, Samuel 169
Colin Creevey 82, 86–89
collections and anthologies 1, 74, 127, 161, 197–201, 204, 207
college 18–19, 130, 141–195
comic books 37, 90, 215
coming of age 17, 137; *see also* bildungsroman; hero's journey
communication 23, 47, 85, 100, 179, 198, 204
community 2, 38, 44, 47, 65, 123, 133, 150, 155, 163, 177, 201, 213, 215
composition 1, 36, 122, 141–151, 188–195
computer games 2, 97, 115, 126
confidence 38, 39, 41, 66, 115, 187
context 25–31, 44, 64, 76, 181, 188–189, 192–194, 199, 205, 207
conventions 13, 57, 191, 210
cooking 2; *see also* recipes
copyright 111, 114
costumes 5, 7, 35, 66, 134

courses *see* school subjects
crafts 6, 127
creative writing 1, 77–78, 82, 84, 90
Critical Perspectives on Harry Potter (book) 67, 127, 197
critical thinking 4, 13, 17, 23–25, 31, 141
criticism 4, 14, 17, 19, 23–25, 31, 123, 126–127, 133, 143, 157, 180–181, 197–207, 213
cross-disciplinary studies 137
cultural studies 99, 180–181, 186, 200–205; *see also* popular culture
curriculum 1, 4, 12, 58, 62, 84, 90, 124, 126, 130–134, 206

Dahl, Roald (children's author) 137
Dante 135
The Da Vinci Code 78, 79
death 19, 40, 44, 49–50, 60, 83, 87–88, 94, 101–102, 162, 172–177
Deathly Hallows 1, 14, 16, 18, 49–51, 56, 61–62, 89, 93, 98, 113–114, 131, 171–176, 189, 209–211, 215
Defense Against the Dark Arts 4, 8, 12, 155
Delirium (YA dystopia) 82
Dementors 30, 136
development 22, 32, 36, 70, 82, 99, 107, 112, 125, 141–144, 149, 165, 169–171, 199, 205
Dickens, Charles 1, 111, 135, 193–194, 210, 213–217
diction 75, 188
digital age 97
disability 35; *see also* ADHD; Asperger's Syndrome; autism; hyperlexia
Disney 35, 45, 50; *see also* fairy tales
Divergent (YA dystopia) 82
divination 12, 43, 44, 62
doppelgangers 36
Dora the Explorer 33
Draco Malfoy 11, 24, 25, 36–37, 58, 60, 74, 102, 145–146, 164, 172, 184–185
Dracula 79, 135
dragons 9, 25–26
Dumbledore, Albus 20, 28–30, 37–40, 50–51, 60, 100, 110, 124, 133, 157, 163, 166, 172–177, 181–182, 186
Dursleys 144–145, 152–153, 164–165, 171–172, 214
dystopias *see* *Delirium*; *Divergent*; *Hunger Games*; *Matched*; *1984*; *Uglies*

ebooks 113
economics 48, 163, 205
education (subject) 1, 8, 131, 137
educational tools *see* teaching tools
Elder Wand 10
elementary school 21, 57, 212
email 18, 85
Enchanted 35
England *see* Britain
English (subject) *see* allusions; archetypes; bildungsroman; Byronic hero; classics; com-

ing of age; composition; context; creative writing; critical thinking; criticism; diction; essays; games; genres; grammar; hero's journey; journaling; language arts; literacy; literary structure; patterns; peer review; plot; reading comprehension; rhetorical devices; satire; spelling; symbolism; themes; tone; vocabulary; writing
English language learners 70, 83
eNotes.com 117–127
entertainment 2, 22, 45, 94–95, 97, 101–104, 207
epics *see* Arthur, King; *Beowulf*; *Faerie Queene*; fairy tales; folklore; *Gawain and the Green Knight*; *Gilgamesh*; Hercules; hero's journey; myth; *Odyssey*; *Robin Hood*; Shakespeare, William; *Sundiata*; *Sword in the Stone*
Eragon (children's book) 15–17
essays 6, 10, 14, 16, 58, 74, 77–78, 84, 91, 118, 126, 136, 138, 141–142, 148–149, 193, 195, 197–205, 216
ethics 23, 48, 95, 101, 107, 113–115, 131, 138; *see also* morality; values
ethnicity 144, 150; *see also* racism
ethnography 81–82, 85, 150, 157
Europe 134, 158, 207; *see also* Britain
evaluations 18

Facebook 7, 10, 89, 107; *see also* social media
The Faerie Queene 193–194
fairy tales 22, 63, 77, 168, 171–172, 191–193; *see also* Disney; folklore; myths
fan culture 83–85, 90, 171
fan fiction 2, 19, 57, 81–90, 109, 111, 114–115, 137, 142, 147–148, 171
fansites 89
Fantastic Beasts and Where to Find Them 9, 26, 31, 155–156, 166
fantasy 14, 15, 22, 45–47, 52, 56, 67, 73, 78–79, 82, 94–95, 98, 101, 103, 122, 125–126, 152, 200; *see also Alice in Wonderland*; *anime*; Arthur, King; *Buffy the Vampire Slayer*; *Chrestomanci* series; comic books; Disney; *Dracula*; dystopias; fairy tales; folklore; Gothic; hero's journey; *His Dark Materials*; Jones, Diana Wynne; Jordan, Robert; LeGuin, Ursula; Lewis, C.S.; *Lord of the Rings*; Meyer, Stephenie; *Midnight Sun*; *Mistborn*; myth; *Name of the Wind*; Nesbit, E.; *Redwall*; role-playing; science fiction; *Star Trek*; *Star Wars*; *Sword in the Stone*; Tolkien; *Twilight*; vampires
feminism 63, 180; *see also* gender
films 7, 19, 22, 34–35, 45–47, 51–52, 56, 59–60, 62, 64–65, 82, 90, 93, 97–98, 103–104, 111, 115, 121, 125–126, 132, 142, 150, 158–159, 171, 179–180, 183, 197, 200, 206
flashcards 37, 72, 75–77
flip charts 19
flying 12, 27
flying car 26–27

folklore 10, 11, 12, 20, 53, 100, 155, 200; *see also* fairy tales; myths
free-choice learning 57
freshman courses 133, 146
friendship 36, 53, 131, 137, 186
Frost, Robert 118
Frye, Northrop (critic) 192

games *see Apples to Apples*; *Attribute*; board games; charades; computer games; games online; Legos; *Once Upon a Time*; *Pictionary*; Quidditch; *Sims*; *Trivial Pursuit*
games online 97
Gawain and the Green Knight 125, 163
GED 147
gender 1, 57, 63–64, 153, 179–186, 205, 212–213; *see also* feminism; Hermione Granger
gender studies 135
genetics 131, 134
genres 84–85, 126, 135, 189, 191, 194, 198
geology 56
Gilgamesh 4, 14, 15, 17, 18
Ginny Weasley 17, 28–29, 184
globalization 83, 85, 90, 131, 152, 204–205
Goblet of Fire 61, 64, 166, 182–183, 196
God 43–45, 48, 96, 99, 136, 170, 174; *see also* Bible; Jesus; spirituality
The Golden Compass (children's book) 15, 177
good and evil 1, 43–50, 94, 101, 120, 131, 135–136, 145, 171–172, 176, 177, 184
Gothic 158, 169
graduation 11
grammar 70, 75–76, 84, 141, 145, 147–148, 211
Granger, John 49, 135, 139
graphic novels 90; *see also* comic books
Grindelwald 50–51
Groosham Grange 8
grounded theory 118–119
Gryffindor 24, 34–36, 39, 41, 98

Hagrid 25–26, 29, 34, 130, 150, 154, 165
Half-Blood Prince 40, 102
Harry Potter books *see Chamber of Secrets*; *Deathly Hallows*; *Goblet of Fire*; *Half-Blood Prince*; *Order of the Phoenix*; *Philosopher's Stone*; *Prisoner of Azkaban*; *Sorcerer's Stone*
Harry Potter and History (criticism) 135, 136, 139, 197, 205, 208
Harry Potter and International Relations (criticism) 204
Harry Potter and Philosophy (criticism) 127, 197, 203, 208
Harry Potter and the Law (criticism) 205
Harry Potter Encyclopedia 114
Harry Potter Fan Zone 93
Harry Potter films *see* films
Harry Potter Lexicon 10, 58, 64, 68, 72, 114
Harry Potter Power (criticism) 41
Harry Potter Wiki 65
Harry Potter's Bookshelf (criticism) 135, 139
Harry Potter's World (criticism) 197, 200, 208

Hawthorne, Nathaniel 134
Heilman, Elisabeth E (critic) 63, 67–68, 126–128, 197–202, 204, 208
Hemingway, Ernest 84, 125
Herbology 12, 160
Hercules 15, 17
Hermione Granger 2, 17, 20, 24–26, 29–30, 36–37, 40, 59, 63–66, 89, 141, 146, 153–154, 157, 160, 164, 173, 176, 179, 182–183, 186, 196, 206
hero's journey 1, 15, 17, 36, 38, 80, 121, 125, 192; *see also* Campbell, Joseph
high school 12, 33, 56–57, 66, 70, 72, 90, 102, 115–127, 132, 134, 143, 146–147, 175, 212
His Dark Materials 48, 134
history 1, 8, 12, 40, 64, 70, 78, 104, 114, 131, 135, 136, 138, 142, 144, 152–157, 205, 206, 208
History of Magic 12
The Hobbit 15, 18, 125, 216; *see also* Tolkien
homosexuality 50, 51, 144, 182; *see also* sexual orientation
horcruxes 36
horror 47, 50, 56
Hufflepuff 145
human condition 38
humanities 211–216; *see also* literary tools
humor 94
The Hunger Games 2, 15, 48, 78, 81–90, 203; *see also* Katniss Everdeen
hyperlexia 33, 35, 37

identity 38, 43, 53, 84, 93, 98–99, 102, 126, 153, 162, 169, 179, 182–186, 205; *see also* confidence; critical thinking; development; ethics; morality; personal awareness; spirituality; values
imagination 22, 47, 53, 85, 87, 98, 126, 176, 214, 216
information overload 97
instant messenger 85
international relations 131, 204
Internet 6, 9, 57–59, 64, 69, 76–77, 81–90, 97, 107, 109–128, 148, 160–161; *see also* eNotes.com; jkrowling.com; Pottermore
intertextuality 90, 193, 194, 200
invitations to Hogwarts 16, 50, 204
IQA (International Quidditch Association) 11–12; *see also* Quidditch
IQA Rulebook 12
iTunes 113
The Ivory Tower and Harry Potter (criticism) 7, 20, 157, 178, 197, 198, 208

Jenkins, Henry (critic) 83, 84, 91, 100, 106, 134, 138, 187
Jesus 44, 46, 48–50, 54
jkrowling.com 107–109, 114
Jones, Diana Wynne (children's author) 8
Jordan, Robert (fantasy author) 15
journaling 34, 145, 146, 147, 148, 149, 150

Jung, Carl (psychologist) 38, 41
junior high *see* middle school

Katniss Everdeen 17, 48, 83, 85; *see also* Hunger Games
King, Stephen 209, 216
Kohlberg, Lawrence (psychologist) 23; *see also* morality

labels 144–145
language arts 117, 119, 122
Latin 1, 2, 8, 10, 52, 71–76, 110, 155, 157–158, 161, 215
law 1, 25–26, 44, 48, 156, 173, 205; *see also* rules
law school 205
leadership 107
The Leaky Cauldron (fansite) 65
Legos 7, 11, 65
LeGuin, Ursula K. (fantasy author) 8, 94–95
Lévi-Strauss, Claude (critic) 192
Lewis, C.S. (children's author) 45–46, 49–50, 94, 135, 137, 152, 213, 217
libraries 44, 63, 117, 127, 153, 210
Lily Potter 7, 172
The Lion, the Witch and the Wardrobe 15, 46, 94; *see also* Lewis, C.S.
literacy 22, 81–85, 90, 122, 125–127, 181, 210, 211, 212
literary devices and tools *see* English
literary structure 132
LiveJournal 85
Lockhart, Gilderoy 35
Looking for God in Harry Potter (criticism) 49, 55
Lord of the Rings 2, 47, 134, 152; *see also* Tolkien, J.R.R.
lying 103, 214

mandrakes 135, 160–161
manuscripts 153–156, 159–161, 163
map-making 156
maps 34, 156, 157, 210
marginalized 63, 156, 162
Matched (YA dystopia) 82
materialism 97, 200
McGonagall, Minerva 5–6, 10, 24–28, 63, 114
media 83, 90, 114, 117, 121, 134, 142, 180, 181–182, 213; *see also* social media
medicine 63, 159
medieval romances 165
medieval studies 18, 65, 137, 152–166, 215
Meyer, Stephenie 15, 110–111, 116
middle school 12, 19, 64, 73, 85, 118, 120, 122–123, 125
Midnight Sun (*Twilight* novel) 110, 116
Milton, John 60, 190, 214, 217
Ministry of Magic 7, 62, 162, 172–174, 185
Mirror of Erised 41, 147, 149
Mistborn (fantasy novel) 79
mixed media 155

monomyth *see* hero's journey
Monster Book of Monsters 154
morality 2, 22–23, 48, 53–54, 95, 98–103, 141, 199, 203, 213; *see also* ethics; values
motivations 22–26, 31, 51, 78, 87, 181
movies *see* films
Muggle Studies 12
Muggles 38, 65, 67, 93, 98, 135, 144–145, 150, 196–197, 203, 208–217
museums 57, 213
music 10, 11, 36, 81, 213
mystery 73, 126, 137, 154, 191
myth 14–15, 18, 53, 60, 73–74, 79, 131, 155, 157, 191; *see also* fairy tales; folklore

The Name of the Wind (fantasy novel) 79
Nancy Drew 48
NASA 59, 61
National Endowment for the Arts 90–91, 126, 212–213, 217
National Science Teachers Association 57
Nazis 135, 144
Nesbit, E. (children's author) 137
Neville Longbottom 11, 24–25, 36–37, 146
newspapers 93, 98
Nicholas Flamel 8, 10, 136, 160–161
Nicholas Flamel series (children's books) 8
1984 125, 135
nursery rhymes 168

occult 44–45, 47–48, 50, 52, 55; *see also* witchcraft
Occupy movement 144
The Odyssey 15, 17, 78, 125
Ollivander 7
Once Upon a Time (card game) 77
Order of the Phoenix 39, 59, 160, 173
Orlando 10, 137
outreach 57–62
owls 9, 34–35, 103, 210
Oxford 50, 105, 158

pagan 6, 43, 45
Pakistan 188–195
Paolini, Christopher (children's author) 15–16, 18
parents 9, 11, 18, 21–31, 40, 42, 45–49, 53, 60, 65, 87, 120, 121, 124, 146, 149, 176, 185, 212, 216
parties 35, 46, 51, 61, 130
patriarchy 63
Patronus 8, 9, 39, 133
patterns 36, 48, 63, 97, 118–119, 122, 152, 189, 193–194, 205, 211
peer review 15, 83, 148
Percy Jackson 17, 78–79
personal awareness 36, 38; *see also* bullying; confidence; critical thinking; development; ethics; identity; imagination; leadership; lying; materialism; morality; motivations; rules; spirituality

personal narrative 149
Peter Pan 15, 18
Philippines 96
Philosopher's Stone 8, 65, 98, 101, 108, 113, 158; *see also Sorcerer's Stone*
philosophy 1, 122, 131, 138, 150, 181, 197, 202–203
Pictionary 75
Pierce, Tamora (children's author) 15, 18
plagiarism 110
planetarium 57–61, 66
Plato 135, 203
plot 10, 14, 24, 34, 36, 51–52, 80, 101, 110, 114, 123, 191
podcast 58, 86
politics 30, 44, 82, 96, 138, 157, 174, 183, 193, 200, 204; *see also* censorship
polls 109
popular culture 13, 21, 36, 56, 64, 83, 104, 125, 138, 151, 169, 180, 186, 197, 200, 202–208
Popular Culture and Philosophy Series (criticism) 202–203
potions 2, 4, 7–8, 12, 36, 64, 113, 135, 210
The Potter Games (fan fiction) 81–89
Pottermore 2, 107, 109, 111–116
PowerPoint 8–9, 13–14, 62
prejudice 137, 144, 145; *see also* gender; homosexuality; labels; marginalized; racism; social issues; stereotypes
preschool 32, 142
presentations 8–9, 11–17, 62, 134
Pride and Prejudice 79, 193
Prisoner of Azkaban 8, 29, 30, 34, 39, 66, 152
propaganda 1, 131, 138
psychobiology 99
psychology 1, 17, 41, 95, 96, 99, 143
The Psychology of Harry Potter (criticism) 197
Pullman, Philip (children's author) 15, 18
punishment 21, 24–29, 162, 184

Quidditch 11–12, 19, 24, 38, 76, 84, 87, 93, 114, 130, 132, 137, 139, 147, 166, 196, 210; *see also* IQA
quizzes 6, 134

racism 1, 65, 131, 138, 144, 153–156, 180, 183, 200; *see also* prejudice; social issues
Radcliffe, Daniel 35
reading *see* literacy
reading comprehension 35, 75, 78
Reading Harry Potter (criticism) 197, 199, 201, 208
Reagin, Nancy R. (critic) 135, 136, 139, 197, 205, 206, 208
recipes 159, 161, 163
Redwall (children's series) 14–15
religion 2, 8, 93–94, 96, 99–101, 104, 144, 183; *see also* Christian; God; Jesus; occult; pagan; spirituality
remix 82, 84–90

research 2, 10, 14–16, 60, 64, 74, 81–85, 90, 99, 118, 126, 133–136, 150, 154–155, 158, 161–166, 192, 197, 201; *see also* essays; scholarship
rhetoric 51, 131, 138
rhetorical devices 75
Rice, Anne (fantasy author) 79
Riordan, Rick (children's author) 15, 18, 73–74, 80
rituals 95, 100, 137
Robin Hood 15, 18, 163
role-playing 66, 81, 83, 84–85
Romantic Movement 168, 169, 193
Romeo and Juliet 77, 79; *see also* Shakespeare, William
Ron Weasley 17, 20, 25–29, 36, 39, 59, 63, 88–89, 141, 153–154, 160, 164, 172, 175–176, 183–185, 206
Rowling, J.K.: announcement Dumbledore is gay 50, 181; internet presence 107–116; interviews with 49, 50, 65, 98, 109, 114, 157, 181; *see also* jkrowling.com; Pottermore
rule-breaking 21–31; *see also* morality; punishment
rules 12–13, 21–30, 48, 70, 76–77, 85, 130, 147, 182

Safire, William (critic) 199, 208
satire 80, 123
scavenger hunt 132
scholarship 122–123, 127, 131, 159, 180, 196–197, 201, 205, 207, 215; *see also* essays; research
Scholastic 127
school *see* college; elementary school; freshman courses; high school; law school; middle school; preschool
school board 117
school concerns *see* ADHD; age-appropriate; Asperger's Syndrome; attention span; autism; bullying; censorship; curriculum; development; English language learners; hyperlexia; libraries; literacy; plagiarism; politics; punishment; rule-breaking; rules; school board; school newspaper; teaching tools; textbooks
school newspaper 84, 137
school subjects *see* architecture; art; chemistry; composition; creative writing; cross-disciplinary; cultural studies; economics; education; English; ethics; ethnography; feminism; folklore; free-choice learning; freshman courses; gender studies; genetics; geology; history; humanities; language arts; Latin; law; medieval studies; politics; popular culture; psychology; rhetoric; science; sociology; theater; theology
science 2, 7, 56–66, 131, 133–134, 137, 142, 215
science fiction 56, 65, 82, 125; *see also* dystopias; fantasy

The Science of Harry Potter (criticism) 65, 133, 139
sexual orientation 50, 144, 182, 183; *see also* homosexuality
Shakespeare, William 1, 125, 135, 157, 190, 216–217
Sherlock Holmes 79
The Sims (computer game) 84–85
Sinistra, Professor 58–59, 64–66
Sirius Black 30, 58
Skype 85
Slytherin 145
Snape, Severus 7, 27, 83, 102, 110, 133, 157, 185
Snicket, Lemony (children's author) 22
social awareness 37–38
social issues 2, 33–37, 40–41, 64, 82, 85, 95–97, 102, 104, 107, 118, 138, 142, 153, 158, 161, 163–164, 171–174, 179, 186, 189, 199–200, 212; *see also* gender; homosexuality; labels; marginalized; prejudice; racism; sociology; stereotypes
social media 85–86, 89, 97, 113; *see also* blogs; email; Facebook; instant messenger; Internet; Livejournal; media; mixed media; podcast; Pottermore; Skype; YouTube
social status 97
social workers 96
Society for Creative Anachronism 166
sociology 99, 122, 131, 137, 205
Socratic method 23, 24, 26, 31
songs *see* music
Sorcerer's Stone 5, 7, 24–25, 34, 37, 39, 42, 52, 59, 130, 142, 144–146, 149–150, 171–172, 175, 177, 179, 184, 209–210, 214; *see also Philosopher's Stone*
sorting 5–6, 10, 18
sorting quiz 6
Spark Notes 76
spelling 38–39, 70, 147, 211–212
spells 1–2, 8, 10, 34, 39, 43, 46, 52, 71–73, 88, 158
spirituality 93–103; *see also* religion
Star Trek 56, 100
Star Wars 1, 33–35, 125
STEM (science and math) 56–57, 64–66, 68
stereotypes 1, 63, 64, 144–145, 182; *see also* gender; homosexuality; labels; marginalized; prejudice; racism; social issues
storytelling 10, 54–55, 77, 131; *see also* folklore; theater
structuralism 192
subjects *see* school subjects
suffrage 144
Sunday school 42; *see also* religion
Sundiata 15, 17
The Sword in the Stone 15
symbolism 6, 135
symposiums *see* conventions

The Tale of the Three Brothers 10, 18
teachers 1, 13, 23–24, 42, 51, 53, 56, 71, 74, 77, 80, 90, 96, 101, 113, 117–127, 143, 146, 163, 179, 181, 189, 200–201, 207, 211
teachers (fictional) *see* Dumbledore, Albus; Hagrid; Lockhart, Gilderoy; McGonagall, Minerva; Sinistra, Professor; Snape, Severus
teaching tools *see* art; charades; costumes; crafts; essays; evaluations; fan fiction; flashcards; flip charts; games; journaling; mapmaking; museums; music; parties; peer review; PowerPoint; presentations; quizzes; scavanger hunt; Socratic method; storytelling; theater; trivia
technology *see* blogs; cellphones; digital age; ebooks; email; fansites; films; Internet; iTunes; media; mixed media; podcast; Pottermore; PowerPoint; Skype; social media; television; YouTube
telescope 61–62
television 33, 47, 50, 56, 90, 142, 180
textbooks 6, 12, 26, 184, 201, 205
textual ownership 111
theater 10, 17–18, 54
theme park 2, 11, 137
themes 2, 9, 18, 36–37, 43, 48–49, 53–54, 58, 66, 81, 83, 90, 94, 102, 120, 122, 125, 127, 131, 135–138, 144, 147, 153, 169, 171, 180; 190–195; 200; *see also* bullying; confidence; ethics; friendship; good and evil; identity; materialism; morality; rules; spirituality
theology 2, 131, 136
Time Turner 30
To Kill a Mockingbird 118
Tolkien, J.R.R. 15, 46, 50, 94, 152, 216
Tom Riddle 29, 58
tone 32, 75–76, 170, 199, 204
tourism 11
Transfiguration 12, 18
translation 64, 158, 161
Treasure Island 177
trivia 6, 126–127, 199
Trivial Pursuit 75, 77
Twilight 2, 15, 48, 77–79, 82, 103, 110, 116, 177, 206, 208

The Uglies (YA dystopia) 82
The Ultimate Guide to the Harry Potter Fandom (criticism) 122

Unforgiveable Curses 39
United States 12–13, 15, 21, 32, 43, 56, 63, 65, 73, 81, 85, 90–91, 96, 117, 118, 123, 126, 131, 134, 136–139, 150, 198, 202, 207
university *see* college

values 2, 48–49, 51, 53, 83, 87, 97, 110, 120, 180–181, 198–200, 205; *see also* ethics; morality
vampires 48, 79, 110
A Very Potter Musical (parody) 111
Victorian era 106, 195
vocabulary 17, 70, 72, 74–77, 80, 158, 193
Voldemort 16, 17, 29, 37, 39, 48–50, 83, 134–135, 149, 158, 162, 166, 172–177

wands 6, 8, 46, 72, 103, 173
Warner Bros. studio tour 158
Western culture 14, 97, 153–154
Whited, Lana A. (critic) 4–20, 157, 178, 197, 198, 208
The Wisdom of Harry Potter (criticism) 21, 31, 138, 151, 166
The Wise Child 8
witch-hunts 152
witchcraft 43, 45, 47, 117, 131, 136, 194; *see also* occult
The Wizard of Oz 2, 15, 18
wizard rock 11
Wordsworth, William 169, 193, 216
The Worst Witch (children's book) 8
writers 10, 45, 84, 86–88, 107, 109, 114, 115, 147–148, 153, 156–157, 161, 190, 201, 210; *see also* authors
writing 4, 11, 13, 21, 39, 45, 50, 57, 70, 73, 77–90, 107, 109, 112, 114–115, 118, 134–138, 142–143, 145, 147–151, 180, 195, 201, 206, 211; goals 88; style 78

young adult literature 18, 42, 48, 55, 81–86, 90, 93, 109, 168, 169, 178, 199; *see also* children's books; dystopias; middle school
YouTube 11, 111

Zipes, Jack (critic) 126, 152, 166, 198

www.ingramcontent.com/pod-product-compliance
Ingram Content Group UK Ltd.
Pitfield, Milton Keynes, MK11 3LW, UK
UKHW041916140426
5217IPUK00013B/182